Women Moralists in Early Modern France

Jean-François de Troy, *La Lecture de Molière* (1730). The painting depicts a group of friends gathered around a central figure holding a copy of one of Molière's plays, from which he has evidently been reading aloud. The reader has paused in his recital; the characters gaze at one another or at the book, suggesting various forms of interest and desire. The woman in blue to the right, however, looks away from the group. Her gaze meets the viewer's, creating a space for interiority and reflection on the scene. She is in this world, but not entirely of it. She has assumed the position of the moralist.

Women Moralists
in Early Modern France

JULIE CANDLER HAYES

OXFORD
UNIVERSITY PRESS

Oxford University Press is a department of the University of Oxford. It furthers the University's objective of excellence in research, scholarship, and education by publishing worldwide. Oxford is a registered trade mark of Oxford University Press in the UK and certain other countries.

Published in the United States of America by Oxford University Press
198 Madison Avenue, New York, NY 10016, United States of America.

© Oxford University Press 2024

All rights reserved. No part of this publication may be reproduced, stored in a retrieval system, or transmitted, in any form or by any means, without the prior permission in writing of Oxford University Press, or as expressly permitted by law, by license, or under terms agreed with the appropriate reproduction rights organization. Inquiries concerning reproduction outside the scope of the above should be sent to the Rights Department, Oxford University Press, at the address above.

You must not circulate this work in any other form
and you must impose this same condition on any acquirer.

Library of Congress Cataloging-in-Publication Data
Names: Hayes, Julie Candler, 1955- author.
Title: Women moralists in early modern France / Julie Candler Hayes.
Description: New York, NY, United States of America : Oxford University Press, [2024] | Includes bibliographical references and index.
Identifiers: LCCN 2023019557 (print) | LCCN 2023019558 (ebook) | ISBN 9780197688601 (cp) | ISBN 9780197688625 (epub) | ISBN 9780197688632
Subjects: LCSH: Ethicists—France—History. | Philosophers—France—History. | Intellectuals—France—History.
Classification: LCC BJ702 .H394 2024 (print) | LCC BJ702 (ebook) | DDC 170.944—dc23/eng/20230831
LC record available at https://lccn.loc.gov/2023019557
LC ebook record available at https://lccn.loc.gov/2023019558

DOI: 10.1093/oso/9780197688601.001.0001

Printed by Integrated Books International, United States of America

Pour l'ami lecteur

Contents

Preamble ix
Acknowledgments xi
A Note on Names xiii
A Note on Texts xv

1. Introduction: The Moralist World 1
   1.1. Moralists and Moralizers 3
   1.2. Unsystematic Philosophy 10
   1.3. Philosophy and Literature in Early Modern France 14
   1.4. Women Moralists and the Canon 16
   1.5. Corpus and Topics: Who Is a Moralist? 22

2. On Self-Knowledge and Knowledge of the Self 31
   2.1. Scudéry: Conversation 34
   2.2. Dupin: Sensation and Belief 42
   2.3. Verzure: Comparison 45
   2.4. Necker: Writing 55
   2.5. Guizot: Doubts 64
   2.6. Introspection and the Act of Writing 68

3. On Friendship 71
   3.1. Foundations of Friendship 74
   3.2. Rituals of Friendship: Reciprocity, Exchange, Secrets 85
   3.3. Sameness and Difference 92
   3.4. The Politics of *Reconnaissance* 104

4. On Happiness and the Passions 112
   4.1. From the Passions to Passion 114
   4.2. The Worlds of Marguerite de La Sablière and Louise Dupin 119
   4.3. Practical Guidance in Du Châtelet and Fourqueux 128
   4.4. The Passions and Their Discontents in d'Arconville 139
   4.5. Staël's Phenomenology of Passion 146

5. On Marriage 157
   5.1. The Philosophical and Legal Critique 161
   5.2. The Implicit Moralist Critique: Lambert and Puisieux 163
   5.3. The Explicit Moralist Critique: Verzure and d'Arconville 168
   5.4. Suzanne Necker on Marriage and Divorce 177
   5.5. On Liberty 182

6. On Age and Experience 191
   6.1. Experience, Knowledge, and the Seasons of Life 195
   6.2. Codes of Conduct 205
   6.3. Not Her Last Word: D'Arconville on Old Age 217

7. On Women's Nature and Capabilities 222
   7.1. Politeness and Embodiment 223
   7.2. Portraits and Mirrors: Pringy's *Les Differens caracteres des femmes du siècle* 227
   7.3. Nature, Culture, and the *désir de plaire* 238
   7.4. *Comment peut-on être femme auteur?* 247

Conclusion 262

Bibliography 265
Index 281

Preamble

The women in this book came from different backgrounds and led very different lives. Most were from Paris, or had taken up residence there by early adulthood. Most were born to privilege, but not necessarily wealth. Madeleine de Souvré, marquise de Sablé; Anne-Thérèse de Marguenat de Courcelles, marquise de Lambert; and Gabrielle Émilie Le Tonnelier de Breteuil, marquise Du Châtelet, were aristocrats to the core. Madeleine de Scudéry was not of noble birth; her keen intelligence attracted a rarified circle of nobles and intellectuals to her salon. Marie de Verzure and her ennobled financier husband moved in court circles. Madeleine de Puisieux's spouse was a lawyer and diplomat. Geneviève Thiroux d'Arconville's father was a financier and her husband a magistrate, thus linking her to the two centers of nonnoble power and influence under the old regime. Pauline de Meulan was the daughter of a count, but after the Revolution she made no scruple of writing for a profession. Her journalistic work led her to meet and later marry François Guizot, bourgeois and Protestant, later a leading liberal statesman. Suzanne Necker, the daughter of a Swiss Protestant clergyman, was the wife of Louis XVI's powerful minister of finance, Jacques Necker; their daughter, Germaine de Staël, would become one of the greatest novelists of the revolutionary generation.

All were thinkers and writers. All sought to have their work read by others, through print publication, manuscript sharing, or by preserving it for posterity.

Most published under their own names, but several used their initials or published anonymously. Émilie Du Châtelet courted intellectual glory. Anne-Thérèse de Lambert famously resisted publication, yet her abundant production and her practice of manuscript circulation evince a strong identification with writing. Geneviève d'Arconville's most-quoted words were a warning to women who published that they would not be taken seriously, and their work attributed to men if they were. Madeleine de Puisieux, whose liaison with Denis Diderot led to imputations that he had a hand in her work, would doubtless have agreed.

Several were accomplished Latinists. Others knew modern languages and would have been familiar with the classics through numerous widely available translations. Du Châtelet and d'Arconville both complained of their lack of early education and embarked on rigorous programs of self-education, especially in the sciences. Several of these women hosted important salons; d'Arconville and Verzure, on the other hand, disliked socializing. Their published works cover a broad spectrum: belles-lettres, translations, criticism, fiction, science, history, and philosophy.

All, however, were drawn to a long-standing tradition of philosophical questions about the human condition, social relations, and emotions.

They were moralists.

Acknowledgments

Long-term book projects incur many debts of gratitude, and it is a pleasure to reflect on them now.

My intellectual home of over four decades, the American Society for Eighteenth-Century Studies, has been the site where initial versions of many portions of this book were first discussed, and I have benefited immensely from audience questions, hallway conversations, epistolary follow-ups, and encounters with the work of colleagues in this diverse, interdisciplinary, and ever-evolving scholarly community. I am also grateful to the anonymous readers for Oxford University Press for their careful comments and to Peter Ohlin for his guidance as the project came into focus.

It is no exaggeration to say that my scholarly life changed in 2008 when I heard Marie-Laure Girou Swiderski give a paper on Geneviève Thiroux d'Arconville's late manuscripts known as the *Pensées, réflexions et anecdotes*. I had been interested in d'Arconville's published work for several years, but gaining access to the unpublished essays transformed my view of her work. To Marie-Laure and to Marc-André Bernier, whose work has inspired so much new scholarship on this important thinker, my deep gratitude. Thanks too to Laurence Vanoflen, Anne-Lise Rey, Colas Duflo, and their fellow dix-huitiémistes at Université Paris-Nanterre for opportunities to present parts of this work to the seminar Litt&Phi and at a memorable conference, "Les femmes et la philosophie des Lumières," in 2017. Patrick Coleman, Faith Beasley, Pierre Saint-Amand, Downing Thomas, Janie Vanpée, and Judith Zinsser have been unstinting in moral and intellectual support over the years.

This book would have been written more quickly, but it would have been the poorer, without the years I spent as department chair, and the decade as dean of the College of Humanities and Fine Arts at the University of Massachusetts Amherst. My colleagues at UMass, as well as the many alumni and friends of the university that I had the privilege of meeting and working with, have broadened my outlook, provided an incomparable intellectual and artistic environment, and supported me during difficult times. Their accomplishments continue to inspire me. That this book was completed on schedule is due entirely to a much appreciated postdecanal research leave: thank you, former Provost John McCarthy! And strong thanks as well to the indefatigable librarians of the W.E.B. DuBois Library, who kept the books and interlibrary loan orders flowing throughout the pandemic shutdown.

I regret only that two people whose influence reverberates through these pages in very different ways did not live to see it completed: my UMass colleague and friend, Eileen O'Neill, whose work on early modern women philosophers changed the field; and my spouse, life partner, and anchor, Claude Bersano.

I owe a special debt to my sisters Mary Leonard and Elizabeth Hayes and to my son Dan Bersano-Hayes. Their love and support make all things possible.

A Note on Names

Even today, it is customary in French academic writing to refer to women of the *ancien régime* by their titles: the marquise de Lambert, madame d'Arconville (or la présidente d'Arconville, a reference to her husband's status as a magistrate). I have followed standard North American usage in referring to women by their last names only, dropping the nobiliary particle "de" in most instances. I respect the French forms of family names: hence, just as the definite article is part of the name for La Fontaine and La Rochefoucauld, we should also refer to La Sablière (not "Sablière"). I follow the common practice of shortening certain aristocratic women's names to what is in effect the husband's title: Émilie Du Châtelet, rather than Gabrielle-Émilie Le Tonnelier de Breteuil, marquise Du Châtelet, or Anne-Thérèse de Lambert, rather than Anne-Thérèse de Marguenat de Courcelles, marquise de Lambert. It is worth pointing out that family names that referenced a particular branch were not always used in their entirety; members of the widely ramified Thiroux family would generally go by the name of their distinguishing title or branch: d'Arconville, Crosne, d'Espersennes. In the case of Marie-Geneviève-Charlotte Thiroux d'Arconville (née Darlus), I use her patron saint's name, Geneviève, the name that her family and familiars would have used.

The most vexing questions concern the appropriate way to refer to women who published under one name, then later married and were known by another. Scholars rarely worry that Germaine de Staël was still Germaine Necker when she wrote *De l'influence des passions*, but for other figures, the usage is less well established. Octavie Belot (née Guichard), widowed young, gained her literary reputation as an essayist and translator during the years preceding her remarriage to the président Du Rey de Meynières, at which point she ceased writing for publication. Although the BNF catalog prefers her last married name, recent scholarship appears to prefer the earlier name under which she published her work, and I have followed that usage. I have taken a similar approach to Sophie de Grouchy, marquise de Condorcet, generally referred to by her maiden name in contemporary scholarship. The case of Pauline de Meulan, later Pauline Guizot, is complex. The BNF catalog prefers her married name; contemporary scholarship uses both. Pauline de Meulan wrote most of her moralist essays for Suard's journal *Le Publiciste*; although anonymous, her authorship was known in at least some circles. Unlike Belot, however, she continued writing and publishing after her marriage to François Guizot and indeed gained a substantial reputation under that name. Following her death, many of her moralist essays were republished under the name Pauline Guizot. I have therefore chosen to refer to her by her married name in most circumstances.

A Note on Texts

All primary source references are to the original French texts; all translations are my own. I have used modern editions whenever possible, and I have benefited from the scholarly apparatus of modern translations of several of the women studied here. (See Bibliography.) Fortunately, despite the lack of modern editions for many figures, the original editions of most key works from the period are readily available from online repositories, especially Gallica, the Hathi Trust, and Google Books; the *Encyclopédie* of Diderot and d'Alembert is available on open access from the ARTFL Project, as is a collection of historical dictionaries.

1
Introduction
The Moralist World

Moralist writing—observations on the human condition—has a distinguished place in French literature and the history of ideas through the work of Montaigne, La Rochefoucauld, La Bruyère, and Pascal, as well as later figures Saint-Évremond, Vauvenargues, and Chamfort. Early modern moralists took inspiration from the Ancients, particularly Cicero and Seneca, but they made the genre their own. They typically eschewed extended treatises in favor of the essay, the maxim, and the portrait, developing an aesthetic of fragmentation, discontinuity, understatement, and irony. Their disabused accounts of human motivation contributed to the shift in mentalities that we associate with the critical consciousness of the Enlightenment.

It is hardly surprising that women would be drawn to participate in a conversation that had its roots in antiquity while engaging contemporary concerns with moral psychology and social relations. Seventeenth-century salon culture saw the flowering of the psychological novel and the moralist maxim, fostered collaborative modes of writing, and expanded women's literary ambitions. Although literary and cultural historians of the past generation have produced voluminous scholarship on women's contributions to the rise of the novel and their role in social and intellectual life, they have paid less attention to philosophical writing. Analogously, even feminist revisions of the history of philosophy have not always taken moralist writing seriously. This study seeks to rectify the imbalance.

Although many moralist writers as well as the genre itself have often been considered the province of literary studies, there are historical and substantive reasons to take a broader view. The passions, happiness, liberty, old age, friendship, and the good life are of intense interest to historians of the emotions, social psychologists, and virtue ethicists—and indeed to many of us, simply as citizens. Women moralists explore not only these traditional subjects but also topics that receive scant attention from male writers, such as marriage. They bring a distinctly gendered perspective. For these thinkers, critical self-consciousness is virtually an ontological condition, given the period's ongoing debates over women's capacity for rational thought. In a context where positions ranged from the claim that "the mind has no sex" to the argument that sexual difference extends into every fiber and inflects every thought, women could never assume that they occupied an unproblematic place in intellectual life. Although they represent a variety of attitudes and approaches, women moralists demonstrate how a marginalized group—however privileged the social standing of certain individuals—were able to claim a position of intellectual authority.

I make two overarching claims in this study: first, that moralist writing, a distinctive genre with certain formal characteristics, holds philosophical significance, particularly in the history of moral psychology and ethics; and second, that women make substantive contributions to that canon.

I make a methodological claim as well: that the writings of women moralists are best understood in terms of the historical, social, and conceptual contexts in which they were written. This is not to say that they can be reduced to their context, or that their work has no relevance to the present, but that the contextual threads clarify the terms of their arguments and help to define their scope.

This chapter lays out multiple layers of that context. The first section defines moralist writing through several lenses: a consideration of the history of the word *moraliste*, the genre's relationship to descriptive versus prescriptive approaches, its formal properties, and the social and political landscape in which it came to prominence. I will distinguish moralist writing from what I call the "moralist impulse" that characterizes a broad range of literary and philosophical texts from the period.

Sections 1.2 and 1.3 place moralist writing in a series of contexts. I consider the relationship of moralist writing, often seen as a literary genre, to the evolution of philosophical writing in France. Enlightenment *philosophes*—a term that was freighted with ideological significance, hence not universally adopted by all who pursued philosophical questions—embraced a wide range of forms and upheld a deliberately antisystematic, exploratory approach. The affiliation of moralist writing with both philosophy and literature becomes even more apparent in Section 1.3, in which I underscore that both disciplines were evolving toward their modern forms during the period of this study, a process that takes place in the context of the complex hierarchies and social relations of the *ancien régime*. Moralist writing, with its roots in the humanistic tradition and its close ties to salon culture, blurs the boundaries between philosophy and literature.

Section 1.4 focuses on the work of women moralists. Despite the association of the emergence of moralist writing with the salon culture in which women played a major role, women's contributions to the genre have rarely received scholarly attention. In this respect, the exclusion of women from the canon of moralist writing parallels the exclusion of women from the western philosophical canon, and the arguments in favor of their inclusion in both have much in common. In addition, the specific writing and publication practices in which women moralists engaged have much to tell us about the opportunities for women philosophers and female intellectuals of all types during the early modern period. The final section discusses the criteria for inclusion and exclusion of thinkers and texts, as well as an overview of the topics studied here.

1.1. Moralists and Moralizers

To a French-speaking public, the word *moraliste* immediately calls to mind the late seventeenth-century pantheon of François VI duc de La Rochefoucauld, Jean de La Bruyère, and Blaise Pascal, although these writers would probably not have used the term to describe themselves.

The French word has a complex history, evolving over time, that includes both a prescriptivist meaning and a more value-neutral descriptive meaning. Awareness of these two semantic poles helps to illuminate certain ambiguities and shifts in moralist discourse. Like its English cognate, the word *moraliste* is entwined with its etymological cousins descended from Latin *mos*, a personal disposition; and from its plural, *mores*: customs, manners. These roots persist in the value-neutral aspect of the term. Cicero used the word *moralis* to translate Greek *ēthikós*, a term whose broader sense is "customs," but which carries the weight of Aristotle's emphasis on integrity of character.[1] French absorbed both strands in the word *moeurs*, which may refer in a neutral sense to manners, social customs, or habits either good or bad, and *morale*, with all its variations, which most often refers to right conduct. The theologian and critic René Rapin sums up the latter meaning: "*La*

---

[1] On Cicero's translations of Greek philosophical terms, see John Glucker, "Cicero as Translator and Cicero in Translation," *Philologica* 10 (2015): 37–53.

Morale teaches us to live, just as Logic teaches us to speak."[2] *Moraliste* appears somewhat tautologically in Furetière's 1690 dictionary as "author who writes on *la Morale*." Furetière then defines *morale* as "The doctrine of *moeurs*, a science that teaches how to conduct one's life and one's actions," in other words, a system of moral precepts.

Around the middle of the seventeenth century, a shift occurs in which the writers now identified as moralists, such as La Rochefoucauld and Saint-Évremond, "begin more clearly to divorce secular ethics from dogmatic morality."[3] By the mid-eighteenth century, d'Holbach defines *la morale* simply as "the system of existing human relationships."[4] The shift to the more neutral sense takes place over the course of the eighteenth century, as evinced by the 1762 edition of the dictionary of the Académie française, which defines *Moraliste* simply as "Writer who treats *moeurs*." The word *moeurs* is never completely value-neutral, but its semantic terrain is now the debate over the relationship between customs, national character, and laws; it takes on increasingly politicized connotations rather than referring to traditional morality.[5] In the later eighteenth century, *moraliste* would even be used by some as interchangeable with *philosophe*. Perhaps because of that politically weighted association, the eighteenth-century writers who consciously saw themselves as inheritors of La Rochefoucauld and La Bruyère use the word infrequently; although it occurs occasionally before 1800, the use of "moralist" to designate a particular group of late seventeenth-century writers (and their successors) only becomes standard during the nineteenth century.[6] Germaine de Staël crystallizes this sense in *De la littérature* (1800).[7] Indeed, the ARTFL database shows a small number of occurrences of *moraliste* before 1750, with substantial numbers after 1750 and throughout the nineteenth century and the greatest relative frequency occurring in the first half of the twentieth century. Like many features of *le grand siècle*, the creation of a unitary group of "moralists" was largely the work of the nineteenth century.

---

[2] René Rapin, "Réflexions sur la morale," in *Oeuvres du P. Rapin*, 2 vols. (Paris: les frères Barbou, 1725), 2:410.

[3] Anthony Levi, *French Moralists: The Theory of the Passions, 1585–1649* (Oxford: Clarendon Press, 1964), 335.

[4] Paul-Henri Thiry, baron d'Holbach, *La Morale universelle, ou les devoirs de l'homme fondés sur sa nature*, 3 vols. (Amsterdam: M.-M. Rey, 1776), 1:1.

[5] Georges Benrekassa, *Le Langage des Lumières: Concepts et savoir de la langue* (Paris: PUF, 1995), 72–83.

[6] Louis Van Delft, *Le Moraliste classique: Essai de définition et de typologie* (Paris: Droz, 1982), 17–37.

[7] Germaine de Staël, *De la littérature considérée dans ses rapports avec les institutions sociales*, ed. Jean Goldzink, in *Oeuvres completes* I.II (Paris: Honoré Champion, 2013), 179.

The prescriptive and descriptive senses of *morale* and *moraliste* thus remain entwined, but the emphasis shifts from one to the other over time.

Despite the anachronism, "moralist" remains a useful term for categorizing writers who share an interest in human nature and human conduct, as well as other commonalities that have perhaps become clearer with the passage of time than they were to themselves or their contemporaries. If anything, however, the term as I have just used it is too broad, since similar interests animate novelists, poets, dramatists, and philosophers of many schools of thought, and not only in the early modern period. Dissatisfaction with the widespread use of the word is the starting point for Louis Van Delft's study, which seeks to rein in the usage through careful "definition and typology." The word "moralist"—in French and even more so in English—is further blurred by its etymological cousins *moraliser*, *moralisateur*, terms that have come to have negative connotations. The OED defines "moralist" both as "teacher or student of morals" but, depreciatively, as "a person given to making moral judgments," and "moralizer" as "a person who seeks to dictate or prescribe the morals of others." The stronger prescriptivist slant of the English terms is a reminder that the phenomenon studied here is peculiarly French. The writers generally referred to as "moralists" in Britain are moral theorists, Cambridge Platonists, and writers on natural religion from Hobbes to Bentham—virtually all of whom have become part of the canon of modern philosophy.[8] French moralists, La Rochefoucauld in particular, were much read in eighteenth-century Britain, but the literary-philosophical movement that they represent does not have a clear equivalent.

French moralist writing emerges at the confluence of Renaissance humanism, aristocratic salon culture, and the Augustinian revival in French Catholicism. While the Augustinian revival took multiple forms, the most widely influential was the austere reformist current centered at the convent Port-Royal de Paris, known as Jansenism. Under the direction of the abbess Angélique Arnauld and her successors, Port-Royal became a spiritual and intellectual center, a place for study and retreat that engaged some of the greatest thinkers of the period, among them Antoine Arnaud, Blaise Pascal, and Pierre Nicole. Controversial from the outset, Jansenism's presence extended far beyond theological debates to politics and culture.[9] The

---

[8] As, for example, in D. D. Raphael's anthology, *British Moralists, 1650 to 1800*, 2 vols. (Oxford: Clarendon Press, 1969).

[9] Although subsequent historical scholarship has nuanced his sociological analysis, the classic account of Jansenism's "tragic vision" remains Lucien Goldmann's *Le Dieu caché* (Paris: Gallimard, 1959). On the contentious relationship of Jansenism to the politics of absolute monarchy, see

Augustinian or Jansenist legacy in moralist writing can be felt in a pervasive distrust of human motivation; a sense that virtuous actions may be performed for self-interested reasons, and hence not truly virtuous; and a belief that our ability to give an account of ourselves and our actions is vitiated by self-love and the passions. This deep-seated posture of suspicion is reinforced by humanist skepticism as well as by the labyrinthine hierarchies of court culture.[10]

Women played a major role in Jansenism, both in its spiritual and theological life and in its cultural diffusion.[11] Nowhere is the intersection between moralist writing, Jansenism, and court culture clearer than in the midcentury Jansenist-leaning salon of Madeleine de Souvré, marquise de Sablé, where she and her friends, François de la Rochefoucauld and the theologian Jacques Esprit, began to exchange short reflections and pithy statements on the complexities and contradictions of existence, both psychological and interpersonal.[12] The strong Jansenist current that runs through moralist writing is significant not so much for any kind of doctrinal purity—"cultural Jansenism" had its secularizing dimension, and moralist writers were nothing if not eclectic in their philosophical affiliations—but because it reminds us that moralist writing is less "descriptive" than is sometimes claimed. While one understands commentators' desire to distinguish moralists from moralizers, one must recognize the deontological aspect of moralist writing, an orientation or world view that may arise from multiple sources, depending on the writer: the ethos of *honnêteté*, a spiritual retreat, a principle of justice, or the urge to unmask hypocrisy and point out the absurdities of modern life.

Daniella Kostroun, *Feminism, Absolutism, and Jansenism* (Cambridge: Cambridge University Press, 2011) and Dale Van Kley, *The Religious Origins of the French Revolution* (New Haven: Yale University Press, 1996).

[10] In a series of studies, Michael Moriarty has explored the Augustinian legacy in seventeenth-century philosophy and literature. See his *Early Modern French Thought: The Age of Suspicion* (Oxford: Oxford University Press, 2003); *Fallen Nature, Fallen Selves* (Oxford: Oxford University Press, 2006); and *Disguised Vices: Theories of Virtue in Early Modern French Thought* (Oxford: Oxford University Press, 2011).

[11] John J. Conley, *The Suspicion of Virtue: Women Philosophers in Neoclassical France* (Ithaca, NY: Cornell University Press, 2002); see also his *The Other Pascals: The Philosophy of Jacqueline Pascal, Gilberte Pascal Périer, and Marguerite Périer* (Notre Dame: Notre Dame University Press, 2019).

[12] On the evolution of Madame de Sablé's salon and the emergence of the maxim as literary form, see Benedetta Craveri, *L'Âge de la conversation* (Paris: Gallimard, 2002), 109–47. See also the chapter on Sablé in Conley, *Suspicion*, 20–44; and Jean Lafond, "Madame de Sablé et son salon," in Jean Lafond and Jean Mesnard, eds., *Images de La Rochefoucauld: Actes du tricentenaire, 1680–1980* (Paris: PUF, 1984), 201–16.

Moralist writing is thus akin to other genres, both in its formal aspect in the use of short forms, and in terms of its focus on social and psychological analysis. Much conduct literature of the period has a descriptive moralist aspect, and certain moralist texts echo or even parody conduct literature, as in the case of Madeleine de Puisieux's *Conseils à une amie*. And, given long-standing traditions of short form spiritual literature of daily devotions and the like, to say nothing of the influence of Pascal and Nicole, it is hardly surprising to find a gray area between moralist writing per se and works of religious and theological inspiration. Both Madeleine de La Sablière's *Maximes chrétiennes* and Madeleine Patin's *Réflexions morales & chrestiennes* fall at different points along this continuum. La Sablière's work, which comments directly on society and human motivations, is included in abridged form in Lafond's anthology of seventeenth-century moralists. Patin is listed in the Toinet corpus, although the second half of her title, "*tirées pour la pluspart des epistres de Saint Paul*," points to a devotional orientation. Most of Patin's chapters concern elements of faith and religious practices, but certain of her topics, such as the virtues and vices, would lend themselves to treatment in works of a more worldly cast.[13]

Ambivalence is inherent in the development of the genre. The period's fascination with the subtleties of human behavior and relationships, its "moralist turn" (*tropisme moral*),[14] occurs at the confluence of multiple strains in seventeenth-century French philosophy, spirituality, letters, and social practices. When La Rochefoucauld elected to publish his work in 1665, he hesitated over what to call these observations. The most obvious model, from Antiquity to the present, were the brief statements of moral instruction referred to as *sententiae*, in French *sentences*, which might be original creations, but were often nuggets from classic writers and biblical texts, anthologized for ease of consultation and memorization. La Rochefoucauld's decision to refer to his aphorisms as "Reflections or sentences and moral maxims" blurred the normal association of *sentence* with dogmatic instruction, leaving the reader to land on

---

[13] Madeleine Hommetz Patin, *Réflexions morales & chrestiennes, tirées la pluspart des epistres de Saint Paul* (Padua: Imprimerie de Jean Baptiste Pasquati, 1682). Patin came from an erudite family and married into another; her father-in-law was Guy Patin, a distinguished physician. She followed her husband into exile in Italy, where she published her *Réflexions morales* simultaneously in French and Italian. She, her husband, and both their daughters were members of the Academy of the Ricovrati. For a later work that similarly adopts the *maxime* for a devotional perspective, see [Marie Prudence Plisson], *Maximes morales d'un philosophe chrétien, par M.D.* (Paris: Chez Lamy, 1783).

[14] Béatrice Parmentier, *Le Siècle des moralistes de Montaigne à La Bruyère* (Paris: Seuil, 2000), 175.

maxime.[15] That *maxime* was also used in a manner that deviated from the usual meaning, "a personal principle of conduct" would have stood out to its readers from the opening sally: "Our virtues, for the most part, are only vices in disguise."[16]

Despite the carping of a few critics for whom the discontinuity of the *Maximes* made it appear to be a "anthology," rather than a "work,"[17] the book struck a chord with readers. The *Maximes* fed a wave of fascination with human psychology, as well as deeper currents of change. Not only guests in aristocratic salons, but also readers of the popular periodical *Le Mercure galant*, pondered and responded to questions on love, friendship, and the ethics of social interactions. The progressive consolidation of royal power forced personal ambitions to seek outlets in the subtle dynamics, shifting alliances, deceptive appearances, and ambiguous motives at court. Moralist writing comes into its own in the wake of the sixteenth-century Wars of Religion, the retreat of the Church as guarantor of state morality, and the new location of personal morality within the individual. The moralist practices the courtier's "art of prudence," both as a form of self-regulation and, through deeper understanding of their motives, as a means to control or surpass others.[18] French political culture, the expansion of absolutism, and a courtly environment "laced with intrigue and a wounding struggle for preeminence," heighten the intensity of the study of others and of oneself.[19] By the dawn of the eighteenth century, the evolution of the royal bureaucracy enhanced opportunities for advancement through the legal and financial professions.

In the intellectual realm, Descartes enjoined fellow philosophers to base their reflections on methodical doubt and to accept as true only that which could be deduced from observation and strict adherence to method; he reached out to readers beyond learned networks by publishing his *Discours*

---

[15] La Rochefoucauld used the term to refer to his and his friends' maxims in his correspondence, however: "l'envie des sentences se gagne comme un rhume." André-Alain Morello, "Actualité de La Rochefoucauld," in Jean Lafond, ed., *Moralistes du XVIIe siècle* (Paris: Robert Laffont, 1992), 110.

[16] François VI duc de la Rochefoucauld, epigraph to the *Maximes*, in Lafond, ed., *Moralistes du XVIIe siècle*, 134.

[17] Alain Brunn, *Le Laboratoire moraliste: La Rochefoucauld et l'invention moderne de l'auteur* (Paris: PUF, 2009), 87–90. Brunn analyzes how the aristocrat La Rochefoucauld approaches authorship in a way that avoids the stigma and the professional associations of "authorship" and contributes to a new, modern concept of the author.

[18] Éric Méchoulan, "La Prudence de l'homme de cour: De Gracián à Amelot de la Houssaye," in Jean-Charles Darmon, ed., *Le Moraliste, la politique et l'histoire de La Rochefoucauld à Derrida* (Paris: Desjonquères, 2007), 96.

[19] Jerrold Seigel, *The Idea of the Self: Thought and Experience in Western Europe since the Seventeenth Century* (Cambridge: Cambridge University Press, 2005), 37.

de la méthode in French, marking a shift to the vernacular for philosophical writing and opening opportunities for women, who were rarely instructed in Latin, to participate in philosophical discussion. Aristocratic virtue was reconfigured as civic virtue during the eighteenth century's "age of the senses."[20] The period saw paradoxical affinities: Montaigne's skeptical humanist recentering of inquiry with the individual at the center—"Que sais-je?"—echoes and transforms practices of Christian spiritual self-examination. A new emphasis on affectivity, exemplified by the rise of the novel, finds an unexpected echo in scholastic philosophy's quest to systematize and classify the passions, reformulated and reimagined in Descartes' *Les Passions de l'âme*.

The moralist impulse, with its focus on the individual and psychological exploration, manifests itself in multiple domains: most visibly in theater, novels, and political theory; privately, in epistolary conversation.[21] Moralist *writing*, however, is associated with certain forms: the fragment or maxim, the literary portrait or "character," the essay. As Jean Lafond has demonstrated in his magisterial exposition of the period's "short forms," the *formes brèves* bespeak a common "aesthetic of density" that stems from both pedagogical and spiritual practices, as well as from a shift from the rolling cadences of Ciceronian style to the terse, abrupt transitions characteristic of Senecan style, privileging brevity and discontinuity.[22] Lafond's study shows the power of the short form in contexts ranging from the worldly, as in Bussy-Rabutin's wildly popular *Maximes d'amour* (1660) to the spiritual, in the marquise de La Sablière's *Maximes chrétiennes*, published posthumously in 1705, to say nothing of the *Pensées* of Blaise Pascal, published posthumously in 1670.

Whether witty, world-weary, or soul-searching, the vogue of "maxims," "reflections," and "thoughts" engaged writers of genius and individuals who found therein a meaningful form for self-expression and intellectual exploration. Jean de la Bruyère's *Caractères* (1688), another short form that claimed inspiration from a classical model, would likewise call forth a host

---

[20] Daniel Brewer, "Virtue and the Ethics of the Virtual," in J. Fowler and M. Ganofsky, eds., *Enlightenment virtue, 1680–1794*(Oxford: Oxford University Studies in the Enlightenment, 2020), 235–51.

[21] To cite one example among many, consider the letters of Louise d'Épinay, a writer and hostess who played a leading role in philosophical circles. Her correspondence with Grimm, Galiani, and others is rich with discussions exemplifying the moralist impulse; see her exchange on happiness and friendship with the Genevan physician Théodore Tronchin, which she published for private distribution in *Mes moments heureux* (Genève: De mon imprimerie, 1759), 94–131.

[22] Jean Lafond, "Le Champ littéraire des formes brèves," in Lafond, *Moralistes du XVIIe siècle*, 21.

of imitators.²³ By redirecting the "portrait" into "character," La Bruyère maintains the lively specificity of the one into the universalizing dimension of the other. The word "character" further references materiality through its original meaning as "distinctive mark," thus underscoring an important feature of moralist writing: its fusion of the abstractly general with the concretely particular.²⁴

"Moralist writing," as I will use the term, is thus distinct from what I call the "moralist impulse" that animates much literary production of the seventeenth and eighteenth centuries. It manifests itself primarily in the short forms. It is rooted in the here and now of contemporary manners and social relations, the lens through which it engages long-standing philosophical issues. It is deeply involved with psychological exploration and knowledge of the self, a quest that draws inspiration from practices of spiritual self-examination as well as from the period's new valorization of the individual. Although moralists purport to render a faithful description or "portrait" of their social milieu, their analysis is suffused with their assessment of that world. They leave the work of interpretation to the reader.²⁵

1.2. Unsystematic Philosophy

Much has been made of the short form as a deliberate rejection of the philosophical treatise. The turn to an aesthetic of open-endedness and discontinuity has distinct philosophical and epistemological implications.²⁶ Feminist philosophers have made the point that early modern philosophizing takes

---

[23] La Bruyère's invocation of Theophrastus conveniently ignores the popularity of literary portraits during the period. See Erica Harth, *Ideology and Culture in Seventeenth-Century France* (Ithaca, NY: Cornell University Press, 1983), 68–128.

[24] On the shift from "portrait" to "character" as indicative of the shift from early seventeenth-century baroque culture to the universalizing ambitions of the *goût classique*, see Bernard Chédozeau, *Le Baroque* (Paris: Nathan, 1989), 221. See also Louis Van Delft, "Caractère et style," in Jean-Pierre Collinet, ed., *Caractères et passions au XVIIe siècle* (Dijon: Éditions universitaires de Dijon, 1998), 13–32. For further discussion of *caractère* in moralist writing, see below, chapter 7, 228, 237.

[25] For a prime example, see Michael Moriarty's discussion of the evolution of conflicting readings of La Rochefoucauld (*Disguised Vices*, 253–75).

[26] For Jean Starobinski, La Rochefoucauld's "aristocratic refusal" to create a coherent system represents "an adequate transcription of man's internal discontinuity" and "the impossibility to achieve complete clarity." "La Rochefoucauld et les morales substitutives," *Nouvelle revue française* 14 (July 1966): 22–23. See also Van Delft, *Moraliste classique*, 103–4; Parmentier, *Le Siècle des moralistes*, 200–208. Andrew Hui takes the long view of the maxim's enduring presence "before, against, and after philosophy," *A Theory of the Aphorism: From Confucius to Twitter* (Princeton, NJ: Princeton University Press, 2019).

place on multiple platforms, such as, to take a famous example, the correspondence of Elizabeth of Bohemia and René Descartes, or, more broadly, the novel, a form that was considered particularly congenial to women. This is certainly one reason to take women moralists seriously as philosophers, a role that stands out all the more clearly when we consider the explicit rejection of "systematic" thought in French Enlightenment philosophy.

Questions of order—how to describe the world, how to understand the relationship between the structures of language and the structures of the mind—are at the heart of Enlightenment thought. The *esprit systématique* for which the period is known is as far removed from the *esprit de systèmes* of seventeenth-century philosophy as from the architectonics of Kant. In the best-known rendering of the distinction, d'Alembert's Preliminary Discourse to the *Encyclopédie*, the "spirit of systems" is taken to refer to the reductive, arbitrary principles of a philosophical style that he and his colleagues rejected, while the "systematic spirit" is an open, exploratory approach unfettered by dogma or preconceived notions—in other words, the enlightened philosophy represented by the *Encyclopédie*. For Ernst Cassirer, this distinction was fundamental to understanding the Enlightenment.[27] As I have shown elsewhere, the eighteenth century's use of the word *système* is far less stable than Cassirer acknowledges, but his basic point is sound: the philosophes were deeply skeptical both of carefully constructed arguments leading from axioms to conclusions and of arbitrary taxonomic structures that purported to describe the world, but—as Buffon claimed of Linnaeus— were unable to account for particulars with any cogency.[28] The philosophes were equally unanimous in their rejection of a Christian theology as a basis for morality; their efforts to lay foundations for an ethical system of behavior while maintaining the impetus of the *esprit systématique* would lead them to propose a variety of arguments and approaches dependent on different contexts.[29]

Why should this matter in a discussion of moralists? Because, as I have suggested, both the moralists' embrace of open-ended forms and their interest in concrete particulars are very much in keeping with a broader

---

[27] Ernst Cassirer, *The Philosophy of the Enlightenment*, trans. Fritz C. A. Koelln and James P. Pettegrove (Princeton: Princeton University Press, 1951), esp. pp. xiii and 8–9.

[28] I explore the semantic shifts of the term *système* and *esprit systématique* as critical consciousness in Hayes, *Reading the French Enlightenment: System and Subversion* (Cambridge: Cambridge University Press, 1999).

[29] See Jacques Domenech, *L'Éthique des Lumières: Les fondements de la morale dans la philosophie française du XVIIIe siècle* (Paris: Vrin, 1989).

rejection of a certain kind of systematicity. In Diderot's account of the universe as a machine infinite in every direction, there is no intrinsic starting point; description involves choices that are arbitrary, heuristic.[30] Diderot's earliest philosophical work, *Pensées philosophiques* (1746), was a series of short, apparently disconnected, reflections. Many of his major works are dialogues; and a preference for parataxis, series of clauses without a governing syntactic structure, would characterize his writing throughout his career. He, Rousseau, Condillac, and their contemporaries experimented with juxtaposing different forms of expository order: synchronous/systematic and narrative/sequential. Rousseau's Second Discourse is a well-known example. Condillac's *Traité des sensations* is another.

This is not to say that the philosophes were entirely of one mind on the issue of method and its applications. In the *Encyclopédie*, the chevalier de Jaucourt defines "Morale" as "la science des moeurs," a phrase echoed in d'Holbach; in his article "Moraliste," Jaucourt goes on to praise figures whom we would more typically classify as political philosophers or moral philosophers (as the term is understood today): Grotius, Pufendorf, Tillotson, and William Wollaston.[31] The legal theorist Jean Barbeyrac, Pierre Nicole, and Jean La Placette (dubbed the "Protestant Nicole" during his lifetime, thanks to his *Nouveaux essais de morale* of 1695 and 1715) are the only French figures considered to be sufficiently scientific by Jaucourt, who dismisses without naming them the authors of "portraits" who seek "less to enlighten than to dazzle." But although Jaucourt is interested in taking *la morale* in a direction that leads toward modern ethics and political philosophy, it remains the case that the open-ended approach of *l'esprit systématique* pervades moralist writing as I have defined it here, particularly in its preference for fragmented forms and the essay—the latter, indeed, exemplified in Jaucourt's list by Nicole and La Placette. For readers of the period, the essay form retains the "experimental" connotation of the word and immediately recalls Montaigne's "reflective methodology" that calls on readers to let go of preconceptions and follow him in his explorations.[32]

---

[30] Denis Diderot, "Encyclopédie," in Denis Diderot and Jean Le Rond d'Alembert, eds., *Encyclopédie ou dictionnaire raisonné des sciences, des arts et des métiers*, 17 vols. (Paris: chez Briasson [et al.], 1751–1772); Denis Diderot, *Oeuvres completes*, ed. Dieckmann, Proust, Varloot (hereafter DPV), 25 vols. (Paris: Hermann, 1975–2004), 7:210–211.

[31] On the Encyclopedists' scientific ambitions for *la morale*, see Stéphane Pujol, *Morale et science des moeurs dans l'Encyclopédie* (Paris: Honoré Champion, 2021), esp. 59–66.

[32] Christia Mercer, "Prefacing the Theodicy," in Larry M. Jorgensen and Samuel Newlands, eds., *New Essays on Leibniz's Theodicy* (Oxford: Oxford University Press, 2014), 15–16.

To take the point a step further, consider Condillac's rewiring of one of the most influential works on philosophical method of the previous century, the Port Royal Logic, published in a series of revised editions from 1662 to 1683. Arnauld and Nicole distinguish two methods of philosophical exposition: analysis, or the "method of analysis or invention," a linear progression from the known to the unknown and back again; and synthesis or geometrical order, the "method of composition or synthesis," in which the exposition proceeds from axioms and logical demonstrations.[33] (Their usage is quite different from the contemporary analytic/synthetic distinction.) The Port Royal logicians consider synthesis to be the more persuasive of the two, and better suited to scientific exposition. For Condillac, however, analysis is more important, as it leads to the discovery of new truths. He further revises the classical method of decomposition and recomposition as a linear association of ideas (*liaison des idées*) based on sensations and observations: induction, not deduction.[34] Synthesis in his account is appropriate for setting forth known truths, but it will not lead us to anything new. Discovery, and hence progress, are only available through the study of particulars.

Moralist writing takes a similar route, seeking a general truth through the study of concrete particulars and inviting readers to puzzle, to interpret, to seek applications in their own lives, and to pause and reflect in the moment of reading. Thus, the later seventeenth-century moralists and their successors will take a different approach than earlier humanists such as Guillaume du Vair and Pierre Charron, who sought "to deduce norms of conduct directly from a general conception of human nature."[35] The study of concrete particulars will inform the moralist project going forward. Moralist works in the treatise format continue to surface in the eighteenth century—for example d'Arconville's *De l'amitié* and *Des passions*, Vauvenargues's *Introduction à la connaissance de l'esprit humain*, or Helvétius's *De l'esprit*—but they lack the systematizing, tightly organized exposition of the traditional treatise. Instead, they offer paratactically segmented chapters virtually indistinguishable from collections of essays.

---

[33] Antoine Arnauld and Pierre Nicole, *La Logique ou l'art de penser*, introduction by Louis Marin (Paris: Flammarion, 1970), 368–77.
[34] Etienne Bonnot de Condillac, "De l'ordre qu'on doit suivre dans la recherche de la verité," *Essai sur l'origine des connaissances humaines*, ed. Charles Porset with introduction by Jacques Derrida (Paris: Galilée, 1972), 278–85. I discuss Condillac's critique of philosophical systems in *Reading the French Enlightenment*, 111–41.
[35] Moriarty, *Fallen Nature*, 65.

1.3. Philosophy and Literature in Early Modern France

Chronologically, the moralist interest in fragments and short forms predates the philosophes' explicit rejection of *l'esprit de système*, but the two participate in the same large-scale cultural shift of modernity. This is hardly surprising when we consider that the forms of writing that we distinguish as "philosophy" and "literature" were both part of the larger world of letters. The first edition of the *Dictionnaire de l'Académie française* (1694) offers "erudition" as a synonym for "literature"; as late as 1800, Germaine de Staël's *De la littérature* surveys the entire field of humane letters. Moralist writing is a key part of the intellectual milieu in which both modern philosophy and the modern literary field emerged. The evolving definitions of both *philosophe* and *auteur* in dictionaries of the period are indicative of their emergent professional status and increasingly separate trajectories.[36]

Moralist writing, through its connection to Montaigne and the humanist tradition, carries forward an older, classically inspired, philosophy as a *mode de vie* or "a way of life," a way of seeing the world independently of (and prior to) the abstraction of philosophical discourse as it emerges in the modern period.[37] It represents ethics understood in a classical sense: not a set of moral injunctions, but rather an ongoing inquiry into the nature of the self, the good life, our ability to discern our own motives and those of others, and the grounds for social relations. It is a form of writing and an activity that holds literature and philosophy, fleetingly, in close contact with one another. Thus, although the seventeenth century sees the emergence of intellectual questions and practices that we identify with the birth of modern philosophy as a discipline—as well as the emergence of the literary field in its modern form—it is not surprising that these compelling topics are no one's exclusive property, but engage a broad range of writers and intellectuals, including women.

Socially, although the seventeenth-century moralists typically represent *mondanité*, worldliness, and salon culture, rather than the realm of

---

[36] Dinah Ribard, *Raconter vivre penser: Histoires de philosophes 1650–1766* (Paris: Vrin, 2003), 17–20. Pointing to the institutionalization of philosophy as an academic discipline after 1800, Ribard argues that nineteenth-century historiographers, exemplified by Victor Cousin, played a major role in structuring the French philosophical tradition in order to emphasize continuity with Descartes and the seventeenth century, and to exclude the eighteenth century (393–403).

[37] Philippe Hadot, *Philosophy as a Way of Life: Spiritual Exercises from Socrates to Foucault*, ed. Arnold I. Davidson, trans. Michael Chase (Malden, MA, and Oxford: Blackwell Publishing, 1995), 264–76.

erudition, science, and philosophy, the boundary between those two worlds was permeable. Aristocrats, *gens de lettres*, learned freethinkers, churchmen, and philosophers were among the men and women who frequented the great salons of the period, such as that of Catherine de Vivonne, marquise de Rambouillet, the model for so many that followed, and those of Madeleine de Sablé, Madeleine de Scudéry, Ninon de Lenclos, Anne-Thérèse de Lambert, and others.[38] Descartes's *Discours de la méthode* (1637) and Cureau de la Chambre's *Les Characteres des passions* (1640) found a wide readership in the worldly public. Treatises on the passions were a broadly popular European phenomenon.[39] Moralists read widely and drew on multiple philosophical traditions in ways that may appear incongruous to us. Montaigne was a model for this approach and a frequent conduit for moralist eclecticism; so too La Rochefoucauld, who offers an "essentially pagan (Aristotelian-Ciceronian)" conception of virtue in an Augustinian framework.[40] Or consider Geneviève d'Arconville, whose broadly Jansenist outlook accommodates a Stoic account of moral development.[41]

I emphasize the cultural rootedness and widespread interest of the questions animating moralist writing for two reasons. First, to underscore that although personal social affiliations tended, with exceptions, to crystallize in different spaces, the salon on the one hand and the official or unofficial academies on the other, the readership for these works crossed those boundaries. What we think of now as the territorial division between philosophy and literature was still in a nascent stage. Both inherit the legacy of skepticism and a sense of the limits of human knowledge from Montaigne, Charron, and the neo-Stoics. The "wisdom" enjoined by Charron in his widely read *De la sagesse* (1601) embraces both the traditional philosophical "way of life" and an emergent emphasis on systematic doubt. In the late seventeenth century, the common ground for *gens de lettres* and *mondains* of a thoughtful persuasion was *honnêteté*, an ethos of civility, carefully attuned

---

[38] See Robert A. Schneider's account of the of the "Generation of 1630" in *Dignified Retreat: Writers and Intellectuals in the Age of Richelieu* (Oxford: Oxford University Press, 2019), in particular the table of social/intellectual affiliations, 30–36. On the social heterogeneity of salon women (old and recent nobility, nonnoble elites), see Carolyn Lougee, *Le Paradis des femmes: Women, Salons, and Social Stratification in Seventeenth-Century France* (Princeton, NJ: Princeton University Press, 1976), 113–37. See also Roger Marchal, *Madame de Lambert et son milieu* (Oxford: Voltaire Foundation, 1991), 105–111; Van Delft, *Moraliste classique*, 151–56.
[39] Marc Fumaroli, *L'Age de l'éloquence* (1980; reprint Paris: Albin Michel, 1994), 381, n.395.
[40] Moriarty, *Disguised Vices*, 380.
[41] Lisa Shapiro, "*L'Amour, l'Ambition* and *l'Amitié*: Marie Thiroux d'Arconville on Passion, Agency, and Virtue," in Eileen O'Neill and Marcy P. Lascano, eds., *Feminist History of Philosophy: The Recovery and Evaluation of Women's Philosophical Thought* (Cham: Springer, 2019), 175–91

social relations, and reasoned exchange.[42] While the intellectual and political environment would evolve dramatically over the course of the eighteenth century, these basic shared understandings remained remarkably stable. Understanding this context provides an important part of the rationale for the period's fascination with the intersection of individual consciousness and the social world.

In her study of seventeenth-century theories of the passions, Susan James notes that contemporary philosophers tend to privilege schools of thought and debates that bear directly on contemporary philosophical questions, to the impoverishment not only of our historical understanding but also of our comprehension of the wider ramifications of those contemporary questions: "The landscape is flattened, stripped of many of the vistas and surprises that enliven a journey, and deprived of the singularity and complexity that makes a region distinctive."[43] By taking up questions that were of compelling interest in the period, but imperfectly appreciated today, James's analyses provide not merely "thick description" or intellectual anthropology, but a fuller understanding of Descartes, Malebranche, and, ultimately, the philosophical traditions that continue to engage with their work. Her focus on major canonical philosophers is explicitly intended to drive home the point about the importance and the pervasiveness of reflection on the emotions. We should also recognize that those now-canonical philosophers moved in a larger world of overlapping social and epistolary networks, and that their writing often spanned genres as well. Pierre Nicole, now better remembered as the coauthor with Antoine Arnauld of the Port-Royal Logic, was also the author of best-selling *Essais de morale*, continuously reprinted through much of the eighteenth century.

1.4. Women Moralists and the Canon

Women rarely appear in discussions of moralist writing, which is typically viewed through the lens of what might be called a Great Man Theory of the genre. Literary history often makes reference to Madeleine de Sablé, but

---

[42] For a succinct account of the place of moralist writing within French neoclassical culture, see Muriel Bourgeois-Courtois, "Réflexion morale et culture mondaine (matériaux pour une synthèse)," *XVIIe siècle*, no. 202 (Jan–March 1999): 9–19.

[43] Susan James, *Passion and Action: The Emotions in Seventeenth-Century Philosophy* (Oxford: Oxford University Press, 1997), 16.

usually as salon hostess and friend of La Rochefoucauld, rather than as the author of her own *Maximes*. The basis for Louis Van Delft's study, a corpus of over 500 seventeenth-century moralists compiled by Raymond Toinet, includes only three women: Madeleine de Sablé, Madeleine de Scudéry, and Madeleine Patin.[44] The genre has been defined in terms of its most illustrious exemplars, La Rochefoucauld, La Bruyère, and Pascal, with a nod to Saint-Évremond and later figures Vauvenargues and Chamfort. Many make references to the popularity of the genre—which La Rochefoucauld quipped people had "caught like a cold"—but generally dismiss lesser-known practitioners as an undifferentiated sea of *minores*.[45]

In short, critics have argued that moralist writing is universally popular and widespread, but that the works of only one or two writers define it. The influence of La Rochefoucauld is palpable in the idea that moralist writing should "aggress" the reader (Coulet), or that paradox (Thirouin) and an ironic twist or *pointe* (Parmentier) are among its defining characteristics. Certainly, these qualities contribute to the success of La Rochefoucauld's style and the "quotability" of his work—qualities to which as a reader I am not immune! But they do not begin to apply to the full range of writing, practiced by many, that seeks to explore and understand the human condition.

Why should we focus on women moralists from the long list of "minor writers"? Broadly speaking, their presence underscores the significance of moralist writing to thoughtful individuals outside the formal institutions of learning—university, academy, seminary—who sought to reckon with personal and social questions. More to the point, moralist writing represents the ground on which women, barred from those institutions, might engage in philosophical discourse on equal terrain with men, since the short forms do not require the formal training needed to produce an academic treatise.[46]

---

[44] Toinet's corpus was originally published in a series of issues of the *Revue d'histoire littéraire de la France*. *RHLF* 23, no. 3–4 (1916): 570–610; *RHLF* 24, no. 2 (1917): 296–306; *RHLF* 24, no. 4 (1917): 656–675; *RHLF* 25, no. 2 (1918): 310–320; *RHLF* 25, no. 4 (1918): 655–671. Van Delft edits and emends Toinet's corpus, 345–369.

[45] Van Delft relies on Toinet's corpus to sketch the general contours of the genre, but his detailed analysis is drawn from the major figures. Henri Coulet comments that the "little moralists" have little to offer the reader: "they do not aggress the reader, nor do they demand the effort of intelligence and sometimes decoding required by a Pascal or a La Rochefoucauld." ("Qu'est-ce qu'un petit moraliste?," in Jean Dagen, ed., *La Morale des moralistes* [Paris: Honoré Champion, 1999], 230.) André-Alain Morello appears to make a similar assumption, or to assume a similar expectation on the part of the reader, in his introduction to Sablé's *Maximes*: "She does not seek to provoke or challenge readers by putting in question the moral foundations of society, like La Rochefoucauld" (in Lafond, *Moralistes du XVIIe siècle*, 244).

[46] On women's modes of participation in intellectual life, see Laurent Vanoflen, "Le *genre* et la philosophie des Lumières," in Laurence Vanoflen, ed., *Femmes et philosophie des Lumières: De l'imaginaire à la vie des lettres* (Paris: Classiques Garnier, 2020), 7–27. On the gendering of cultural

Some women did produce formal treatises, of course—Gabrielle Suchon and Émilie Du Châtelet are important examples—but the treatise is hardly the only genre of philosophy during this period.[47] John J. Conley has argued that the salon, the world in which many women worked out their ideas, should be seen as a "philosophical site," and moralist writing understood as women's platform for making statements in ethics and moral psychology.[48] Indeed, the freedom and variety of moralist forms may have been particularly appealing to women.

The methodological issues surrounding the focus on women moralists parallel discussions of the inclusion of women in the history of early modern philosophy. In a classic article, Eileen O'Neill argued for a new understanding of history that would show "both how women's contribution to early modern philosophy are relevant to our present philosophical concerns and how their contributions are a vital part of the internal dialectics of philosophy."[49] Part of this work involves rethinking the foundations of present concerns and opening them to new questions; part involves opening up the canon to genres that modern philosophy has ignored or cast aside. As Lisa Shapiro and others have noted, many of the issues debated by women intellectuals, such as education and spirituality, have not been taken up—or were suppressed—by the philosophical mainstream. The work of women philosophers serves to remind us of the contingency and constructedness of the canon. So, too, a closer look at the work of women moralists sheds light on the aims and methods of the genre that extend beyond historical interest, to engagement with questions of enduring import.

It would not be appropriate to insist too heavily on "influence" or "contributions" to social or epistemic questions, if these are understood as public contributions known to contemporaries, as criteria for consideration, however. "Influence" is retrospectively constructed and replicates

---

and intellectual spaces, see Erica Harth, *Cartesian Women: Versions and Subversions of Rational Discourse in the Old Regime* (Ithaca, NY: Cornell University Press, 1992), 15–33.

[47] There has been broad recognition of the need for the history of philosophy to broaden both its corpus and its interpretive frameworks. See, among many others, Christia Mercer, "The Contextualist Revolution in Early Modern Philosophy," *Journal of the History of Philosophy* 57.3 (2019): 529–48; Lisa Shapiro, "Revisiting the Early Modern Philosophical Canon," *Journal of the American Philosophical Association* 2.3 (Fall 2016): 365–83; Sarah Tyson, *Where Are the Women? Why Expanding the Archive Makes Philosophy Better* (New York: Columbia University Press, 2018).
[48] Conley, *Suspicion*, 1–19.
[49] Eileen O'Neill, "Disappearing Ink," in Janet A. Kourany, ed., *Philosophy in a Feminist Voice: Critiques and Reconstructions* (Princeton, NJ: Princeton University Press, 1998), 43.

exclusionary practices.⁵⁰ Certainly, a number of these women were both famous and widely read. However, although the act of writing was vitally important for all of them, their opportunities for the circulation and publication of their work varied widely. Social rank, material circumstances, and the evolving shape of the literary field all play a part. Manuscript circulation, particularly in the seventeenth century, was a major driver in cultural and intellectual life. Among the figures of this study, Anne-Thérèse de Lambert participated avidly in this practice, as did Madeleine de Sablé. Lambert, famously, expressed dismay when one of her manuscripts was leaked to a publisher, and sought to purchase the print run herself. Although the episode has traditionally been viewed as Lambert's aristocratic fear of reputational harm—which, indeed, was a well-founded fear—it has been argued that her resistance to print publication stemmed more from her deep-seated sense of herself as a writer and desire to control the circulation of her work.⁵¹ Madeleine de Scudéry, one of the most admired writers of her day, established a model that others might follow, but the route to publication, particularly outside the domain of the novel, remained difficult and circuitous for women throughout the eighteenth century.

That not all engaged in print publication during their lifetimes, or that some of their works remained relatively obscure, does not negate their intrinsic interest or preclude their being worthy of study. In the chapters to come, we will see how all display writerly self-consciousness and deliberate participation in the formal and discursive conventions of moralist writing. Not all women participated in the same manner. Like Lambert, several withheld, or attempted to withhold, their work from print during their lifetimes; it was published posthumously by friends or family. Such was the case with Madeleine de Sablé, Suzanne Necker, and Marie-Louise de Fourqueux. Geneviève d'Arconville published her extensive body of work anonymously, then returned to writing for an audience of friends and family in the final years of her life.⁵² Although at an early stage of this project I had thought to exclude unpublished "personal" texts—*écrits du for privé*—I came

---

⁵⁰ Rebecca Wilkin, "Impact, influence, importance: Comment mesurer la contribution des femmes à l'histoire de la philosophie?" in Marie-Frédérique Pellegrin, ed., *Repenser la philosophie du XVIIe siècle: Canon et corpus*, special issue of *XVIIe siècle* 296 (2022/3), 435–50.

⁵¹ Marchal, 167–72, 197.

⁵² D'Arconville's manuscripts, bound in twelve volumes with the title *Pensées, réflexions et anecdotes* (hereafter PRA), are housed in the Morisset Library at the University of Ottawa. On the provenance of the PRA, see Marc André Bernier and Marie-Laure Girou Swiderski, "Présentation," *Madame d'Arconville, moraliste et chimiste au siècle des Lumières* (Oxford: Oxford University Studies in the Enlightenment, 2016), 6–10; the volume includes the table of contents of the PRA, 221–25.

to recognize the structuring influence of the moralist tradition as a hallmark of authorial agency and conscious participation in a philosophical tradition. One of the "private" projects discussed here is Dauphine de Sartre's *Recueils de choses morales*. Although they bear features of a commonplace book, her *recueils* contain a "Dissertation sur l'amitié" and general observations on moralist topics. In an important sign of authorial agency, Sartre thought her writing significant enough to have it copied; one copy found its way to North America, while another remained in the municipal archives of Marseille.[53] Even more "private" are the voluminous reflections and observations left by Suzanne Necker and published by her husband after her death, yet, as we shall see, her practice of writing was both intensely self-conscious and crucial to her involvement in intellectual discussion.[54]

In addition to achieving a more complete view of women's intellectual achievements and the work of individual women thinkers, I believe it important to set their work as moralists in the larger context of the genre as a whole, an ongoing conversation whose origins reach back over the centuries. Moralist writing, like the institution of the salon, is inextricably bound up with conversation. Not as a salon activity per se—scholars have discarded the once-prevalent idea that La Rochefoucauld and his friends improvised maxims in company—but as an awareness of and engagement with other writers, texts, and traditions. That engagement reflects their identification with larger intellectual networks, past and present, and nourishes the emergence of the woman writer as a conceptual category.

Women writers of the *ancien régime* were visible participants in the literary field, but the field was hardly a level one. In his landmark study of the emergence of the professional writer in seventeenth-century France, Alain Viala enumerates various "strategies of success," such as academies and patronage networks, but these were open primarily to men.[55] In his study, women figure as salon hostesses, hence a key element in establishing men's literary reputations. As Myriam Dufour-Maître has shown, women's "strategies of success" and the pathways that led them to write, to publish, and to decide

---

[53] Dauphine de Sartre, marquise de Robiac, *De sa propre main: Recueils de choses morales*, ed. Nancy M. O'Connor (Birmingham, AL: Summa Publications, 2003).

[54] As Catriona Seth points out, despite the formal differences among many "personal writings," many of the motives behind them respond to the same societal pressures that inhibited women from seeking publication. "La Fabrique de l'intime" (editor's introduction), in *La Fabrique de l'intime: Mémoires et journaux de femmes du XVIIIe siècle*, ed. Catriona Seth (Paris: Robert Laffont, 2013), 7–46.

[55] Alain Viala, *La Naissance de l'écrivain: Sociologie de la littérature à l'âge classique* (Paris: Editions de minuit, 1985).

whether or not to use their own names operated under very different rules.[56] Despite the challenges, women published their work and, over the course of the next century, became identified as professional writers and "authors" in the full sense given by Michel Foucault, as authors of ideas and founders of discourse.

Awareness of other women intellectuals was central to the decision of many to devote themselves to study and writing. Recent scholarship points to a European network of learned women well before the emergence of the distinctive concept of the "woman author" in the later eighteenth century.[57] Female authorship held a positive value in the seventeenth century's "intellectual feminism," before increasingly pejorative connotations became attached to the expression *femme savante*.[58] By the early eighteenth century, however, personal and institutional memories of earlier female intellectual networks were fading. Even among women writers, women's cultural production in the seventeenth century is more often rooted in salon life, rather in than the Republic of Letters. The Enlightenment brought in new models of cultural and intellectual production and participation, as *gens de lettres* and *philosophes* took the place of humanist *érudits*; new literary genres emerged; men's and women's roles, associational practices, and communication protocols shifted.

Women's intellectual production had long been highlighted in the tradition going back at least as far as Boccaccio of compendia of famous women that include figures from antiquity as well as more recent times. In the seventeenth century, grammarian Marguerite Buffet concluded her *Nouvelles observations sur la langue française* (1668) with a series of discourses in praise of illustrious learned women, ancient and modern. In 1690, the academician Gilles Ménage dedicated his history of women philosophers, *Mulierum philosopharum historia*, to the great classicist Anne Dacier, but he discusses figures from antiquity only. The genre proliferated through the eighteenth

---

[56] Myriam Dufour-Maître, *Les Précieuses: Naissance des femmes de lettres en France au XVIIe siècle*, new ed. (Paris: Honoré Champion, 2008). Dufour-Maître's study covers the same period as Viala's work and is an indispensable complement to it. See also the essays in Nicole Racine and Michel Trébitsch, eds., *Intellectuelles: Du genre en histoire des intellectuels* (Bruxelles: Editions Complexe, 2004).

[57] Carol Pal, *The Republic of Women: Rethinking the Republic of Letters in the Seventeenth Century* (Cambridge: Cambridge University Press, 2012).

[58] Linda Timmermans, *L'accès des femmes à la culture sous l'ancien régime* (1993; new ed., Paris: Champion, 2005), 19–86. Timmerman's study covers the period 1698-1715; for the eighteenth century, see Adeline Gargam's equally monumental *Les Femmes savantes, lettrées et cultivées dans la littérature française des Lumières, ou la conquête d'une légitimité (1690–1804)*, 2 vols. (Paris: Honoré Champion, 2013).

century, but only at the century's end and in the post-Revolutionary period do we see the woman-authored literary histories by Louise-Félicité de Keralio, Fortunée Briquet, and Félicité de Genlis. Over time, the category of the woman of letters comes into focus, emerging from the broader categories of "famous women" and "learned women." Even so, "femme de lettres" was a relatively novel expression, and the term "femme auteur," which came into use toward the end of the eighteenth century, was not always used as a compliment. These developments tell us that "women writers," however designated, formed a conceptual category that, by the post-Revolutionary period, had become controversial. The hundreds of names catalogued by the compendia remind us that the field of women intellectuals appeared much more populous to their contemporaries and near contemporaries, than it would be two centuries later.

1.5. Corpus and Topics: Who Is a Moralist?

I have chosen to treat as wide a variety of thinkers as possible, while restricting the list of topics. Other approaches would be possible, such as a series of in-depth studies on a smaller number of important figures, along the lines of Nina Gelbart's recent study of women of science, *Minerva's French Sisters*, which examines the contributions of six women to different fields in science and mathematics.[59] A number of the women in this study would lend themselves to such a treatment. (Gelbart and I share an interest in Geneviève d'Arconville.) To restrict the cast of characters to those who left a substantial body of moralist work or a single major contribution to the genre (for example, Scudéry, Lambert, Du Châtelet, d'Arconville, Necker, Staël) would not allow me to make my point about the widespread participation of women moralists in philosophical issues and would leave out numerous interesting figures. By presenting a larger number of thinkers, many of whom are "understudied," I hope to inspire further work.

Several of these women are not "minor" figures at all, but are quite well known, although often for other forms of writing. Madeleine de Scudéry was one of the mothers of the novel, but also produced collections of "conversations," philosophical dialogues on social life and the emotions.

---

[59] Nina Rattner Gelbart, *Minerva's French Sisters: Women of Science in Enlightenment France* (New Haven: Yale University Press, 2021).

Anne-Thérèse de Lambert, a prominent salon hostess, wrote influential essays on friendship, aging, and the status of women. Émilie Du Châtelet, scholar, mathematician, and scientist, wrote a powerful essay on happiness. Germaine de Staël, a major novelist and public intellectual of the post-Revolutionary period, wrote a treatise on the passions. Others, while less well known, have more recently become the focus of scholarly attention, especially Geneviève d'Arconville and Suzanne Necker. Even those women whose work has received significant scholarly attention have never been studied together as a group, nor has their collective contribution to moralist writing been recognized.

It is important to observe, however, that although early modern women produced philosophically significant work in a wide range of genres, not all of those works are moralist writing. Moralists are philosophers, but not all philosophers, even those focusing on women or topics related to those discussed in this book, are moralists. Given the parameters of the genre as defined here—prose, with a preference for the short form or essay; general observations anchored in the here-and-now of contemporary social practices; and an approach that may pass judgment, implicitly or explicitly, but is not didactic—there are important philosophical works by women that are not discussed here, or discussed only briefly. These include Marie de Gournay's *Égalité des hommes et des femmes*, Gabrielle Suchon's *Du célibat volontaire*, Louise Dupin's *Des femmes*, and Sophie de Grouchy's *Lettres sur la sympathie*. Similarly, although I have learned a great deal from his study, my corpus includes only two of the exemplars of "salon philosophy" studied by John J. Conley in *The Suspicion of Virtue*: Madeleine de Sablé and Marguerite de La Sablière. I discuss Françoise de Maintenon briefly, but the pedagogical and didactic aim of her conversations excludes them from moralist writing as defined here. While recognizing that the distinction between genres is not absolute, my focus in this study is primarily on secular or "worldly" moralist writing. I will have less to say about works with a clearly pedagogical aim, such as Lambert's *Avis à sa fille*, or works of an exclusively religious character. On the other hand, I discuss "hybrid" works of moralist reflections or essays that include formal elements of other types of writing, such as those of Henriette de Marans and Marie-Louise de Fourqueux.[60]

---

[60] Marans's *Pensées errantes* (1758) are a series of reflections offered as a sort of antipreface to a brief epistolary novel, "*quelques lettres d'un Indien*," but constitute three-quarters of the text: Bonne-Charlotte de Bénouville [and Henriette de Marans], *Pensées errantes; avec quelques lettres d'un Indien*, ed. Huguette Krief (Paris: Classiques Garnier, 2014); Fourqueux's *Confessions*, published

Although I will have more to say in later chapters about the significance of these women's writings to themselves and their contemporaries, an account of some of the kinds of connections that can be drawn among them offers food for thought. Certainly, the major salonnières (Lambert, Dupin, Necker) were highly visible in their day, as were a number of others as writers and intellectuals: Scudéry, Du Châtelet, Staël. Among women moralists, Lambert is undoubtedly the most frequently quoted by other women moralists. During her lifetime, Émilie Du Châtelet had an international reputation as a scientist and philosopher; long after her death, her name would be cited, often along that of the classical scholar Anne Dacier, as a model of the *femme savante*. Although her *Discours sur le bonheur* would be published long after her death, references to its prior manuscript circulation appear in Fourqueux's *Confessions* and the correspondence of Julie de Lespinasse.

Other connections are less visible, but have left traces either in women's writings or in the scholarship on their lives. Not surprisingly, La Sablière and Marie-Madeleine-Gabrielle de Rochechouart de Mortemart, abbesse de Fontevraud, two brilliantly educated, well-connected women who turned to a life of spirituality, knew one another. Du Châtelet and her husband purchased the Hôtel de Lambert from Louise Dupin and her spouse. Somewhat surprisingly, given her aversion for socializing aside from the select company of close friends and men of science, Geneviève d'Arconville was a connection for several women moralists. We know that she knew Marie-Louise de Fourqueux from a Paris police report noting that the two young women enjoyed a lively evening out in 1743. She probably knew Henriette de Marans, who was a lifelong friend and correspondent of her brother-in-law, Louis-Alexandre Angran d'Alleray. (D'Alleray appears to have facilitated the publication of Marans's *Pensées errantes* in 1758.) She knew Octavie Belot, later de Meinières, whom she eulogizes in one of her late essays, written not long before her own death in 1805. The journalist and man of letters Jean-Baptiste-Antoine Suard connects several figures: it was he who, at the request of Du Châtelet's lover Saint-Lambert, refrained from publishing the *Discours sur le bonheur* in 1764; a friend of Suzanne Necker, he was a regular in her salon and reprinted some of her early belle-lettristic writings in the *Variétés littéraires* that he coedited; in the years following the Revolution, he invited the young Pauline de Meulan, later Guizot, to become a regular contributor

---

posthumously, begin with a pair of autobiographical essays, then shift to a series of moralist essays on classical topics. Marie-Louise Auget de Monthyon de Fourqueux, *Confessions de Madame *** Principes de morale pour se conduire dans le monde*, 2 vols. (Paris: Chez Maradan, 1817).

to his journal *Le Publiciste*; and at the end of his life, he oversaw the long-delayed posthumous publication of Fourqueux's *Confessions*.

I offer this suggestive, but inevitably incomplete list, in order to signal the importance of looking beyond "influence," beyond publication histories, and beyond citation networks, in order to understand the variegated fabric of relationships that shaped the lives and ideas of early modern women thinkers. Their awareness of one another extends beyond celebrity and beyond the popular compendia of women writers, although these too played an important role in widening their horizon of possibilities and expectations. It has often been observed that famous women philosophers and intellectuals, like Dacier and Du Châtelet, might be admired, but were also considered unnatural and unfeminine. The problem did not soon disappear; both Germaine de Staël and Pauline Guizot complained about it in the early nineteenth century. Women novelists were undoubtedly more visible in the literary marketplace, but women moralists were crucial in broadening the purview of what constituted "women's writing." By their example they demonstrated that women's ideas on the major philosophical topics of the age as well as on the simple structures of everyday life were worth printing, reading, and discussing.

The topical organization of this study is intended to underscore the engagement of a wide range of women thinkers with issues of long-standing philosophical interest, as well as their ability to bring the moralist lens to issues that spoke directly to their experience as women. Each chapter begins with an overview of how the topic was framed in the period and, occasionally, how it has been framed in our own.

I have taken two approaches to the women moralists' responses to these topics, alternating close readings of individual texts, extended discussions on individual figures, and analyses of specific topics or subtopics that involve a wide number of women's voices. It would be simpler, undoubtedly, to focus on major figures such as Scudéry, Lambert, Du Châtelet, d'Arconville, and Staël, but also harder to make the point that a much broader spectrum of women were drawn to moralist writing and had significant insights to share. Each chapter has a roughly chronological organization that provides a sense of the changing tenor of moralist discourse and the evolving philosophical context; each features a varying cast of characters, since some women wrote on a wide range of topics, while others left a single work. The summary that follows will help readers locate extended discussions of major works and figures.

The first three topics stem from philosophical investigations of ethics and the good life; the topics reach back to antiquity, but also hold profound relevance to the changing social and political environment of seventeenth and eighteenth-century France.

1.5.1. Self-Knowledge and Knowledge of Others

We begin at the heart of the moralist enterprise. These texts are shaped by a philosophical landscape that leads from humanist skepticism and Jansenist "suspicion," to the foundational role of introspection in Cartesian thought and the Enlightenment's focus on materiality and sense perception. I analyze works by five women who offer different responses to the question of whether or not we are truly able to know ourselves, and who propose different techniques for seeking that knowledge: Madeleine de Scudéry's philosophical dialogue, "De la connoissance d'autruy et de soy-mesme"; Louise Dupin's short essay, "Réponse à une dame de mes amis," on the role of the senses in human understanding; two substantial essays by Marie de Verzure on the nature of the "heart" and the "soul," as well as her broader reflections on the value of introspection; a range of essays and brief reflections by Suzanne Necker, including her account of a conversation with Diderot on the nature of the soul; and an ironic take on the role of "experience" in moralist writing by Pauline Guizot.

1.5.2. Friendship

One of the most venerable topics in the moralist tradition, friendship comes with a canon of reference points in Aristotle, Cicero, and Montaigne, as well as questions that achieve quasi-canonical status as well: what are the proper foundations of friendship? What are the practices and obligations incurred by friendship? To what extent do sameness and difference (especially sexual difference) help or hinder friendship? Responses to these questions reflect a changing world, from an environment in which friendship may offer a refuge from the instrumentalizing relationships of court culture to the "new affectivity" of the eighteenth century. I argue that a preference for "difference," thematized in different-sex relationships drives much of the writing by women moralists, despite historical and biographical evidence of the importance of female friendship, because it offers not only an alternative to the classical insistence on male friendship, but also a theoretical space for recognition and separateness.

Many women wrote on friendship, some briefly and others in a more extended fashion: Madeleine de Sablé, Dauphine de Sartre, Louise Dupin, Elisabeth Guibert, Marie de Verzure, Marie-Louise de Fourqueux, Sophie de Grouchy, Constance de Salm, Germaine de Staël, Pauline Guizot. I offer detailed readings of several conversations by Madeleine de Scudéry, Anne-Thérèse de Lambert's *Traité de l'amitié*, and Geneviève d'Arconville's *De l'amitié*.

1.5.3. Happiness and the Passions

The early modern period inherits views on the relationship between the passions and happiness from both Stoic and Epicurean traditions. Moralists respond to that legacy, but also to the new medicalized taxonomies of the passions in Cureau de la Chambre and Descartes, as well as to the later valorization of Passion (singular), or intensity of feeling. I analyze the ways in which both Marguerite de La Sablière and Louise Dupin, for all their differences, share an interest in the effect of the passions on self-possession and personal integrity, as well as in the intersection of the passions, happiness, and temporality, an issue that also arises for Émilie Du Châtelet. Du Châtelet and Fourqueux each approach the question of happiness in terms of a practical guide of advice offered to oneself and the need to construct a "program." Here, too, the question of personal autonomy proves to be significant. The chapter offers detailed readings of Du Châtelet's *Discours sur le bonheur*, d'Arconville's *Des Passions*, and Staël's *De l'influence des passions sur le bonheur des individus et des nations*.

Although gender is clearly an element in women's treatment of these canonical topics, I turn in the second half of the book to topics in which women's experiences are the central focus of philosophical inquiry. While their reflections on the female condition draw to some extent from the long-standing *querelle de femmes* that exercised both men and women writers since the Middle Ages, the moralist perspective gives them a different slant than the traditional pro- or antiwoman stance of many earlier texts.

1.5.4. Marriage

Marriage is a noncanonical topic for moralist writing. Largely ignored, or treated ironically, by male writers, the subject is of weightier import to women, who cast a pitiless eye both on traditional arranged marriages and on the emergent ideal of companionate marriage. Although I take into account the political and legal critiques by Gabriel Suchon and Louise Dupin, my primary focus is on implicit and explicit critiques of the institution of marriage by moralists: Anne-Thérèse de Lambert, Madeleine de Puisieux, Marie de Verzure, and Geneviève d'Arconville. I also look in detail at the defense of marriage, or, more precisely, the arguments against the 1792 law permitting divorce, by Suzanne Necker. In the concluding section, I set the moralist analysis of marriage in the context of larger concerns with the nature of liberty by Émilie Du Châtelet, Octavie Belot, Sophie de Grouchy, Germaine de Staël, Constance de Salm, and Pauline Guizot.

1.5.5. Age and Experience

Classical antiquity, especially the writings of Cicero and Seneca, provides much of the agenda for moralist inquiry, with questions of the conduct appropriate to different stages of life, the need to lay foundations for old age in one's youth, and the preparation for death. As Anne-Thérèse de Lambert points out, however, the advice of the Ancients rarely applies to women, a lacuna that she proposes to fill in her *Traité de la vieillesse*. In this chapter, I look at works by Madeleine de Scudéry, Dauphine de Sartre, Marie de Verzure, Henriette de Marans, Suzanne Necker, Geneviève d'Arconville, and Pauline Guizot, with a special focus on Scudéry, Lambert, and d'Arconville. For all, the moralist reflection on old age becomes a means to critique the status of women in society.

1.5.6. Women's Nature and Capabilities

The early modern literature on "women's nature" is immense, as is the scholarship on the subject. Given the entwinement of moralist writing with social practice, I begin by grounding this chapter in seventeenth-century court culture, the ethos of *honnêteté*, politeness, and the "desire to please" (*désir de plaire*) that was considered by some as fundamental to women and by all as crucial to maintaining social relations. This chapter introduces two new figures from the later seventeenth century: the abbesse de Fontevraud, who wrote a brief essay on politeness, and Jeanne-Michelle de Pringy, author of a substantial work, *Les Différents caractères des femmes du siècle*. I offer a detailed reading of Pringy's work, which gives a sharp critique of women's propensity to *amour-propre*, but a sharper critique of the society that requires and rewards such behavior; her approach to moral psychology includes a pedagogy aimed at enabling women to progress toward greater self-awareness and virtue. Anne-Thérèse de Lambert's *Réflexions nouvelles sur les femmes*, written in response to Malebranche's dismissal of women's intelligence, falls at a transitional moment between the Cartesian feminist philosopher Poulain de la Barre's assertion that "the mind has no sex" and the eighteenth century's increasing emphasis on biological determinism. I argue that Lambert seeks to have it both ways, defending women's intelligence while upholding their cultural authority in matters of taste and proclaiming the importance of "feeling," a harbinger of the Enlightenment to come. Other figures studied include Madeleine de Scudéry, Marie de Verzure, Geneviève d'Arconville, and Françoise-Albine Benoist, author of *Lettres sur le désir de plaire*, a set of moralist portraits posing as a novel.

One of the overarching arguments of this book is that through their critique of institutions and practices, their valorization of introspection and self-expression, and their distinctive engagement with philosophical issues, women moralists carve out an important space for the public exercise of their reason. Something crystallizes in the late eighteenth century, as evinced by the emergence of the term "woman writer" (*femme auteur*). The final section thus moves beyond moralist writing per se to examine that moment and the acrimonious debates that flared around the phantasmatic figure of the woman writer. At issue are all the questions discussed in the chapter: women's intrinsic qualities, intelligence, and proper station and duties in life. I close with a discussion of three major figures of the post-Revolutionary era: Germaine de Staël, Félicité de Genlis, and Pauline Guizot.

I view the intellectual projects of these women as feminist. They contribute to a female intellectual tradition and broaden the space for women's participation in the public sphere. That they themselves represent a broad range of views is hardly surprising, given the diversity of their backgrounds and historical circumstances. Some might be at odds with contemporary notions of feminism and female agency. We need to consider them with an inclusive, historically sensitive approach.

The classical moralist perspective is founded on a paradox. It offers authoritative, universalizing observations on the human experience, but always in a distinctly individual, "partial," authorial voice, grounded in the present. Both particularity and mastery pose special traps for women writers, too often assumed to be overly attached to the former, incapable of the latter. The "short forms"—maxim, essay, dialogue—of the moralist tradition prove to be a valuable tool for asserting women's claim to a distinguished tradition and their own right to observe and analyze.

2
On Self-Knowledge and Knowledge of the Self

At the confluence of humanist inquiry, devotional practice, post-Fronde politics, and Cartesian philosophy, the Delphic maxim "Know thyself" resonates throughout seventeenth-century France. The imagery of interiority, the "hidden folds of the heart," takes root in the writings of mystics, in post-Tridentine spirituality, and in the rich complexities of Baroque art, with its interplay of surface and depth, interior and exterior, light and shadow. The metaphor of the heart's "depth" spreads from the writings of Catholic mystics to the Augustinian theology of Port-Royal and on through a widening semantic field that ultimately encompasses metaphysics, psychology, and literary representation in a discourse of secrecy, unknowability, and tragic consciousness.[1] The Enlightenment carries forward the examination of psychological depth, while eschewing its tragic aspect and focusing on what can be elucidated in the *science des moeurs*.

Seventeenth-century philosophical and theological approaches to the question of self-knowledge point to the intrinsic connection of what are now viewed as separate spheres, psychology and ethics: understanding the workings of the mind in pursuit of understanding the good life.[2] Self-knowledge can be construed in two ways: as insights gained from the study of one's own character and motivations, on the one hand; and as understanding the nature of the self, its operations, and its relation to the body-mind distinction, on the other. In this chapter, I focus on works by Madeleine

---

[1] Benedetta Papasogli, *Le "Fond du coeur": Figures de l'espace intérieur au XVIIe siècle*, trans. Claire Silbermann and Marie-Pierre Benveniste (Paris: Honoré Champion, 2000). Originally published in Italian (1994).
[2] See Moriarty, *Fallen Selves*, 95–98. For Moriarty, the period's approaches tend to fall into two general categories, "descriptive" (with a strong normative dimension) and "problematic." The thinkers who incline to the latter approach, for whom "human nature is problematic because it is not easy to identify its essential features," are typically those whom we associate with the emergence of modernity: Montaigne, Descartes, Pascal. The approach also has deep ties to Augustinianism. The two approaches combine in a figure like Charron, whose *De la sagesse* probes both the elusiveness and the necessity of self-knowledge.

de Scudéry, Louise Dupin, Marie de Verzure, Suzanne Necker, and Pauline Guizot, whose works reflect different dimensions of the topic and echo the changing philosophical landscape. Among the questions they confront are the nature of self-awareness and the reliability of our self-perception; the existence of "thoughts" that are not available to consciousness; the nature of belief and the question of whether the self is material or nonmaterial; and the techniques and benefits of introspection. Introspection and a proper understanding of oneself, a long-standing requirement of religious practice, continue to be foundational to virtue in an increasingly secular age.

As discussed in the previous chapter, the neo-Augustinian Jansenist movement brings a deep-seated suspicion to the possibility of human self-understanding. Pierre Nicole's extended essay "De la connaissance de soi-même" ("On Self-Knowledge") from his influential, oft-reprinted *Essais de morale*, exemplifies the Jansenist view.[3] Like his friend Blaise Pascal, Nicole views our inability to see within ourselves, or more accurately, our reluctance to do so, as a sign of our fallen state. Nicole's point of departure is our avoidance of self-knowledge and the many strategies with which self-love, *amour-propre*, causes us to deceive ourselves, both in our interactions with others and in our innermost meditations. We commonly assent to the proposition that self-knowledge is a good thing—but only for other people, whose faults we assess with a clarity that we withhold from ourselves. Our self-examination is founded on vanity and provides no true self-knowledge: "Man desires to see himself, because he is vain. He avoids seeing himself, because his vanity cannot bear the sight of his failings and misery" (Nicole, 342). For Nicole and the Port-Royal theologians, self-love can only be overcome by God's grace—indeed, it is only through grace that we find within ourselves the desire to overcome it. For Nicole, the human psyche's mystery resides within subconscious "imperceptible thoughts" (*pensées imperceptibles*), a forerunner of modern notions of the unconscious.[4]

The manifold disguises of *amour-propre* are a perennial topic of moralist reflection. Nowhere was this more powerfully expressed than in the extended maxim that La Rochefoucauld included in the first edition of the *Maximes* (1665), but cut from subsequent editions, now known as "Maxime

---

[3] Pierre Nicole, "De la connaissance de soi-même," in *Essais de morale: Choix d'essais*, ed. Laurent Thirouin (Paris: Encre marine, 2016), 337–412. Nicole's essay appeared in the third volume of the *Essais de morale*, published in 1675, five years after the publication of Blaise Pascal's *Pensées* by Nicole and a committee of Pascal's family and friends at Port-Royal.
[4] On Nicole's theory of the unconscious, see Béatrice Guion, *Pierre Nicole, moraliste* (Paris: Honoré Champion, 2002), 121–85.

supprimée 1," that concludes with an evocation of self-love as fundamentally undescribable: "Nothing is as impetuous as its desires, nothing more hidden than its plans... its cunning cannot be described, its transformations surpass metamorphosis, and its subtlety greater than chemistry" (La Rochefoucauld, *Maximes*, 179–80). More easily evoked via negations and analogies, in language pushed to the edge of representability, coming to an unstable conclusion in the final image of the sea, *amour-propre* undermines any form of interiority and self-mastery.[5]

While women moralists are also mindful of the problem of the distortions wrought by self-love, their approaches vary. Although highly sympathetic to Jansenism, Madeleine de Sablé suggests that self-knowledge may be uncommon, but it is not impossible: "It is possible to know oneself well, but we do not examine ourselves sufficiently to achieve this, being instead concerned about appearing as we should, rather than being as we should."[6] A century later, Geneviève d'Arconville, also deeply influenced by Jansenism, argues that although self-love is a character flaw, it also drives exploration and scientific progress: "a dangerous gift, but often useful."[7] The difficulty of the pursuit of self-knowledge makes it no less imperative. To anticipate arguments in later chapters, women moralists remain mindful of the moral and epistemological pitfalls occasioned by *amour-propre* in a variety of contexts, but self-understanding remains key to their goal. Their continued effort echoes the more optimistic Cartesian position that defects in our self-understanding may be countered through the exercise of one's reason.[8]

Indeed, even moralists who consider the innermost self as ultimately unknowable often refer to their task as the anatomy of the human heart. While the French word *anatomie* initially referred simply to the human body or a representation thereof, in the sixteenth century it came to refer to the practice of medical dissection. As "anatomists," moralists engage in a positive project allied with the ambitions of modernity: the will to know, to analyze, and to describe.[9] The inquiry into human psychology and human behavior is

---

[5] Starobinski, "La Rochefoucauld et les morales substitutives," 19.
[6] Madeleine de Sablé, Max. 19, *Maximes*, in Lafond, *Moralistes du XVIIe siècle*, 248.
[7] D'Arconville, *Discours sur la chimie*, in *Mélanges de littérature, de morale et de philosophie*, 7 vols. (Amsterdam: Au dépens de la compagnie, 1775), 3:88. (All references to d'Arconville's published works will be to the *Mélanges*, the collected edition produced under her supervision.)
[8] On self-knowledge as an essential component of individual agency and liberty in the Cartesian philosopher François Poulain de la Barre's feminist agenda, see Martina Reuter, "François Poulain de la Barre on the Subjugation of Women," in Jacqueline Broad and Karen Detlefsen, eds., *Women and Liberty, 1600–1800* (Oxford: Oxford University Press, 2017), 33–49.
[9] Louis Van Delft, "La Rochefoucauld et l'anatomie du coeur," *Littératures classiques* 35 (Jan 1999): 37–62.

thus marked, on the one hand, by Jansenist suspicion of human motives and capabilities, and on the other, by the emergent Enlightenment confidence in our capacity to know ourselves and the world. As many have observed, the will to know is also a will to power; in the context of the *ancien régime*, the ability to know oneself and others provides a crucial practical advantage in navigating the labyrinth of protocols and motivations that shape public life. The self is contested territory: inspired by Montaigne's elusive *Que sais-je?* but also, increasingly, by philosophical investigations into the mechanisms of knowledge and perception, moralists explore what Charles Taylor terms "radical reflexivity" as the inner self is seen less as a manifestation of unchanging human nature and increasingly as an individual product of time and circumstance.[10]

In the readings to follow, I will discuss how Madeleine de Scudéry's philosophical dialogue on knowledge of the self and others responds to her contemporaries' deep-seated skepticism regarding such knowledge. She acknowledges the pervasive distorting influence of self-love, while offering a potential solution to the problem. Louise Dupin's short essay, written a few decades later, grounds both mental operations and the nature of belief in sensation and feeling. Marie de Verzure seeks to establish a comparison between self and other in order to understand mental operations. Like Dupin, she considers the possibilities of a physiological base for thought and feeling, as well as a social and political program derived from her approach. In a wide-ranging series of reflections and short essays, Suzanne Necker meditates on mental operations, the nature of the self, and the interplay of introspection and the act of writing. Pauline Guizot evinces doubts as to the knowability of the self, but in a manner that reflects a newer understanding of the problem in the early years of the nineteenth century. In conclusion, I will consider more broadly the ways in which the practice of moralist introspection played an important role in women's self-construction and sense of agency.

2.1. Scudéry: Conversation

In the final decades of her long and distinguished career, Madeleine de Scudéry (1607–1701), perhaps sensing a sea-change in the literary

[10] Charles Taylor, *The Sources of the Self: The Making of Modern Identity* (Cambridge, MA: Harvard University Press, 1989).

marketplace in which her multivolume *romans fleuves* had seen such success, began publishing collections of worldly philosophical dialogues that echoed the ideal sociability cultivated in her salon. Several of these pieces were drawn from her earlier novels, *Artamène ou le Grand Cyrus* (1649–53) and *Clélie* (1654–60), but increasingly they were new works.[11] Scudéry's *Conversations*, published in ten volumes under various titles from 1680 to 1692, touch on topics ranging from the norms governing polite conversation to time-honored subjects such as anger, the passions, jealousy, love, friendship, and the desire for glory.[12] In two of the later conversations, "L'histoire de deux caméléons" (Scudéry 1688, 2:496–541) and "L'histoire des papillons" (Scudéry 1692, 2:196–333), her observations of the natural world form the basis for contesting Descartes's theory of animal machines. The *Conversations* have been viewed as a sort of vulgarization or translation of moral and philosophical issues into the language of salon conversation,[13] but the nuanced working-through of the topics goes beyond vulgarization to offer carefully constructed explorations of moral psychology and ethics.

"De la connoissance d'autruy, et de soy-mesme," appears in Scudéry's first anthology, *Conversations sur divers sujets* (1680). While the organization of topics in *Conversations sur divers sujets* is not that of a systematic treatise, it is far from accidental. For example, it is clear that each of the first three conversations sets up a different aspect of Scudéry's program. The first, "De la conversation," provides the grounding principles of sociability and enlightened exchange among peers. The egalitarian give-and-take among women and men already represents the philosophical position that "the 'soul has no sex.'"[14] Although her characters express multiple views on the subject at hand, there is invariably a normative center: usually an older, wiser man or woman or couple in the role of *raisonneur*, as in a play by Molière. Which is

---

[11] Nicole Aronson, *Mademoiselle de Scudéry, ou le voyage au pays de Tendre* (Paris: Fayard, 1986), 300–319. On the reception of the *Conversations*, see Elizabeth C. Goldsmith, *Exclusive Conversations: The Art of Interaction in Seventeenth-Century France* (Philadelphia: University of Pennsylvania Press, 1988), 41–43.

[12] Each of the five collections contains two volumes; I will refer to them by date. For full details, see the Bibliography.)

[13] See Chantal Morlet-Chantalat, "Parler du savoir, savoir pour parler: Madeleine de Scudéry et la vulgarization galante," in Colette Nativel, ed., *Femmes savantes, savoirs de femmes* (Genève: Droz, 1999), 177–95.

[14] Eileen O'Neill, "Women Cartesians, 'Feminine Philosophy,' and Historical Exclusion," in Susan Bordo, ed., *Feminist Interpretations of René Descartes* (University Park: Pennsylvania State University Press, 1999), 248. For an overview of Scudéry's philosophical positions, see John Conley, "Madeleine de Scudéry," in Edward N. Zalta, ed., *The Stanford Encyclopedia of Philosophy* (Fall 2019 Edition), https://plato.stanford.edu/archives/fall2019/entries/madeleine-scudery/.

not to suggest that the conversations are didactic. Readers are responsible for exercising discernment, identifying the "reasonable" characters, and drawing their own conclusions. In Scudéry's conversations, the examination of the topic produces a cartographic exploration of the matter at hand, with various characters offering different perspectives, personal narratives, and exempla, as they plot a trajectory that ultimately brings them into harmony and produces what Elizabeth Goldsmith has called "euphoric" sociability.[15]

The second conversation, "Des plaisirs," follows the model prescribed in "De la conversation," as characters map out different aspects of the topic, such as whether or not one can have too much or too many pleasures, the distinction between pleasure and mere diversion (*divertissement*), and the relationship between pleasure and virtue. Scudéry's characters seek not to define the essence of pleasure itself—whether it consists of "a movement of the soul" or in "repose" (Scudéry 1680, 1:49)—but, in keeping with the norm of moralist inquiry, they instead analyze its operations in lived experience. "Des plaisirs" focuses on both individual psychology and group dynamics and begins to touch the deeper question of our capacity to understand our own motives and those of others. These become the focus of the third conversation, "De la connoissance d'autruy et de soy-mesme" ("On the Knowledge of Others and Oneself").

"De la connoissance d'autruy et de soy-mesme" goes straight to the heart of the moralist enterprise. A select company of men and women explore the epistemological foundations of social relationships: our ability to know one another, to gain insight into our own motivations, and to learn from past experiences. Scudéry, whose settings always bear a subtle relationship to the topic at hand, stages the encounter of "a fine group" bearing classical names who have just come from viewing the Nemean Games; they stroll through an ideal landscape worthy of Poussin, where nature and art combine to enhance the pleasure of recent acquaintanceship. The conversation departs subtly from the "euphoric" model, as it foregrounds a debate between two female characters that explicitly mirrors the games of athletic prowess that the company has just witnessed.

Scudéry underscores the fact that the members of the group do not know each other well, and some do not know each other at all, but that their collective participation as spectators for the athletic competition has put them at

---

[15] Goldsmith borrows the term from sociologist Erving Goffman's account of "focused encounters" that seek to minimize any disjuncture between the group and external or individual idiosyncrasies, maximizing the "euphoria function" of the group's interactions. *Exclusive Conversations*, 47.

ease with one another. The newness of their acquaintance sets up one of the central questions of the conversation, whether we can possess true knowledge of others. As in other conversations in this collection, "De la connoissance d'autruy" contributes to an overarching reflection on the practices of sociability, its requisites and rules. The friendly exchange of ideas reminds us that, although (as the characters will eventually agree) other people are fundamentally unknowable to us, the limits of our knowledge are no obstacle to participating in a community.

In the discussion that follows, I will follow the text closely. Scudéry's philosophical dialogues follow a pattern: exploration of different aspects of the main topic, examples, alternatives, and resolution. Attentive readers will not be in doubt as to which characters are the most "reasonable," but they will not find "arguments" in the manner of the Platonic dialogues. Instead, her characters follow sometimes circuitous routes to arrive at understanding and consensus (or near-consensus). This approach represents not only a statement about the collective construction of knowledge, but also a pedagogy for achieving it.

Our attention is drawn to two central female figures. On the one hand, we have the lively Céphise, who claims to judge everything "sur l'événement" and praises superficial judgment as the least likely to lead us into the bitterness of disappointment (Scudéry 1680, 1:91). Céphise's claims are however immediately nuanced by the more thoughtful Télésile, who in turn is supported by the victorious athlete Arate, who is clearly in love with her. Banter on whether it is better to look beneath the surface of love and friendship shifts to the deeper question of whether such knowledge is even possible.

The question of knowledge arises within a discussion of civility, with which it remains closely linked. Céphise denies praising superficiality as such, but argues that one is usually better off not probing too deeply into the motives behind friendship and love, for fear of "destroying one's own pleasure" (Scudéry 1680, 1:93). When Télésile protests that we cannot possibly love or enjoy friendship with people if we do not know them thoroughly, Céphise quips that this is invariably the case: "I will prove that everyone loves everyone, and no one knows anyone" (Scudéry 1680, 1:94). Timocrate—the mature *raisonneur* of the group—suggests that self-knowledge is even more difficult than knowledge of others. Céphise and several others find this strange. As one puts it, "I do not hide from myself in the way that others disguise themselves" (Scudéry 1680, 1:94–95).

These early episodes allow us to understand the characters' roles, establishing Télésile and Timocrate in the space of good judgment, with Céphise as the clever but superficial friend in need of guidance. The group takes on the project of understanding Timocrate's seeming paradox: after all, why should it not be the case that our self-awareness gives us better insight into our own selves than into others, especially given that they often deceive us? Télésile sides with Timocrate, noting the roles played by self-love, *amour-propre*, which shields us from unpleasant truths, and habit, which dulls our perception, citing as analogy our failure to attend to the beauties of nature that we see every day, "the Sun, Moon, and stars" (Scudéry 1680, 1:97–98). The point has to do with the effects of habit, but the metaphor of the sun will return at a key moment in the conversation. Furthermore, Timocrate observes that our familiarity with our own "inclinations," even a major one like self-love, is what prevents us from seeing them (Scudéry 1680, 1:101). Habit, pride, and a banal "civilité universelle" are the principal barriers to insight.

Change over time proves to be a complicating factor. As an example of the difficulty in knowing others, Céphise cites the common occurrence of discovering an unpleasant quality possessed by someone whom we have known for many years; Timocrate notes that what we take to be a hitherto unrecognized quality may simply be the effect of change (Scudéry 1680, 1:132); Télésile will later point out that Céphise herself has changed in her attitude toward certain friends (Scudéry 1680, 1:151–52). Despite the uncertainties wrought by change, however, all the characters appear committed to a notion of the self as a continuous personal identity. Neither Céphise nor Télésile challenges our awareness of the continuity of the self; Télésile points out that our attitudes change over time, yet a sense of one's identity persists. This is an important claim for Scudéry. In the preceding conversation, "Des plaisirs," the lead character reminds the others that the things in which one takes pleasure—considered to be the key to understanding a person—will vary constantly throughout one's lifetime (Scudéry 1680, 1:57). The constant variation and change in one's tastes and desires are thus no obstacle to the persistence of identity.

With their positions broadly staked out, and neither giving signs of conceding, Télésile and Céphise engage in a formal debate, presided over by Timocrate, on two questions: Which is more difficult, knowledge of others or self-knowledge? And which of the two is the most useful? Throughout, Scudéry's interlocutors maintain both their lofty ideals of friendship, love, and social relations, and their skepticism as to the possibility of true knowledge of self or others, given the complexities of interpersonal exchange, social masks, and *amour-propre*. Céphise defends the proposition that knowledge of others is most difficult: "Knowledge of those whom we see the most often is more often than not an art of conjecture" (Scudéry 1680, 1:133) and ultimately, "the heart is impenetrable" (Scudéry 1680, 1:137). Others agree.

Télésile, on the other hand, argues that as difficult as it is to know other people, the ruses of self-love make it far more difficult to know oneself: "Because the self-love hidden within our heart creates illusions in our mind without our realizing it. Other people deceive us when we attempt to know them, but we deceive ourselves sometimes without thinking—and sometimes, deliberately" (Scudéry 1680, 1:140–41). Céphise, firmly grounded in a sense of herself based on the immediacy of her lived experience and knowledge of her own mental states, argues that she knows what she thinks, what she likes, what she hates, what she does and does not want (Scudéry 1680, 1:146). At this point, Télésile counters with the full force of Augustinian psychology:

> Against you are arrayed your senses, your pleasures, your inclinations, your temperament, as well as that self-love that cannot be emphasized enough. It is so well disguised that it occupies all our heart and mind and infuses our sentiments: we do not feel it, we do not know it, and we do not want to know it. (Scudéry 1680, 1:147)

Like the theologian Nicole and the Jansenist-leaning La Rochefoucauld, Scudéry's characters—other than Céphise—are persuaded that our own motivations, our own passions, are largely hidden from our view. Self-love is one explanation for our failure, but Timocrate points to an additional problem, the elusiveness of thought during even the most rigorous self-examination: "some thoughts succeed one another so rapidly that we are only aware of the last one that impels us to action" (Scudéry 1680, 1:115) Scudéry thus offers two explanations for our lack of insight. One is framed in terms of Augustinian psychology, but Timocrate's comment suggests that our ignorance is a function of the operations of the mind.

The contest between Télésile and Céphise reaches its apogee with a return to the sun imagery from Timocrate's earlier comments on how habit dulls our perception of the natural world. Céphise insists that she sees herself "as easily as I see the Sun" (Scudéry 1680, 1:148). Télésile responds,

Be aware that at first glance the Sun—to use your comparison—appears brilliant and luminous. But one must examine it closely over time in order to see its spots. Thus, if we examine ourselves only for an instant, we will know ourselves imperfectly. (Scudéry 1680, 1:148–49)

Télésile possesses the knowledge and technique needed to be able to gaze "avec application" at the sun without being dazzled, and by extension, to examine herself. The observation of the heavens and the science of optics yield powerful metaphors for knowledge and indeed for the moralist enterprise, traditionally evoked in terms of portraits, vision, and spectatorship.[16] Céphise admits that she has never undertaken any of the techniques of self-examination recommended by Télésile, who for her part concedes that it is certainly easier to *prove* that knowledge of others is more difficult; Timocrate awards points to both of them, but clearly Télésile has conceded only a secondary matter; her overall arguments are weightier.

The second debate question, on whether knowledge of others or of oneself is more useful, is dispatched more quickly. Predictably, Céphise argues in favor of the former, pointing out the practical advantages of being able to steer one's course, whether in love, friendship, business, or advancement at court (Scudéry 1680, 1:154). Télésile politely points out that, given Céphise's doubts regarding our ability to know others, this advantage is quickly nullified; in any case, even if knowledge of others is useful for improving one's material circumstances, self-knowledge is essential "to advance in virtue" (Scudéry 1680, 1:156). All concur that the goal of fortifying one's virtue trumps material concerns. According to Télésile, if we are aware of our failings, we will correct them, just as Céphise would adjust her hair if she happened to see it out of place while passing by a mirror. Dismissing arguments that we do not always possess the strength of character required to combat "a bad inclination," Télésile asserts that true virtue depends on self-examination; without self-understanding and intention, virtuous acts are not truly virtuous. "No one is virtuous by accident" (Scudéry 1680, 1:161).

Despite the skepticism of many of her pronouncements ("One must distrust one's heart in order to know it" (Scudéry 1680, 1:150), Télésile offers

---

[16] Bernard Roukhomovsky, "Portrait du moraliste en opticien," in B. Roukhomovsky, ed., *L'Optique des moralistes de Montaigne à Chamfort* (Paris: Honoré Champion, 2005), ix–xix.

two alternatives to the prospect of ignorance and self-deception. One is found in a strong, carefully cultivated will, *la volonté*, which can guard us against most ills, save, perhaps "a grand passion" (Scudéry 1680, 1:160). The other is sociability itself, *le commerce du monde*, which allows us to see ourselves in others' eyes and to compare ourselves to others. The "friendly jests" provide agreeable instruction ("les corrige en les divertissant," Scudéry 1680, 1:164). This idea reassures Céphise, who feared that self-knowledge was only available to those who abandoned society (Scudéry 1680, 1:165). Conversation itself thus becomes the central model for a knowledge that remains aware of its limits, but is not crippled by them, that is founded on the exchange of ideas and "the liberty that makes society pleasant" (Scudéry 1680, 1:84–85).

Timocrate has the final word. First, he cautions his friends—and the reader—that it is easier to gain general knowledge than knowledge of particulars: "it is easier to know national character than a single individual from a given country" (Scudéry 1680, 1:167). Second, returning to the optical analogies that he favors, he reminds us of the need for a just perspective:

> The greatest difficulty in knowing others, and oneself, is the same as with physical objects that we see confusedly at too great a distance, and that we cannot properly discern when they are too close to the eye. (Scudéry 1680, 1:170)

Other people are too far, we ourselves are too close, for us ever to achieve perfect understanding of either. The reader thus embarks on the journey of the *Conversations*, knowing what can be seen, and the limits of our vision.

Scudéry shares with the Jansenists and their fellow travelers a profound doubt in our ability to arrive at the deepest levels of self-understanding, or to chart the causes of our drives and passions. The shadow of *amour-propre* prevents us from clearly seeing uncomfortable truths. She differs from them, however, in her belief that we are able to make progress in approaching those truths. One can "advance in virtue" through an exercise of the will and through participation in the ideal social exchanges embodied in salon conversation. Her poised courtiers, for all their classical dress, are in many respects looking ahead beyond the waning rays of the Sun King's reign, to the Enlightenment's preoccupation with the phenomenal world, time, and change.

2.2. Dupin: Sensation and Belief

The short essay by Louise Dupin (1706–1799), "Réponse à une dame de mes amies" ("Response to a Female Friend"), is one of the undated manuscripts included in the collection of her papers and correspondence, *Le Portefeuille de Madame Dupin*, published nearly a century after her death by her great-grandnephew Gaston Villeneuve-Guibert.[17] Best known during her lifetime as the hostess of a brilliant salon, Dupin employed a young Jean-Jacques Rousseau as her secretary in the late 1740s; several of the pieces in the *Portefeuille* are in his handwriting, with her corrections. One of Rousseau's chief duties during his employment was to serve as research assistant for Dupin's planned magnum opus, *Des femmes*, a critique of women's legal and social status in France based on cross-cultural comparisons and an exhaustive historical survey.

The question to which Dupin is responding appears to concern our ability to know God; the faintly defensive turn of one passage and her statement that her view "does not favor Atheism" (*Portefeuille*, 123), suggests that her interlocutor had evinced some doubt as to the solidity of her religious convictions. In addition to a statement of faith, Dupin's essay offers an account of the fundamental role of the senses in human understanding, a reflection on the limits of knowledge, and an argument that we are able to have awareness of phenomena of which we do not have immediate sensory evidence.

Dupin begins by stating the central role of the senses as "the gateways of human understanding" (*Portefeuille*, 120). Mind (*l'esprit*) and imagination, which are "parts" of our understanding, both "work" on perception; they can either cloud or disfigure it, or they can correct it and make distinctions. Her preference for "imagination" rather than Lockean "reflection" suggests a creative, imagistic faculty. The emphasis on Imagination echoes that of the *Encyclopédie*'s Tree of Knowledge, where Imagination replaces Will as the third faculty after Memory and Understanding, in a revised trinity of faculties. She cites two examples of how understanding operates: the notion that stars in the sky might be worlds similar to ours is born of *esprit* and imagination together; but when we see a stick in the water, apparently bent, our *esprit* corrects our perception, for we know the stick to be straight. Thus, the senses can both teach and mislead us, as can our *esprit*. From this

---

[17] Louise Dupin, "Réponse à une dame de mes amies," in *Le Portefeuille de Madame Dupin, Dame de Chenonceaux*, ed. Gaston de Villeneuve-Guibert (Paris: Calmann Lévy, 1884), 120–23.

observation, she concludes that "the truth of that which is hidden from us is not necessary to us" (*Portefeuille*, 121).

This statement requires some unpacking. Dupin is not saying that those things of which we have no immediate knowledge are meaningless, but, to the contrary, that we do not need absolute certitude, *la verité*, about that which lies beyond our direct knowledge, in order to consider it meaningful. This reading is borne out by her observation that, although much remains outside the limits of our knowledge ("we are surrounded by the unknown," *Portefeuille*, 121), that which is best and greatest in us inspires us to believe in that which remains unseen. In an implicit rejoinder to Pascal's account of human *misère*, lost in the infinite universe, Dupin tells us that she sees no reason why this aspect of the human condition should lead one to think less of what we do know, and no reason why one should seek out reasons to find humans "small, abject, and contemptible":

> Nor do I understand how the pettiness and limited faculties of humanity are supposed to give us a sense of grandeur and the extent of other possible faculties; rather, I believe that the greatness within us and the best in our faculties enable us to believe in that which we cannot see. (*Portefeuille*, 121)

Her statement exemplifies the Enlightenment reaction to Pascal, whom Voltaire famously referred to as a "sublime misanthrope." Her point is our sense of something greater than ourselves comes not from an abject awareness of our shortcomings, but instead from that which is best in our abilities.

Among those abilities are our senses, which, Dupin suggests, may be "a significant part of my mind." Recalling her earlier observation that the mind "works on" sensory perceptions, she underscores the centrality of the senses in human understanding; *esprit* and imagination are secondary. She offers three examples of phenomena that are not available to our senses—the perceptions of animals, polar magnetism, the state of the soul after death—observing that although she lacks personal experience of these, she does not regard them as nonexistent.

Dupin thus offers an inductive argument for the existence of God, extrapolated from her awareness of the existence of phenomena beyond the reach of her immediate perceptions. Although unable to affirm absolute knowledge of either the existence of God or the ultimate nature of matter, she nevertheless professes her faith. She looks forward to the moment of death, not because of certitude in the afterlife, but because it seems possible that she might "learn something" ("il me paroît possible que ce grand moment m'instruise de quelque chose," *Portefeuille*, 122).

The remaining paragraphs of the "Réponse" are constructed from a series of clarifications ("I am not saying this . . . but rather that," etc.) that suggest the nature of the conversation that led her to write the essay. She denies that atheists have any sort of "system," since negatives are not susceptible to proof, and indeed they offer none. Being unable to describe God does not compel one to accept only that which one can see; our ignorance of any entity does not constitute an argument against its existence. Belief is based on our acknowledgment of the limitations of our perception, the existence of phenomena that we cannot perceive, and the possibility or even probability of phenomena that lie beyond our immediate perception. Ultimately, it is a matter of "feeling": "One senses divinity more than one knows it" (*Portefeuille*, 123).

As the hostess of a brilliant salon that included Voltaire, Condillac, Montesquieu, and other leading philosophers, it is not surprising that Dupin would incline to a form of the natural religion favored by many of her contemporaries. But although she grounds all knowledge squarely in the sensations, she does not offer an ontological argument or argue that we take our belief in God from our perception of the order and harmony of creation. Rather, she focuses on an internal sentiment or feeling, a sensation generated from within. A "feeling" is not knowledge, but it can suffice for belief.

Dupin's concept of belief is rational in that it relies on induction and extrapolation, but it remains limited in its claims. As she points out, she lacks a "clear and certain" idea of God and hence "affirms" nothing other than the fact of her religious experience: "J'adore, je jouis" (*Portefeuille*, 122). *Jouir* puts the focus back on sensation and anticipates the conclusion that we feel the divine rather than having actual knowledge of it. She firmly rejects the older notion that the senses are a source of confusion: "I respect my senses" (*Portefeuille*, 122). The forthright association of the senses with pleasure returns in her final example of knowledge of things unseen: "am I not certain that pleasure exists in the world, even if I am not aware of it and I do not know whence or how it comes, or how to find it, when I do not possess it? (*Portefeuille*, 123).

Self-knowledge, for Dupin, consists then in an understanding of mental operations and the nature of belief. She is not perturbed by the idea that hidden motives may cloud our perceptions or direct our desires; hers is a mental world that functions rationally; true knowledge is possible, even in the absence of complete certitude. In a new version of the ancient dictum that philosophy is a preparation for death, the *possibility* of learning something of the nature of the cosmos suffices for her to look forward to that moment.

2.3. Verzure: Comparison

The year 1766 saw the publication of an anonymous work, *Réflexions hazardées d'une femme ignorante, qui ne connoît les défauts des autres que par les siens, et le monde que par relation et par ouï-dire* ("Chance reflections by an ignorant woman who only knows others' faults through her own, and the world from others' accounts and hearsay"). Its reception was mixed, most commentators seemingly unable to get past the title. The reviewer of the *Correspondance littéraire* had only scathing remarks: "There's nothing to add to the title."[18] Since he proceeds to attribute the work to Madame Bontemps, "the good friend of the marquis de Mirabeau," one can only wonder what personal animus may have colored the review.

The reviewer for Bachaumont's *Mémoires secrets* was less overtly hostile than the writer for the *Correspondance littéraire*, since he faulted the *Réflexions* not for a lack of ideas, but rather for a lack of originality: "The title suggests an original work, but . . . the author seems to have read a great deal and perhaps too much."[19] It is fair to say that, despite its unconventional title, the *Réflexions* is a traditional moralist work: a two-volume collection of essays on time-honored topics such as happiness, the passions, self-love, gratitude, social vices and virtues, youth and age. The most positive reaction was that of Joseph de la Porte, writing a decade after the work's publication, who found in it "a profound and extensive understanding of the heart and of the world."[20]

The reviewer in the *Mémoires secrets* may have objected less to a lack of "originality," per se, than to the absence of any clear reference to the predecessors that the author had evidently consumed, but not acknowledged. Instead, she calls attention to the solitary nature of her quest. Insistence on her singularity is the hallmark not simply of her moralist persona

---

[18] December 1765, in Maurice Tourneux, ed., *Correspondance littéraire, philosophique et critique par Grimm, Diderot, Raynal, Meister, etc.* (Paris: Garnier Frères, 1878; reprint 1968), 6: 455.
[19] Louis-Petit de Bachaumont, *Mémoires secrets pour servir à l'histoire de la République des Lettres en France depuis 1762 jusqu'à nos jours* (Paris, 1784), 3: 25–26.
[20] Joseph de La Porte, *Histoire littéraire des femmes françoises*, 5 vols. (Paris: Lacombe, 1769), 4: ix.

but also of her method, a quality that sets her apart from other writers in a genre characterized by the acknowledgment of a shared set of questions extending back over the centuries. Its unprepossessing title notwithstanding, the *Réflexions* is a rich set of essays that include observations on social issues alongside classical topics such as friendship, love, and the passions. Ostensibly a series of observations on human behavior, the *Réflexions* is also an exploration of the nature of the self and of our capacity to know ourselves and others.

The veil of anonymity was lifted in 1778 in Hébrail and La Porte's *La France littéraire*, which identified her as "Madame de Verzure."[21] In her 1804 historical dictionary of French women writers, Fortunée Briquet also lists Madame de Verzure as the author of the *Réflexions*, describing her as the "wife of a Genoese banker," a description that was repeated without further elaboration in later nineteenth-century catalogues and literary dictionaries. It's worth observing that, although "ignorance" and "obscurity" are the hallmarks of her authorial persona, Madame de Verzure was not obscure at all and probably knew the "world" quite well. The "Genoese banker" was Nicolas Bonaventure de Verzure, sieur de Vaudry (1696–1778), born in Genoa and naturalized French in 1726. A successful financier, he was a royal secretary, tax collector, and syndic of the Compagnie des Indes. His wife, Marie Pannier d'Orgeville (1712–1770), was a native of Lyon. They moved in high circles. When their eldest daughter, Marie-Émilie, married the marquis de Tracy, the king and queen signed the marriage contract.

I will explore three aspects of Marie de Verzure's elaboration of the nature of the self. First, I examine her self-presentation, which, as her title suggests, is unusually self-effacing but also involves a complex dynamic with other people. Second, she analyzes the mental operations that constitute the self in a pair of essays, "Notions sur l'âme" ("Notions on the Soul") and "Sur le coeur" ("On the Heart"). In the third part of this discussion, I will focus on the social and ethical implications of her ideas as she explores a range of social issues. Throughout, she remains preoccupied by the question of method: What is the most effective means to attain self-understanding and understanding of the world? Can either be achieved with any certitude?

Verzure's preface sets up the basic terms of her approach. While there is nothing especially unusual in the eighteenth century about an élite woman

---

[21] Jacques Hébrail and Joseph de la Porte, *Supplément à la France littéraire* (Paris: Chez la Veuve Duchesne, 1778), 185.

preferring to remain anonymous in her publications, Verzure goes to such lengths to emphasize her obscurity and avoidance of the social world that she draws attention to herself.

> Born with little to recommend either my wit or my face, I recognized early on the indispensable need for me to develop resources that would depend on myself alone. . . . Unable to contribute anything amiable in society, one result of my self-assessment was an extreme timidity, reinforced by *amour-propre*, which added to my other disadvantages a great difficulty in speaking.[22]

As we will see in later chapters, the topos of "resources" occurs fairly frequently among women moralists as a hedge against a lonely old age. For Verzure, it represents the first statement of her intellectual autonomy, *moi seule*. One might ask why someone so obsessively shy would seek publication at all, but the author claims that her solitude is precisely the reason for publishing her book. "My ignorance may undoubtedly have mistaken as discoveries ideas that everyone has already had. And I may have misjudged people, since I analyzed them in my own way, based on my own sensations, passions, and imperfections. This is what I do not know, and my uncertainty leads me to take the public as judge" (Verzure, 1:xii–xiii). The anonymous public is cast in the role of confidant, "a friend whom I beg to let me know my true worth" (Verzure, 1:xvii).

The *Réflexions* is based on a paradox. On the one hand, Verzure presents herself as a spectator of social mores, an anatomist of character types, an impartial observer of the hypocrisies, inconsistencies, vanities, and misperceptions that characterize human interaction: a moralist. On the other, she claims to know little or nothing of the world and to derive any insights that she might have from introspection.

> Before knowing others, I wished to know myself to the greatest extent possible. Although through the lenses of *amour-propre* we see ourselves to the greatest advantage, I found an infinite number of defects in myself; I confess, to my shame, that most of the reflections that I risk putting before the public are based on myself. (Verzure, 1:xi)

---

[22] Marie de Verzure, *Réflexions hazardées d'une femme ignorante*, 2 vols. (Paris, 1766), 1: ix–xi.

Over the course of the *Réflexions*, Verzure returns often to the double-sided question of self-knowledge and the knowledge of others. Unlike Scudéry, for whom the two issues remained distinct, for Verzure they are inextricably linked.

The dynamic relation between self and other is a constant feature of the essays. Introspection appears to offer the royal road to understanding, yet Verzure concedes the need for some degree of social stimulation. Thus, despite an obvious and reiterated preference for solitude as the only place where one sees oneself "au naturel" (Verzure, "Le Monde et la solitude," 2:186), she argues that uninterrupted solitude is less useful than an existence "interrupted and deferred by socializing" (Verzure, 2:187). A certain amount of worldly distraction is needed, she tells us, to help us appreciate and benefit from solitude. On occasion she even appears to lend greater weight to observation. In "Sur la société" (Verzure, 2:138–41), she describes the parade of character types and behaviors as "a continuous lesson" offering both positive and negative examples. These lessons may even make a stronger impression than those arrived at through self-examination, since the latter tend to be tainted by the distortions of *amour-propre* (Verzure, 2:141).

Furthermore, our judgments of others' motivations may provide insight into our own, since we would not necessarily perceive others' defects and qualities if we did not already possess the same: "How could we imagine them?" ("L'Amour propre," 2:226). We have seen in Dupin a similar argument that perception of something external to us is rendered possible by something in the nature of the self, even if we are not directly aware of it. The apparently simple program of inferring what we know of others from knowledge of oneself is thus shown to operate from a complicated back-and-forth dynamic.

To sum up Verzure's program: the self-understanding gained through introspection is key to her enterprise, but it is complicated both by the subterranean impulses of self-love and by an unavoidable need to compare and contrast the experiences and actions of others. The relationship between self and other is also complicated by the question of congruency. On the one hand, given her account of herself as "knowing the world only through hearsay," her claim to moralist spectatorship requires some degree of congruency between herself and others, so that she can draw correct conclusions based on her self-understanding. On the other hand, she regularly calls attention to the ways in which she is different. "I do not like to follow others' thinking" (Verzure, 2:200). One way to resolve the dilemma is to distinguish between her individual judgments and the underlying mental framework common to all. She elaborates this framework in a pair of essays in the second volume, "Notions sur l'âme" and "Sur le coeur," which together provide an account of the operations of the mind, an epistemology of thought and feeling.

"Notions sur l'âme" anatomizes the components of the "soul"—will (*volonté*), taste or inclination (*goût*), feeling (*sentiment*), reason, reflection, passion, imagination, etc.—indicating that each is based on either mind (*esprit*) or heart (*cœur*), and occasionally on both. Like Dupin, Verzure proposes a model for mental activity in which the rational faculty, although primary, is offset by appetitive and imaginative faculties. For Verzure, the "heart" is instinctive and instantaneous in its operations, a "sudden preference," even "a sort of electrical shock" (Verzure, 2:91), when experienced simultaneously by two people. Unreflective in its initial impulse, its impressions are not necessarily lasting and may eventually fade or be tamed by the mind and will. The heart "feels," while the mind judges, distinguishes, and chooses; mind may operate without heart, but not vice versa. While mind is the "tutor" of the heart, the heart is "an imprudent pupil" whose tendency to stray (*écarts*) places the tutor in "a continual agitation" (Verzure, 2:96). Reflection, on the other hand, may either be entirely free or subject to the will; it distinguishes among the objects that appear to the senses, sorts out and develops ideas, produces discernment.

Not only does the heart play an important role in the generation of ideas; so too does the imagination, which is described as "willful" and "lacking direction," but also as "the mother of ideas" (Verzure, 2:98–99), without which the mind would be at a loss. Verzure makes an important distinction between "ideas" and "thoughts" (*idées, pensées*). The former represent unorganized perceptions; the latter, cognition: "Ideas are converted to thoughts, once they have undergone examination and correction from our reflection, reason, and judgement" (Verzure, 2:99–100).

If self-examination alone can lead us to form coherent thoughts from the raw material of ideas, then Verzure's introspective approach should be validated; yet again she draws back from claiming certainty: "These are the most distinct notions that it is possible to have when one knows nothing." Describing her "notions" (evidently less than "ideas" or "thoughts") as belonging entirely to "nature" and without "*principes*," she regrets that she is only able to derive a faint glimmer (*foibles lueurs*), not true enlightenment (*lumières*) (Verzure, 2:100). "Notions" is, of course, the term used in the essay's title, suggesting that the goal of providing a clear description—"thoughts"—of mental operations may not be attainable.

In her initial presentation, Verzure's essay has elements in common with treatises of an earlier era in its approach to human mental operations as a general system of operations and faculties, describing the parts and their articulating principles.[23] If that initial program proves not to be available, what remains? The context of the *Réflexions hazardées* suggests an effort to reconcile the deductive, systematic approach of philosophers to what Susan James has called the "retreat from generality to particularity" of moralists such as La Rochefoucauld and La Bruyère, whose fragmentary style and skeptical posture cast doubt on the possibility of an overarching, all-encompassing account.[24] For the moralists, the particulars generate the greatest intellectual and philosophical interest; general schemes are less informative. Scudéry, it will be recalled, commented that it is easier—hence less meaningful—to lay out general rules or a framework, than to penetrate the complexities of individuals. Discovery, as we earlier saw in Condillac, proceeds from induction and particulars.

Verzure frames her retreat from the general to the particular as a limitation due to her own isolation and lack of insight:

I fear getting lost in attempting to unravel the operations of the mind.
It is easy to wander from the truth, when one has no guiding principles and takes one's ideas from nature alone, without any external assistance. Never mind; I will feel my way forward, at the risk of stumbling. (Verzure, 2:96)

There are two important points here. First, despite her caveat, Verzure persists ("N'importe"!) in the elaboration of her model. Second, we should note the strikingly modern stance that informs this moment of apparent self-doubt. Like her contemporaries, Verzure upholds the value of *la nature seule* over (artificial) "principles": *l'esprit systématique* over *esprit de systèmes*. The

---

[23] For example, Martin Cureau de la Chambre, *Le Système de l'âme* (Paris, 1665), the work that brought the technical scientific term "système" into widespread fashionable use. A few decades later, Etienne de Gamaches's *Système du coeur* (Paris, 1704) would take a less "systematic" approach, but like Verzure, examines the role of the heart in perception. I discuss the use of the term "system" in Cureau and Gamaches in *Reading the French Enlightenment*, 23–24, 26–28.

[24] Susan James, "Reason, the Passions, and the Good Life," in Daniel Garber and Michael Ayers, eds., *The Cambridge History of Seventeenth-Century Philosophy* (Cambridge: Cambridge University Press, 1998), 2: 1361.

absence of *principes* and the image of feeling her way in the dark—an analogy dear to Diderot—place her squarely in the Enlightenment mainstream, despite her wish for a firmer foundation.

The other distinctively modern aspect of Verzure's cosmos of mental operations is the tilt toward the heart as the center of mental phenomena. Thus, "Notions sur l'âme" treats the heart as one of two principles that undergird the operations of the soul; the subsequent essay, "Sur le coeur," explores it in depth. While the distinction between mind and heart may initially have appeared to be a conventional distinction between reflection and sensation, the heart proves to represent considerably more than "sensation." The heart is fundamental, but not, as it is in many writers of the period, as a metaphor for the emotional life, nor in the sense that *Nihil est in intellectu quod non sit prius in sensu*. Instead, Verzure argues that it provides a physiological basis for thought, a site for the interaction of body and mind.

She introduces this view after an extended preamble in which she warns the reader that her thoughts on the heart are the opposite of all that she has been taught and that normally she ought to conclude that her idea is "as wrong as it is bizarre" (Verzure, 2:101).

> As I am perhaps the only one who has dared turn away from the ordinary route on a much-studied topic, I do not flatter myself that others will approve; it is therefore simply a kind of dream that I will describe.
>
> It is absurd to imagine that the soul has sensation/a feeling (*un sens*), and that its sensation is the heart; this is my wild proposal. (Verzure, 2:101–2)

The imagined criticism is reminiscent of the self-doubting moment in the preface where she expresses concern that in her ignorance she has perhaps taken as novelties "ideas that everyone else has had" (Verzure, 1:xii). Here, however, she announces her certainty that her ideas are not those of "tout le monde," and that they are certain to be rejected by the reader. The approach is *tâtonnement*, feeling in the dark, thinking a question through in the manner of Montaigne. Her rhetoric also functions both to deflect criticism and to stimulate the reader's curiosity.

What does it mean to argue that mental phenomena have sensations, and that their sense organ is the heart? She takes us through the relationships between the heart—that instant, immediate impulse, preference, or disinclination—and the full range of mental faculties. "Through discernable relations (*rapports sensibles*), if we pay attention, it enters into all that we think, all that we say, and all our actions" (Verzure, 2:103). The heart is not equally "interested" in every movement or decision, but it is indifferent to none; it takes "satisfaction" or feels pain in every act or event.

Ultimately, we might define the heart as embodied unconscious: "Reason, judgment, reflection, mind, will, imagination, you believe yourselves free, but you are its slaves; it governs you without your knowledge" (Verzure, 2:107). Its domination of mental and emotional states renders it "nobler" than mere physical sensations, but Verzure closes by confirming that it is "the only sense (*le sens unique*) of body and soul"; other sensations are merely its mechanisms (*ressorts*). Like her moralist predecessors, Verzure argues that much of what motivates our desires and decisions lies outside our immediate awareness, but her account is startlingly different from that of Nicole, La Rochefoucauld, or Scudéry. While Verzure considers *amour-propre* to be a significant force in our psychological makeup, she sees it primarily as an obstacle to self-assessment, rather than as an overarching sign of the limitations of the human condition. The heart, on the other hand, is both psychological and physiological.

Verzure's essays are nourished by the impetus that drove Montaigne: What do I know, how do I know it? As we have seen, her initial response to the latter question appears simple: I know what I know through rigorous self-examination. As she discovers, introspection alone cannot lead to certainty; she must rely on observation of society and a series of "parallels" comparing herself with others (Verzure, 1:xii). The act of comparison allows extrapolation of the insights gained from introspection, but in a kind of feedback loop also suggests new zones for self-examination. How would she be able to identify others' defects if she did not possess the same? she asks. Both observation and introspection reveal inner complexity, a world of mental operations and faculties in thrall to a "sense" that remains largely unavailable to thought, but is perceptible through its effects. Although her starting point is not far removed from that of Descartes, *seul dans un poêle*, Verzure finds a firm foundation (*principes*) unavailable and thus turns to advancing *à tatons*.

If the search for first principles proves vain, this does not prevent her from pursuing the moralist project of social spectatorship and analysis, to which we now turn. Verzure's essays tend to fall into two broad categories, not unlike her dual epistemological program of introspection and observation. In the first group, "introspective" essays explore the meanings of terms, particularly terms that are closely related: for example, what is the difference between *mensonge* and *fausseté*? or *ingénuité* and *innocence*? Verzure's method in these pieces is similar to that of the articles classified under the rubric "Grammar" in the *Encyclopédie*, teasing out distinctions between pairs of closely related terms and together contributing to the general linguistic claim—by Du Marsais, Condillac, and Diderot among others—that no true synonyms exist in a universe of infinite particulars. Similarly, she explicates key topics in the moralist repertory, such as friendship, gratitude, moderation, and liberty. Here too, insights can be gained through analysis, an explication of the predicates attached to a term.

In the second category are essays that display a distinctly "outward-facing" orientation, with commentary on social and political institutions: observation of the world. The very first essay, "Le Monde," for example, immediately contradicts the claims to ignorance of the title, with a series of detailed satirical scenes and portraits, and an evocation of the immensity of the subject: "So many worlds within the world!" (Verzure, 1:2). The universe is composed of particulars; the moralist's goal is to see relationships among them and to determine a basis for ethical judgment.

It's worth recalling that Verzure dedicated the *Réflexions* to the marquis de Mirabeau; the allusion in the dedicatory epistle to his wildly popular work, *L'Ami des hommes* (1756) is the only reference to another text anywhere in her book.[25] A number of essays touch on physiocratic themes that echo Mirabeau, in particular the connections between luxury, decadence, and depopulation. In "Sur les besoins" and "Sur le bonheur," she criticizes luxury as having a detrimental effect on the physical well-being of the wealthy, mocking the decorative items that the woman of fashion "needs": "So many lovely porcelains! So many Chinese figurines!" (Verzure, 1:159). Ultimately, the proliferation of useless objects, clothes, servants, and other accoutrements of the noble lifestyle leads to degeneration: "Most encourage and increase softness (*mollesse*); softness weakens and enfeebles man and in the long term leads to decline of the species" (Verzure, 1:160).

Other essays of explicit social commentary include "Sur le célibat et le marriage," about which I will have more to say in Chapter 5; "La Subordination," and "Sur les Loix." The latter pair present the social order and its legal system as necessary evils. Hierarchy is necessary for the maintenance of order, as humans left to their own devices would seek to dominate one another. How

---

[25] On Mirabeau's work as both political economics and "a true cultural event," see Michael Kwass, "Consumption and the World of Ideas: Consumer Revolution and the Moral Economy of the Marquis de Mirabeau," *Eighteenth-Century Studies* 37.2 (2004): 187–213.

does this political framework relate to moralist dimension of *Réflexions*? In addition to the obvious topics of luxury and population, the physiocratic thread allows us to notice certain thematic resonances: a certain pragmatism, or groundedness, that manifests itself in the examination of both Verzure's own and others' behavior. A solitary search is preferable, but recourse to the world is still necessary. There are other resonances as well. (Like the reviewer from the *Mémoires secrets*, I tend to believe that she has read a great deal more than she admits.) Part of what is happening throughout the text is the effort to reconcile traditional themes and topoi, such as the need to free oneself from the passions, with newer concepts, such as the physiocratic denunciation of useless luxury. We can see a similar effort to reconcile modern and traditional ideas in Verzure's redefinition of the heart as more than a metaphor for the emotional life. Indeed, it is tempting to see in her efforts to describe a physiological ground for mental phenomena, a foretaste of what would become one of the founding principles of her grandson, the philosopher Antoine Destutt de Tracy, founder of *l'Idéologie*, a "science of ideas" rooted firmly in physical experience, for whom "to think is always to sense (*sentir*), and only to sense."[26]

In her reading of the preface to the *Réflexions*, Florence Lotterie draws connections between Verzure and various fictive avatars of the self-taught, self-made woman, figures that she situates within a broad "Cartesian program."[27] For Lotterie, Verzure's presumption to dedicate her work to Mirabeau while downplaying its worth is in fact a ruse, allowing the author to hide a declaration of intellectual equality behind a modest façade. While I agree that the preface and dedication contain elements of both self-promotion and self-effacement, I am less sure that they represent a ruse as such. As we have seen, Verzure's "Cartesian program" ultimately takes a different path; her journey into the innermost self produces insights that open new pathways, rather than indubitable principles. The inner journey requires an ongoing series of checkpoints with others; not dialogue in any conventional sense, but "parallels," subjects for observation, and ultimately a public. Whatever regret she might express for elusive "principles," Verzure makes it clear that uncertainty is no vice. As she explains in "L'Incertitude," a lack of certainty or indecisiveness based on one's suspension of judgment when

---

[26] Antoine Destutt de Tracy, *Élemens d'idéologie, Première partie: Idéologie proprement dite*, 2nd ed. (Paris: Chez Courcier, 1804), 25.

[27] Florence Lotterie, *Le Genre des Lumières: Femme et philosophe au XVIIIe siècle* (Paris: Classiques Garnier, 2013), 94–97.

faced with a complex situation or stemming from one's own "lack of confidence in one's abilities," represents reason, fairness, and modesty (Verzure, 2:251–52).[28]

For Verzure, the quest for self-knowledge becomes a pathway to knowledge of the self. Recognizing that uncertainty must remain to some degree ineluctable, she elaborates a method rather than a system, refines her positions, and finds a voice in the world.

2.4. Necker: Writing

Suzanne Necker, née Curchod (1737–1794), was well known during her lifetime, but not as a writer. The daughter of a Swiss pastor who came to Paris as the companion of a young widow, she met and married the banker and later finance minister Jacques Necker, embarked on a rigorous program of acculturation to Parisian society, and created one of the most brilliant salons of the late *ancien régime*, where Diderot, Raynal, Buffon, Mably, and Marmontel were among the regular guests. She was equally known for civic engagement and the founding of the charitable hospital that today bears her name, l'Hôpital Necker. She wrote extensively but published little; after her death her husband edited and published five volumes of her writings, the *Mélanges* (1798) and *Nouveaux mélanges* (1801). Today, she is most often remembered as a prominent salon hostess and as the mother of Germaine de Staël.

In his preface to the first volume of *Mélanges*, Jacques Necker emphasizes his late wife's piety, intelligence, modesty, and charity: in a word, her ideal womanhood. In his view, the authenticity of her writing stems directly from its private nature.[29] He presents her writing as "an emanation of her virtue," describing her as entirely free from the desire for literary fame.[30] Largely on the basis of one of Suzanne Necker's letters from 1779 and a comment in her daughter's *Journal de jeunesse*, it is thought that she sacrificed her

---

[28] Similarly, the debaters in Scudéry's "De l'incertitude" largely concede victory to "les Incertains" (Scudéry 1686, 1:493).

[29] Jacques Necker, "Observations de l'éditeur," in Suzanne Necker, *Mélanges extraits des écrits de Mme Necker*, ed. J. Necker, 3 vols. (Paris: Charles Pougens, 1798), iv. Based on the success of the *Mélanges*, Necker published a second selection, *Nouveaux mélanges extraits des écrits de Mme Necker*, 2 vols. (Paris: Charles Pougens, 1801). Subsequent references will identify the two collections by their publication dates.

[30] Dena Goodman, "Suzanne Necker's *Mélanges*: Gender, Writing, and Publicity," in Elizabeth Goldsmith and Dena Goodman, eds., *Going Public: Women and Publishing in Early Modern France* (Ithaca, NY: Cornell University Press, 1995), 221.

literary ambitions in deference to her husband's wishes. However, both these references date from before the appearance of Suzanne Necker's published essay against premature burial (1790), as well as the documents and reports concerning the Hospice de Charité that she founded in 1778, suggesting that the claims for her self-effacement have been exaggerated.[31] She also prepared for publication her *Réflexions sur le divorce*, a defense of marriage in response to the Revolutionary government's 1792 legalization of divorce; it appeared a few months after her death in 1794.[32]

It is worth noting that early in her marriage, she published (anonymously) a translation of Gray's *Elegy Written in a Country Churchyard* and a portrait of her friend Paul Moultou; both appeared in the *Gazette littéraire* and were reprinted in J-B-A Suard's *Variétés littéraires*.[33] While her decision to refrain from further literary efforts after 1769 may have been in keeping with her spouse's preferences, it seems equally if not more likely that she did so in the understanding that a reputation as a woman of letters was incompatible with her role as a hostess to the salon that she launched in 1765. She would have been well aware of the fate of Anne-Marie du Bocage, whose salon suffered a steep decline in prestige, becoming reduced to a small circle of close friends and a subject of mockery among others, as her literary career took flight in the 1750s and 1760s.[34]

Suzanne Necker may not have had any intention of publishing her personal writings, but she took care to preserve them over many years and made a point in her will of leaving them, along with her letters, to her husband to do with as he saw fit. As the manuscripts are presently unavailable to scholars, we do not know the extent of his editorial interventions.[35] Jacques

---

[31] Sonja Boon, "Does a Dutiful Wife Write; or, Should Suzanne get Divorced? Reflections on Suzanne Curchod Necker, Divorce, and the Construction of the Biographical Subject," *Lumen* 27 (2008): 59–73.

[32] I will discuss Necker's *Réflexions sur le divorce* in Chapter 4 below.

[33] [Suzanne Necker], "Elégie écrite sur un cimetière de campagne, traduite de l'anglois de M. Gray," and "Portrait de mon ami," *Gazette littéraire de l'Europe*, vol. 5 (April–May 1765): 217–23, 269–73. Reprinted in Jean-Baptiste Suard and Antoine Arnauld, eds., *Variétés littéraires*, vol. 4 (Paris: Lacombe, 1769), 486–94, 495–501. Both pieces, originally anonymous, were later included in Necker 1801, 2:231–41, 242–49).

[34] On Du Boccage, see Antoine Lilti, *Le Monde des salons: Sociabilité et mondanité à Paris au XVIIIe siècle* (Paris: Fayard, 2005), 119–20. On Suzanne Necker as salonnière, see Valérie Hannin, "Une ambition de femme au siècle des Lumières: Le cas de Madame Necker," *Cahiers staëliens* 36 (1985): 5–29; and Catherine Dubeau, "L'Épreuve du salon ou Le monde comme performance dans les *Mélanges* et les *Nouveaux mélanges* de Suzanne Necker," *Cahiers staëliens* 57 (2006): 201–25; see also Craveri, *L'Âge de la conversation*, 381–85.

[35] Catherine Dubeau, who was able to begin studying the manuscripts prior to the current embargo, describes their physical state and observes that the published *Mélanges* generally reflect the organization of the manuscript volumes. Dubeau, "Les *Mélanges* (1798) et *Nouveaux mélanges* (1801)

Necker, who refers to the manuscripts as *journaux* and mentions her practice of writing daily, indicates that he had initially thought to organize the short essays and fragments by subject, but abandoned the idea, given that "moral and metaphysical subjects" require elaboration and nuance beyond what these "scattered thoughts," written at different times, might offer. Stating that his wife wrote with no intention beyond "setting down her reflections and noting the direction of her daily opinions," he opts to leave them in their fragmentary, disorganized state as "detached thoughts." The *Mélanges* also include society anecdotes as well as large excerpts from her extensive correspondence with important men of letters, which he admits to having freely edited for "the primary ideas" (Necker 1798, 1:iii–v).

By referring to his wife's writings as *pensées détachées*, he has explicitly invoked over a century of moralist writing and shaped the reader's expectations accordingly. He reinforces the point in his introduction to the *Nouveaux mélanges* with an extended comparison between his wife's *pensées détachées* and La Rochefoucauld's *Maximes*.[36] Sharing the general eighteenth-century distaste for La Rochefoucauld as "humanity's censor," he argues that his late wife's greater range of topics constitutes a "cours varié de notre nature morale." Whatever her thoughts may have been about eventual publication, Suzanne Necker was certainly conscious of this dimension of her writing; she shaped her reflections in keeping with literary norms. We see this explicitly in the "sketch" (*esquisse*) titled "Maxims Imitated from Marcus Aurelius" (Necker 1798, 3:238–40), setting forth the qualities of the Stoic sage: gentleness, strength of character, modesty, the cultivation of virtue, indifference to material wealth and to ill-treatment by others. Scholars have compared Suzanne Necker's personal writing to Calvinist practices of moral "accounting," but the *Meditations* of Marcus Aurelius—similarly written for the author's personal use, in no particular order, as an exercise for self-improvement—suggest classical and literary models as well.[37] Stylistically, her maxims are closer in form and spirit to eighteenth-century *pensées détachées* than to the

---

à rebours: Un florilège à quatre mains . . . et deux voix?," in Diane Desrosiers and Roxanne Roy, eds., *Ventriloquie: Quand on fait parler les femmes (XVe–XVIIIe siècles)* (Paris: Hermann, 2020), 209–29.

[36] Jacques Necker, "Avertissement de l'éditeur" (Necker 1801, 1: ix–xiii). On the Enlightenment's ambivalent reception of La Rochefoucauld, see Jean Deprun, "La Réception des *Maximes* dans la France des Lumières," in Lafond and Mesnard, *Images de La Rochefoucauld*, 39–46.

[37] On the *Meditations* as philosophical praxis, see Philippe Hadot, "Marcus Aurelius," in *Philosophy as a Way of Life*, 179–205.

Meditations; they represent her distillation of its precepts in a contemporary form.

The variety of genres present in the *Mélanges—pensées détachées*, letters, society portraits, anecdotes—have perhaps made its place within the moralist tradition less obvious to readers.[38] Nineteenth-century readers seem less bothered by the work's format than by its tendency to slip away from observations of social life to more abstract philosophical concerns. Writing shortly after the publication of the *Mélanges*, Fortunée Briquet offers praise with reservations:

> This collection reveals a beautiful soul and proves that Madame Necker, had she wished, would have been at the first rank of women of letters; it includes, however, a number of untrue maxims, false wit, and obscure and overly complicated metaphysics.[39]

Among the most "metaphysical" pieces is a short essay, "De l'âme," whose two parts reflect two aspects of the *Mélanges*: personal reflection and salon conversation—in this instance, a debate between Suzanne Necker and "Monsieur D***," evidently her friend Diderot, who (not surprisingly) is attempting to persuade her of the materiality of the soul.[40] "De l'âme," explores the nature of the self or soul—Necker uses the words *âme* and *moi* interchangeably—and its persistence over time. It is one of many short pieces in which she considers the operations of the mind, on the one hand, and specific techniques for introspection, on the other.

Let us look first at "De l'âme." Suzanne Necker's inquiry into the nature of the soul, or self, is shorter and less detailed than Verzure's, but represents a similar anatomizing approach.

---

[38] Even a sympathetic reader like Geneviève Soumoy-Thibert, in search of a systematic set of ideas, finds the text off-putting, "a disordered, incoherent genre" (Soumoy-Thibert, "Les Idées de Madame Necker," *Dix-huitième siècle*, no. 21 [1989]: 358). Valérie Hannin similarly finds it a "tedious read—it's the nature of the genre—but especially frustrating" in her efforts to understand Suzanne Necker as an intellectual and as a woman (Hannin, "Une ambition de femme," 6).

[39] Fortunée Briquet, *Dictionnaire historique, littéraire et bibliographique des Françaises, et des étrangères naturalisées en France* (Paris: Treuttel et Würtz, 1804), 252–53. See Soumoy-Thibert on other nineteenth-century responses, "Les Idées de Madame Necker," 358.

[40] The essay appears in truncated form (lacking the conversation with Diderot) in Necker 1798 (3:234–38), where it immediately precedes the "Maximes imitées de Marc-Aurèle," and in an extended version in Necker 1801 (1:106–14), the version to which I will refer.

> The soul is a simple being (*être*); it is our sentiment of existence: existence is not the same as thought, because thought involves combinations, which a simple being cannot do alone. (Necker 1801, 1:106)

Like Malebranche, to whose work she refers elsewhere,[41] Necker makes a distinction between self/soul and thought. The former is the pure sentiment of existence or *sentiment intérieur*; it perceives "thoughts" or "ideas," which themselves are material in origin ("the traces of sensations on the organ of the brain").[42] Her interest lies in reflecting on moments when the simple self is distinguishable from cognitive operations. These observations in turn become an argument for the persistence of the self/soul over time. Although the *moi* precedes thought, which it "receives" and "approves or rejects," it is incapable of imposing its will on the thinking mind—otherwise, it would be able to substitute agreeable notions for painful ones. The self/soul must instinctively strategize (*user d'adresse*) in order to arrange to receive pleasant thoughts, which arise from the senses.

Necker asserts that the persistence of the self is an initial proof for its distinctiveness. One's ideas and feelings change, sometimes radically, yet "it is the same *moi* who was thinking yesterday and who thinks today." For all the turnover in one's ideas over time, she tells us that if she were to be reminded of a crime committed in the distant past, "remorse would inform me of my continued existence (*coexistence*)." She does not explore the issue of remorse per se, but it would appear to be an example of an unpleasant feeling excited by an idea. Unpleasant though it may be, it serves as a reminder of the self's continuity.

The persistence of the self underscores its distinctness from its physical substrate, the brain. The connection between the self and the brain's "fibers" can be relaxed or broken during moments of delirium, fever, madness, and sleep.[43] At such moments, the self/soul is undisturbed by thoughts or information from the senses. This state represents "a kind of death" that if it were to last, would result in actual

---

[41] Elsewhere in the *Mélanges*, Necker refers to Malebranche and the occasionalist view that all that we are, any talent that we possess, is due entirely to God. "This system is particularly appealing for pure, timid, and sensitive souls" (Necker 1798, 3:251).

[42] On Malebranche's account of the soul, see Jean-Louis Vieillard-Baron, "L'Âme et l'amour selon Malebranche," *Les Études philosophiques* 4 (1996): 453–72.

[43] Elsewhere, she describes the *âme* as having two parts: the *moi* "that compares, judges, and determines" and the *fibres*, which she compares to Peruvian *quipos*, the knotted communications that play a central role in Françoise de Graffigny's popular novel, *Les Lettres d'une Péruvienne* (Necker 1801, 2: 55).

death.[44] Even in this detached state, we retain our inner awareness ("the sentiment of one's existence"). Observing that profound sleep is itself deeply pleasurable and that we dislike being torn from it, Necker describes inner awareness as "pure happiness" in which time ceases to have any reality, noting that such reflections can ease the fear of death. Continuing the inventory of altered states of consciousness, she cites the "momentary death" induced by deliberately preventing the *âme* from receiving the brain's stimuli; or by concentrating entirely on a single idea to the exclusion of all others, as occurs via the passions, madness, and unreason.[45] Returning to consciousness, *se rappeler*, does not however represent an act of will on the part of the soul; it occurs via an increasingly pronounced movement or disturbance (*ébranlement*) of the fibers. She concludes this section, which is the entirety of the text in the shorter version published in 1798, by characterizing the *âme* as the feeling (*sentiment*) intended by the creator to help us not simply to find our existence bearable, but to cherish it.

The central feature of Necker's reflections on the self is the primacy of self-awareness as distinct from cognitive activity, "thoughts," which arise in the physical brain. She is interested in two aspects of this scheme: the intrinsically pleasurable quality of the pure sentiment of existence, and the altered states of consciousness produced by the sliding degrees of connection between self/soul and brain. Suzanne Necker's particular interest in these questions becomes clear in the second half of the full version of the piece published in the *Nouveaux mélanges*, her debate with Diderot.

> Monsieur D*** and I argued for a long time about the future; he wants to prove to me that I have no soul and that after the dissolution of this weak body, nothing will remain of me but a memory. I appeal, and summon him to meet me at the foot of the celestial throne. (Necker 1801, 1:110)

---

[44] Suzanne Necker's experience with the administration of the Hospice de Charité led her to consider a potential real-world consequence of this idea: premature burial. In one of the rare works published during her lifetime, she proposes legal and medical protocols to avoid the hasty burial of those who appear dead, yet are in an intermediate stage where they remain conscious of their surroundings. *Des inhumations précipitées* (Paris: De l'imprimerie royale, 1790).

[45] Necker refers to the first of these states, in which one prevents one's soul from receiving thoughts from the brain, as "le secret de ce curé espagnol dont parle Descartes" (*NM* 1:109). I have been unable to track this reference beyond Descartes's reference to the Spanish Jesuits ("the Coimbrans, Toletus and Rubius") in a 1640 letter to Marin Mersenne. The spiritual exercises of Ignatius Loyola, which formed an important part of Descartes's education at La Flèche, are a tempting example, but he never mentions Loyola explicitly. Roger Ariew, "What Descartes Read: His Intellectual Background," in Steven Nadler, Tad M. Schmaltz, and Delphine Antoine-Mahut, eds., *The Oxford Handbook of Descartes and Cartesianism*, online ed. (Oxford: Oxford University Press, 2019).

Diderot lays out a position that is familiar to us from his works: that nature is composed of matter that is sensate to lesser or greater degree, from stones to human beings, and that matter alone suffices to account for all phenomena, including sensation and thought. It is possible that his resolutely materialist stance pushes her to a dualist position. Necker concedes that all ideas come from the senses (via the "fibers" in the first part of the essay), but argues that ideas are distinct from both sensations and things. The fact that, in certain preoccupied states, we carry out various activities and receive even painful sensations without being conscious of them, points to the existence of an entity of some sort that receives "the tribute of the senses" (Necker 1801, 1:112). That entity, she argues, is unique and distinct from the senses themselves; it is a place (*un foyer*) where they are brought together that prevents confusion among them. It cannot itself be material, for then it would be divisible, not simple, and unable to receive and compare them all: it is "a collective sense (*sens*)." At the same time, she acknowledges that she has more questions than answers regarding the ultimate nature of "this sense" and how, exactly, it performs its operations and communicates with the senses. Her exclamation "Ah, Monsieur D***!" brings us back to the world of salon conversation. With a comparison of the multitude of metaphysical speculations to the confusion of tongues at Babel, she enjoins her friend to acknowledge that neither of them possesses the answers to the question.

What can "Sur l'âme" tell us? Its diptych structure exemplifies in miniature the philosophical dimension of salon conversation; it may also reflect Suzanne Necker's much-discussed preparation for conversation. It has become something of a trope of Necker scholarship to cite an anecdote told by the marquis de Chastellux to Félicité de Genlis, of coming across a little notebook that she had accidentally left out, with all of her notes on what she planned to say to whom, a program that he saw methodically carried out over the course of the evening.[46] Many of the *pensées détachées* concern the importance of writing as a technique for understanding what one has read, for clarifying one's own ideas, and for preparing oneself to discuss them with others.

Necker's interest in the mind's functioning goes far beyond finding an interesting topic with which to engage the materialist philosopher Diderot, however. The nature of the soul/self is a recurring topic throughout the *Mélanges*, as are the mind's faculties, particularly memory. Consider, for

---

[46] Dubeau, "L'Épreuve," 215 n.44.

example, her discussion of two kinds of memory: *réminiscence*, or a literal transcription of events, and "true memory" that judges, makes connections, and creates meaning; developed through experience, only the latter is able to bring objects into "our permanent ideas" (Necker 1801, 2:189). These two kinds of memory correspond to two types of wit: the literal, boring recital of details, and true wit, which selects and arranges ideas (Necker 1798, 2:251–52). Similarly, she regards genius as the capacity to master details, understand their relationships, and organize them (Necker 1798, 3:12–15).

As we see in "Sur l'âme," Necker is fascinated by mental operations that are not available to conscious thought. She returns on multiple occasions to the ways in which apparently new ideas are constituted without our knowledge, *à notre insu*, via the accumulation over time of "fleeting ideas" and "secondary perceptions" (*aperçus accessoires*) that we would be incapable of rehearsing in their complexity (Necker 1798, 1:2; 2:6–7; 3:252–53). She explores this process in detail in her essay, "Sur l'utilité et de la nécessité de s'examiner attentivement" ("On the Utility and Necessity of Careful Self-Examination," Necker 1798, 1:363–70). Neither an Augustinian indicator of our fallen state nor a Leibnizian epiphenomenon of the complexity of the universe, Necker's "imperceptible judgments" are the source of human judgment and creativity. "We are far from understanding all the treasures that we possess" (Necker 1798, 1:363).

> Let us turn our attention to the secret work that takes place within us; we will learn better to understand the presiding agent. So many things occur in this little universe without our knowledge! (Necker 1798, 1:364)

The mind, for Necker, is constantly aware of all that escapes our immediate attention: "our soul . . . reaches out and gathers riches of all sorts without our knowledge" (Necker 1798, 1:365). Understanding this process, studying it within oneself, leads to "wonder" at one's own intelligence and to greater self-possession. Necker contrasts this intimate self-study, which allows one to discover the connections within ourselves and with nature, with life in society, in which connections dissolve and simplify themselves before our eyes. Society shows us the "theater" of machines and stage equipment, but reveals nothing meaningful; likewise, we might become aware of the mechanisms of the body, but we need to descend to the level of the soul to understand our place in the universe. As in "Sur l'âme," Necker considers the effects of (physical) thoughts on the (immaterial) soul; upon arriving at deep introspection, "you will be present at the creation of thought," a process that will instruct us and, if we allow ourselves to be guided by virtuous thoughts, make us better.

Necker's reflections on the techniques and benefits of introspection occur throughout the *Mélanges*, but one of the most striking passages is the essay, "Sur un nouveau genre de spectateur" ("On a New Type of Spectator," Necker 1801, 1:62–70), in which she reimagines Addison and Steele's periodical as a model for introspection and writing the self, a "Spectateur intérieur." "The Spectator [i.e., the original English *Spectator*] saw the full exterior; this one would see the full interior" (Necker 1801, 1:65). The essay has been read as a programmatic text for the entire body of writings that compose the *Mélanges*, in which the daily practice of writing on "all of life's objects" becomes a means for self-examination and self-improvement.[47] Necker returns on multiple occasions to the importance of self-mastery and the need to be vigilant regarding one's desires and motivations. Catherine Dubeau correctly describes her personal moral system as a syncretic "composite of paternal Calvinism and Stoic philosophy,"[48] but while Necker's "war with herself" is one way to frame introspection, it is not the only way, as we have seen. In "Sur l'âme" and "De l'utilité et de la nécessité de s'examiner attentivement," the inward gaze is one of fascination, enthusiasm, and the quest for understanding.

Noting the large number of observations in the *Mélanges* on how to stimulate conversation or make guests feel comfortable, Necker's work has been termed "one of the last manuals of *savoir-vivre* from the period before the Révolution."[49] Such "preparatory notes" for salon conversation suggest to some a difficult, tormented personality. We know that she had a complicated relationship with her daughter, whose passions and ambitions were quite foreign to her, but this characterization seems to stem more from accounts in the memoirs of contemporaries than from the *Mélanges*—and may tell us more about their response to the daughter of a Calvinist pastor whose social "performance" may not have conformed to Parisian norms, but whose

---

[47] Dena Goodman, "Le Spectateur intérieur: Les journaux de Suzanne Necker," in Benoît Melançon, ed. *L'Invention de l'intimité au siècle des Lumières* (Nanterre: Université Paris X, 1995), 91–100; Catherine Dubeau, "Mrs. Spectator: Journal, comptes moraux et tyrannie de l'introspection dans les *Mélanges* et les *Nouveaux mélanges* de Suzanne Necker," in Virginie Dufresne and Geneviève Langlois, eds., *Influences et modèles étrangers en France sous l'Ancien Régime* (Québec, QC: Presses de l'université Laval, 2009), 145–62. Whereas Goodman sees Necker's combination of writing and introspection as a means for defining her personal autonomy, Dubeau offers a darker interpretation, "the tyranny of introspection" and a drive to self-control motivated by self-hatred and "painful acuity."

[48] Dubeau, "Mrs. Spectator," 149.

[49] Craveri, *L'Âge de la conversation*, 382.

power was undeniable, than about Necker herself.[50] When read in the context of moralist writing and the practice of maxims and *pensées détachées*, Necker's observations on social behavior, on writing and style, on one's own and others' habits of learning, writing, and thinking fall very much within the tradition of the moralist *spectateurs de la vie*.

Given Necker's vast culture and her early literary ambitions, these writings appear to represent more than grimly dogged preparation for a social role with which she was ill at ease. Like Verzure, Necker sees introspection as a means for pursuing both self-understanding and knowledge of the world: "Sometimes by studying oneself, one becomes able to understand others" (Necker 1801, 1:23). A woman of action who channeled her formidable intellectual and managerial abilities into her salon and her charitable work, Suzanne Necker is also, undeniably, a writer and thinker for whom writing and thinking were inextricably entwined: "The only way to know one's thoughts is to write them down" (Necker 1798, 1:119).

2.5. Guizot: Doubts

I will round out this account of women's writings on self-knowledge with a short look at the most prolific of the post-Revolutionary moralists. Pauline Guizot, née de Meulan (1773–1827), was the well-educated daughter of a nobleman who turned to writing as a means of supporting herself and family members in the wake of the Revolution. A successful novelist and translator, her moralist essays and works of criticism appeared in J.-B.-A. Suard's periodical *Le Publiciste* (1799–1810) and were subsequently collected in volumes that enjoyed considerable success. Sainte-Beuve, the leading French literary critic of the nineteenth century, would declare her one of the finest moralists that France had produced.[51] Her essays are characterized by their verve, forthrightness, and variety. Writing anonymously during her years with *Le Publiciste*, Guizot took on many authorial personas, male and female, young and old. She published an anonymous collection of her moralist pieces and

---

[50] On Necker's ambivalent relationship with the world of Parisian salons, see Boon, *The Life of Madame Necker: Sin, Redemption, and the Parisian Salon* (London: Pickering and Chatto, 2011), 17–38.

[51] "De cette famille illustre et sérieuse des moralistes, qui, de La Rochefoucauld et de La Bruyère, se continue par Vauvenargues et par Duclos, Mme Guizot est l'auteur le dernier venu." Charles-Augustin Sainte-Beuve, "Madame Guizot," in Gérald Antoine, ed., *Portraits de femmes* (Paris: Gallimard, 1998), 273.

criticism as a two-volume *Essais de littérature et de morale* (1802). After her marriage in 1812 to academic and rising political star François Guizot, she produced political essays and collaborated with her husband on a wide range of projects, but did not publish under her name until he (temporarily) left politics, when she became well known for a series of thoughtful tales and novels for young people.[52] These eclipsed her early work, until François Guizot edited the two volumes of her *Essais et conseils de morale* following her death. Her work continued to be reprinted throughout the century, with a further collection of literary, moralist, and political essays by both Guizots appearing under the title *Le Temps passé* (1878) after his death.

Two essays, both presumably from the *Publiciste* years and republished later, offer an ironic perspective on the value of observation and introspection for the moralist. "Des inconvéniens de l'Expérience" ("On the Inconveniences of Experience") begins bluntly: "To write on *la morale*, it is best not to have seen too much of the world."[53] The spectacle of other people's problems, vices, and passions wears on the observer; we begin to see others only in terms of what they can do for us and we risk losing our moral compass. Instead, she continues, the moralist should look within and seek to preserve a "precious model" by maintaining self-mastery and avoiding the influence of others. Another essay, dated 1806 but republished many years later, suggests the futility of such a program, however. In "À quel point on est étranger à soi-même" ("The Extent to Which We Are Strangers to Ourselves"), Guizot maintains that we are never able to know or understand ourselves, that we are constantly changing: "Often, from evening to the next day, from one hour or minute to the next, we change opinions, feelings, resolutions."[54] We exaggerate our good qualities and minimize the bad, but (paradoxically) *amour-propre* is not our main motive. After all, she reasons, if it were, then surely we would stake our self-love on things that make us happy, rather than running after that which makes us unhappy. And, in any case, what is *amour-propre*? Is there anything in us that we could reasonably love? Why, in the end, are we so attached to "this particular assemblage of qualities and defects that constitute our being?" Guizot compares our attachment to our imperfect selves to

---

[52] On the couple's collaborations and the political intertext of Pauline Guizot's works for young readers, see Robin Bates, "Madame Guizot and Monsieur Guizot: Domestic Pedagogy and the Post-Revolutionary Order in France, 1807–1830," *Modern Intellectual History* 8.1 (2011): 31–59.

[53] Pauline Guizot, *Essais et conseils de morale*, ed. François Guizot, 2 vols. (Paris: Pichon et Didier, 1828), 1:7–9.

[54] Pauline Guizot, *Le Temps passé, mélanges de critique littéraire et de morale par M. et Mme. Guizot*, ed. Henriette de Witt, 2 vols. (Paris: Perrin, 1887), 2:505–508.

an unhappy relationship that we maintain out of habit and because we fear "divorce." Ultimately, the only people with a sense of self are "methodical types" whose ideas and attachments are as inconsistent as anyone else's, but whose routine never varies—"that is what they call fidelity."

Guizot's deft irony suggests why Sainte-Beuve saw in her the inheritor of La Rochefoucauld and La Bruyère. If experience of the world causes the moralist to lose perspective and self-love is based on the mere illusion that something like a self exists, what remains, and what is possible? There is a sense in which Guizot has both closed one tradition, by dismissing *amour-propre* as essentially meaningless, and opened a new one. The doorway to the new has two aspects. First, the semantic field of *la morale* has begun to shift: although the phrase "écrire sur la morale" continues to evoke a certain tradition, the essay "Des inconvéniens de l'Expérience" makes it increasingly clear that *la morale* is to be understood as in its modern sense, as "morality" rather than disinterested spectatorship. Indeed, the speaker dismisses the possibility of such disinterest—our own interests inevitably surface in our interactions with others. Furthermore, although conceiving the self as an "assemblage" of qualities is not without an echo of La Bruyère—or Diderot, for that matter—the randomness of change, the dissolution of "interest" as an overarching motivation, the lack of coherent volition ("So many unforeseen circumstances, sudden urges, cowardly accommodations, weaken a will that should be absolute!") point to the restless sensibility of the decades following the Revolution.

* * *

Madeleine de Scudéry, Louise Dupin, Marie de Verzure, Suzanne Necker, and Pauline Guizot pursue different aspects of the topic of self-knowledge. Scudéry's characters debate the extent to which the self, understood as one's innermost desires and motivations, is knowable; given the limits of our knowledge, she offers the means to acquire at least a contingent understanding of oneself and of others. Verzure develops a dialogical method by which self-examination and observation of others provide a measure of understanding. Dupin, Verzure, and Necker seek to anatomize the operations of the mind, but whereas Dupin and Verzure suggest a physiological basis for mental operation, Necker's account of the mind insists on its immateriality. Guizot's ironic persona dissolves the self into an "assemblage" of qualities held together by habit, but she recommends maintaining an inward gaze in order to avoid developing an instrumentalizing approach to others.

The limits of our knowledge, the contours of what remains unknown, and how we can navigate those limits are recurring issues. For Scudéry and her seventeenth-century contemporaries, self-interest and *amour-propre* are the primary obstacles that prevent us from seeing clearly into our character and motives: we cannot bear the knowledge. When Scudéry's Céphise claims that she knows herself as clearly as she sees the sun, the wiser Télésile points out that looking at the sun is hardly a simple matter and that, like sunspots, *amour-propre* is always hidden beneath the bright surface. On the other hand, Scudéry's character Timocrate also points to the elusiveness and rapidity of our thoughts as a factor, placing the problem in the nature of mental operations. Dupin's short essay focuses on how we can "feel" or be aware of that which lies beyond our immediate knowledge. Verzure's approach is the most "operational": her regret for the lack of clear "principles" does not prevent her from seeking a way forward by combining introspection and observation of others.

Necker is concerned with the thoughts and feelings that escape our consciousness. For her, our mental universe is rich in the proliferation of "fleeting thoughts" and "imperceptible judgments." Her *jugements imperceptibles* echo Pierre Nicole's *pensées imperceptibles*, which are also mental events occurring out of the range of consciousness. In Nicole, however, they are part of the fundamental unknowability of the self; for Necker, they are an explanation for how a "new" idea arises through subconscious mental fermentation.[55]

Necker's concept contrasts with a similar idea in Vauvenargues, for whom the sheer rapidity of mental processes is the only reason why our feelings and desires are not entirely transparent and accessible to us. In his 1744 *Traité du libre arbitre*, he claims that "what hides from the mind the motivation for its actions is nothing but their infinite speed."[56] Like Scudéry's Timocrate, Vauvenargues points to a rapid succession of ideas that passes out of awareness almost instantaneously. For Vauvenargues, however, the existence of the succession of ideas guarantees that our actions are based on reasons, not

---

[55] The issue of "imperceptible" thoughts arises in many contexts. Béatrice Guion discusses Nicole's *pensées imperceptibles* in relation to Cartesian *idées accessoires* (*Pierre Nicole*, 127–35). See also Geneviève Rodis-Lewis, *Le Problème de l'inconscient et le cartésianisme* (Paris: PUF, 1985). We find yet another model in the Leibnizian *petites perceptions*, which Du Châtelet refers to as *représentations obscures* in her *Institutions de physique*. As Rodis-Lewis points out, the models are quite different—*pensées imperceptibles* take us into the hidden folds of the heart, while *petites perceptions* arise in the fundamentally different mental universe of the monadology (Rodis-Lewis, 259–65). Nevertheless, all are useful frameworks that remind us of the historicity of more recent concepts of the unconscious.

[56] Luc de Clapiers, marquis de Vauvenargues, "Traité du libre arbitre," *Oeuvres complètes de Vauvenargues*, ed. Jean-Baptiste-Antoine Suard, 2 vols. (Paris: Dentu, 1806), 2:248.

chance. Furthermore, he argues that decisions come about as the result of a struggle among ideas which we experience as uncertainty:

> Everything is present to the mind, everything is depicted simultaneously, [or] at least objects follow one another with great speed and create a swarm of urges; these urges are in combat. None is actually the will, for the will is what decides; they are uncertainty, anxiety. The strongest, most complete, and liveliest ideas ultimately vanquish the others. (Vauvenargues, 2:258)

The strongest ideas carry the day, forming the basis for our choices and enabling us to take any sort of action, even the most trivial. There is no mystery here, but rather a sort of optimizing mechanism that deletes unnecessary mental subroutines from our consciousness.

While Vauvenargues's agonistic account has a certain clean efficiency, it lacks the subtlety and nuance of Necker's, for whom interactions too complex to describe in simple combative terms interact and combine to produce new, creative ideas. It is their willingness to make a cartography of the unknown, the unconscious, to experiment with its texture and test its boundaries, that distinguishes the women studied here. For them, it is not the case, as it is with Vauvenargues, that "everything is present"; rather, much remains hidden. Their goal is not to simplify, but to find language adequate to the complexity of mental phenomena and the depths of the self.

2.6. Introspection and the Act of Writing

The value of introspection is practical, since it grants insights into the motivations governing the behavior of others. More importantly, as we have seen, it is ethical. Although the examination of one's conscience had long constituted a religious obligation, in Scudéry it becomes a means "to advance in virtue" in an entirely worldly context. Necker and Guizot will similarly underscore the need to look within in order to maintain one's integrity. The "anatomists" Dupin and Verzure make the point implicitly, by linking their accounts of the operations of the self to the perception of unseen truths, for Dupin, and the ability to frame social and ethical judgments in Verzure.

Knowledge of self and others—the particularity of observation—is foundational to the moralist project. Many of the thinkers whom we will encounter in subsequent chapters began their projects as personal writing that became a springboard for broader, more ambitious analysis, as we have already seen in Necker. Marie-Louise Fourqueux's *Confessions* are emblematic in this regard.

> By writing, one deepens one's thought, thus developing within oneself an infinite number of ideas that one would never have had without writing them down. (Fourqueux, 1:93)

What begins as an introspective dive into her own history and character later evolves into a far more general series of analyses and observations of her world—moralist essays on happiness, virtue, friendship. The inward journey provides her with the means and authorial confidence to describe and assess her world.

Women who did not consider publication for their personal writing practice nevertheless pursued topics and shaped their observations in keeping with the conventions of the genre. Henriette de Marans (1719–1784) made the leap from personal writing to publication, drawing on years of personal reflections to create the idiosyncratic "Préface qui contient tout" for an experimental collaborative novel, *Les pensées érrantes; avec quelques lettres d'un Indien*.[57] Although comparison of the novel with the manuscripts shows that she revised her text for publication, the presence in the manuscripts of ornate title pages and other features of print publication reveal that publication was on her mind, if only as an aspiration or fantasy, from the beginning.[58] Likewise, among her letters and papers Dauphine de Sartre (1634–1685) carefully preserved her commonplace book, to which she gave a title, *Recueil de choses morales*, as well as a short, but formal "Dissertation sur l'amitié." In looking at these works, what matters is less the form of each writer's engagement with the world of print publication, than her engagement with the

---

[57] The authorship of the *Pensées errantes* has a complicated history. Published anonymously in 1758, the novel was attributed by nineteenth-century bibliographer Antoine Barbier to Bonne-Charlotte de Bénouville, an attribution that held until quite recently, including in the excellent modern edition of the work by Huguette Krief. Working independently in the Marans family archive, Mathilde Chollet made the connection between Henriette de Marans's manuscripts and the published novel. The present assumption is that the two women, who moved in the same social circles, coauthored the work, with Marans providing the long "preface" (the "wandering thoughts" of the title) and Bénouville, the short epistolary section. Mathilde Chollet and Huguette Krief, *Une femme d'encre et de papier à l'époque des Lumières: Henriette de Marans (1719–1784)* (Rennes: Presses universitaires de Rennes, 2017), 93–107. References to the *Pensées errantes* will be to Krief's edition (Paris: Classiques Garnier, 2014), but I will refer to Marans as the author.

[58] Marans, "Memorial à mon usage particulier," in *Une femme d'encre et de papier à l'époque des Lumières*, 110.

moralist tradition: a turn of mind and a form of writing marked by that tradition. Although Jacques Necker refers to his wife's writings as *journaux*, they are not a diary in any usual sense, but, literally, "daily writings." The unbound pages, neither dated nor numbered, reflect her interests, her reading, and her desire to set down in writing her observations about the world.

In her earliest moralist work, *Pensées et réflexions morales* (1760), Geneviève d'Arconville saw a dual utility in such writing:

> Everyone should write down their ideas and observations regarding the various objects that present themselves from the moment they begin to think. In addition to the benefit of keeping track of the progress of one's mind, one would produce the history of one's soul, the study of which is undoubtedly the most useful and interesting of all. (D'Arconville, 1:406)

Nearly half a century later, looking back on her long life and a publishing career that was no less distinguished for having been entirely anonymous, she remembered her earliest attempts at writing, and regrets having destroyed the manuscripts, "because I would have been able to read the story of my brain, more interesting perhaps than the story of my life, and to which one's ideas in childhood contribute more than is usually thought."[59]

"The story of my brain": the desire to write, to read, and to return to oneself in later years infuses women's moralist projects with a particular energy. Other forms of writing offer opportunities for self-fashioning and agency, of course. The novel assumes a major role in psychological and social analysis, and the publication of Rousseau's *Confessions* opened a door into new dimensions of self-disclosure. Moralist writing, however, enabled one to walk a careful line between the personal and the philosophical and to examine oneself while exploring larger questions, both social and epistemological. Necker:

> By writing down one's thoughts as they come on all kinds of topics, one creates without realizing it the portrait of one's soul, of which one would never have a clear notion otherwise. (Necker 1801, 2:52)

To paint a self-portrait is to achieve self-understanding, but also to demonstrate one's mastery and capacity for judgment.

---

[59] D'Arconville, "Histoire de mon enfance," PRA 3:311–489. Also in Marc André Bernier and Marie-Laure Girou Swiderski, eds., *Madame d'Arconville, moraliste et chimiste au siècle des Lumières* (Oxford: Voltaire Foundation, 2016), 45–46.

3
On Friendship

Reflection on the nature of friendship and its significance for one's sense of self, intersubjective relations, and the social order has been part of the Western philosophical tradition since its beginnings. Eclipsed by the epistemological and scientific concerns of modern philosophy in the wake of Cartesianism, it remains a central preoccupation of seventeenth and eighteenth-century moralists. "Friendship" is both the name of a relationship and an "emotive" or articulation of feeling; the understanding of friendship in a given period is inflected by social and political theory, by notions of selfhood, and by the affective regime, however ostensibly distinct the discursive domains may be. The texts I examine here bear a profound relationship to the evolving public sphere and the sense of self of those who participated in it.

It is thus hardly surprising that friendship should surface as a key theme at a time when the fundamental principles of the body politic are being subjected to critical analysis, when social relations in both *la Cour* and *la Ville* are undergoing significant shifts, and when European culture is about to experience what William Reddy termed the "affective revolution" of the eighteenth century. The ability to discern the contours, the limits, the privileges and the responsibilities of friendship takes on a special significance in the rigidly hierarchical world, especially court culture, of the *ancien régime*. In such a world, forms of association outside the dangerous confines of court intrigue, such as friendship—true friendship—would be revalorized as an emotional refuge.[1] The eighteenth century's profound reframing of social relations ensures that the topic remains richly relevant, as an intensified focus on the discourse on friendship is tightly bound up with the constitution of the literary public sphere and the new sociability—salons, cafés, print journalism—fostering openness and exchange.[2] The personal is very much the political, especially in a context where the political is still seeking the

---

[1] William Reddy, *The Navigation of Feeling: A Framework for the History of the Emotions* (Cambridge: Cambridge University Press, 2001), 145–54.
[2] Anne Vincent-Buffault, *L'Exercice de l'amitié: Pour un histoire des pratiques amicales aux XVIIIe et XIXe siècles* (Paris: Seuil, 1995).

discourse in which its goals may be articulated. Affectivity, family relations, and gender are intimately connected to the classical language of politics.[3] Thus the world of the moralists intersects with broader concerns, which it subtends and by which it is affected.

The classical legacy connecting friendship with virtue and equality resonates strongly in this period. In the *Nicomachean Ethics*, Aristotle distinguishes among friendships based on utility, pleasure, and virtue—the last being the truest form—and reflects on the link between friendship and justice. As a voluntary relationship, friendship signifies freedom and autonomy. One's friends reveal something of one's character; in a famous passage, he tells us that the friend is "another self." Cicero too bases friendship on virtue, arguing that friendship is based in our nature, rather than in any "need" for the other person, hence securing freedom and equality as key elements. Similarly, in his *Moral Epistles*, Seneca seeks to reconcile our desire for friendship with Stoic self-sufficiency. An additional key reference is Montaigne's essay "De l'amitié," a meditation on his personal experience of friendship in the moving evocation of his late friend Etienne de la Boétie. Montaigne's oft-cited words, "Par ce que c'estoit luy; par ce que c'estoit moy" ("Because it was he; because it was I") become a touchstone for describing friendship in terms of fusion and identification with the other.[4] As we will see in the readings ahead, these texts echo and re-echo in the writings of moralist thinkers.

Despite the echoes, however, the foundation of friendship shifts distinctively from virtue to affectivity, beginning in the *ère du soupçon* that characterizes seventeenth-century court culture through the eighteenth century's emphasis on sentiment and the separation of public and private life.[5] Given women's central role in social life and the ongoing associations between femininity and sentiment, it is hardly surprising that friendship becomes a key topic in their moralist writings. In addition to reimagining the foundations of friendship, they reframe the concern with need versus self-sufficiency as a focus on the dynamics of reciprocity and obligation. What do we owe our friends, what is the role of gratitude in friendship, and, assuming that friendship implies special obligations, how can it be prevented from falling into a vulgar form of exchange? Indeed, during the Enlightenment,

---

[3] Jacques Derrida, *Politiques de l'amitié* (Paris: Galilée, 1994).
[4] Michel de Montaigne, *Essais*, ed. M. Rat, 2 vols. (Paris: Classiques Garnier, 1962) 1:204.
[5] Jean-Charles Darmon, "Moralistes en movement: L'Amitié entre morale et politique," in Darmon *Le Moraliste*, 31–68.

the Stoic avoidance of "need" as constitutive of friendship is completely reversed by figures such as Vauvenargues, who classifies friendship as a passion based on the "insufficiency of our being," and Helvétius, who declares bluntly, "To love is to need."[6] Need and obligation become vexed problems to solve in a world of complex social hierarchies and protocols for the giving and receiving of favors.

Crucially, there is the question of whether women have any place in this conversation at all. Aristotle raises the question of friendship between men and women briefly in the *Nicomachean Ethics*, but only in the context of asymmetrical power relations, and hence not a friendship in the fullest sense, since that requires freedom and equality. Can women and men be friends? Although his thinking on the question was more nuanced elsewhere, Montaigne gave a strong "no" in "De l'amitié": women's souls are too weak to sustain the connection and, in any case, as Harry said to Sally, the sex part always gets in the way. La Bruyère granted the possibility, but claimed that such relationships could not truly be considered friendship and were "une classe à part."[7] For the female moralist, then, the appeal of exploring a subject that not only had inspired the Ancients but also offered plenty of relevance to her own lifeworld, comes with the implicit requirement to justify her place in the conversation, her claim to know friendship and be able to say something about it.

In this chapter, I discuss three aspects of the moralist account of friendship: first, the swerve away from the classical model of friendship based on virtue and free will to models that increasingly reflect the new affectivity; second, the practices characteristic of friendship, in particular the thorny issues surrounding reciprocity and exchange; third, the role of gender and of difference more broadly. In conclusion, I consider the place of *reconnaissance*, gratitude, initially broached by Madeleine de Scudéry as one of the foundations of friendship, and reflect on its implications for the moralist understanding of friendship.

This chapter is organized differently from the previous one. Because friendship is probably the topic on which more women moralists wrote than on any other, each subtopic involves a large cast of characters. These will provide a broader context to several key texts that will be the object

---

[6] Vauvenargues, *Introduction à la connaissance de l'esprit humain* (1747), ed. Jean Dagen (Paris: Flammarion, 1981), 93; Helvétius, *De l'esprit* (1758), ed. François Châtelet (Paris: Marabout université, 1973), 279.

[7] Jean de La Bruyère, *Des caractères*, in Lafond, *Moralistes du XVIIe*, 739.

of extended readings: in the discussion of the foundations of friendship, the conversations of Madeleine de Scudéry; in the discussion of difference and gender, Anne-Thérèse de Lambert's *Traité de l'amitié* and Geneviève d'Arconville's *De l'amitié*.

3.1. Foundations of Friendship

Let us first consider a text that reflects the classical legacy of friendship based on virtue. Madeleine de Souvré, marquise de Sablé (1599–1678), is primarily remembered as the hostess of an influential intellectual salon with Port-Royalist sympathies, the milieu in which La Rochefoucauld crafted his *Maximes*. In her apartment adjacent to Port-Royal de Paris, she welcomed not only the leading Jansenist intellectuals but also Jesuits and Protestants; she played a central diplomatic role in the Peace of the Church of 1669. Her eighty-one *Maximes*, anterior to those of La Rochefoucauld, were published at the time of her death; beginning in 1690, they were frequently reprinted with La Rochefoucauld's *Maximes*. With the important exceptions of a chapter in John Conley's book on women and salon philosophy and an article by Lewis Seifert, there have been few contemporary readings of her work, though recent scholarship on salon culture has done a great deal to reestablish her intellectual prominence.[8] Her reflections on friendship are to be found partly in her *Maximes*, but primarily in a short manuscript, "Sur l'amitié."[9]

Sablé's maxims offer a striking example of what Lucien Goldmann called "le refus intramondain du monde" ("rejection of the world from within the world") of Jansenist sympathizers.[10] The worldly genre of the maxim bespeaks a social setting and conversation, yet serves to critique social façades, purposive exchanges of favors, and worldly ambition. As the first

---

[8] Conley, *Suspicion*, 20–44; Lewis C. Seifert, "The Marquise de Sablé and Her Friends: Men and Women Between the Convent and the World," in Lewis C. Seifert and Rebecca M. Wilkin, eds., *Men and Women Making Friends in Early Modern France* (London: Routledge, 2015), 219–45. See also Faith E. Beasley, *Salons History, and the Creation of 17th-Century France* (Aldershot: Ashgate, 2006), 216–19, 225–26; and Jean Lafond, "La Marquise de Sablé et son salon," in Lafond, Moralistes du XVIIe siècle, 201–16.

[9] For Sablé's *Maximes*, I cite the text in Lafond, *Moralistes du XVIIe siècle*, 243–55. For "Sur l'amitié," see *Maximes de Madame de Sablé (1678)*, ed. Damase Jouaust (Paris: Librairie des bibliophiles, 1870), 57–61. The manuscript to "Sur l'amitié" was initially uncovered by Victor Cousin and published in his *Madame de Sablé: Nouvelles études sur les femmes illustres du dix-septième siècle*, 3rd ed. (Paris: Didier, 1865), 111–12.

[10] Goldmann, *Le Dieu caché*, 66.

reader and valued editor of La Rochefoucauld's maxims, her own maxims and short fragments on friendship are thought by some to be a response to La Rochefoucauld and a corrective to his cynicism. Sablé however sometimes seems to have scarcely more confidence in the possibility of authentic human relations than her friend; many of her maxims offer an *art du monde* emphasizing the need for defensive strategy. Compare La Rochefoucauld on friendship:

> What people name friendship is only a form of socializing, a reciprocal management of each other's interests, an exchange of services; it is ultimately no more than a form of commerce where *amour-propre* always sees something to gain. (Max. 83; La Rochefoucauld, *Maximes*, 142)

with Sablé:

> Society, and even friendship for the majority, is only a form of commerce that lasts only as long as the need for it. (Max. 72; Sablé, *Maximes*, 254)

Already in Sablé we see the laconic style, the reductive unmasking gesture of "ne ... que" ("only") that would characterize La Rochefoucauld, minus his characteristic *pointe* or witty, paradoxical final twist. Neither holds out much confidence in society as a whole, although in the maxims just cited, Sablé leaves open the possibility that despite the distortions of friendship by "la plupart des hommes," a more authentic form of attachment might nevertheless exist outside the corrupt sphere of ordinary social relations.[11]

Sablé makes clear in her first Maxim that the truths of the world are diametrically opposed to fundamental, eternal truth: "Just as nothing is weaker or less reasonable than submitting one's judgment to others without employing one's own, so too nothing is greater or more reasonable than submitting oneself blindly to God and taking his word for everything" (Sablé, *Maximes*, 246). The opening statement of faith casts the remaining eighty maxims in a certain light: not so much cynical as a practical, realistic commentary on

---

[11] Conley draws a sharper distinction between the two, arguing that Sablé is far more "moderate" in her critique of human motivations than La Rochefoucauld (*Suspicion*, 39). I am arguing that her critique is hardly less severe, but that she makes an explicit distinction between the hypocrisy and self-deception of the world and an authentic virtue enabled by faith. For Seifert, Sablé's moderation lies in her willingness to evince the possibility of authentic friendship and virtue outside the realm of *le monde*, whereas La Rochefoucauld and their mutual friend Jacques Esprit held "(at best) ambiguous" positions on this point (Seifert, "The Marquise de Sablé and Her Friends," 226).

human interaction in "the world," urging us to be wary of the deceptions of others as well as our own propensity for self-deception. Sablé's comments on friendship show both sides: the *Maximes* present the disabused critique of inauthentic, worldly "friendships" (Maxims 43, 44, 46, 77, and 78), whereas the manuscript "De l'amitié" offers an account of the genuine article in eight short passages. Sablé's key intertexts are Montaigne and classical writings on friendship, many of whose themes she echoes. Thus, like Aristotle, she defines friendship as a form of virtue, affirming that it must be founded on esteem and "qualities of the soul . . . and the good qualities of the mind" (Sablé, "De l'amitié," 57). Friendship is always reciprocal, "because in friendship it is impossible to love—as it is in love—without being loved" (Sablé, "De l'amitié," 58). The only true friendships are those founded on virtue, rather than on pleasure or interest. Like the Stoics, she maintains that friendship should be an expression of one's free will. The discourse of seventeenth-century affectivity imparts however a particular nuance to the argument:

> We should not give the name of friendship to natural inclinations, because these depend on neither our will nor our choice; although they render friendship more agreeable, they cannot serve as a basis for it. (Sablé, "De l'amitié," 58–59).

Sablé is making what is in some ways the same point as Montaigne, for whom friendship is the truest expression of free will (Montaigne, 1:200), but whereas he emphasized our choice as the difference between the affection we feel for family that what which we feel for friends, her use of the term *inclination* points rather to the contemporary psychology of love that both privileged and warned against the sort of "inclination" that leads inexorably to a passion as blind as the physical forces of nature; the notion that *inclination* might render a friendship more "agreeable" further suggests that she is speaking of friendship between the sexes. Although she specifically excludes inclination from the foundations of true friendship, hers will prove to be a minority view.

The winds of salon conversation were shifting away from the neo-Stoic account. In the short "Dissertation sur l'amitié" of Dauphine de Sartre, marquise de Robiac (1634–1685), a highly educated member of Montpellier intellectual circles, friendship is entirely separate from reason, and is a matter of *coeur*, not *esprit*. Friendships may vary depending on individual dispositions, time, and circumstance, but ultimately there are no "varieties" of friendship, simply degrees of intensity. So-called friendships based on merit, duty, or gratitude are insipid, pale reflections of the kind of deep feeling that consoles us and "takes the place of all things" (Sartre, 44). In a reversal from those for whom friendship is based in virtue, she declares that friendship is neither a passion nor a virtue: it is "a simple natural movement whose effects may be either good or bad" (Sartre, 43). Sartre does not use the word *inclination*, but *mouvement de la nature* is a close paraphrase of the word, whose usage had shifted during the period from a physical disposition or tendency to the urging of the heart.

One of the best-known uses of *inclination* in its newer sense is by Madeleine de Scudéry, who might well be termed the preeminent theorist of friendship of the seventeenth century and a thorough revisionist of the classical legacy. In the famous *Carte de Tendre* from her novel *Clélie* (1654–1661), multiple pathways lead from the town of "new friendship," *Nouvelle Amitié*, to variations of friendship, or *Tendre*; two slow, circuitous routes lead to towns on the small rivers of *Estime* and *Reconnoissance*, Esteem and Gratitude (See Figure 3.1.). The most direct way, however, is to be swept down the large, swiftly flowing river of *Inclination*—which, if one is not careful, may carry

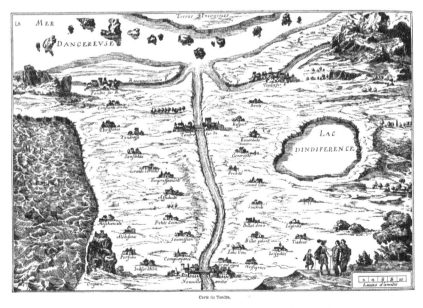

Figure 3.1 *La Carte de Tendre* illustration, Madeleine de Scudéry, *Clélie, histoire romaine* (1654). Public Domain

one straight into the "dangerous sea" of passion, beyond which lies *terra incognita*.

In this section, I examine Scudéry's multiple reworkings of this basic framework in her *Conversations*. In these late works, Esteem and Gratitude tend to yield to Inclination as the most powerful force in a relationship, yet all three pose different problems to be solved. For example, although virtue is a given in Scudéry's world, the form of friendship that most explicitly recognizes it and places the emphasis on free choice, friendship based on Esteem, is the most tepid of the three. Gratitude for services rendered risks becoming indistinguishable from a transactional relation that invalidates friendship. Inclination, while warmer than Esteem and more instantaneous than Gratitude, is closely associated with passion and hence incurs other risks. Scudéry's reworking of the triad marks her effort to come to terms with the dangers of Inclination, on the one hand, and the complex nature of obligation and gratitude, on the other.

The most elaborate reworking occurs in the multilayered "Histoire et conversation d'amitié" from her third collection of conversations, *La Morale du monde* (1686). In an explicit reference to *Clélie*, we find the verbal representation of an allegorical map depicting three towns, three rivers, and three models for attachment: *Estime, Reconnoissance, Inclination*. First, however, we encounter a group of friends who read and reflect on the story of Belinde, a cautionary tale. Belinde makes the mistake early in life of marrying the man who seems to be most in love with her. He turns out to be a terrible husband, but he conveniently goes off to war and is killed. An attractive young widow, Belinde, inspired by reading *Clélie*, renounces love in favor of friendship; as one of her friends advises: "Ordinary love ends ... but friendship ... can become eternal in the right kind of heart." Belinde understands that esteem and gratitude arise in the mind; inclination, in the heart (Scudéry 1686, 2:920).

In search of the perfect friendship, Belinde experiences all of friendship's vicissitudes—the "best friend" who falls in love with her and must be sent away, the old friend who might be in love with her but is wise enough not to say so, the new friend who uses her to advance in society, and many more. Ultimately, she renounces friendship just as she has renounced love and the tale ends on an ambiguous note. Although she is more beloved of her friends than ever, Belinde "loved nothing" (Scudéry 1686, 2:993) and no longer takes the same pleasure in her life as before.

Belinde's story appears to offer little encouragement for either love or friendship, but the group of friends who read her story together seem not to lose heart at her withdrawal from relationships; instead, they take it as a springboard for discussion and focus on the triad of *Estime, Reconnoissance, Inclination*. One of the women present, Elpinice, promises to show the others a fan, which reproduces a text that her mother had painted on a screen; but rather than waiting to see the curious object, another woman present, Asterie, who has seen the screen, describes it from memory, recalling that it represents "a certain Map that cleverly shows how esteem, gratitude, and inclination give rise to all the different kinds of friendship" (Scudéry 1686, 2:996–97). Elpinice lets herself be prevailed upon to recite the verses from her fan from memory and the group of friends revisits one of Scudéry's most celebrated creations, first proposed a quarter century earlier.

Why the elaborate framework, the interpolated story, the digression about the mother's screen, the daughter's fan? As we have seen, the story does not provide a model to emulate, and Scudéry could have let Elpinice recite the verses without the roundabout introduction. She often bestows great care on the physical setting of her conversations, but neither of these two objects is actually present; Elpinice's description is all we have. Just as Belinde's story offers a model for the "use" of literature not as an example to be blindly followed, but a text to be pondered and its applications to be adopted or dismissed, so too the triple ekphrasis (a narration of a description of a visual representation) foregrounds the act of artistic representation. The fan is both utilitarian and fashionable, but the mother's screen is noteworthy for its beauty rather its usefulness ("a beautiful screen that my mother keeps in her study without using it"). The generations of women and of objects remind us of the passage of time since the original Carte in *Clélie*; the evocation of a mother–daughter relation suggests a feminocentric inheritance as well.[12]

The painting on the screen echoes the earlier map, but differs in significant ways. Instead of representing a landscape dotted with cities and traversed by three rivers, we are told that it depicts a Temple of Friendship with three doors, each of which is reached by a different route: a quick river to one— Inclination, needless to say—and long paths to the others. Each route calls

---

[12] For Laura Burch, Belinde's inability to find a real friendship equal to those she had read about in *Clélie* and the subsequent updating of the Carte de Tendre as a fan constitute Scudéry's self-critique, both of the ideology of friendship and of the outdated literary form of her earlier *roman-fleuve*. Burch, "New Pleasure in Life Unfolding: Madeleine de Scudéry's Friendship Fan," *Seventeenth-Century French Studies* 36.1 (2014): 4–17. See also Barbara Piqué's discussion of how Scudéry's settings encode aesthetic principles: "Les Cadres allégoriques dans les *Conversations* de Madeleine de Scudéry," in Delphine Denis and Anne-Elisabeth Spica, eds., *Madeleine de Scudéry: Une femme de lettres au XVIIe siècle* (Artois: Artois presses université, 2002), 59–67.

out to the sentimental traveler to follow its path and ignore the two others. Both *Reconnoissance* and *Estime* claim to speak to "a noble and generous heart." Inclination, however, mocks them both:

> If you imagine that you can arrive at Tendre,
> Without Inclination,
> What error, what illusion! (Scudéry 1686, 2:1003)

The friends weigh the advantages of inclination against its chief drawback, its tendency to metamorphose into love. At last, they agree that perfect friendship is "rare" and that, referring to Montaigne, in order to achieve the ideal of a "total community of goods" (Montaigne, 1:206), all three of the pathways—inclination, esteem, and gratitude—must combine to produce *une amitié héroïque* (Scudéry 1686, 2:1014–15). In a significant shift from Montaigne, however, the "community of goods" has become a community of affective resources.

Scudéry was far from finished with the topic of friendship or the triad *estime-inclination-reconnoissance*, all of which reappear in her final collection, the *Entretiens de Morale* (1692). One of the longest conversations, "De la diversité des amitiez" begins with a scene in which "wise and beautiful Melicrite" treats her friends to a musical performance that includes a dialogue between Love and Friendship, in which each proclaims its superiority to the other. The question arises whether or not love and friendship indeed have separate claims on the heart, or are inextricably linked. Although the familiar echo of love's dangers recalls the image of *La Mer dangereuse* awaiting those who are swept away by Inclination in *La Carte de Tendre*, the conversation keeps sliding from the topic of friendship to that of love, despite Melicrite's repeated attempts to keep the two separate. Her recurring complaint is a discursive embodiment of love's constant "attraction" and the tendency of friendship to stray into love.

Like her classical predecessors, Scudéry finds friendships based on either (mere) pleasure or self-interest imperfect and wanting. Both love and friendship are vulnerable to ingratitude and thrive on *reconnoissance*; both require mindfulness, a commitment to "not forgetting" the gifts and good actions of one's friend or lover (Scudéry 1692, 1:78). Even so, it is Melicrite who in the final pages declares that a friendship based on gratitude pales in comparison with one based on inclination; although reason prompts us to prefer the former, inclination (by definition) guides one's will, *volonté*. Friendship and love appear to be simultaneously fused and distinct, and no longer subject to one's free will. Possibly because of the impossibility of maintaining the delicate balance, or deciding the question, the only conclusion that the group finds is that "friendship is rare" (Scudéry 1692, 1:118). Just as the conversation began with a musical interlude, so it ends with "a fine Ode" evoking the famous words attributed to Aristotle by Diogenes Laertius:

> I half believe
> The Greek gentleman:
> Friends, there are no friends,
> Said he to all who were near. (Scudéry 1692, 1:117)

Like Sablé, Scudéry worries about the implicit scorekeeping suggested by the need for "reciprocal favors" in friendship, and numerous are the conversations that examine how to avoid the fall into exchange. Echoing her classical predecessors, Scudéry enjoins us to forget favors given, but to remember favors received, and to surpass our friend with new displays of generosity in a relation that one might term "reciprocity without exchange."

If "De la diversité des amitiez" appears to be leaning toward love, or at least toward an account of friendship from which love cannot be excluded, the conversation "Des Désirs," describes sincere friendship as a relationship that springs from all three sources: "born from inclination, augmented by merit, and cemented by favors" (Scudéry, 1692, 1:365–66). The familiar triad thus appears as a sequence, *inclination, estime, reconnoissance*, in which inclination provides the stimulus and gratitude represents the crowning moment. Unlike "De la diversité des amitiez," "Des désirs" does not condemn appetitive drives, but sees them as natural, which corresponds to the shift toward a more positive treatment of inclination in the later texts as well.[13]

Scudéry's final volume covers a wider range of topics than any of the earlier volumes, including works of fiction and natural history, so it is all the more striking that she returns to familiar territory in the very last piece, "De la reconnoissance" (Scudéry 1692, 2:334–403). The treatment of gratitude goes into greater depth than in her earlier conversation, "De l'oisivité et de

---

[13] This more positive view of inclination nuances the account in Scudéry's earlier conversation, "De l'inclination," in which the term is used in its older sense, as "tendency." Here, Scudéry observes that we all have various kinds of inclinations, but none can be seen as either virtuous or vicious since all are simply natural instincts; virtue can only be ascribed to actions "led by Reason" (Scudéry 1684, 1:325).

l'ingratitude," in *Conversations sur divers sujets* (1680), where the somewhat awkward juxtaposition of topics and the restriction of "ingratitude" to affective relations limited the scope. Part of the awkwardness of this early conversation stems from the unavoidable sense that both love and friendship imply forms of obligation, even purposiveness. While the absence of gratitude may be condemned, Scudéry would like to remove love and friendship from the realm of quid pro quo.

Such is the task of "De la reconnoissance." The group of friends who engage the hermit Periandre in conversation shift the ground of the discussion by agreeing that gratitude is founded on justice and that the first and highest form is gratitude to God and to the King as God's image on earth (Scudéry 1692, 2:340–42). While the conversation will turn again to the context of human desires and relationships, this initial context provides a higher moral plane for the understanding of *reconnaissance*. Thus, when Lisimene asks if it is possible to "settle the debt" of gratitude, Periandre replies that such a tit for tat approach is tantamount to ingratitude, since clearly such a person is seeking to forget the favor and be rid of any obligation. A truly "noble reconnoissance" both insists on reciprocity and denies it by unbalancing the equation in various ways. For example, we should always strive to return, not favor for favor, but, in a Ciceronian "rivalry of virtue," a hundred favors for one; we should forget the favors that we give, remembering only those that we receive (Scudéry 1692, 2:345–46). Memory is thus inextricably linked to gratitude; ingratitude is a form of forgetting.[14] *Reconnaissance* is, literally, remembering: "knowing again." Ultimately the question comes back to the peculiar asymmetry of gratitude: "the main rule is always to aim to surpass those whose favors we accept" (Scudéry 1692, 2:359). In this manner, grateful relations are forever removed from the world of nonnoble exchange and instead sent spiraling out to infinity.

A proper expression of thanks is the first step toward gratitude. Again, the interpolation of a text allows Scudéry to make both explicit and implicit points: Periandre shares a manuscript given him by a friend, part of which is missing, making it impossible to identify either its author or its intended recipient (Scudéry 1692, 2:361). As it happens, the text was indeed "by a friend"; Nicole Aronson has identified the text as having been written

---

[14] The one exception is in the aftermath of a love affair, when men are under a moral obligation to forget "ladies' favors" (2:354)—but in such circumstances, "forgetting" is a form of remembrance, with the intimacy of a secret.

by Scudéry's friend Paul Pellisson, and originally intended for the disgraced former finance minister Nicolas Fouquet, a somewhat startling element.[15] The inclusion of Pellisson's text thirty years after Fouquet's dramatic fall and imprisonment by the Sun King bespeaks the entwinement of gratitude, memory, and a web of friendships. Scudéry literalizes her point through an extended allegory of a visit to the *Pays de la Reconnaissance*, whose architectural wonders include "columns of memory" engraved with letters of gold (Scudéry 1692, 2:376). No longer a tributary river in the *Pays de Tendre*, *reconnaissance* is now an extensive territory of its own, enabling Scudéry/Pellisson to explore the taxonomy of expressions of thanks (Scudéry 1692, 2:379–87). Like many other of her conversations, "De la reconnoissance" concludes with a panegyrick to the King; the creative reuse of the text parallels the redirection of artistic projects from Fouquet's chateau Vaux-le-Vicomte to Versailles, but also, silently, remembers Fouquet.[16]

Although Scudéry's propensity to reuse her own earlier materials and characters in the *Conversations*, especially in the early volumes, makes it difficult to speak of a clear evolution in her thinking, the reconfigurations of *estime*, *inclination*, and *reconnaissance* point both to an ongoing concern with the ambiguous place of inclination in friendship and to a deepening interest in gratitude over and above esteem. If in the "Histoire et conversation d'amitié" friendship is defined as "a sentiment of reciprocal tenderness" (Scudéry 1686, 2:962), the concept of "reciprocity" becomes much more complicated in "De la reconnaissance." Esteem attracts less attention than either inclination or gratitude—"Votre estime me fait pitié," sneers Inclination, the clear winner in the "Histoire et conversation d'amitié"—and is all but forgotten in "De la diversité des amitiez." Scudéry's ideal friendships are "tender and ardent" ("Des désirs," Scudéry 1692, 1:365), constantly skirting the dangerous border between friendship and love. Gratitude, with its reciprocity-without-exchange, offers a structurally similar example of a potentially destabilizing contradiction whose provisional containment enlivens the affective bond. The nature of that affective bond continues to be a topic of discussion, but Scudéry has definitively shifted it into the zone of inclination and attraction.

---

[15] Aronson, *Mademoiselle de Scudéry*, 318.
[16] See Claire Goldstein, *Vaux and Versailles: The Appropriations, Erasures, and Accidents That Made Modern France* (Philadelphia: University of Pennsylvania Press, 2008). On Scudéry's successful integration into the "Versailles literary budget" after having been associated with Fouquet, see 138–53.

We see this shift away from the Stoic tradition quite clearly in later writers. In the shift away from friendships based purely on esteem/virtue, however, they must wrestle with the distinction between friendship and love. In her essay "Idées sur l'amitié" (Ideas on Friendship), from the late 1740s, Louise Dupin argues that there should be a new word, since the terms *amour* and *amitié* are used in ways that are too distinct from one another to evoke a lived experience in which they are fused.[17] Ideally, we should abandon the word *amitié* in favor of *amour*, since ultimately "there exist only friendship on the one hand and desires on the other"—in other words, we shouldn't use *amour* to refer to feelings of sexual attraction, which are simply "desire." Having dismissed mere desire as unworthy, for Dupin there is only one thing. She settles on the phrase *amour ou amitié* ("love-or-friendship") to convey a phenomenon rooted in both physical and psychological reality, using language of the natural world analogous to *inclination*: "all that we call impulse, attraction, growth (*végétation*), could be called love" (Dupin, *Portefeuille*, 69). Similarly, Marie de Verzure, despite cautionary language about the "masks" of friendship, claims that the foundations of friendship lie in the heart, not the head: "This sentiment of the heart does not wait for the mind's consent" (Verzure, 1:60).

Elisabeth Guibert (1725-1788), governess of Louis XV's children, dramatist, and author of a 1771 volume of *Pensées détachées*, offers the contrary view, a clear distinction between love and friendship: "Love arises in the heart; it is possible that friendship arises in the mind only." More crudely, she makes it clear which of the two is preferable: "Friendship is the miscarriage of love."[18] Germaine de Staël, however, returns friendship to the affective realm: "those pure and true attachments, born from the heart's choice alone."[19] Friendship falls in an intermediate space for Staël: neither a passion nor an "internal resource" (because it depends on another person) to console one for an unhappy passion, true friendship infuses all areas of life. At the same time, friendship teeters on the verge of passion, and—unlike love—it requires reciprocity. Like Sablé, Staël finds that "Love is better able to manage

---

[17] Louise Dupin, "Idées sur l'amitié," in *Portefeuille*, 65–97. The manuscript is in Rousseau's hand, with Dupin's corrections, placing its composition during the time that Rousseau was employed as her secretary, 1745–1751.

[18] Elisabeth Guibert, *Pensées détachées de Madame Guibert* (Bruxelles: Couturier fils, 1771), 41–42, 13.

[19] Germaine de Staël, *De l'influence des passions sur le bonheur des individus et des nations*, in *Oeuvres completes*, ed. Florence Lotterie et al. (Paris: Honoré Champion, 2008) 1:243.

without reciprocity than friendship" (Staël, *De l'influence*, 248). Which, in the end, renders it almost unattainable.

It is the philosopher and translator Sophie de Grouchy, marquise de Condorcet (1764–1822), who reframes the question. In her *Lettres sur la sympathie* (1798), not a moralist work per se, but sharing certain key issues with moralist writing, she reformulates both love and friendship as "individual sympathy" and offers "a theory of the encounter with the other": in the immediacy of visual apprehension, we decode the signs that suggest whether or not another person shares our outlook and what the potential for pleasure or pain might be in situations involving the other.[20] De Grouchy's emphasis on sudden *enthousiasme* originating in the senses infuses the traditional moralist discourse on friendship with Enlightenment sensibility. In the present context, one of the most striking features of De Grouchy's account is her rehabilitation of esteem as an important foundation of friendship. As we have seen, esteem came in last for Scudéry, and gets short shrift elsewhere. For De Grouchy, however, esteem is not only "the firmest basis for individual sympathies" but also is extremely pleasurable to experience: "it is the unique element in which our affections can develop and our heart give itself free rein and thus develops completely."[21]

In effect, De Grouchy has returned virtue, the basis for esteem, to the foundations of friendship. I do not mean to suggest that virtue has been entirely absent: most moralists consider friendship to be a virtue, or see a common love of virtue as a significant element of friendship. Even since Montaigne, however, the emphasis has shifted toward the affective—the ineffability of his "Parce que c'estoit luy, parce que c'estoit moy," quoted and echoed throughout the period. Mutual recognition of moral worth has nothing like the centrality that we find in Aristotle. By reimagining esteem for the other's excellence as a form of pleasure, De Grouchy makes explicit a hitherto unstated current in the discourse of friendship: pleasure.

3.2. Rituals of Friendship: Reciprocity, Exchange, Secrets

As we have already seen in considering the foundations of friendships, the relationship between generous, open reciprocity between friends and the

---

[20] Vincent-Buffault, *L'Exercice de l'amitié*, 116.
[21] Sophie de Grouchy, Lettre 4, *Lettres sur la sympathie*, ed. Marc André Bernier and Deidre Dawson (Oxford: Voltaire Foundation, 2010), 51.

purposive exchange of favors remains vexed. Aristotle had attempted to clarify the distinction by insisting on the intention of the donor, who gives without expectation of return.[22] Cicero would strive to resolve the problem by insisting on the removal of affective relations from the economic sphere: "we are not led to friendship by the hope of material gain."[23] Seneca's *De Beneficiis* provides detailed instructions for the proper way to give and respond to gifts and favors, and the many nuances and permutations of the relationship between giver and receiver. Montaigne, on the other hand, condemns as inimical to friendship any references to favors, obligations, gratitude, or thanks, as "words of division and difference" (Montaigne, 1:206).

Seneca's approach, however, resonated with seventeenth and eighteenth-century moralists, who were deeply attuned to the complexities of both tangible and intangible favors. At the same time, the period's tectonic shifts in social relations, subterranean but inexorable, lead to a special scrutiny and reconsideration of all interactions. The legacy of both Stoicism and Epicureanism for moralist discourse came into increasing tension with the specific circumstances and social configurations that had led to the interest in the classical figures.[24] In a further sign of tension, although the ability to give and receive favors correctly and to show gratitude in the appropriate degree and form demonstrates one's innate worth and inner nobility, in the hands of Rousseau and other writers, "gratitude could be a means of challenging as well as confirming status hierarchies."[25]

Women were considered to have a special role in this regard. Because elite women's responsibilities typically involved cultivating and maintaining not only their own personal friendships and alliances, but also those of their broader networks, even those who were not hostesses of salons often oversaw their families' interests in multiple spheres. As her correspondence shows, Émilie Du Châtelet managed an exceptionally complex "portfolio" that included her family's legal interests and social obligations, her children's and

---

[22] Aristotle's distinction may have been more ideal than real; even in classical Greece "the norm of reciprocity is not entirely self-evident and unambiguous." Tazuko Angela van Berkel, *The Economics of Friendship: Conceptions of Reciprocity in Classical Greece* (Leiden and Boston: Brill, 2020), 4. In Van Berkel's analysis, *philia*-relationships undergo inflection from the tremendous changes in the economic structures undergirding Athenian society in the fifth and fourth centuries BCE, leading to an unavoidable monetization in the discourse of affiliation and spillover into the world of moral obligations and affect.

[23] Cicero, "On Friendship," in *On Old Age* and *On Friendship*, trans. Frank O. Copley (Ann Arbor: University of Michigan Press, 1971), 60.

[24] Darmon, "Moralistes en movement," 60–61.

[25] Patrick Coleman, *Anger, Gratitude, and the Enlightenment Writer* (Oxford: Oxford University Press, 2011), 22.

husband's advancement, her social and intellectual networks, and Voltaire's complicated public role. Thus, while the dynamics of social interactions are of keen interest to all moralists throughout the period, it is hardly surprising that women seem especially interested not only in the affective phenomenon but also in the external practices and mechanics of friendship.

In this section, I consider the practice of friendship most often discussed in moralist writing: various forms of reciprocity and exchange, whether of services and favors, compliments, advice, or secrets and confidences. Just as the shift in the foundations of friendship from the rational to the affective brought with it the risk of destabilizing passion, so too does the centrality of exchange carry the potential for the relationship to devolve into something purposive and utilitarian.

In "Idées sur l'amitié," Louise Dupin refers to the ideal friendship as fusion, "le commerce des coeurs," crediting the marquise de Lambert with the expression (Dupin, *Portefeuille*, 80). She argues that *amour ou amitié* should be the model for all society, in which "all men have but one soul" (Dupin, *Portefeuille*, 70). Unlike Scudéry and Lambert, for whom the exchange of favors risks degrading friendship, in her essay "Sur les sentiments de l'âme," Dupin sees *mutuels services* simply as an "advantage of friendship" that does not reduce friendship to vulgar self-interest (Dupin, *Portefeuille*, 112). Others, however, find it more difficult to separate the two. Marie de Verzure denounces the entire structure of "friendly" exchange: "Overattentive and eager attentions, offers of services, yielding to others, seductive praise, affectionate words, preferences, tender or flattering expressions" are all too often simply "means of seduction," propelled by self-interest, *intérêt* (Verzure, 1:55). She distinguishes these manipulations from true friendship, *l'amitié véritable*. While the latter is "neither as precise nor as methodical" (Verzure, 1:57), it appears to rely on a high degree of almost psychic awareness of the needs and wishes of the other:

> If he offers his services, it is because he is certain that you are not in a position to demand anything from him, or that you do not like either to ask or to owe anything.
>
> His attentions for you will often be irrelevant, offered more to make you notice them than in order to be agreeable for you. (Verzure, 1:57–58)

The gifts and services of true friendship here have an oddly gratuitous quality ("hors de propos"), defined by what is not said and what is not needed—filling needs without neediness, as it were. All these approaches have in common an effort to surpass the banality of what was presumably everyone's lived experience of actual social relations with their status-laden nuances and potential for error or insult.

Marie-Louise de Fourqueux (1728–1798) offers a detailed account of the practical aspects of friendship in her posthumously published *Confessions de Madame ****. A successful society hostess and patroness of the arts in the decades preceding the Revolution, she frequented philosophical gatherings at the Baron d'Holbach's; she and her husband, a high-ranking financier, were close to Turgot and other economists. Such was her reputation for a brilliant social life that some who had known her had difficulty accepting she had had the time or inclination to write the substantial *Confessions*.[26] The chapter "De la manière de se conduire avec ses amis" ("On How to Conduct Oneself with One's Friends") is the final chapter, probably written in the mid-1770s, after the *Confessions* had shifted from a personal confessional project to a broader reflection on virtue, happiness, and social relations. For Fourqueux, friendship is undoubtedly an emotional refuge, but a refuge with clearly defined protocols and rules of engagement.

Observing that families can be "bizarre and insensitive," Fourqueux sees friends as the family that we choose.[27] Choice, however, remains less significant in the foundations of friendship than something resembling *inclination*, an "appeal that is as powerful as undefinable" (Fourqueux, 2:223). Sensibility is fundamental to the good life: "The sensitive person alone knows existence" (Fourqueux, 2:235). But although shared feelings and the ability to express them openly are key to friendship, so are friendship's duties and obligations. Chief among these are giving advice, managing conflict, and offering criticism as needed.

Fourqueux takes an individual's character as a given. Because a person's basic nature is a constant, one must not offer advice that one's friend is

---

[26] For an account of Fourqueux's life and work, see Laurence Croq, "Mme de Fourqueux (1728–1798), femme du monde et écrivain," in Frédéric Barbier, ed., *Histoire et civilization du livre: À travers l'histoire du livre et des Lumières* (Geneva: Droz, 2011), 157–77. Fourqueux also wrote two novels, *Julie de Saint-Olmont* (1805) and *Amélie de Tréville* (1806), which were published by her literary executor. The executor died before publishing the *Confessions*, which were brought to print by J.-B.-A. Suard a decade later. Croq, 175–76.

[27] In her introductory autobiographical chapter, Fourqueux describes an idyllic early childhood that comes to a swift end when she is married at age twelve and finds herself bullied and miserable in the household of her father-in-law. Her unsparing assessment of her character flaws and determination to "work on my character" may owe something to the thirteen years of his tyranny and emotional abuse.

incapable of following, or that one would be incapable of following oneself. While we should seek to bring out the best in our friends, we cannot change them: "however much influence one may have over another, it is impossible to create a single quality; one should not attempt to do more than develop and bring out what nature placed there" (Fourqueux, 2:232). The art of giving advice thus relies on a profound study of human nature in general and a detailed understanding of individuals in their particularity.

While attraction and mutual sympathy may launch a friendship, maintaining the connection requires careful attention. "How does one manage to be loved? Is it not from the pleasure and happiness that one provides?" (Fourqueux, 2:252). Pleasure, or more accurately, pleasing (*plaire*) and being pleasant and accommodating (*aimable*) are at the heart of the social qualities recommended by Fourqueux. The chapter on friendship is third in a series on "ways of pleasing," which she examines in general ("par rapport à la morale") and in the familial context, before turning to relationships with friends. (I will have more to say on the period's focus on the importance of "pleasing" in Chapter 7.) Although a modern reader might find the emphasis on being pleasing to others somewhat less than satisfying, for Fourqueux it is part of a carefully researched system of self-presentation and relationship-building. As she reminds us, she was taught nothing; her comments are based on instinct, personal observation, and reflection.

> Married at age twelve, living under the reign of a difficult father-in-law, I spent my youth being scolded and taught nothing. All I brought into society was a friendly disposition for others and a wish to be loved. I have relied entirely on my instincts for what I should do or avoid. (Fourqueux, 2:130)

The details on how to give compliments, give and receive favors, receive confidences, and complain (gently) as necessary thus represent a form of self-creation and self-assertion. They also remind us of the power of the model of the self-taught woman, consciously directing her movements and discovering her path, not only in novels such as Graffigny's *Lettres d'une Péruvienne* or Laclos's *Liaisons dangereuses* ("Je suis mon ouvrage") but, repeatedly, among women moralists who decry their lack of early education and weave their search for knowledge into the fabric of their understanding of the world.

The end of the *ancien régime* did not see the end of the complex protocols of "friendship." Pauline Guizot makes the point in a pair of essays, "Des amis dans le malheur" ("Friends in Misfortune") and "Des amis dans le bonheur" ("Friends in Good Fortune") (Guizot, *Essais et conseils*, 1:111–17; 1:117–24). Like many of the essays that she published in Suard's periodical *Le Publiciste* in the 1790s, both pieces have a satirical dimension—Guizot's sharp wit makes her a worthy inheritor of La Rochefoucauld (whom she quotes). The first piece, a first-person narrative by a male persona, recounts how his personal disasters have attracted a seemingly endless parade of "friends," who derive a sense of superiority and self-satisfaction by offering useless advice: "I was overcome by proofs of friendship," bemoans the narrator (Guizot, *Essais et conseils*, 1:115). The second essay is written in the form of a letter "from an old woman to a young man." She writes to congratulate him on his recent wealth and good fortune, but primarily to warn him that none of the people who stood by him in misfortune are likely to remain his friends. Any favors that he does for them will engender obligations and hence inevitable resentment; an older woman, "Madame de Ch**," who once took pleasure in introducing him in society when he was a complete unknown, now feels lost in the crowd of his new admirers. Any attention or deference that he shows her will seem like "gratitude," in other words, something owed her rather than a spontaneous demonstration of affection: "you are already at the stage of empty formalities (*être aux procédés*) once you get to gratitude" (Guizot, *Essais et conseils*, 1:122). Neither essay offers an escape from the burden of debt and obligation.

Trust and the sharing of secrets are a special case of exchange with profound significance in the long literature on friendship.[28] For Seneca, "if you think that a person is a friend when you do not trust him as much as you trust yourself... you do not know the meaning of friendship."[29] Scudéry saw trust and confidences as essential to "heroic friendship" between men and women. La Rochefoucauld noted the flattery implicit in the sharing of a secret with a friend: "Confiding a secret always pleases the recipient; it's a tribute to his

---

[28] On confidentiality and the friendship tradition, see Peter Shoemaker, "From My Lips to Yours: Friendship, Confidentiality, and Gender in Early Modern France," in Seifert and Wilkin, *Men and Women Making Friends*, 247–65. For Shoemaker, the frequent description of confidences as *dépôt*, a term with fiduciary implications, suggest that the discourse of confidentiality "is not so much on the idea of secrecy, per se, as on entrusting others with one's business" (264).

[29] Seneca, Letter 3, *Letters on Ethics*, trans. Margaret Graver and A.A. Long (Chicago: Chicago University Press, 2015), 27–28.

merit" (La Rochefoucauld, *Réflexions diverses*, 202). Telling one's secret is thus a high compliment paid to the other. A century later, Verzure will similarly observe that sharing a confidence shows our recognition of our friend's discretion and probity. She notes, however, that although there can be good reasons for imparting a secret, such as when we seek the advice of someone wiser than ourselves, most people are simply indiscreet, making the practice unwise (Verzure, 2:119–23).

Attentive to the rules that govern the conduct of friendship and the importance of pleasing others, Dupin observes that, just as there are good and bad ways to give advice, there are right ways and wrong ways to give and receive confidences: when we receive the confidence of a friend, we should avoid either a passionate (and unhelpful) identification with the friend's situation or a coldly dispassionate response. A confidence is an ethical engagement; if we were truly mindful of the implied commitment, we would be less curious about others' secrets (Dupin, *Portefeuille*, 91–92).

For Fourqueux too, shared confidences and "the liberty to express all one's feelings" are central to friendship. Unlike Dupin, Fourqueux believes that total sympathetic identification with a friend's situation is appropriate; one should not take the sharing of confidences as an occasion to attempt to lecture to one's friend: "If there is a time for reason, there is even more for indulgence" (Fourqueux, 2:240). It quickly becomes evident, however, that the rules governing male and female friendships are different. It is permissible for a woman to hear the secrets of a man in love with someone else, but "a decent woman (*une femme honnête*) must never become the confidant of a woman friend involved in an affair" (Fourqueux, 2:242). Indeed, she goes on to explain, none of her women friends, even those that she knows are having love affairs, have ever spoken of their situation to her; clearly something in her manner makes it clear that she would reject such revelations. She makes exceptions only in the case of women who are recovering from having been abandoned by their lovers and whose conduct, aside from this one misstep, has been irreproachable: "love alone could have led them astray" (Fourqueux, 2:244).

The question of exchange is thus complicated by several factors: unstated motivations, the potential for misunderstanding, the importance of avoiding "need" of any sort, and the delicate moral balance between "indulging" a friend and receiving confidences that represent an affront to virtue. The fusion or "commerce des coeurs" remains the sought-after goal, but it is an elusive one.

3.3. Sameness and Difference

Let us look more closely at the issue of sameness and difference, especially sexual difference, in friendship. As we have seen, the rules of exchange can be different for men and women; the "danger" of affectivity reflects an unstated heteronormativity. "Sameness" or total identity of tastes, opinions, and, of course, commitment to virtue, has long formed the primary foundation to friendship, from the classical writers to Montaigne, whose "Parce que c'estoit luy, parce que c'estoit moy," continues to be repeated as one of the principal topoi for evoking the fusion of souls in friendship. Women moralists often make the same point. Guibert adds age to the list of identical qualities: "We feel friendship for someone when one feels the same degree of sensibility, same tastes, same opinions. Such connections can only be found among those who have similar age and status in life" (Guibert, 80). For Dupin, the commonalities that underpin friendship are a model for an ideal society: "People who share the same ideas, the same tastes, the same needs, must necessarily love one another; all humanity should come together as one soul" (Dupin, *Portefeuille*, 70). Verzure too stresses the importance of "equality in age, status, and manner of thinking" "(Verzure, 2:276). In the long history of writing on friendship, gender—male gender—was long considered fundamental to friendship. As Cicero flatly put it, "friendship can only exist between good men" (Cicero, 53). How does the language of sexual difference inflect the discourse on friendship?

Salon culture offered flourishing examples of mixed-gender friendship. Nevertheless, few male moralists gave more than a passing or ambiguous acknowledgement to its possibility. In a notable departure from the classical tradition, Scudéry is explicit in privileging friendship between men and women as "plus douce" than any other relationship, so long as it does not turn into passion (Scudéry 1692, 1:46). For her, this equilibrium, while delicate, is eminently possible. Given the rather more complex representations of female same-sex friendships in her narratives, particularly the "Histoire de Sapho" in *Clélie*,[30] the insistence on deferred, unconsummated heterosexual relations may be a form of shorthand to indicate the subtle erotic charge that animates any "ardent" friendship.

---

[30] See Joan DeJean, *Fictions of Sapho 1546-1937* (Chicago: University of Chicago Press, 1989); Leonard Hinds, "Female Friendship as the Foundation of Love in Madeleine de Scudéry's 'Histoire de Sapho,'" *Journal of Homosexuality* 41.3-4 (2001): 23-35.

In this section, I will first examine in detail two key statements on friendship, Anne-Thérèse de Lambert's *Traité de l'amitié* and Geneviève d'Arconville's *De l'amitié*, followed by a survey of other thinkers. Almost without exception, difference, framed in various ways, is viewed as intrinsic to friendship, whether as obstacle or as enabling condition—or both.

Complex layers of sameness and difference structure one of the most-cited works on friendship of the eighteenth century, the *Traité de l'amitié* of Anne-Thérèse de Marguenat de Courcelles, marquise de Lambert (1647–1733). She appears to have written her *Traité de l'amitié* in the late 1690s or early 1700s, when she was in her fifties, about the time that she took up residence in the Hôtel de Nevers and a few years before she would launch one of the most celebrated literary salons of the age. The treatise—actually a relatively short essay—emerged from her long-standing friendship with Louis de Sacy, who dedicated his *Traité sur l'amitié* (1702) to her and whose dedicatory epistle incidentally made her hitherto invisible intellectual life visible to the reading public.[31] Lambert's work would not be published until after her death, in a collection of short texts on love and friendship by several hands.[32] Like her other "Ciceronian" essay from the same period, the *Traité de la vieillesse*, the *Traité de l'amitié* manifests a certain world-weary tone and awareness of the passage of time: "The further one advances in life, the more one feels the need for friendship."[33] By its form, its references to Seneca and Montaigne, and many of the topics it examines, Lambert's essay places itself firmly in the classical tradition.

Friendship's ideal fusion of souls is here most felt by its absence, however. Echoing Seneca, she initially couches her discussion in the form of a letter. The opening words suggest that, like Seneca's Epistle XVIII or Cicero's *De amicitia*, she is writing in the wake of a friend's death: "Monsieur, you owe me consolation for the loss of our friend" (Lambert, 155). We quickly realize, however, that Lambert is not writing of a dead friend, but a dead friendship: "I call loss, any lessening of friendship, because normally any weakened sentiment falls away." Is it my fault? she wonders, asking her interlocutor for advice. Lambert's first sentences prefigure two features of her treatise: a recurring emphasis on the ending of friendship and an increasingly

---

[31] Louis de Sacy, *Traité de l'amitié* (The Hague: Chez Louïs et Henry van Dole, 1703); Marchal, *Madame de Lambert et son milieu*, 160–61.

[32] Thémiseul de Saint-Hyacinthe, ed., *Recueil de divers écrits, sur l'amour et l'amitié* (Paris: Veuve Pissot, 1736). On the publication history, see Marchal, *Madame de Lambert et son milieu*, 177–78.

[33] Lambert, "Traité de l'amitié," *Oeuvres*, ed. Robert Granderoute (Paris: Honoré Champion, 1990), 155.

clear privileging of male–female friendship over exclusively female friendship. Lambert's male addressee disappears entirely from the text after the first paragraph, but the lost *amie* continues to haunt the text as a reminder of failure. With the disappearance of the interlocutor, the requested "consolation" remains unfulfilled, unless we take the treatise, which is structured as a series of questions and answers, as Lambert's self-consolation. Friendship itself has a consolatory or compensatory aspect for Lambert, who observes that it makes up, not for the loss of love, but for the deliberate refusal to let oneself be "carried away" by love. "Friendship is enriched by love's losses" (Lambert, 156).

Friendship, then, fills an empty space. Lambert is at pains, like her predecessors, to exclude "need" (*les besoins*) as a basis for true friendship. At the same time, she has asserted friendship's primacy in meeting our emotional needs, characterized as "an emptiness that only friendship can fill" (Lambert, 156). There would thus seem to be two types of need: material or utilitarian needs, which are illusory and distracting, and "the needs of the heart," which are intimately connected to our well-being. In its opening depiction of the "advantages of friendship," Lambert describes the relationship in terms of sharing and exchange, such as the "charm of baring one's soul to one's friend, of reading in his heart, of seeing him as he is, of showing one's own weaknesses" (Lambert, 157). Friendship is "a society, an exchange (*un commerce*), reciprocal commitments where no one keeps count" (Lambert, 158). Like reciprocity without accountability or exchange ("où l'on ne compte rien"), friendship meets needs which both are and are not real needs, similar to Verzure's superfluous "needs without neediness."

Lambert's account of friendship is not unusual for its depiction of intimate sharing, as she herself makes clear from her citation of Montaigne, rendered vividly by a misquotation in the present tense—"'c'est que c'est lui; c'est que c'est moi'" (Lambert, 157).[34] Her reflections on the dynamic of need and self-sufficiency reflect her manifest affiliation with the Stoic tradition. Unlike the predecessors that she cites, however, her text opens with the evocation of a failed friendship; even her (very classical) insistence on the importance of a solid moral foundation for a durable attachment brings her back to the topic of friendship's end: "There is no breakup that doesn't reflect badly on us; it's always the fault of one or the other; one cannot avoid the shame of having made a mistake and having to go back on one's word" (Lambert, 159). Why

---

[34] Dupin, who quotes Lambert, also echoes her misquotation (Dupin, *Portefeuille*, 116).

should there be such shame in a broken friendship? Because, she tells us, our choice of friends reveals our character, "our portrait, the admission of who we are." Although in Aristotle, the notion of the "other self" betokens the congruence of a virtuous person's internal integrity and ability to relate to others, here the "other" self also suggests an internal estrangement and the revelation of a lack or defect within oneself, one's internal lack of consistency. As Giorgio Agamben terms it, "an otherness immanent in self-ness, a becoming other of the self."[35] For good or for ill, the friend reveals who and what we are to the public.

Time is another agent of difference. Unlike Scudéry, Sablé, or their classical predecessors, for whom friendship is impervious to the passage of time, Lambert laments the temporality of affections. For Lambert, time is a factor in friendship in two ways. First, because we are capable of true friendship only after we have reached a certain age and are able to free ourselves from too great a reliance on pleasure and passion (Lambert, 162), and second, because friendship has its own life cycle. "There are three stages in friendship: the beginning, the duration, and the end" (Lambert, 163). Both factors remind us of change in ourselves and in others.

As Lambert recounts the ways in which common character flaws can strain a relationship, her discussion of friendship's duties shifts to a discussion of what we owe after a friendship has ended, whether on account of irreconcilable differences or because a friend has died (Lambert, 167–68). The recurring motif of *rupture* reminds us of the reference in the opening paragraph of the "the loss of our friend" and the discussion takes on an increasingly personal tone as Lambert blames herself for her tendency to "give too much of herself" ("je me livre trop," Lambert, 168) and for being too trusting.

It is at this point, possibly at the thought of the failed friendship with another woman, that she takes up the question of whether there can be friendship between the sexes. Since Lambert earlier commented that friendship is the reward of "virtuous love" and especially in the light of the fact that the treatise is addressed to a male friend, her affirmative answer does not come as a surprise. Such a relationship is "rare" and "difficult," but as long as it is founded on virtue, the friendship between a woman and a man is "the most delicious" of all friendships and "a degree of vivacity that cannot be found

---

[35] Giorgio Agamben, "Friendship," *Contretemps* 5 (2004): 6. See also Eric Méchoulan: "la célébration de l'ami comme *alter ego*, qui exige de trouver, dans l'autre, le murmure insistante de la ressemblance, et de voir apparaître, dans le moi, le miroir troublante de l'autre." "Le Métier d'ami," *XVIIe siècle* 205.4 (1999): 634.

between persons of the same sex" (Lambert, 169). She holds little hope for friendships among women: "Women have the misfortune of not being able to count on one another for friendship.... They come together from necessity, never from affection (*goût*)." The treatise ends with praise for women's capacity for sentiment and proclaims that "nature" is responsible for friendship between the sexes, "those secret ties, sympathies, an irresistible sweet penchant "(Lambert, 170)—the final admonition that one should be *en garde* lest friendship become passion seems almost an afterthought.

Lambert would make much the same point in one of her few works that was published during her lifetime, her *Réflexions nouvelles sur les femmes* (1727). Here too she privileges a deeply felt virtuous attachment between a woman and a man, while seeing scant possibility for friendship among women: "Needs bring them together, not feelings" (Lambert, 231). Clearly the "needs" in question are of the material, purposive sort that, like the "necessity" decried in the *Traité de l'amitié*, are antithetical to real intimacy. The broader context of the *Réflexions nouvelles* suggests that this failure is not due to an innate deficiency on the part of women, whose capacity for sentiment she praises elsewhere, but to a poor education that prevents self-understanding, and to social pressures that require them to compete for attention and stay on guard against one other. Women are not alone in their failure to rise to the demands of a profound, durable friendship: "Most men are only capable of a vulgar form of love" (Lambert, 232). The ideal relationship that transcends "the senses" and takes the form of "the union of hearts" (Lambert, 231) is viewed as realizable, but rare.

Having begun the *Traité de l'amitié* with a request that her male interlocutor console her for the loss of her female friend, Lambert thus ends by denying the possibility of durable friendship between women and asserting the natural foundation for "invisible ties" (Lambert, 169) between the sexes. Although her addressee disappeared after the opening lines, a second person pronoun crops up unexpectedly in the final paragraph:

> Women who set their duty against love and who offer you the charms and sentiments of friendship, if you find in them a merit equal to that of men, what better could one do than attach oneself to them? (Lambert, 169)

While the elision of *vous* by *on* suggests that it does not refer to as specific an interlocutor as the "Monsieur" of the beginning, *vous* is clearly gendered as male, giving the question ("peut-on mieux faire ... ?") the effect of an invitation and reminding us of the request for "consolation" with which the essay began. Even if the ending of a relationship suggests that it was not a "true" friendship to begin with, she is left with the realization that, try as one may to base one's relationships on solid foundations, one cannot know in the first stages how things will ultimately transpire. Lambert tells us that she simply does not know how to "distrust my friends" (Lambert, 168); mistrust would be an obstacle to "l'union des coeurs." Friendship implies an element of risk, and it is possible that one may be duped.

Sexual difference thus plays a major role in Lambert's concept of friendship. It is the most tangible form of difference that she discusses, but as we have seen, it is not the only one. Multiple factors disturb the ideal meeting of heart and mind: time, change, loss. The destabilizing peril of sexual attraction is no less a danger to friendship than the rupture of affective bonds. And yet, it is also clear that difference is an enabling condition of friendship. This is clearest in mixed-gender friendship, where the "vivacity" of the erotic undercurrent enhances feeling and the capacity for sharing. More subtly, the various changes and disappointments evoked throughout the essay not only point to the risks and vicissitudes of friendship, but also remind us of its ability to provide consolation and an impetus to renew or create relationships, as Lambert's closing invitation to her interlocutor suggests.

If difference plays an ambivalent role in Lambert's *Traité de l'amitié*, it is writ large throughout the treatise *De l'amitié* by Marie Geneviève Charlotte Thiroux d'Arconville (1720–1805). Few relationships rise to her high standards for friendship, instead remaining enmeshed in snares of difference. A polymath and prolific writer, d'Arconville's earliest publications were literary and scientific translations; moralist writing marks her first entry into original publication, first with her well-received[36] *Pensées et réflexions morales* (1760), followed quickly by *De l'amitié* (1761) and a companion work, *Des Passions* (1764). She would go on to produce original scientific research, novels, and works of history, always anonymously.

D'Arconville offers a grim view of a society guided by ambition, pride, and frivolity: "The habit of mutual deception is so common in the world that it

---

[36] While less than enthusiastic about works of "pensées détachées" in general, an early reviewer finds that the *Pensées et réflexions morales* stands apart from the usual run, praising the author's style, quoting numerous passages, and encouraging the (presumptively male) author to develop some of his more original insights. *Journal encyclopédique* (Mai 1760), 77–84. D'Arconville's moralist treatises were evidently considered strong enough to be attributed to Diderot in a pirated edition (Frankfurt, 1770). Dismay at the misattribution may have been the impetus for her to arrange for a collected edition of her works to date, her *Mélanges* (1775).

affects that which is most sacred; friendship has no retreat so obscure as to hide it from the general corruption."[37] Her treatise, the longest and most fully elaborated philosophical statement on friendship by an eighteenth-century woman, goes further than any of her predecessors in raising the bar for friendship, classifying not only need, habit, *amour-propre*, vanity, and self-interest, but also *reconnaissance* as extraneous motivations that too often "pass" for friendship.[38]

D'Arconville's concept of friendship aims at complete disembodiment. She tells us in her introduction that it is a suited only to "souls purified from their seditious flame" (D'Arconville, 2:6) and goes on to define it as "a sentiment that affects only the soul" (D'Arconville, 2:8). The emphasis on the evacuation of the senses paradoxically implies their lingering presence, complicating different-sex relationships. Over the course of her treatise, she examines the potential for friendship at different life stages, with chapters on friendship between children and their parents, between brothers and sisters, between spouses, and among people in different walks of life: elites, bourgeois, writers and intellectuals, even fools (*sots*). Other scenarios reflect different affective foundations: *reconnaissance, estime, goût*. (*Goût* should be understood as roughly synonymous with *inclination*.) The chapters offer varied formats: some are analytic, while others offer literary portraits or "characters" in the manner of La Bruyère. As Marc-André Bernier points out, however, like the variety of relationships and frameworks in *De l'amitié*, her *caractères* reflect her scientist's fascination with human variety, rather than classificatory typology.[39]

In Chapter 8, "De l'amitié des Femmes pour les Hommes, & celle des Hommes pour les Femmes," ("On the friendship of women for men, and of men for women") she holds out little encouragement that such a relationship might actually be possible.

> Friendship, which requires strength of soul, upright thinking, consistency in one's principles, truth in one's character, constancy in one's conduct, and discernment in one's choices, little suits a sex that is weak by nature,

---

[37] Geneviève d'Arconville, *De l'amitié*, in *Mélanges*, 2:178–79.

[38] Lisa Shapiro is right to point out the Stoic foundations of d'Arconville's view of friendship as "character friendship" based on the friends' mutual recognition of virtue, rather than on pleasure or utility. She understates, however, the complications wrought by sex. Shapiro, "*L'Amour, l'ambition* and *l'amitié*," 188–91.

[39] Marc-André Bernier, "Mme d'Arconville et la question des limites de l'esprit humain," in Vanoflen, *Femmes et philosophie des Lumières*, 43–54.

frivolous by education, thoughtless from pretentiousness, flirtatious from vanity, and inconstant from idleness. (D'Arconville, 2:82)

Like Lambert, d'Arconville finds that women's weakness of character is compounded by their poor education and by society's misplaced values; as far as friendship is concerned, she clearly feels that "the sex part gets in the way." Men and women may claim to feel friendship, but they are either deliberately duplicitous or simply deluding themselves: "the mutual attraction that nature placed between the sexes has too much power over us to let us easily disentangle the physical from the mental (*le physique du moral*)" (D'Arconville, 2:83). Only after youth has fled and age has "deadened the fire of passion" will friendship between men and women be possible, because "sexual difference has become null for them" (D'Arconville, 2:86).

Despite the need to "nullify" sexual difference for friendship to flourish, d'Arconville does not see same-sex relations, presumably free from the temptations of the flesh, as offering better soil for friendship to take root. To the contrary, relations among men, she tells us, are marred by ambition, just as relations among women are by jealousy. Thus, although sexual difference sparks a sensuality that derails true friendship, sexual "sameness" is fraught with competition, a need to distinguish oneself, and a mistrust of the other. Her rare depictions of sincere friendship are thus between men and women who are no longer susceptible to passionate feelings, either because of age or because, as physical desire gradually cools, as it inevitably must, "they have had the time to know one another and to learn to love one another before ceasing to desire each other" (D'Arconville, 2:91). The friendship that comes after love is the rarest and most precious of all in d'Arconville's lexicon, based as it is not simply on virtue, but on virtue regained. "Where better to find consolation than in the arms of the lover whom virtue has rendered our friend, and who is no longer a danger?" (D'Arconville, 2:92). As in the case of friendship that comes with age, sexual difference and sexual desire are both present and absent; difference is the unconditional foundation, but also an all-but-insuperable obstacle to true attachment.

As noted earlier, each of the twenty-five chapters looks at friendship in a different life stage or a different interpersonal situation. Each of these relationships, from the friendship between parents and children to the *amitié d'estime*, is defective in some way, undermined by ulterior motives, unruly desires, or *amour-propre*. In the final pages, having recapitulated all the cases of "amitiés simulées," d'Arconville echoes Aristotle: "O mes amis, il n'y a point d'amis!" (D'Arconville, 2:184). Nevertheless, despite her respect "the great Philosopher," she disagrees with him and proclaims that, however rare it may be, true friendship does exist. After the detailed analyses of the preceding twenty-four chapters, however, the final pages offer a very abstract evocation of "celestial Friendship." Assimilated with virtue, we are told that friendship consists of complete reciprocity and that it stems from "an invincible attraction" that cannot be analyzed or articulated (D'Arconville, 2:177). The closest we come to an example is a citation of Montaigne—the famous "parce que c'étoit lui, parce que c'étoit moi" (D'Arconville 2:187)—but the citation expresses the ineffable, inexplicable nature of friendship rather than offering a concrete example. Despite the increasing abstraction, the closing lines seem to reverse the elision of lived experience and indeed of gender, by sending us back to the idea that friendship is available only those whose passion has burned itself out, to all appearances a pair of former lovers: "Your heart, worn out by pleasures that you were only able to enjoy through the error of your senses, which are now lost to you, will take on a new life; the path of happiness is still available to you (D'Arconville, 2:190).

D'Arconville presents her (anonymous) self as capable of friendship. Both *De l'amitié* and her next moralist treatise, *Des passions*, are dedicated to "mon ami" ("You owe my heart not to chance, but to my choice," D'Arconville, 2:195), and the dedications of other works express great affection for her sister and niece.[40] Indeed, in the unpublished essays she left at the end of her life, she took great pleasure in recalling past friendships:

> I was born with too sensitive a heart and too lively an imagination not to further augment my sensibility. I admit that it brought me much pleasure, because I had both men and women friends who offered me great proofs of their attachment and constancy. I thoroughly enjoyed it all, and never had any reason to complain of them. (D'Arconville, "Mes souvenirs," PRA 9:330–31)

In her published work, however, her view of human relationships remains bleak. She is often harsh in her judgments of women. Her reflections on women in her early *Pensées et réflexions morales* (1760) manifest impatience

---

[40] The likely dedicatee of *De l'amitié* and *Des passions* was d'Arconville's brother-in-law, François Thiroux d'Espersenne, whom she refers to "le bien aimé de mon coeur" and with whom she planned to live out her days; his sudden death in 1767 left her profoundly depressed and unable to write for a long time. D'Arconville, "Histoire de ma littérature," PRA 5:169–226.

with the vanity of worldly women, their trivial preoccupations, their lack of self-awareness. Reading her indictment—which, like Lambert's, is an indictment of the society that does not simply encourage, but demands such behavior from women—one reflects that the erudite translator and scientific writer might well have never encountered another woman whose interests were anything like her own. Her assessment of the possibility of friendship among women is dire: "it is so rare than it may be considered as nonexistent" (D'Arconville, 1:336). For d'Arconville, friendship remains a tantalizing possibility, preferably between a man and a woman, but only if both ignore any form of erotic attachment.

We find the same preference for mixed-gender friendships in other women moralists. Dupin sees no obstacle to mixed-gender friendships, especially at ages when gender is irrelevant—childhood or old age—and assuming that "a good education and proper socialization" prevent the formation of inappropriate impulses (Dupin, *Portefeuille*, 116). Fourqueux prefers her friendships with male friends, since, according to her, women only want to talk about themselves: "I spent ten years listening to one of my friends recount her vapors, and during the whole time I spoke of myself on a handful of occasions" (Fourqueux, 2:245–46). Staël will make a similar complaint, noting that for women, confidences are often the heart of a friendship, but the situation is problematic, since in order to speak of one's own heartache, one must listen to another; conversation becomes "an alternating sacrifice made by the listener in hopes of being able to have a turn to speak" (Staël, *De l'influence*, 246). Henriette de Marans, on the other hand, finds it difficult to be friends with men who prefer flirtation over engaging in deeper conversation: "I would like to be a man for them" (Marans, *Pensées érrantes*, 93).

Pauline Guizot paints a portrait of a long-term friendship in "Des vieilles amitiés" (Old Friendships), an essay purporting to be a letter "from an old woman to an old (male) friend" (Guizot, *Essais et conseils*, 1:186–95). Like many of her other moralist essays, this piece demonstrates her ability to adopt other personae, since Guizot herself never lived to the age imagined for her narrator. Here, her adopted perspective enables her to analyze the changing dynamics of friendship over time. The letter is ostensibly written to patch up a quarrel: the narrator's friend of forty years has reproached her for having put her family (which he frames as *habitude*) ahead of their long-standing relationship. By way of response, the narrator claims that "reconciliation" is for trivial quarrels and that, having reached old age with a long shared history, they are beyond such things. She looks back on a series of unsuccessful friendships with men in her youth, all characterized by an equivocal and uneasy balance of friendship and flirtation.

That said, her relationship with her old friend is not precisely platonic. She has been aware from the beginning of his unspoken feelings: *goût, penchant*. In a deeply moving passage, she describes how they have aged together:

> And thus, time has passed on, we have grown old together, always the same. The changes in you did not let you see the changes in me.... As you never thought of me in a particular way [*sous un point de vue déterminé*], you never had to think of me otherwise; your ideas kept pace with your situation, but without changing their nature: the same pleasure and *amour-propre* that you had in pleasing me, and that has never faded, is still there.... You come over to my house with a certain sweet little agitation.... My old friend, you will laugh if I say that with me you are still almost gallant; with you, I might be tempted to believe myself a coquette. (Guizot, *Essais et conseils*, 1:193–95)

What made this relationship different from the others where sexual attraction similarly hovered in the background? Time is a factor. For young people time is an "open door"; they experience events as infused with either hope or fear. For the old friends, "the future is set" and imagination has lost its power (Guizot, *Essais et conseils*, 1:187). In addition to the fact that their relationship deepened later in life, it appears that the very aimlessness of her friend's desire, the lack of "un point de vue déterminé" distinguished his feelings from those of men who expected a particular scenario or resolution to the story. This friendship endures because it occupies a space outside of expectations. If the erotic charge were entirely lacking, however, "you might look at me with less interest; I might welcome you with less grace" (Guizot, *Essais et conseils*, 1:194). On the other hand, had they given into the erotic subcurrent and experienced "a livelier sentiment," then they would have found themselves in an unequal dynamic in which the woman is always the loser after having "given all": "On your side would have been the power of the man who may or may not give something, while on mine the discontent of the woman who can only ask" (Guizot, *Essais et conseils*, 1:194–95). Instead, she reminds him, they are both able to experience equal pleasure in the relationship. "So let us enjoy our situation, my friend; in truth, it is rather spicy for our age" (Guizot, *Essais et conseils*, 1:195).

Guizot thus confirms the widespread preference among women moralists for mixed-gender friendship animated by an unspoken flirtation or erotic undercurrent. It may be argued that such friendships were the "best" women could hope for, given heteronormative assumptions, the sexual morality that defined women's virtue in terms of chastity, and the dim view that many women moralists took of marriage (as we shall see in Chapter 5). While these elements undoubtedly factor in, however, it would be reductive to claim that they are the whole story. It would also be incorrect to attribute the preference to internalized misogyny, given the many attestations of the importance of female friendships during the period. Rather, and more profoundly, the moralist insistence on mixed-gender friendship reflects a moral psychology inherited from the seventeenth-century *précieuses*, that the "danger" of an overwhelming passion or "inclination" far exceeds sexual morality. As Scudéry's work and the exemplary story of La Fayette's *Princesse de Clèves* demonstrate, yielding to inclination represents the loss of one's will and personal integrity—one's true virtue. And, as I shall argue in the following section, this preference has a deeper political and ideological dimension as well.

It is only the writer Constance de Salm (1767–1845), an early feminist and champion of women's political rights, who makes an unambiguous statement in favor of friendship between women.

For a woman, there is no friendship preferable to that of another woman.[41]

Indeed, according to Salm, male friends are distinctly less helpful than female friends. An unhappily married woman, for example, will rarely find in a male friend the consolation that she needs. Men, however well-meaning, will unconsciously adopt the position of other men; a woman's plight can only be understood by another woman, "because their position and their destiny are the same, and because nature has given them the same sensations, tastes, and essential needs, which open their souls to the same sentiments and the same pains that they alone can feel" (Salm, *Pensées*, 152–53). By assuming that men have their own *parti pris*, Salm has changed the terms of the equation in which others had imagined the egalitarian nature of friendship.

---

[41] Constance de Salm, *Pensées* (Paris: A. René, 1846), 48–49.

3.4. The Politics of *Reconnaissance*

As we have seen, women moralists examine three distinct but interrelated issues, each of which represents a revision of the classical model of friendship. First, the shift from a model of friendship based on merit to friendship grounded in affect has the effect of moving the basis of friendship from a rational decision to something involuntary and ineffable. Second, although a concern with exchange surfaces in classical writers, it is infinitely more pronounced in the early modern period, to the extent that one might speak of an anxiety of reciprocity. This "anxiety" is exacerbated on the one hand by the protocols of *ancien régime* sociability, and on the other by the role of affect, since transactional relations appear entirely at odds with friendship based on sentiment. Last, they study the ramifications of inserting forms of difference—writ large as gender, but apparent in other forms as well—into a relationship that has traditionally been framed in terms of resemblance. The discourse of friendship is beset by paradox and contradiction: reciprocity and nonaccountability, equality and excess, sameness and difference, secrecy and visibility, memory and forgetting. It is not surprising that the rarity of true friendship is a recurring theme, often framed by the words attributed to Aristotle, "O my friends, there are no friends."

I have been suggesting throughout this chapter that women moralists' thinking about friendship should be seen as part of the much larger pattern of social and political change in the late *ancien régime*. While it is true that although the "ideology of the salons" of Lambert and others evinced certain "egalitarian social implications," the salonnières did not themselves draw out those implications to their conclusion in ways that would be immediately recognizable as emancipatory today.[42] On the other hand, it is not necessary to argue that Scudéry, Lambert, d'Arconville, and the others had an explicit political agenda as they reimagined the classical definition of friendship. Change may come into the world via dramatic events or a striking, visionary document that forces us to see things anew. But change also comes into the world subtly, incrementally, and through shifts and changing uses of language—thereby providing the discursive framework that enables a striking, visionary document to be conceived and written. It is this emergent form of change that is ushered in by the moralist redefinition of friendship.

---

[42] Karen Green, *A History of Women's Political Thought in Europe, 1700–1800* (Cambridge: Cambridge University Press, 2014), 72.

Friendship in the *ancien régime* is simultaneously public and private. It is ineluctably public because of the unavoidable visibility of social life, the need for alliances, patronage, and the exchange of favors. For most commentators, such utilitarian grounds for friendship tend to diminish its worth, yet such relationships cannot be ignored. The shift to affect and interiority as the basis for authentic friendship is concomitant with the role of friendship as "emotional refuge" from public life. At the same time, friendship never entirely ceases to be "public," in the sense that even in its most private moment, it is bound up with a profound reimagining of social relations, both in terms of the broader political framework and in terms of an individual's sense of self that characterizes the long eighteenth century. The mistrust of one's own and others' motives that we saw in the previous chapter exacerbates the search for authentic relations.

It is hardly new to consider friendship as a fundamentally political topic. In the *Nicomachean Ethics*, Aristotle aligned virtuous male friendship with the principles of a just society. Seventeenth-century moralists are less explicit in drawing that parallel, but the notion resurfaces in the eighteenth century. As we have seen, Dupin offers friendship as a model for the ideal society. Fourqueux explicitly portrays friendship in terms of egalitarian social relations: "In friendship, freedom of thought and tolerance should be limitless. . . . Equality is the basis for friendship; despotism makes it flee" (Fourqueux, 2:266). Resituating the grounds for friendship in affect, rather than in virtue and merit, marks a shift away from classical definitions of citizenship and civic participation based on an ideal of masculine virtue.[43] Women rewrite the classical script from which they have been, as Derrida put it, doubly excluded—denied friendship with men on the one hand and with other women on the other—and effectively cut off from participation in the *polis* (*Politiques de l'amitié*, 323). The ramifications of that exclusion spread far and wide beneath the tree of liberty, equality, and fraternity. When women claim access to friendship, the basis of friendship changes from sameness to difference. This shift echoes throughout their writings.

Now, it might reasonably be expected that women's revision of classical friendship would valorize female friendship as a means to female empowerment. As we have seen, however, other than in Salm's account, this is generally not what happens, despite the undeniable cultural power of depictions

---

[43] For an overview of scholarship on classical masculine virtue and the republican ideal of citizenship, see James Fowler and Marine Ganofsky, "Virtue and the Secular Turn, 1680–1794," in Fowler and Ganofsky, *Enlightenment Virtue*, 1–36.

of women's friendship in fiction, exemplified by Richardson's Clarissa and Anna and Rousseau's Julie and Claire. Similarly, women's lived experience of deep friendships with other women is amply attested in correspondences and journals of the period.[44] Why would women moralists take a skeptical view and instead promote different-sex friendship as superior?

There are undoubtedly many answers, both practical and theoretical, to this complicated question. From a practical perspective, mixed-gender socializing with an undercurrent of mild flirtation, *la galanterie*, was a major cultural narrative, viewed and valorized both in France and abroad as a defining feature of French society. The theorizing thus draws on and reinforces an existing cultural narrative. And it is also simply the case that, in the highly visible public worlds of *la Cour et la Ville*, women were socialized to compete with one another, as Lambert and d'Arconville complained. At a deeper level, however, to lay claim to mixed-gender friendship is to counter not only the age-old belief that men and women cannot be friends but also the equally ancient principle that friendship, hence the polity, is based on "sameness." A focus on mixed-gender friendship removes women from the zone of dependency in which traditional narratives (coquetry, romantic love, marriage) leave them. There are thus philosophical reasons to claim the superiority of friendship between men and women.

The discourse of sameness and similarity does not disappear, of course. Numerous moralists underscore the importance of having "même degré de sensibilité, même goûts, mêmes opinions" (Guibert, 80). In the context of mixed-gender friendship, however, *conformité des goûts* does not elide a fundamental difference. Difference is complex, potentially destabilizing. When framed in terms of gender, its positive aspect, the *je ne sais quoi* of sexual attraction, is shadowed by the risks of passion. Difference, as we have seen, appears in other forms, such as time and change, which must be managed and dealt with. Often held up as a barrier to friendship, as in d'Arconville, it is also key to women's participation in friendship and, ultimately, society.

Let us consider the related themes of mourning and temporality. Mourning is a motif in all the key classical texts—Cicero, Seneca, Montaigne. Of the works examined here, Lambert's essay is the most classical in inspiration and the one that echoes this theme the most explicitly. While she does take up the

---

[44] See Janet Todd, *Women's Friendship in Literature* (New York: Columbia University Press, 1980). On young women's correspondences, see Dena Goodman, *Becoming a Woman in the Age of Letters* (Ithaca, NY: Cornell University Press, 2009).

subject of death as she reflects on our obligation to respect the memory of a dead friend, the emotional poignancy of her essay is most keenly felt in the discussion of the death of friendship, rather than the death of a particular friend. Indeed, our memory of past happiness consoles us in the wake of a friend's death, but cannot help us emerge from a wrecked friendship. The notion that friendship itself might "die," that I might be left, as after the death of a loved one, with feelings that go unreciprocated or are even betrayed, points to the connections between mourning and other situations wherein the self is painfully exposed and alone. Social intrigue and trickery in Sablé, forgetting and especially ingratitude in Scudéry provide structurally similar dilemmas in which we are forced to confront the world's indifference to our feelings—to difference, in fact.

Another classical touchpoint, Cicero's condemnation of the precept that "one ought to love in the expectation of someday hating" (Cicero, 72) circulates in a number of moralist texts: Montaigne, La Bruyère, Scudéry, Sacy, Lambert. Seeing a potential enemy in the friend is a dangerous form of otherness. Without exception, moralists roundly reject the notion that one might distrust a friend, which is viewed as holding back from giving oneself unreservedly to a relationship; following Cicero in condemning the idea, which Montaigne declared "abominable," is part of the trope.[45] At the same time, its tendency to surface in these texts from around or before 1700 points to the felt tenuousness of relationships and the fear of a hidden other or of changing circumstances.

Difference thus figures both in the reimagining of friendship and as a challenge to friendship. So too, the related issues of need, self-interest, and exchange. As we have seen, need and debt are the most intractable issues in the discussions of friendship. Throughout the centuries, commentator after commentator declares that true friendship is not founded on "need." Like *amour-propre* in the world of Sablé and La Rochefoucauld, however, self-interest, *intérêt*, haunts these texts like an unwanted guest. Echoing Montaigne, Scudéry, Lambert, and d'Arconville offer a number of stories and classical exempla depicting relationships that contain a transfer of material wealth without debt or obligation, as gift. But how can one obviate debt without either obviating gratitude or falling into endless cycles of obligation? Seen in these terms, the debt/gratitude dilemma poses as deep a problem to

---

[45] See Montaigne, *Essais*, 1:206; La Bruyère, *Des caractères*, 745; Scudéry 1688, 1:145; Sacy, *Traité sur l'amitié*, 49–57; Lambert, "Traité de l'amitié," 168.

the moderns as the question of "need" did for the ancients. The idea that the gift, by imposing the obligation of gratitude, cancels itself out as gift,[46] is not far removed from the concerns that lead Scudéry to envision what I called reciprocity without exchange, in which favors circulate, but are forgotten and not "counted" by the giver (although they must be remembered by the receiver).

In what initially appears to be a more positive evaluation of reciprocity, Sablé emphasizes "reciprocal favors" as an important indicator of friendship. In her Maxim 44, however, she observes that while we shouldn't love our friends for the favors that they bestow, it's nevertheless a sign of their lack of friendship when they do not bestow favors when they have the means to do so (Sablé, *Maximes*, 251; "De l'amitié," 59). This seems perilously close to the sort of accounting that Scudéry deems "low," yet there is a kind of inevitability to it. Scudéry's "De la reconnoissance" explores ways to avoid exchange, to "forget" favors given, and to surpass one's friend in generosity. For both women, the fall into exchange is to some extent conditioned by status (calculated exchange is nonnoble), but also bespeaks an intimation of the problem of the gift. Gratitude thus highlights "the tensions between autonomy and dependence."[47] Friendship needs to exceed any and every form of exchange, even gratitude, with which it nevertheless remains inextricably linked.

It is therefore not surprising that one of the leitmotivs in the discourse of friendship is the difficulty and rarity of friendship. As we've seen, after excluding nearly all categories of relationships, d'Arconville locates authentic friendship in the high-wire act of a friendship that comes after a love affair; Dupin returns on multiple occasions to the notion that true friendship is felt only by the happy few *belles âmes*: "a form of happiness unknown to most people" (Dupin, *Portefeuille*, 118); Staël paints friendship in glowing terms, but describes with equal eloquence why it is nearly impossible in every circumstance. Just as the familiar words from Montaigne, "Parce que c'estoit luy, parce que c'estoit moy" are emblematic of friendship's ineffable quality, so the words attributed to Aristotle by Diogenes Laertius, "O my friends, there are no friends," are cited in multiple contexts from Montaigne to d'Arconville.[48]

Both Lambert and d'Arconville seek to move beyond gratitude as conventionally understood as the imposition of an obligation, in search of a

---

[46] See Derrida's critique of Mauss, *Donner le temps: 1. La Fausse monnaie* (Paris: Galilée, 1991); and on the "gift without a gift" in Montaigne. Derrida, *Politiques de l'amitié* (Paris: Galilée, 1994), 204.
[47] Coleman, *Anger, Gratitude, and the Enlightenment Writer*, 73.
[48] On the history of the quotation, see Agamben, "Friendship," 2–7.

solution to the problem. For Lambert, true friendship consists in "reciprocal commitments where no one keeps count" (Lambert, 158). Mutual "services" should come as a result of friendship, and not the reverse (Lambert, 161). The implication is that friendship cannot be founded on gratitude, but must precede it. Lambert acknowledges the moral debt incurred by someone who has been pardoned by a friend whom he has wronged; it is then incumbent on the friend not to let him feel in any way "dependent" ("faire sentir sa dépendence,"Lambert, 165). Such delicate forms of equilibrium are hard to sustain; Lambert confesses her own tendency to destabilize her relationships: "I give too much of myself" (Lambert, 168). In her *De l'amitié*, d'Arconville goes the furthest in the elimination of gratitude: just as "accounting" is unworthy of friendship, so even gratitude is listed as one of several motivations "foreign" to true friendship, along with need, habit, *amour-propre*, vanity, and self-interest (D'Arconville, 2:10–11). In her *Pensées*, she describes friendship as "the commerce of souls," but immediately envisions the potential for asymmetry and the need to end a relationship "if we assume all the costs" (D'Arconville, 1:230).

Reconnaissance, which is both gratitude and recognition, is a word and a concept rich in "semantic density." Its association with knowledge, *connaissance*, is made explicit by François de Sales in his *Introduction à la vie devote*: "La connaissance engendre la reconnaissance."[49] Ostensibly an observation that our understanding of divine grace leads to gratitude for God, de Sales suggests broader implications as well. *Re-connaître*, literally to "know again" is also remembrance, as we have seen in Scudéry. Although *reconnaissance* yields to inclination in Scudéry's theories of friendship, it persists in their common quality of acknowledgement of the other. As such, it becomes one discursive locus among many in the growing insistence on acknowledgment of the other's personhood, and, increasingly, equal respect of the other's rights as an individual: the "politics of recognition" that Charles Taylor sees emerging in Rousseau.[50]

Reconnaissance is both more and less than political "recognition." It carries both residual and emergent understandings of relationships in the world as they become absorbed into a modern understanding of personal authenticity. Just as the discourse of friendship carries forward a subcurrent of difference, revising classical notions of friendship based on sameness, *reconnaissance*

---

[49] Coleman, *Anger, Gratitude, and the Enlightenment Writer*, 72–73.
[50] Charles Taylor, "The Politics of Recognition," in Amy Gutman, ed., *Multiculturalism: Examining the Politics of Recognition* (Princeton: Princeton University Press, 1994), 25–73.

may be seen as a structure enabling us to navigate difference and to be sustained, rather than destabilized, by it.

In a well-known essay, Maurice Blanchot describes friendship as an articulation of difference:

> Friendship, the relationship without dependency, without episodes, yet containing all the simplicity of life, comes through the recognition of the shared strangeness (*étrangeté*) that permits us not to speak about our friends, but to them ... the movement of understanding (*entente*) where, in speaking to us, they maintain, even in the greatest intimacy, the infinite distance, the fundamental separation from which that which separates becomes relation.[51]

Reconnaissance/recognition, reverberating in its multiple meanings and connotations, becomes the means, not of overcoming difference as such, but of holding it in equilibrium, maintaining the call for separateness and recognition while enabling a connection, via knowledge and memory, with the other.

Intimacy, fusion, sharing and mingled "commerce" are set against the externalizing forces of exchange and obligation. How is one to overcome the antinomies of friendship? For Sablé, an Augustinian critique of worldliness may show the way. For all of these women, a carefully managed expression of difference, most often figured as sexual difference, may be another. While moralists from Scudéry to Guizot laud friendship between the sexes as "la plus douce," they also assume sublimation, or at least a careful negotiation, of "inclination." Sablé, without addressing the question, implicitly frames friendship as a relation between a woman and a man; d'Arconville posits such relationships as well-nigh impossible, but no less to be wished for.

Sexual difference is a more tractable form of difference than "the fissure of death,"[52] yet both oblige us to confront our limitations, our incapacity to remake the world with ourselves as a model; both summon us at the deepest level to appear, to confront that which is strange and unlike us. In this there is something like what Derrida once called the "law of intimation." *Intimare*: both the judicial summons to appear in public, to bear witness, to justify oneself, and, from *intimus*, the interior, the personal, the intimate. The

---

[51] Maurice Blanchot, *L'Amitié* (Paris: Gallimard, 1971), 328.
[52] Blanchot, 329.

English verb "to intimate" calls on both branches of the etymological family tree: the subtle suggestion, hidden and private, yet perceptible and deliberately aimed at bringing that which is hidden into the open. In elaborating this idea, Derrida is describing his relationship to a particular text, a correspondence between two of his friends in which he is sometimes referred to, but has no active role. The letters both summon him forth and require that he remain silent, "the excluded-middle-latecomer that I remain."[53] I have argued elsewhere that he is in effect describing the act of reading,[54] one that is cast dramatically in relief by the particular situation of reading a correspondence, but that is found in other circumstances, as we find ourselves interpellated, described, and shaped in our innermost selves, and yet drawn out into the world to identify with others that we experience as different from ourselves. Friendship, too, calls on us in this way.

One of Scudéry's figures for the fusion of public and private is the secret. In both "De l'inclination" and "De la reconnoissance," solitary individuals are induced to give up the secret motives for their reclusion and gradually allow themselves to be incorporated in the group of friends. Lambert also evokes the sharing of secrets as the first form of reciprocity in friendship ("the charm of baring one's soul to one's friend," Lambert, 157), underscores its significance as a precious "dépôt" (165) over the course of a friendship, and its enduring imperative after a friendship has ended ("the secret is a debt from the former friendship," Lambert, 167). For d'Arconville, the link between inside and outside is a total apprehension of the other, as immediate as self-knowledge and having as little need of language: "Without speaking, we say that we love one another; without seeing each other, we still say it: our mere existence is a proof" (D'Arconville, 2:188).

Such is intimacy, or intimation: transparent communicability, a mutual recognition that both incorporates and maintains sexual difference and exceeds the faint trace of exchange lurking within reciprocity.

---

[53] Jacques Derrida, "Cher Jean-Luc, cher Simon," afterword to Simon Hantaï and Jean-Luc Nancy, *La Connaissance des textes* (Paris: Galilée, 2001), 145.

[54] J. Hayes, "The Body of the Letter: Epistolary Acts of Jean-Luc Nancy, Simon Hantaï, and Jacques Derrida," *Postmodern Culture* 13.3 (2003), doi: 10.1353/pmc.2003.0018.

4
On Happiness and the Passions

Between the first two printings of her treatise, *De l'influence des passions sur le bonheur des individus et des nations*, Germaine de Staël changed her epigraph from Seneca, *De beata vita*:

> Inde ista tanta coacervatio aliorum super alios ruentium
> ("This is the cause of those great heaps into which men rush till they are piled one upon another," Aubrey Stewart translation)

to a very different scene, from Vergil's *Aeneid* IV:

> Quaesivit coelo lucem ingemuitque reperta
> ("Her gaze went wavering as she looked for heaven's light / And groaned at finding it" Fitzgerald translation).

Neither a crush of people misled by rumors nor Dido's painful suicide would appear to offer obvious insight, beyond ominous foreboding, into the relation of the passions to happiness. While the substitution might appear to show the "individual" side of passion (love lost) taking precedence over the collective, it remains nevertheless the case that Dido's tragedy is also a political event, both for the kingdom over which she reigns and for Rome, since her death is part of the price of Aeneas's destiny as founder of Rome. The same Vergilian passage, freighted with multiple meanings, was a key referent for Diderot, who used it in his 1751 *Lettre sur les sourds et muets* in the elaboration of his concept of the "hieroglyph," an emblem of language's capacity to resonate on multiple levels whose meaning cannot be entirely circumscribed: a theorization of the sublime.[1]

The sublime, the sensation of "extending the limits of human destiny" as Staël would later write in reference to Kant (*De la littérature*, 331), was already very much part of her philosophy and aesthetics. Staël began *De l'influence*

---

[1] Diderot, *Lettre sur les sourds et les muets*, DPV 4:183.

des passions in exile in 1793, completing it in 1796. When she published it, she was feeling the aftershocks of the Revolution, the recent death of her mother, and tumult in her personal life.[2] It is noteworthy that she chooses neither to write on political events nor to embark on a major work of fiction, whose philosophical potential she had begun to envision in her 1794 *Essai sur les fictions*, but, rather, to produce a moralist treatise that explores the relationship between two venerable topics. In her introduction, she notes that it may seem strange to write about happiness at this particular moment in history; and yet, she observes, the century that is drawing to a close exemplifies "the hope or the need for happiness," both individual and political.

Staël initially planned a two-part work, a first volume on individual happiness and a second on the collective. Although she never completed the second volume, the political is never far from her analysis of the individual. The two operate somewhat differently. Certain passions, such as vanity, are detrimental to the individual but useful at the collective level.[3] On the other hand, a similar temporal dilemma confronts both the personal and the political. Individual happiness, as we shall see, requires a grounding in the present moment, displaced neither by anticipation of the future nor by regret for the past; the implicit goal of *De l'influence des passions* is to help passionate individuals move toward this state. France, too, has yet to heal from the divisions and violence of the immediate past; it can only, for now, exist as an ideal, a hope, a potential fulfillment of democratic ideals. Post-Revolutionary France, in Staël's vision, exists as a work in progress whose never-fully-realized status provides the impetus for its ongoing, but never complete, process of realization, in the mode of what Derrida called "Lumières à venir."[4] Happiness, whether personal or political, is always *à-venir*, or as Staël would later term it, in the realm of *perfectibilité*.

Staël's moralist treatise comes at an intellectual crossroads, a nodal point that marks the convergence of multiple threads in Enlightenment thought and an opening into new ways of imagining the individual in the polis. Reflection on the passions extends back to classical antiquity, but the term

---

[2] Catherine Dubeau, "The Mother, the Daughter, and the Passions," trans. Sylvie Romanowski, in Tili Boon Cuillé, and Karyna Szmurlo, eds., *Staël's Philosophy of the Passions* (Lewisburg, PA: Bucknell University Press, 2013), 19–38.

[3] Christine Dunn Henderson, "Passions, Politics, and Literature: The Quest for Happiness," in Cuillé and Szmurlo, 57–73.

[4] Jacques Derrida, *Voyous* (Paris: Galilée, 2003). I discuss "Lumières à venir" and the related concept, "démocratie à venir," in "Unconditional Translation: Derrida's 'Enlightenment to Come,'" *Eighteenth-Century Studies* 40 (2007): 443–55.

evolved and took on entirely new meanings over the course of the seventeenth and eighteenth centuries. Concepts of what constitutes happiness similarly evolved in the early modern period in a reorientation of happiness from bliss to be enjoyed in the afterlife to an earthly paradise in the here-and-now and a human right.[5] It has been said that the eighteenth century took an almost "obsessional" interest in happiness.[6] Throughout their vicissitudes, happiness and the passions have ever been entwined. My goal in this chapter is not to rehearse the full histories of either—the work of many scholars—but rather to consider the contributions of women moralists to these major conceptual shifts.

This chapter examines multiple configurations of the relation of the passions to happiness. Through its engagement with predecessors, whether by emulation or opposition, moralist writing carries forward both residual discursive formations and emergent ideas. The discourse of the passions shows this clearly. Eighteenth-century moralists continue to set up systems and taxonomies of the passions, even as newer vocabularies for mental and physical states become established in what has been termed the transition from "passions to emotions." As Amélie Rorty put it, "Instead of being something external to the self, passions became the very activities of the mind."[7] Although the ongoing taxonomic impulse bespeaks an older formation, the shifts in the taxonomies and changing understandings of the terms reflect an evolving philosophical and cultural landscape.

4.1. From the Passions to Passion

As is well known, philosophical accounts of the emotions have their roots in Aristotelian thought, modulated through or influenced by Stoicism, Augustinianism, Scholasticism, and evolving theories of the body and its humors. Until well into the eighteenth century, "emotion" is a purely physiological term, rarely used; the operative semantic field is that of the passions, the perturbations within the soul. For the Stoics, the passions' disturbance is

---

[5] Darrin M. McMahon, *Happiness: A History* (New York: Grove, 2006).
[6] Robert Mauzi, *L'Idée du bonheur dans la littérature et la pensée françaises au XVIIIe siècle* (1960; rpt. Paris: Albin Michel, 1994), 80. Although scant on women thinkers, Mauzi's book remains the indispensable reference for the period.
[7] Amélie Rorty, "From Passions to Emotions and Sentiments," *Philosophy* 57.220 (1982): 159–72; see more recently, Thomas Dixon, *From Passions to Emotions: The Creation of a Secular Psychological Category* (Cambridge: Cambridge University Press, 2003).

inimical to the detached equilibrium of the good life and so must be carefully regulated. In Aristotelian and Thomistic thought, the passions take place within the sensitive soul, and thus operate apart from the rational soul, setting up a long-lived dichotomy between passion and reason. The discourse of the passions is closely bound up with ethics, going back to the Stoic condemnation of the passions in pursuit of an ideal of detachment; the passions also play an important role, both ethical and aesthetic, in the art of rhetoric from Antiquity to the early modern period.[8] From the beginning, the passions are associated with the body; they furnish part of the account of the interaction of body and soul. The seventeenth century saw a powerful renewal of the theory of the passions via mechanical-corpuscular philosophy and understanding of the body.[9] As Susan James argues in *Passion and Action*, the analyses of the passions by Descartes, Malebranche, Hobbes, and Spinoza all led to different psychologies and different accounts of the relation between body and soul.

In France, the transition from Scholasticism to the new philosophy can be seen in a series of influential treatises that preceded Descartes's *Les Passions de l'âme* (1649); Jean-Pierre Camus, *Traité des passions de l'âme* (1614); Nicolas de Coeffeteau, *Tableau des passions humaines* (1620); Jean-François Senault, *De l'usage des passions* (1641); and Marin Cureau de la Chambre, *Les Characteres des passions* (1640). For Coeffeteau and Senault, the passions are neither good nor bad in themselves; even the "negative passion," hate, has a proper use when directed against vice. Cureau de la Chambre's *Characteres des passions* is distinctive, first because of his revised taxonomy, which juxtaposes primary passions and "passions mixtes"; second, because of his medicalization of the passions and stress on their physical "characters," which include feelings, changes in internal states, gestures, and facial expressions. (Cureau, a physician, also wrote works on physiognomy.) Both features are reflected in Descartes's *Les Passions de l'âme*.[10] Rejecting Scholastic classifications of the passions as either concupiscible or irascible

---

[8] See Gisèle Mathieu-Castellani, *La Rhétorique des passions* (Paris: Presses universitaires de France, 2000).
[9] See Gabor Boros, "The Passions," in Desmond M. Clark and Catherine Wilson, eds., *The Oxford Handbook of Philosophy in Early Modern Europe* (Oxford: Oxford University Press, 2011), 182–200.
[10] Carole Talon-Hugon, *Les Passions rêvées par la raison: Essai sur la théorie des passions de Descartes et de quelques-uns de ses contemporains* (Paris: Vrin, 2002). For Talon-Hugon, Descartes is embarked on two incompatible projects: the ostensible goal, the elaboration of a scientific discourse to rationalize the passions, and an unacknowledged connection with earlier theories or "doxa" on the passions.

appetites, Descartes posits six "primitive" passions from which all others are derived and describes their physiological basis.

Madeleine de Scudéry's conversation, "De la haine," offers insight into the diffusion and evolution of the new philosophy in salon culture. Scudéry's mouthpiece Aspasie cites Cureau de la Chambre's *Charactères des passions* approvingly, claiming that "only God surpasses him in his understanding of the human heart." She describes her own approach more modestly, in terms that Verzure will echo nearly a century later: "I speak simply as an ignorant woman who knows only what the world has taught her, what she feels in her heart, or what she sees in others" (Scudéry 1686, 2:530–31). Scudéry thus rejects the philosophers' *esprit de système* while remaining no less committed to an understanding gained through observations and comparisons drawn from experience. This seemingly more circumscribed approach bespeaks the moralists' preference for observed examples of behavior that enable a profounder, more nuanced, account of human experience, and points toward a new empirical approach.

As moralists continue to view the passions as one of the key forces underlying human behavior, they also contribute to the semantic slippage of the word. This is particularly evident in the Jansenist and Jansenist-leaning writers. For Pascal, the passions are part of the world's "noise and movement" (Pascal n.168, 358) that obscure our ability to seek the truth (Pascal n.151, 352). The passions, with *amour-propre* at the forefront, are central to La Rochefoucauld's moral psychology: "The heart perpetually generates passions, so that the end of one is nearly always the birth of another" (La Rochefoucauld, *Maximes* n.10, 135). Scudéry, however, takes a different, more naturalistic approach in "Des passions que les hommes ont inventées": "I call passion ... whatever one prefers the most and that directs nearly all our actions" (Scudéry 1680, 1:275–6). Scudéry's passions do not disturb, but are simply part of our basic humanity.

As we move into the eighteenth century, the passions continue to attract the interest of moralists and philosophers, but the traditional passions, other than love, figure less and less prominently as they are displaced by new entries to the list. Among the newcomers are *gloire, ambition, amour-propre, avarice, amitié,* and *envie*. Vauvenargues opens the discussion of the passions in his *Introduction à la connaissance de l'esprit humain* (1747) by citing Locke to argue that all the passions are based on either pleasure or pain, and that all goods and ills stem from sensation and reflection. Virtually all his passions are expressions of desire: *l'ambition, l'amour du monde, l'amour de la gloire, l'amour des sciences et des lettres, l'avarice, la passion du jeu, l'amour paternel,* and even *l'amitié qu'on a pour les bêtes* (Vauvenargues, 83–101).

What emerges from these evolving accounts? The roster of the passions undergoes a significant shift in the eighteenth century, away from the canonical eleven to an array of new "feelings," some of which are not feelings per se, but social relations and even pastimes. No longer perturbations of the psyche caused by physical or external forces, the passions stem from sensation and reflection, rather than humors or *esprits animaux*. Love becomes "the quintessence of all passions . . . elevated to the point of activity."[11] "Passion" requires no further explanation. Under the newer dispensation, "bad feelings" are acknowledged, but are viewed more as vices (avarice, pride, gambling) and folded into social and interpersonal narrations (anger, envy, ambition), if mentioned at all. "Passion" can be promoted.[12]

While some maintain the notion that the passions are not simply dangerous or detrimental to good judgment, others begin to view them as good in themselves. Helvétius observes that although they can lead us into error, they can also inspire us to seek the truth (Helvétius, 30). D'Holbach goes so far as to argue that the passions are not simply useful but indeed necessary to the social order: "A man bereft of passions or desires, far from being as perfect as some thinkers have claimed, would be useless to himself and to others, hence little suited for society" (D'Holbach, 33). The ambiguity of the passions emerges in the *Encyclopédie*'s article PASSIONS. A traditional account in some respects, it offers an extended taxonomy and finds that the passions "set a thousand obstacles to our understanding and our happiness." And yet, the author acknowledges, we are deeply attached to them. The most painful passions are secretly pleasurable: "If one can find pleasure in sadness, hatred, or vengeance, what passion is exempt from pleasure?" The passions are "rationalized," in the sense of being made acceptable and even desirable; their irrational, uncontrollable aspect is validated and their ultimate cause becomes even less knowable than the movement of animal spirits.

There is a long-standing relationship between the passions and notions of happiness. Whether one emphasized the Stoic ideal of mastery of the passions or the Epicurean of moderation, passions and desires were to be

---

[11] Niklas Luhmann, *Love as Passion: The Codification of Intimacy*, trans. Jeremy Gaines and Doris L. Jones (Cambridge, MA: Harvard University Press, 1986), 62.

[12] On the evolving discourse of affectivity eighteenth-century France and its inheritance from the seventeenth century, see Philip Stewart, *L'Invention du sentiment* (Oxford: Voltaire Foundation, 2010), esp. "Au-delà des passions, et en deçà," 45–81.

wisely regulated in the interests both of peaceful enjoyment and virtuous citizenship. Both threads were largely compatible with Christian teaching. The passions, recoded as emotions, become essential to the pursuit of happiness.[13] The rehabilitation of the passions, their redistribution, and their reframing as sentiments further reinforce the conviction that happiness is not only available in this world but also a basic need and a right, a notion we find in Dupin. For Du Châtelet, the passions are essential to happiness; d'Holbach claims broadly that "Man is born to be happy" (D'Holbach, xv). The abbé Jean Pestre wrote in his article BONHEUR for the *Encyclopédie*, "Our happiness is Nature's law." The abbé Pestre was careful to distinguish between happiness and pleasure; happiness being understood as a state of being, "a situation such that we would desire its unchanging duration," while pleasure "is only a pleasant, but brief and temporary feeling." Both the materialist philosopher d'Holbach and the liberal churchman Pestre emphasized the alignment of happiness and virtue.

This distinction, which we will see elsewhere, is not so easily maintained, however. The many possible configurations of the passions, happiness, pleasure, and virtue echo in each chapter of this study. To take just two examples, our susceptibility to the passions and their ability to lead us into error exacerbates the difficulty of self-knowledge, essential both for virtue and for authentic being in the world. And as we have seen, love forms the basis of friendship, but must be properly guided and moderated in order to meet certain conditions.

Women find themselves at the intersection of all these issues. Cast in the role of guardians of virtue, excluded from many of the institutions of public life, assumed to possess an innate capacity for sentiment and feeling, and, especially as Rousseau's ideas gained influence, believed to find their greatest fulfillment in domesticity, it is hardly surprising that these questions arise in their moral and philosophical writing, in their personal writings, and as situations to be worked through in the novel. In this chapter, we will see two primary areas of interest: the nature of happiness and the role of temporality. Although most deem the passions to be antithetical to happiness, the relationship is complicated by the rehabilitation of emotion as intrinsic to one's true self. As we saw in the ambiguous role played by inclination—closely

---

[13] Ritchie Robertson, *The Enlightenment: The Pursuit of Happiness, 1680–1790* (New York: Harper Collins, 2021), 36.

related to passion—in the previous chapter, the key element here is not "virtue" in the conventional sense, but rather self-possession and personal integrity.

The following series of roughly chronological close readings foregrounds the originality of women moralists' treatment of the question. First, Marguerite de La Sablière and Louise Dupin offer distinct, yet complementary, views on the role of the passions in the individual's relation to the social world and the forms of happiness available therein. Next, I examine Émilie Du Châtelet's *Discours sur le bonheur*, emphasizing its structure as a practical guide and arguing against interpretations that find Du Châtelet inconsistent in her reasoning; I find a similarly "practical" approach in Marie-Louise de Fourqueux. The last two sections turn to two major theoreticians of happiness and the passions: Geneviève d'Arconville and Germaine de Staël.

4.2. The Worlds of Marguerite de La Sablière and Louise Dupin

Born into a family of Protestant bankers, brilliant and highly educated in both letters and the sciences, Marguerite de La Sablière (1636–1693) hosted a salon of literary and philosophical luminaries in the 1670s; she is remembered in literary history as the patron of the poet Jean de La Fontaine, who dedicated to her his "Discours à madame de La Sablière," a critique of the Cartesian theory of animal machines. Following reverses and personal crises, she moved to a more modest residence, converted to Catholicism, and led a life increasingly devoted to penitence, first under the spiritual direction of the Jesuit and eminent man of letters René Rapin and, following Rapin's death in 1687, Armand-Jean de Rancé, the reforming abbot of the Abbaye Notre-Dame de la Trappe. It is probably during this last period of her life that she wrote her *Maximes chrétiennes*, which were first published anonymously in a 1705 volume that included the *Maximes* of La Rochefoucauld and Madeleine de Sablé as well as the *Pensées diverses* of the abbé d'Ailly.[14]

---

[14] *Réflexions ou sentences et maximes morales de monsieur de la Rochefoucault. Maximes de madame la marquise de Sablé. Pensées diverses de M.L.D. et les Maximes chrétiennes de M. **** (Amsterdam: Chez Pierre Mortier, 1705). "M.L.D." is the churchman Nicolas d'Ailly, a member of Sablé's circle; his *Pensées diverses* had been included in editions of Sablé's *Maximes* beginning in 1679; both Sablé's and d'Ailly's works were included with La Rochefoucauld's *Maximes* beginning with the fourth edition of the *Maximes* in 1690. Those three, plus La Sablière's *Maximes chrétiennes*, would continue to be published together throughout the eighteenth century, but La Sablière's name would not appear with the text until 1777.

As John Conley has observed, La Sablière's maxims have features in common with more worldly examples of the genre: their concision, their use of irony, and their exploration of issues in moral psychology; he argues that she "transformed the genre by theologizing it."[15] Conley exaggerates somewhat—maxims of religious inspiration are common in the period[16]— but it is certainly the case that La Sablière's maxims evince her literary culture even as they put forth a philosophy of contemplation and moral rigor.

A single unnumbered statement prefaces ninety-nine numbered maxims: "The birth that we receive at baptism and that makes us Christians, raises us up above all that we are by nature and by fortune."[17] The epigraphic statement sets the tone and the context for the maxims to follow—a framing function similar to that of La Rochefoucauld's famous epigraph, "Our virtues, for the most part, are only vices in disguise" (La Rochefoucauld, *Maximes*, 134). Many of La Sablière's maxims will also unmask the self-interest and hypocrisy of many apparent "virtues." By setting her maxims in the context of the transformative rebirth of baptism, however, she emphasizes the rift between the Christian life and *le monde*. Her *Maximes* explore both sides of the rift: the worldly tumult that feeds our vanity and obstructs self-knowledge, on the one hand; and the peace that enables us to hear the inner voice of conscience, on the other. The same objects, viewed from each side, are completely different: "Faith makes us see as good that which the world regards as ill; from this difference in ideas comes the different conduct of the righteous and of sinners" (La Sablière, *Maximes* n.10, 282–83).

The passions are the epitome of the world's distractions and misdirections. *Orgueil*, pride, is the passion most often named individually, but as a group they represent the destabilizing forces of desire: "It is difficult to defeat one's passions, but it is impossible to satisfy them" (La Sablière, *Maximes* n.35, 291). Passions are insatiable appetites that lead us away from confronting our situation. Disbelief and skepticism are merely symptoms of our inability to face the truth: "We seek to retain our passions while ridding ourselves of our

---

[15] Conley, *Suspicion*, 82.
[16] For Jean Lafond, "Entre la maxime religieuse et la maxime morale, il n'y a en effet d'autre différence celle du point de vue" ("Le Champ littéraire des formes brèves," 63).
[17] La Sablière, *Maximes chrétiennes*, 279. Numerotation and page numbers are from the original 1705 edition (see note 14 above), available via Gallica. The *Maximes chrétiennes* can also be found in Samuel Menjot d'Elbenne, *Madame de La Sablière, ses pensées chrétiennes et ses lettres à l'abbé de Rancé* (Paris: Plon-Nourrit, 1923), 252–62. Menjot d'Elbenne renumbers the maxims 1–100 (rather than an unnumbered epigraphic maxim followed by 99 numbered maxims) and inserts headers that do not appear in the original edition. Conley also includes the *Maximes chrétiennes* in the appendix to his book (*Suspicion*, 181–87), but follows Menjot d'Elbenne's numerotation and headers.

remorse" (La Sablière, *Maximes* n.18, 285). "Remorse" is in any case a misleading symptom, more often a sign of disappointment and frustration than of true penitence (La Sablière, *Maximes* n.29, 289). As Conley observes, the passions render the will inoperative, underscoring the "voluntarist cast" of her philosophy.[18] "We enjoy the idea of virtue, but as soon as there is a passion to combat, our resolution weakens and we no longer feel capable of carrying out a plan that was easy to make but cannot be executed without pain" (La Sablière, *Maximes* n.25, 287–88). The passions produce willful ignorance and avoidance: "We cannot bear for others to avoid us with the same care that we avoid ourselves by dispersing ourselves outside (*nous répandant au dehors*)" (La Sablière, *Maximes* n.24, 287).

That outside into which we attempt to "disperse" ourselves is the world where La Sablière lived for many years. The phrase "le torrent du siècle"—in which *siècle* is used in its etymological sense of "secular world"—speaks to the blinding distractions and activity of *le monde*. Those who are the most caught up in the torrent are aristocrats and the élite of the Court, whose self-understanding, difficult for everyone, is further hampered by the fact that they are surrounded by sycophants. "The great almost never reflect on their lives, and yet they are required to look into themselves more than others, in order to learn certain truths that they will not hear elsewhere" (La Sablière, *Maximes* n.3, 280). Although social customs and standards, *l'usage*, reinforce these tendencies, the ignorance of *les Grands* is no less a choice and as such condemnable (La Sablière, *Maximes* n.5, 281).

To the exteriorizing forces of *le monde*, La Sablière opposes the peace of *les justes*, who have chosen to receive the new life that was conferred through their baptism as Christians. "A heart lifted up by grace considers that nothing in the world is beneath it" (La Sablière, *Maximes* n.49, 295). As in the epigraph to the *Maximes chrétiennes*, the Christian life is "lifted up" and separated from *le monde*; this "elevation" contrasts with the notion that nothing is "below" one—the key virtue of humility. (The paradox is in keeping with the expectations of the maxim genre.) The efficacy of grace, as we have seen, does not relieve individuals from the responsibility of dedicating their will to achieve this state. Numerous maxims explore the difficulty of separating oneself from the world, given our susceptibility to self-deception and the passions, especially pride, *orgueil*.

---

[18] Conley, 87.

The obvious solution is to withdraw entirely: "We must separate ourselves from the world and in a sense from ourselves, in order to hear God in our retreat. The tumult of the world and of our passions often prevents us from hearing him" (La Sablière, *Maximes* n.75, 303). At the same time, she recognizes that complete withdrawal is not the only option. There is a less obvious, more difficult, solution: "It is easier to separate oneself from interaction with the world than to live in the world with as little attachment as if one were completely separated; yet one or the other is necessary for our salvation" (La Sablière, *Maximes* n.56, 297). She describes living in the world as if one were separated from it, even amid worldly banter. "Contemplation is a kind of solitude, to which one should often retreat in the midst of the world's profane conversations, in order to avoid becoming infected by the contagion in the air" (La Sablière, *Maximes* n.63, 299).

To concentrate oneself within is the antidote to "dispersing oneself without." This practice is more difficult than a literal retreat, since the temptations and distractions of the world remain present; withdrawal must be constantly lived and renewed. This would appear to have been La Sablière's personal practice. Although she spent an increasing amount of her time in her lodgings at the Hôpital des Incurables, she herself never completely abandoned her apartment in town. Her approach resembles what Lucien Goldmann saw as a key element of Jansenism, the *refus intramondain du monde*: remaining in the world, but not of the world; holding a vision of totality within a fragmentary world; transcending the world while being part of it.[19] She describes the spiritual journey as a process, during which one gradually loses one's interest in the world's pleasures, just as one ceases to care about childish amusements.

La Sablière does not speak of "happiness." Instead, she evokes "peace," *la paix*, or *repos*: a perfectly quiet state, conferred by humility, that transcends human happiness. It is the opposite of the *agitations* created by pride (La Sablière, *Maximes* n.74, 303). The final stage of La Sablière's journey is suggested by her *Pensées chrétiennes*, a manuscript that came to light in the twentieth century and appears to be part of her correspondence with the abbé de Rancé.[20] Composed of twenty *pensées*, it is less polished, more

---

[19] Goldmann, *Le Dieu caché*, 62–67.
[20] La Sablière's biographer Samuel Menjot d'Elbenne uncovered the *Pensées* in a manuscript collection at the château de Chantilly; he includes it in his biography along with the *Maximes chrétiennes* and the correspondence with Rancé (Menjot d'Elbenne, 265–66). All references are to this edition, available via Gallica.

fragmentary, than the *Maximes chrétiennes*. The *Pensées* describe the soul's union with God in a series of austere images: disengagement, renunciation, emptiness, forgetting. All created things are to be regarded as if they no longer exist, with God as the "unique principle"; one should consider only the action of God in the soul, rather than one's own reflections. This state of contemplation is achieved in solitude, but, as John Conley points out, "[t]his solitude ... does not suppress moral outreach to the neighbor";[21] La Sablière enjoins solitary meditation in the service of others:

> To be in solitude as much as possible, for that is where God communicates with the soul. . . . [O]ne learns more in solitude and one will obtain more grace by being united with God in order to live with others, than in speaking to them; we mustn't flatter ourselves that we speak only of God; we should speak only to God, unless he inspires us to do otherwise or our station in life requires it. (La Sablière, *Pensées* n.12, 266)

La Sablière's emphasis on contemplative silence may represent an echo of the guidance of her spiritual director the abbé de Rancé, best known for bringing the Strict Observance to the Abbaye de la Trappe. Her injunction to silence is not absolute; one should seek silence "as much as possible," but speak if so moved by God, or if required by one's role. This final qualifier echoes the idea that we saw in the *Maximes chrétiennes* that spiritual retreat is available to all, even those who remain in *le monde*.

In the long history of the relation between the passions and happiness, La Sablière's account echoes both Classical and Christian notions that the passions are antithetical to happiness, but with significant distinctions. La Sablière does not define her goal as happiness or bliss, but as the peace achieved through union with God, described as both *paix intérieure* and *repos*; it is not relegated to a hoped-for afterlife, but must be sought in a present that is "lifted up" by the awareness of eternity. The word *repos* has a special resonance in seventeenth-century France, drawing on Stoic and Epicurean influences, modulated through Jansenism, and infused throughout secular culture—famously, in Marie-Madeleine de La Fayette's 1678 novel *La Princesse de Clèves*.[22] La Sablière's concern with the passions is in keeping with one of the major intellectual preoccupations of her age,

---

[21] Conley, *Suspicion*, 93.
[22] See Domna Stanton, "The Ideal of 'repos' in Seventeenth-Century Literature," *Esprit Créateur* 15.1/2 (Spring–Summer, 1975): 79–104.

but with a difference. As we have seen, she generally refers to the passions in the plural as the forces that distort our vision, vitiate the will, and attach us to the world. To echo La Fayette's heroine, lucid as she strives to combat her passion: "I confess . . . that the passions may lead me, but they cannot blind me."[23] Strikingly, the only passion that La Sablière singles out, *orgueil*, is not considered a passion in either the classical texts or the numerous seventeenth-century treatises with which she would have been familiar. *Orgueil*, pride, is instead one of the seven cardinal sins, generally deemed the most serious of them; its corresponding virtue in the teachings of the Church is, as in La Sablière, humility. The *Maximes chrétiennes* thus recast traditional Church teaching in the contemporary framework of the passions. Analogously to her *refus intramondain du monde*, La Sablière's *Maximes chrétiennes* gesture toward a reality beyond the world in a language firmly anchored in it. She remains in both worlds.

Louise Dupin (1706–1799) inhabited a world not very different from La Sablière's in the 1670s, prior to her conversion. Like La Sablière, she was raised in a family of wealthy financiers. Superbly educated, she hosted a salon frequented by writers, philosophers, and visiting dignitaries. Dupin's salon endured from the 1730s until her retirement to her château de Chenonceau a few years before the Revolution.[24] Her essay, "Idées sur le bonheur," was among the writings published by her great-great nephew nearly a century after her death; he estimates its date as 1736, which would situate it in the early years of her salon. Addressing her thoughts to her son, stepson, and nephews, she begins by asserting not only that happiness is possible in this world, but also that it is available to all and that all have "the same rights to pleasure" (Dupin, *Portefeuille*, 39–40). In addition to the statement that happiness is to be found in this world, three features stand out: that it is universally available, regardless of one's status; that it is equated with pleasure; and that there is a fundamental right to it.[25]

The right to happiness would become one of the most potent concepts of the Enlightenment; although Dupin would not publish her essay, it suggests the tenor of discussions in her salon. The equation of happiness and pleasure

---

[23] La Fayette, *La Princesse de Clèves* (Paris: Garnier-Flammarion, 1966), 174.

[24] Antoine Lilti mentions the elegance and magnificence of Dupin's salon as exemplifying the aristocratic lifestyle of the moneyed elite and as an important crossroads for visiting foreign dignitaries, which brought it under the eye of the Paris police. Lilti, *Le Monde des* salons, 151, 384–95. For a detailed discussion of Dupin's social networks, see Frédéric Marty, *Louise Dupin: Défendre l'égalité des sexes en 1750* (Paris: Classiques Garnier, 2021), 37–82.

[25] On Dupin's politics as a reforming monarchist with republican tendencies, see Marty, 270–74.

may represent an echo of the highly influential work by Louis-Jean Levesque de Pouilly (1691–1750), *La Théorie des sentiments agréables*, first published in 1736.[26] The "most concise statement of 'philosophical happiness'" of the Enlightenment,[27] extended portions of the work would find their way into the articles PASSION and PLAISIR of the *Encyclopédie*. Pouilly proposed a thoroughly rationalized account of "pleasant feelings," claiming for moral philosophy the same precision and accuracy as the physical sciences. As his subtitle, "On the pleasure attached to virtue," makes clear, this is no hedonistic account of happiness such as would later be put forth by the materialist Julien Offray de La Mettrie. The subtitle of the later edition of the work would go further, underscoring his goal to align "the principles of natural theology and those of moral philosophy." *Sentiments agréables* are occasioned by the display of noble actions, demonstrations of wisdom and insight, the perception of beauty, and the penchant to harmonize our own happiness with that of other people (Pouilly, 143).

In equating happiness with pleasure, Dupin also assumes that both are grounded in virtue. She ascribes happiness to following *les bons principes* and practicing justice and *bienfaisance* (Dupin, *Portefeuille*, 43); she concludes the essay by claiming that those who seek happiness in ignoble pursuits ("la folie et les sottises," Dupin, *Portefeuille*, 63) will not find it. At the same time, her essay is clearly and resolutely focused on earthly pleasure. Following Locke, Dupin sees pleasure and pain as the basic principles that regulate human existence. Reason is an important principle, but given that humans are not born with a fully functioning reason, but must develop it over time, and given that it may decline in later life, she sees it as less fundamental to our being than pain and pleasure, which are constants (Dupin, *Portefeuille*, 57). Relegating reason to second place does not imply less importance to our mental faculties, however, as pleasure and pain have both mental and physical dimensions. Just as body and mind act upon one another, but are also

---

[26] Levesque de Pouilly's work was initially published without his permission in the *Recueil de divers écrits sur l'amour et l'amitié* edited by Thémiseul de Saint-Hyacinthe—the same collection that saw the original publication of madame de Lambert's *Traité de l'amitié* and Marie Madeleine Gabrielle de Rochechouart de Mortemart (abbesse de Fontevraud), "Question sur la politesse." The reception that greeted Pouilly's work, as well as a second unauthorized publication, persuaded him to expand his initial short essay into a formal treatise. This final version appeared in 1747. Because of the likely influence of the work on Dupin and Émilie Du Châtelet, both of whom use the expression "sentiments agréables," I cite the 1736 version that they would have encountered as they were writing their works on happiness; this version is available as an appendix to Françoise Gevrey's critical edition of the 1747 version. Louis-Jean Levesque de Pouilly, *Théorie des sentiments agréables*, "Deuxième état du texte," ed. Françoise Gevrey (Reims: Université de Reims Champagne-Ardenne, 2021), 131–61.

[27] Mauzi, *L'Idée du bonheur*, 240.

independent, Dupin finds that ideas affect feelings, *sentiments*, more often than the reverse: in most circumstances, "it seems to me that a feeling is simply the adoption of an idea" (Dupin, *Portefeuille*, 40). The preeminence of cognitive phenomena leads her to associate happiness with clear and accurate thinking: "our errors create our misfortunes" (Dupin, *Portefeuille*, 41).

Mental pleasures, *les plaisirs de l'esprit*, are therefore the most significant. Among these are our "inner resources": the sense that our minds are free even under difficult circumstances; *sensibilité*, the ability to feel deeply; and even the belief in the afterlife, which she finds to be "useful" for society and "delicious" for individuals (Dupin, *Portefeuille*, 55). Dupin observes that when we take pleasure in any "object," whether a material object or an idea, our pleasure stems from our "disposition" rather than the thing itself; we need our reason in order to judge whether a perceived pleasure is worth the "cost," hence the need for "idées claires" in the pursuit of happiness.

The social world plays an important role in Dupin's idea of happiness, because relationships with others offer one of our greatest sources of pleasure. Here, too, Dupin focuses on the roles of pain and pleasure. Having a good reputation gives us pleasure, because of its effect on the way that others treat us. We seek to please (*plaire*) others, further increasing mutual happiness. Both pain and pleasures are shared "by a certain organic disposition" or *sympathie* that leads us to "enter into unison with one another" (Dupin, *Portefeuille*, 49). Although we are naturally attuned to others, especially to our friends, good manners (*la politesse*) teach us not to display our pain or sorrow to others. Dupin observes that this reticence is in our best interest. Not only does maintaining the appearance of good cheer reinforce the "happiness feedback" of sociability, but such positive distraction is linked to mental function: "since we can only feel or think one thing at a time, we do not feel our pain if we hide it from others" (Dupin, *Portefeuille*, 49–50).

Temporality has a central place in Dupin's definition of happiness. Happiness is not "a fixed state" but rather "series of different pleasures, pleasant ideas, agreeable feelings [*sentiments agréables*], and various notions that amuse the mind; all this creates a state in which we are at ease" (Dupin, *Portefeuille*, 56). Her concept of happiness as constituted by the variety and successivity of pleasures may initially appear at odds with her insistence elsewhere that calm and tranquility form the basis of happiness (Dupin, *Portefeuille*, 42). As we shall see, however, "variety" is not incompatible with "tranquility."

The passions are antithetical to calm and therefore to happiness. Dupin regards the passions as immoderate attachments that appear to lead us toward our goal of happiness, but actually lead us away; they create social disorder (Dupin, *Portefeuille*, 43). She also refers to them as "simple" thoughts or sentiments, the only kind known to the majority of people (Dupin, *Portefeuille*, 47). The "simple" sentiments include three traditional passions: fear, desire, hope. These prevent happiness because they "pull us toward the future and disrupt our sense of reality" (Dupin, *Portefeuille*, 47–48). The temporality of the passions is thus different from that of happiness: happiness consists in a series of present moments, while the passions pull us away from the present toward an uncertain future. She terms the inability to appreciate one's present situation "disquiet" (*inquiétude*).

The apparent tension between happiness as calm and happiness as successivity echoes one of the "antinomies of happiness," movement and repose, that emerge in the period's definitions of happiness.[28] The appeal of tranquility or Epicurean *ataraxia* coexists with the rise of *inquiétude* as an aesthetic notion that blends into moral psychology.[29] Dupin's resolution of the dichotomy differs from others such as Levesque de Pouilly, who resolves the dichotomy through a judicious mixture of social and private life. For Dupin, happiness consists in a complex understanding of temporality, in which appreciation of the present is key to happiness. Even "sad hours" are part of the time of our lives, and we should not attempt to hasten their passing (Dupin, *Portefeuille*, 55). Remaining in "a calm situation" enables one to appreciate the present, just as adjusting one's desires and expectations to fit one's circumstances enables one to live peacefully and in the present. At the same time, happiness is not a "state"; it involves change, variety, and being fully conscious of each moment. Happiness is now: a vividly experienced, constantly changing present.

Louise Dupin and Marguerite de La Sablière are undoubtedly worlds apart in many respects, but there are unexpected resonances between them. Without evincing La Sablière's skepticism of virtuous appearances or seeking to unmask hidden motives, Dupin is also keenly aware of the inconsistency (*inconséquence*) between people's expressed principles and their behavior (Dupin, *Portefeuille*, 42), and she enjoins clarity and the use of one's judgment in relations with others. While La Sablière's rejection and Dupin's embrace of

---

[28] Mauzi, 125–35.
[29] See Jean Deprun, *La Philosophie de l'inquiétude au XVIIIe siècle* (Paris: Vrin, 1979).

sociability are a key difference, there are nuances in Dupin's positive view of social relations. She advises that we carefully gauge the degree of our closeness to and dependency on others: "Often our happiness is disturbed because we either count too much on others, or not enough" (Dupin, *Portefeuille*, 45). Furthermore, the natural sympathy or "unison" that connects people is not absolute. In an extended analogy, she describes the individual as a sovereign state with responsibility for his inner organization and external relations:

> For him, other men are neighboring countries who must sort out their own interests with regard to him and who come together for the general commerce of common interests. Life and society are a commerce where we all have our own interests; one trades on one's talents, one's advantages, one's qualities; hence it is necessary to know the value of what one possesses. (Dupin, *Portefeuille*, 50)

"Le commerce du monde" is a term frequently used in the period to describe sociability; Dupin's literalization of the metaphor speaks not only to the enhanced cultural status of trade, but also to the need for internal regulation and judgment, just as in trade and diplomacy. While La Sablière proposes to abandon the world while remaining within it, Dupin embraces the world while maintaining an inner distance.

4.3. Practical Guidance in Du Châtelet and Fourqueux

Émilie Du Châtelet's *Discours sur le bonheur* was not published during her lifetime. She either gave or bequeathed the manuscript to her lover, Jean-François de Saint-Lambert, but copies came into circulation after he imprudently showed it to others. When Saint-Lambert learned that Jean-Baptiste-Antoine Suard planned to include it in a volume of related texts in 1764, he wrote to ask him to refrain from publication. We cannot know whether he wished to shield Du Châtelet's family from the personal revelations in the text, as he claimed, or to prevent Voltaire from learning of it—Voltaire had an influential vote in the Académie française to which Saint-Lambert hoped to be elected—but in any case, Suard acquiesced. The text was published in 1779, the year following Voltaire's death, but seems to have escaped critical notice until later editions in 1796 and 1806. The 1961 critical edition by Robert Mauzi, who termed it the only philosophical treatment on happiness by an eighteenth-century woman (not quite the case, as we see) contributed to the rise of scholarly interest in the text, which has often been disregarded or seen as less than "philosophical" because of intensely personal passages in which Du Châtelet evokes the waning of her relationship with Voltaire and discusses personal predilections such as food, gambling, and collecting bibelots.

Scholars disagree as to the date of composition. Going on a quotation from Voltaire's play *Sémiramis*, begun in 1746, Mauzi places it in the period from 1746 to the first months of 1748, claiming that the elegiac tone of the final section could not have been written in the flush of her passionate new relationship with Saint-Lambert in the spring of 1748.[30] Judith Zinsser, on the other hand, sees the text as having been written in multiple phases, with the earliest sections dating from the early 1740s, when happiness was one of the topics that Du Châtelet and Voltaire discussed with their frequent visitor Helvétius. In Zinsser's chronology, Du Châtelet returned to the text after 1746 to reflect on the evolution of her relationship with Voltaire, and completed the final section in the spring of 1748 as she contemplated the possibility of new love with Saint-Lambert.[31] While I agree that the final section, in which she discusses the pros and cons of yielding to one's *goût* (a term that, in this context, refers to sexual desire) takes on a certain resonance if one imagines that she has a specific decision in mind, the text stands on its own merits regardless of how one sees its relation to the author's life. Recent scholarship on the *Discours* has focused on its intertextual relations with works by Helvétius, Voltaire, and La Mettrie.[32] Other fruitful approaches analyze

---

[30] Robert Mauzi, "Introduction," Émilie Du Châtelet, *Discours sur le bonheur* (Paris: Les Belles lettres, 1961), lxxiv–lxxix. All references to the *Discours* are to this edition.

[31] Judith Zinsser, *La Dame d'esprit: A Biography of the Marquise Du Châtelet* (New York: Viking, 2006), 244–46, 265; see also her editorial comments to the English translation of the *Discours*, in Émilie Du Châtelet, *Selected philosophical and Scientific Writings*, ed. and trans. Judith Zinsser and Isabelle Bour (Chicago: University of Chicago Press, 2009), 345–46. As evidence that Du Châtelet composed the final section of the *Discours* in the early months of her relationship with Saint-Lambert, Zinsser cites the numerous echoes between the *Discours* and the letters to Saint-Lambert. The editors of the recent edition of Du Châtelet's correspondence also note the similarities (Letters 552, 553, 587, 588, 590, 599, 633). *La Correspondance d'Émilie Du Châtelet*, ed. Ulla Kölving and Andrew Brown, 2 vols. (Ferney-Voltaire: Centre international d'étude du XVIIIe siècle, 2018). It is impossible to know, of course, whether Du Châtelet was writing the *Discours* at the same time as these letters (dated from June 1748 to February 1749), or if the ideas that she had developed in a recently composed text remained uppermost in her mind.

[32] See Barbara Whitehead, "The Singularity of Mme Du Châtelet: An Analysis of the *Discours* sur le bonheur," in Judith Zinsser and Julie C. Hayes, eds., *Émilie Du Châtelet: Rewriting Enlightenment Philosophy and Science* (Oxford: Voltaire Foundation, 2006), 255–76; Ana Rodrigues, "Du Châtelet und La Mettrie: Letzte Replik in Potsdam," in Ruth Hagengruber and Hartmut Hecht, eds., *Émilie du Châtelet und Die Deutsche Aufklärung* (Wiesbaden: Springer Vieweg, 2019), 389–413. Whitehead and Rodrigues concur that Du Châtelet's greater affinity is with La Mettrie, but that she comes to

the arguments of the *Discours* in terms of Du Châtelet's philosophical principles as elaborated in her *Institutions de physique* and other works.[33] In this reading, I focus on the role of temporality in the relation between happiness and passions.

Du Châtelet begins the *Discours* by taking a practical approach:

> Happiness is generally considered difficult to achieve, and for all too many reasons; but it would be easier to become happy, if reflection and a plan preceded one's actions. We are pulled along by circumstances, and we give ourselves over to hopes that yield only half of what we expected; finally, one only perceives the means to be happy once age and self-imposed limits become obstacles. (Du Châtelet, 3).

The problem of happiness, as Du Châtelet sees it, is a problem of sequence and temporality: our actions all too often precede a *plan de conduit*; and we only realize what we need in order to be happy after age and self-inflicted limitations have exacerbated the difficulty. Note the complex dynamic of the central sentence: "pulled along" by circumstances, we are "given over" to hopes for a future state that will be imperfectly realized at best. The problem is double: one must seize control of one's agency and develop a plan of action prior to taking unreflective steps. The references to the passage of time continue: we must anticipate (*prévenir*) reflections that typically come too late or too slowly, and avoid wasting our "brief and precious time" on earth.

Du Châtelet echoes many of her contemporaries in stating that we are on earth in order to be happy: "we have nothing to do in this world but to procure pleasant sensations and sentiments [*sentiments agréables*]" (Du Châtelet, 4). The echo of Pouilly is likely no accident. Not only would his emphasis on "pleasant sensations" have appealed to her, but also his thoroughly

---

significantly different conclusions. Véronique Le Ru focuses more on Du Châtelet's "hedonist, materialist" commonalities with La Mettrie, rather than on the differences in their views; Le Ru, "*Le Discours sur le bonheur* ou le déploiement d'une morale hédoniste et matérialiste à travers deux questions," *La Lettre clandestine* 30 (2002): 87–97; see also Le Ru, *Émilie Du Châtelet philosophe* (Paris: Classiques Garnier, 2019), 151–60. Ann Thompson urges "caution" in claiming a relationship between the two ("Émilie Du Châtelet and La Mettrie," in Ruth Hagengruber, ed., *Époque Émilienne*[Cham: Springer, 2022], 377–89).

[33] Marcy P. Lascano reads the *Discours* through the lens of Du Châtelet's use of the "two great principles," the principle of contradiction and the principle of sufficient reason, "Émilie Du Châtelet on Illusions," *Journal of the American philosophical Association* 7.1 (2021): 1–19; Tracy Rutler considers the implications of the principles of indiscernables and continuity for the *Discours* in "Happiness and Disability: Émilie Du Châtelet's Adaptive Worldbuilding," *Esprit créateur* 61.4 (2021): 140–52.

rationalized approach to moralist reflection. For him, the study of moral sentiments "is of the same sort as the physico-mathematical sciences" and "susceptible to the same certitude" (Levesque de Pouilly, 133). Like Pouilly, Du Châtelet emphasizes the use of reason and the importance of choice in charting a course for happiness. Other than an axiomatic assumption that happiness is aligned with virtue, however, she is not interested in his goal of providing a theological framework to moral philosophy. As we have also seen in Dupin, the language of "pleasant feelings" lends itself to an emphasis on happiness in the secular here and now.

Du Châtelet sums up the basic requisites for happiness: to free oneself from *préjugés* and false ideas; to be virtuous; to be in good health; to have desires (*goûts*) and passions, and to be susceptible to illusion (Du Châtelet, 4). She refers to these components as "les grandes machines du bonheur" (Du Châtelet, 16). While she shares the first three elements with Louise Dupin, the last two are more unexpected. Dupin, it will be recalled, stresses the need for "clear ideas" and the avoidance of error. Even as sympathetic a reader as Pauline Guizot would find inconsistency in Du Châtelet's injunction to eliminate prejudice while maintaining illusions; for Guizot, Du Châtelet had allowed herself to be dazzled intellectually by "maxims that contradicted her heart."[34] Critics from Sainte-Beuve to Robert Mauzi have voiced similar ideas. As Marcy Lascano has pointed out, however, Du Châtelet discusses multiple types of illusion in the *Discours*, offering examples of the ways in which we allow ourselves the pleasure, as in the theater, of the voluntary suspension of disbelief. Du Châtelet points to optical illusions as the closest correlate of love's illusions: they represent a natural property of our vision and they produce pleasure, but we are able to dispel them by use of our reason: "Reason may determine that we have to vanquish some of our illusions in order to be happy. We may have to leave love behind and turn to other sources of pleasure. But reason will allow us the illusions that truly do increase our happiness."[35] As we shall see, even the most emotionally weighted sections of the *Discours* involve the careful use of reason.

Let us turn to the question of the other unusual "machine" of happiness, the need for desires (*goûts*) and passions. *Goût* is an intractably untranslatable term in the eighteenth-century lexicon. Du Châtelet clearly indicates that it is a weak substitute for a passion: "in the absence of passions, one must

---

[34] Pauline Guizot, "Lettre d'une femme sur les femmes qui ont de la reputation, et en particulier sur Mme du Châtelet" (1806), *Le Temps passé* 2:500–504. I discuss Guizot's essay in Chapter 7.
[35] Lascano, "Émilie Du Châtelet on Illusions," 17.

content oneself with *goûts*" (Du Châtelet, 5). *Goût* is, however, more than simply a "preference," as Lascano has it. The historical Littré dictionary cites a 1690 definition of *goût* as an "inclination that one prefers not to call love," and as a "simple inclination, fleeting amusement, a term used at court." While the range of meanings in period dictionaries is vast, the erotic connotation of *goût* is quite clear in the final pages of the *Discours*, when Du Châtelet asks, "What is your goal when you yield to your desire (*goût*) for someone?" (Du Châtelet, 35).

Although Du Châtelet is very clear that happiness comes not simply from having passions and desires, but from satisfying them ("Happiness comes only from satisfied desires and passions"; Du Châtelet, 4), her approach is not a full-throated "hedonistic" apology of the passions on a par with La Mettrie, as Véronique Le Ru has argued. Just as her recommendation to indulge in salutary illusions represents an equilibrium between reason and pleasure, so too her approach to the passions relies on careful reflection, even calculation.

The eighteenth century's focus on happiness often turned to questions of how to provide the greatest amount of happiness for the greatest number of people, the "felicific calculus" of which Jeremy Bentham's utilitarianism is the best-known example.[36] Du Châtelet is no Bentham and, beyond her definition of virtue as whatever contributes to the good of society, she is not interested in political happiness—she is quite clear in defining her intended audience as individuals (implicitly, women) of her social class. She is, however, a utilitarian of individual happiness. Her emotional calculus appears in multiple contexts, as she discusses the need to maintain the proper proportionality of one's desires to one's estate, to substitute one pleasure for another should one not attain the object of one's desire, and to weigh the degrees of pain and pleasure that result from a particular choice. "You calculate badly" if you choose great pain for temporary pleasure, for example (Du Châtelet, 8). Her criticism of Montaigne's injunction to prepare oneself for death comes in the context of advice to avoid unpleasant thoughts, but she frames it in terms of the investment of one's time and effort: if our mental capacity declines, either from sickness or old age, we will not reap the benefit of Montaigne's preparation and "we'll have nothing for our trouble" (Du Châtelet, 19).

Avoiding unpleasant thoughts is one of the "special skills" ("adresses de détail") that contribute to happiness. Decisiveness, with its corollary, the avoidance of regret (*repentir*) (Du Châtelet, 16–17), and the ability to

---

[36] McMahon, *Happiness*, 212–21.

moderate one's desires to one's estate in life (Du Châtelet, 23) are others. Adjusting desire and accommodating it to one's means represent a form of calculation, whereas decisiveness reflects Du Châtelet's concern with time. To be indecisive is to waste one's time in "an ocean of uncertainty": "making mistakes (*sottises*), correcting them, regretting them" (Du Châtelet, 16). Regret is a useless emotion because it too represents a waste of time: given the diversity of circumstances, we rarely learn anything by mulling over our mistakes. If there is something to be learned, we should take the point and move on (Du Châtelet, 17).

"Wisdom should always have the chips in hand" (Du Châtelet, 19). The image is of Wisdom at the gaming table, ready to play: significantly, it marks the beginning of the discussion of the passions. Desires and passions are among the *grandes machines* that make happiness possible; the key thing is to make them serve happiness ("les faire servir à notre bonheur," Du Châtelet, 19), a phrase that occurs multiple times.

Ambition, for example, is a passion that can produce significant enjoyment, but Du Châtelet cautions that of all the passions, it makes us the most dependent on others (Du Châtelet, 20). In order to maintain one's independence, the best passion is the love of study, which offers a pathway to fame (*gloire*). In a famous passage, she points out that study is more important to women's happiness than to men's, even though most are denied the education that would open this door. Men have multiple pathways to achieve renown and happiness. Women, on the other hand, "are excluded by their state from every form of fame; and when by chance there comes one with an elevated spirit, she has only her studies to console her for all the exclusion and dependency to which her state condemns her" (Du Châtelet, 21). She concedes that the desire for literary or intellectual *gloire* is also dependent on others and is to a great extent illusory. If one can restrain oneself from needing the approval of one's contemporaries, one can take pleasure in imagining the applause of future generations. "Philosophically speaking," she acknowledges the vanity in this thought, but the thought itself is pleasant—and that pleasure is not an illusion.

There is an important temporal dimension to her reasoning here. Although happiness is "in the present moment," this present involves both pleasurable hope (*espérance*) and reminiscence; it is thus "enriched by the past and the future" (Du Châtelet, 22). *Espérance* is here used in a different sense than in her opening paragraph, where she pointed to unfulfilled hopes as one of the obstacles to happiness. The special weight of the pleasurable, hopeful moment will play an important role in the final section of the *Discours*, where she considers what is at stake in yielding to desire.

Since happiness consists in satisfying one's desires and passions, "making them serve" implies that the pursuit of one's desires is to be undertaken in such a manner as best to ensure the desired result—with alternatives and substitutions, if needed. Like Dupin, Du Châtelet argues that contentment with one's situation in life enables one to avoid the contrary situation, that of disquiet (*inquiétude*) or perpetual dissatisfaction, an enemy of happiness (Du Châtelet, 25). Given that Du Châtelet has just advocated for making the best of one's situation and avoiding disquiet, it may come as a surprise that she promptly turns to what she terms "une passion très déraisonnable," gambling (Du Châtelet, 25). Furthermore, although she has just said that we should seek to accommodate ourselves to our situation, she points to high-stakes gambling "le gros jeu" as being particularly compelling.

But Du Châtelet's passion for gambling is less paradoxical than it may seem. Her pleasure in gambling is enhanced, not restricted, by her comparatively modest fortune, since with infinite riches, there would be nothing significant at stake and gambling would be meaningless. The appeal of high-stakes gambling is that it places one between hope and fear, intense feelings that produce an elevated sense of existence. Intensity of feeling represents "one of the great principles of happiness" (Du Châtelet, 26). It is the intensity of the moment, full of possibility, rather than the ultimate result, positive or negative, that matters. The ability to appreciate the richness of the moment, whether at the gambling table or in imagining one's *gloire* for future generations, is thus quite different from the kind of hope evoked in her opening paragraph, a hope that loses sight of the present by grasping at the future, a form of *inquiétude*.

Du Châtelet's analysis of the pleasure of gambling enables us to understand the stakes in her analysis of love. The last part of the *Discours* first evokes the passion of love and the joy of two beings who reciprocate one another's desire, then shifts to a personal mode: "for ten years, I was happy in the love of the man who conquered my soul.... When age, illness, and perhaps to some degree the facility of pleasure had diminished his desire, I did not notice for a long time; I loved enough for two" (Du Châtelet, 31–32). Having come to the realization that perhaps she alone possesses an unchanging heart able to "destroy the power of time" (Du Châtelet, 32), she gradually accommodates herself to the "peaceful sentiment of friendship" and consoles herself with her passion for study (Du Châtelet, 33).

Is friendship truly ever enough? she however goes on to ask. Seemingly not: "we are only happy through lively, agreeable feelings" (Du Châtelet, 33). The final section—which Judith Zinsser argues was written for Saint-Lambert—takes up the question of whether one should commit oneself to love. Whether or not she already had Saint-Lambert in mind, the tone here changes from elegiac reminiscence to argumentation and persuasion. Given all that one knows about love's vicissitudes, she notes, there are certain practical steps to take before embarking on a new relationship, such as gaining a thorough knowledge of the character of one's prospective partner; there are also steps that one must take if a relationship begins to cause one pain. We are again in the realm of calculation and strategic decisions: where does the greater pleasure lie; how much pain will cause us to break off a relationship? Here the "special skill" of decisiveness comes into play: "One must cut to the quick, break off without looking back" (Du Châtelet, 37).

One gambles. One gambles not to win a fortune—although one may hope for it—and despite the fear of losing. One gambles in love, as at the gaming table, for the experience of the moment.[37] Experience teaches us what the outcomes may be, but it also teaches us to "give an accounting" of oneself ("à compter avec nous-mêmes") and to "make our passions serve our happiness" (Du Châtelet, 34).

> What is your goal in yielding to your desire for someone? Is it not to be happy through the pleasure of loving and the pleasure of being loved? It would be ridiculous to deny oneself that pleasure out of fear of a future misfortune that you might not experience until after having been very happy, which would be compensation. (Du Châtelet, 55)

Far from being "inconsistent" in her reasoning, Du Châtelet shows herself to be utterly rational. An able mathematician, Du Châtelet was well aware of the intersection of chance and logic in probability theory. The self-knowledge gained from experience enables her to "account" for herself, to herself, and decide accordingly.

> Every gambler plays with certainty to win with uncertainty. (Pascal, *Pensée* n.680, 516)

---

[37] Thomas M. Kavanagh explores the significance of the gambler's "moment" in the fiction of the period. *Enlightenment and the Shadows of Chance: The Novel and the Culture of Gambling in Eighteenth-Century France* (Baltimore: Johns Hopkins University Press, 1993).

The outcome of Du Châtelet's Pascalian wager is immaterial: the sensation of the moment, the enhanced sense of existence, will have been sufficient in itself, and provide a "compensation" should happiness prove brief.

Marie-Louise de Fourqueux was among those who read the *Discours* during the years that it circulated in manuscript. In her first chapter, "Aveu de mes défauts," she cites Du Châtelet as a model for one of her goals for self-improvement: to banish her tendency for irresolution and second-guessing.

> Madame Du Châtelet says in her treatise on happiness that one should never repent one's actions. She was right: one should only repent culpable or imprudent acts. If it is useless for the past, it becomes a lesson for the future. (Fourqueux, 1:78)

Although she does not cite Du Châtelet in later chapters, there are other echoes of the *Discours* in the *Confessions*. Fourqueux, it will be remembered, began the *Confessions* as a purely private writing project with the intention of clarifying her *principes* and defining a course of self-improvement. Although Du Châtelet's *Discours* has a more formal structure, at least in its first half, both it and the *Confessions* have a distinctly practical, "how-to" approach. Like Du Châtelet, Fourqueux associates happiness with a form of sociability that does not result in dependency, and a particular concept of time as multilayered and purposive.

Happiness is Fourqueux's aim: "My primary goal is to make myself as happy as possible in all situations" (Fourqueux, 1:100–101). Or, as she writes in a later chapter, "my intent is to work on the improvement of my soul, in order to deserve being better loved" (Fourqueux, 2:130). Being cherished by friends and family is essential to Fourqueux, for whom sociability is the first element mentioned in her Chapter 2, "Resources that Can Contribute to Happiness":

> Everyone always says that one should be self-sufficient and find happiness within oneself; I cannot imagine a form of happiness enjoyed in solitude. (Fourqueux, 1:85)

Fourqueux defines happiness as "a succession of agreeable moments that continues for a long time" (Fourqueux, 1:93). Like both Du Châtelet and Dupin, she emphasizes the pleasant sensation of the moment; like Dupin, she frames duration as a succession of distinct moments. Given her stated need for other people and her self-described emotional nature (*sensibilité*), it may come as a surprise that half of the chapter is devoted to deciding on a program of reading. Goals and projects, such as the reading program, are however also key to happiness: "The present is never sufficient; we always need to extend our existence into the future" (Fourqueux, 1:100). Fourqueux's "moment," although similarly complex, is thus structurally different from Du Châtelet's present moment, "rich with the past and the future." Fourqueux's *avenir* involves not simply pleasurable anticipation, but a clear trajectory toward a specific goal. Just as she finds other people necessary to happiness, so too the present moment needs to point toward a defined future, a plan.

Throughout the *Confessions*, Fourqueux expresses regret for her lack of early education; one wonders if the "passion for studies" described in the *Discours sur le bonheur*—as well as Du Châtelet's reputation as a singularly brilliant intellectual, even decades after her death—served as a model. Du Châtelet had felt no need to detail the studies she found engrossing; by the time she began writing the *Discours*, she had already charted her course in philosophy and mathematics. Fourqueux scans the horizon of subjects, finding the sciences "too foreign" (although she thinks she might like chemistry—possibly an echo of her friendship with Geneviève d'Arconville[38]), and considers the intrinsic interest and utility of various subjects.

Fourqueux prefaces her reading program with reflections on the nature of learning itself. In order to learn, she observes, we need to choose subjects that are suited to our talents and interests, that "connect to what is already in our soul." Noting that the operation of the mind requires logical connections from one proposition to the next, she argues that *sensibilité* works via similarly connected steps: "to see, to feel, or to understand, nothing happens without successivity" (Fourqueux, 1:88–89). Given her interests, she is most attracted by the study of the knowledge of God's existence, of medicine, and of *la morale*—here in the sense of ethics. Because she prizes utility, she dismisses the first as unknowable and the second as too uncertain, settling on *la morale*, since it helps one become "objective (*juste*) toward oneself and generous toward others" (Fourqueux, 1:90).

It is worth noting that, even at this point, Fourqueux had already embarked on a program of ambitious reading and self-education. She notes that, when she was younger, the mathematician Clairaut expressed "astonishment" at

---

[38] Laurence Croq cites a 1743 police report on the (anodyne) activities in town of the two young married women (Croq, "Mme de Fourqueux," 160).

reports of her understanding of geometry; in this chapter alone, she refers to a number of readings, among them Charron's *De la sagesse* and Gilbert-Charles Le Gendre's six-volume *Traité de l'opinion* (1733), which she criticizes as superficial (*Confessions*, 1:99).[39] She also comments on Nicolas-Antoine Boulanger's *Antiquité dévoilée par ses usages*, posthumously published by the baron d'Holbach in 1766, just as Fourqueux was beginning her *Confessions*. Boulanger's work is remembered for his argument that religious practices, like superstitions, were founded on natural events and primeval terror. For Fourqueux, the book is interesting but overly tendentious, fixated on imposing a "system," as opposed to an exposition that aims at discovery ("ideas must yield to facts, not facts to ideas," Fourqueux, 1:98). She may have been developing her ideas on Boulanger for an evening at d'Holbach's salon, which she occasionally frequented in the company of her daughter and son-in-law, Trudaine de Montigny (Croq, 164).

D'Holbach himself appears in the next chapter, "Influence de la religion sur le bonheur," separated from the previous chapter by a hiatus of eight or nine years. She notes the progress that she has made on her goals and credits a religious conversion as the most important event in her personal life, ending her earlier concerns about the lack of certainty in religious truth. Her readings include the classics and the works of Saint Theresa d'Avila, but she discusses two contemporary works at length, Louis-Claude de Saint-Martin's *Des erreurs et de la verité* (1775) and d'Holbach's *Système social* (1773). Conceding d'Holbach's contention that wise legislation alone may lay the groundwork for an ordered society, she argues against his claim that religion is useless and even dangerous. For Fourqueux, since legislation and government controls cannot alone produce a love of justice or a desire to act virtuously, these feelings must have been instilled in us by God. "How else to explain the pleasure that we necessarily feel in accomplishing a good action?" (Fourqueux, 1:116–17).

Fourqueux emphasizes her sense of inner well-being ("bien-être intérieur," *Confessions*, 1:112), but her overall framework is social. Just as in her earlier discussion of different kinds of reading she recommended that novels be read as a collective activity with friends and that solitary reading, if practiced, should lead to conversation with others (Fourqueux, 1:102), here in her virtual debate with d'Holbach she describes the love of virtue as "necessary"

---

[39] For a list of works referenced in the *Confessions* and mentioned in the inventory of the Fourqueux library, see Croq, 170–72.

to individual happiness and "indispensable" to *bonheur général* (Fourqueux, 1:117). Virtue is not only a "sentiment agréable," but a social disposition; later chapters will describe the importance of "pleasing" for ethical behavior with friends, family, and others. The "désir de plaire" is not simply a "project" with a specific aim, but rather "a permanent feeling that guides our discourse and actions without our realizing it" (Fourqueux, 2:208).

Fourqueux describes the pathway to virtue as the "annihilation" of egoism (Fourqueux, 1:121), a defect that she sees as the source of tyranny, injustice, and crime. Egoism is dangerous because it is incapable of mastering the passions; it leads one into a vicious cycle of unsatisfied desire. The egoist's restless pursuit from one object to another thus offers a negative reverse image of the succession of moments that constitutes happiness. Neither state can be removed from its existence in time, but whereas the egoist's experience of time is a meaningless empty series, the happy and virtuous person's experience is of "full" moments leading forward with structure and purpose.

4.4. The Passions and Their Discontents in d'Arconville

Geneviève d'Arconville wrote on the passions and happiness throughout her life, from her early moralist texts through the essays composed in her final years. It is striking, however, that her initial engagement with the topic comes as a series of reflections on unhappiness. For d'Arconville, happiness is so foreign to our being ("étranger à notre être") that we can scarcely imagine it other than in vague terms. We have a much keener sense of the many forms of unhappiness, which is why we respond so deeply to tragic depictions in art and theater: "It is our native language." As for happiness, we know only the "A, B, C."[40] Why is it so difficult to be happy, or even to imagine happiness? As we shall see, the answer stems from d'Arconville's concept of happiness and its relation to time.

The first two editions (1760 and 1766) of *Pensées et réflexions morales* feature reflections on unhappiness ("les chagrins et le malheur"), but she would not take up the question of happiness until much later, when she added an essay, "Sur le plaisir et le bonheur," to the expanded edition included in the *Mélanges* of 1775. Two additional essays, "Sur le plaisir et le bonheur" and "Sur le chagrin et le malheur," appear in the first volume of her late essays

---

[40] Geneviève d'Arconville, "Sur les chagrins," *Pensées et réflexions morales sur divers sujets*, 1:389.

(D'Arconville, PRA 1: 136–43, 145–59), and related topics arise in other late essays. Given her Stoic and Jansenist sympathies, it comes as no surprise that she finds the passions to be antithetical to happiness. Like the other women studied here, she focuses on the ways in which temporality intersects with concepts of happiness and unhappiness. Her particular interest lies in exploring the intersection of physical and psychological states, as well as concepts of selfhood and personal autonomy.

The 1760 "Sur les chagrins," like the other chapters in the volume, consists of a series of loosely connected "thoughts" or maxims. D'Arconville's observations take up the omnipresence of human pain, our limited capacity for joy, the paradoxical relationships between pleasure and pain, and our tendency to "embody" pain ("les chagrins *s'incorporent*," D'Arconville, 1:393). One observation will recur in later writings, signaling an ongoing preoccupation: quoting Charles Pinot Duclos, "pleasure is a situation, happiness is a state," d'Arconville notes that, similarly, *le chagrin* is a "situation," or punctual event, while unhappiness, *le malheur*, is a state of being (D'Arconville, 1:393).[41] The distinction between the moment and duration distinguishes her thinking from the moralists who frame duration as a succession of moments; for d'Arconville, successivity and duration are distinct and incommensurable.

The physical, psychological, and temporal dimensions of happiness and unhappiness are woven throughout the 1764 treatise *Des Passions*. A sequel to her 1760 *De l'amitié*, *Des passions* is dedicated to a close friend, possibly her brother-in-law François Thiroux d'Épersenne, and begins by indicating a very different approach to its subject from the previous treatise. Observing that virtuous friendship is the pathway to happiness, she makes it clear that the "wild delirium" of the passions will lead in the opposite direction. "Every excessive sentiment is a passion, however respectable its origin may be, because reason, the only principle worthy of governing us, does not allow excess." D'Arconville takes her epigraph from Seneca's *De ira*:

---

[41] The quotation is from Charles Pinot Duclos's *Mémoires pour servir à l'histoire des moeurs du XVIIIe siècle* (1751), a novel—the title notwithstanding—written as a follow-up to his highly successful moralist treatise, *Considérations sur les moeurs de ce siècle*. D'Arconville would have been struck by the episode in which the line occurs, a scene between the libertine hero and a woman with whom he has had a brief affair, who rejects him because he refuses to accept her Platonic friendship with another man; the woman's reflections on love and friendship are very close to d'Arconville's own. D'Arconville is evidently quoting from memory; the exact sentence is "Le plaisir n'est qu'une situation, le bonheur est un état." Duclos, *Mémoires pour servir à l'histoire des moeurs du XVIIIe siècle*, ed. Henri Coulet (Paris: Desjonquères, 1986), 77–78.

Aristotle says that some passions, if used well, serve as weapons. And this would be true if, like the arms of war, they could be taken up and put off at the judgment of the one who dons them.[42]

Once we have stepped outside the governance of reason, the natural order imposed by our creator, "we no longer deserve to be happy" (D'Arconville, 2:199). Like Seneca, d'Arconville emphasizes that there is no legitimate use of the passions, however "respectable." Reason alone should guide us; the passions are "double-edged" and cannot be trusted.

For d'Arconville, there are only two passions: love and ambition. Throughout the treatise, she describes the passions as tyrannical forces to which people submit themselves willingly out of a sense of "their insufficiency of being" (D'Arconville, 2:201). She appears to give two different accounts of virtuous action, emphasizing choice and volition in her discussions of friendship, but a naturalistic Stoic understanding of agency as alignment with the natural order in *Des Passions* (Shapiro, "L'Amour, L'Ambition, L'Amitié, 186–90). As the epigraph from Seneca suggests, d'Arconville inclines to the Stoic ideal: to be governed by reason, free of the "excessive" passions. After a brief introduction, the treatise consists of two long chapters, one on love, the other on ambition. In the introduction, she explains that both passions have two dimensions, physical and psychological, *le physique et le moral*, which generally correspond to the life stages of youth and maturity, but vary according to individual temperaments. There is no innate difference between the sexes, whose vastly different experiences are the result of education and socialization (2:223). The physical dimension is most obvious in the passion of love, but its psychological intensity lifts it above a simple "need" and creates its dangerous force. Each chapter is organized as a series of examples drawn from literature and history that demonstrate the danger of the passions in increasing order of destructive intensity.

Memory is one of two key elements in the temporality of the passions. It is "the source of all the passions, especially of love" (D'Arconville, 2:210). The memory of a pleasant experience enhances desire and stimulates the imagination, so that "the conflagration spreads" (D'Arconville, 2:211). Imagination is the counterpart to memory. While memory enflames passion by returning to the past, imagination exacerbates the situation by projecting us into the

---

[42] Seneca, "On Anger" (1.17.1), in *Anger, Mercy, Revenge*, trans. Robert A. Kaster and Martha Nussbaum (Chicago: University of Chicago Press, 2010), 29.

future: both lead us to repeat scenes in our mind, drawing us into an endless spiral of desire from which there is no escape. Imagination is doubly dangerous because it leads us to fixate on something that never happened, a fiction. Both memory and imagination remove us from the present moment and render us incapable of being present to ourselves. In an apostrophe to imagination, d'Arconville claims that through its effect, "the present is nothing to us; it escapes us without our having appreciated it; transported into the future, we live only for illusions" (D'Arconville, 2:257–58). Even more than love, ambition carries one away from the present: the ambitious person "lives only in the future; the present is merely a passage leading to the glory that he expects" (D'Arconville, 2:296). She argues, especially in the case of love, that the working classes are less susceptible to the passions, and hence have happier marriages, because they do not spend their time in "indolence and inaction" that foment dangerous erotic revery among the elites (D'Arconville, 2:236). The sense of time is however a human attribute; animals experience "momentary desire that leaves no trace of the object that excites it" (D'Arconville, 2:209–10)—a description that echoes Rousseau's account of sexual encounters in the state of nature where, similarly, a sense of time does not exist.

Memory and imagination are, of course, two of the three branches of the "système figuré" of knowledge in the *Encyclopédie*—an echo of Bacon's tree of knowledge and a distant echo of the Augustinian trinity of Memory, Understanding, and Will—where imagination takes the place of will, becoming the encyclopedic site for poetry and the visual arts. In d'Arconville's psychology, memory (past) and imagination (future) must be held in check by reason, the present. The key to mental health, reason makes possible the virtue of the Stoic sage, who lives "without regrets for the past, untroubled by the future" (D'Arconville, 2:294). The evacuation of the present, whether by an imaginative leap toward an illusory future or a useless rehearsal of the past, represents the subjugation of reason by the passions.

Freedom and subjugation are the terms of the dialectic determining the degree of moral danger in the various scenarios and examples. Following the pattern of progressive destructiveness, ambition follows love as the passion with direst consequences. For d'Arconville, ambition, the "insatiable desire to govern" (D'Arconville, 2:298) is despotic by definition.[43] As we shall see in the

---

[43] As Lisa Shapiro points out, d'Arconville concedes that love and ambition were instilled in us by the Creator suggesting a potential positive role for ambition via collaboration and emulation

chapter on marriage, liberty is the highest good for d'Arconville. Ambition as she defines it is therefore antithetical to liberty and to happiness. "A sage was never a conqueror, because a sage is always happy and finds within himself all the advantages that he would seek in vain through the pursuit of grandeur" (D'Arconville, 2:308–309). Tellingly, in her series of historical examples of the evils of ambition, Richelieu is placed in the final culminating position, following Cromwell, whom d'Arconville blames for the death of Charles I. How is Richelieu's crime greater than regicide?[44] Placing Richelieu last indicates that the worst crime is not to kill one's king (*mal physique*), but to dominate him in order to serve one's own will to power (*mal moral*).

For d'Arconville, the loss of liberty, physical or (especially) psychological, represents the worst that can befall one; the usurpation of another's liberty, the worst crime. How can either fate be avoided—how do we master the passions? She offers no easy answer to the question. The closing invocation to virtue describes it as a supernatural force, a "celestial emanation" that rescues humans from being "slaves of themselves" (D'Arconville, 2:387). While she offers no specific set of rules or techniques to achieve the state, she does provide a counterexample to passionate beings dispossessed by memory and imagination: the self-possessed individual whose attention is grounded in the present.

Des Passions is d'Arconville's most extensive reflection on the passions and (un)happiness, but she would continue to develop her ideas, first in the essay "Sur le plaisir et le bonheur" included in the 1775 *Mélanges* edition of *Pensées et réflexions morales*, and later in the essays written in her final years. She made many changes, both stylistic and substantive, to the works that she included in her *Mélanges*; the addition of a new chapter to *Pensées et réflexions morales* is one of the most significant. Between the original editions of the *Pensées* and the *Mélanges* she had matured as a thinker and writer, having produced the two moralist treatises of the 1760s, her scientific work, and two novels. "Sur le plaisir et le bonheur" is a fully realized essay, setting it apart from the chapters of loosely connected "thoughts and reflections."

Just as she had earlier emphasized the incommensurability of "situation" and "state," here d'Arconville declares that pleasure is not on a continuum

---

(Shapiro, "L'Amour, l'ambition, l'amitié," 183). It seems clear, however, that this potential is never realized, through what might be seen as d'Arconville's equivalent of the Fall.

[44] Writing *Des passions* twenty-five years before the French Revolution, d'Arconville believes the French to be incapable of such excesses (2:353–54).

with happiness and indeed is totally unrelated to it. Evincing her continued interest in the intersection of physical and mental phenomena, d'Arconville notes that pleasure may arise either in the senses or the imagination, but is always experienced in the senses. She thus differs from Levesque de Pouilly, for whom true *sentiments agréables* are mental.[45] An intense sensation, pleasure both surprises and moves us and "tears us away from ourselves, carries us with ardor, and fixes us on the object that pleases us" (D'Arconville, 1:467–68). Pleasure's action, "tearing us away from ourselves," is reminiscent of the action of the passions, but d'Arconville does not denounce pleasure as innately harmful. Although it is quickly sated and fades quickly, hence unable to produce happiness, pleasure is nevertheless "un bienfait du Créateur" for which we should always be grateful; it leads to unhappiness only when we do not put it to good use (D'Arconville, 1:465–66). Pleasure should be appreciated like the view of a beautiful landscape that a traveler encounters en route, a refreshing moment that gives one the energy to continue one's course.

But whereas pleasure is universally understood and sought after, happiness is virtually unknown. Happiness supposes perfection, which only God can know. As d'Arconville claimed in "Des chagrins et du malheur," we have only a confused notion of what happiness might be. To those who might conclude that, happiness being impossible, we should abandon its pursuit and devote ourselves entirely to pleasure, she responds with a pair of analogies. First, she points out that the fact that we do not have the vision of a lynx does not lead us to close our eyes; and more pointedly, the fact that we are unable to comprehend all the marvels of the universe does not deter us from striving to make progress in the sciences—an analogy of profound importance to d'Arconville, a woman of science.

> I therefore conclude that, despite the impossibility of attaining an impassive state, happiness, to the extent that our weak nature is capable of it, merits that we devote all our abilities to discovering the surest methods for arriving at it. (D'Arconville, 1:460).

---

[45] D'Arconville notes that she does not discuss purely physical pleasures—"Personne ne les ignore"—observing wryly—and echoing La Rochefoucauld—that the taboo on speaking of physical pleasure is at odds with people's actual behavior: "C'est un hommage que le vice rend à la vertu" (D'Arconville, 1:468–69).

Happiness is "impassive," nonpassionate, a constant state not of bliss but of the Horatian "happy medium" (*heureuse médiocrité*). Happiness is like clear daylight, while pleasure dazzles the eye (D'Arconville, 1:463). Both the ideal of happiness and the reality of pleasure are necessary for our well-being. In the conclusion to the essay, she returns to the image of a beautiful landscape. She points out that our ability to perceive the landscape as beautiful relies on the imagination; otherwise, we would look out on "a bizarre assemblage of heterogeneous objects" (D'Arconville, 1:483). Imagination produces the relations and associations that constitute beauty, just as sorrow (*le chagrin*) changes everything to drab ugliness. Despite imagination's dangerous role in inflaming the passions, it like pleasure has its positive potential and proper use.

The power of imagination and its effect on perception remain key points in d'Arconville's late essays. Several of their titles echo those of her earlier pieces, but her thinking has evolved. "Sur le plaisir et le bonheur" and "Sur le chagrin et le malheur" appear in the first volume of the *Pensées, réflexions et anecdotes*, composed in 1801 (D'Arconville, PRA 1:136–43, 145–53). At this stage of her life, d'Arconville finds that, just as no two leaves are exactly the same, so no two human beings, given the endless variety in physical and emotional make-up, will have exactly the same experience of pleasure.[46] Like Du Châtelet, she finds that illusion is a necessary element of pleasure, since without it, "life would be very monotonous" (D'Arconville, "Sur l'illusion," PRA 1:309–27). Her skepticism regarding the possibility of happiness, however, is deeper than before. Recalling the passage in Duclos that had caught her attention forty years earlier,[47] she now doubts that a "state" of happiness could ever exist, since even if we were to achieve happiness, we would inevitably be anxious about losing it, and hence unable to maintain it. Happiness is thus only an ideal figment, "un être de raison," (D'Arconville, PRA 1:142–43). Unhappiness, however, often becomes a permanent state. Beyond the "supernatural courage" offered by religion, she wonders why people continue to want to live (D'Arconville, PRA 1:152–53).

Numerous passages in the PRA reflect the dark moods that affected d'Arconville in her final years, but she also has many occasions to speak of her pleasures—if not happiness. The pleasures of friendship and the reminiscence of times past console her for her poor eyesight and infirmities. "Thinking and

---

[46] She returns to the idea of infinite human variety, with the same analogy of leaves, in "Sur les caractères" in one of the last volumes of the PRA (PRA 11:260–83).

[47] See note 41 above.

feeling" characterize her in old age as in her youth (D'Arconville, PRA 6:10); the urge to write, "le désir de *faire*," carries her forward. In "Sur les projets," she reflects that it is absurd, at her age, to plan more than a week in advance, yet paraphrases an old saying—

> If it is true, "One dies when one no longer loves," then it is just as true that one dies when one no longer makes plans. (D'Arconville, PRA 6:368)

In one of the last essays in the final volume of the PRA—volume 7, evidently misnumbered by another hand[48]—she reflects on her good fortune in having had loving friends: "few people have enjoyed the happiness of being loved with as much tenderness and constancy as I have been" (D'Arconville, "Mes souvenirs," PRA 7: 346–47). Having abandoned the idea of an enduring state of happiness, d'Arconville comes to terms with the idea that such pleasurable moments might suffice.

4.5. Staël's Phenomenology of Passion

Staël's 1796 *De l'influence des passions sur le bonheur des individus et des nations* has an analytical goal, to study the passions' role in both private and public life, and a therapeutic goal, to show how their damage may be healed or at least mitigated. Ostensibly aimed at "passionate souls" who seek to free themselves from the passions in search of happiness, she acknowledges that the "agitated souls" who read her will have recognized in her a fellow traveler, and that "it is I whom I wished to persuade" (Staël, *De l'influence*, 293). Like the other thinkers examined in this chapter, she is deeply concerned about the passions' corrosive effect on individual autonomy, the dangers of dependency in interpersonal relationships, and the individual's sense of self in time. She shares with others, in particular d'Arconville, the conviction that the passions are detrimental to our well-being; yet she echoes Du Châtelet in her affinity for the enhanced sense of existence that they afford. Throughout, despite the plan announced in the book's introduction to treat the political

---

[48] Both internal and physical evidence—a reference to "thirteen volumes" (PRA 7:335) and traces of modifications to the title page—indicate that "volume 7" was originally the thirteenth and last volume. It is probable that the original volume 7 was lost as the set changed hands during the nineteenth century, and a bookseller renumbered the thirteenth volume in order to give the appearance of a complete set of twelve.

arena in a separate volume, the political dimension is never far removed from the question of the individual.[49]

Staël defines the passions as fundamentally antithetical to personal autonomy: "that impulsive force that pulls people along independently of their will" (Staël, *De l'influence*, 136). It is the loss of autonomy that constitutes the "obstacle to happiness," implying an equation between autonomy and happiness. The closest that she comes to giving an explicit definition of happiness is, however, curiously indirect:

> Happiness, as we wish for it, is the union of opposites: for individuals, hope without fear, activity without disquiet, fame (*gloire*) without calumny, love without infidelity, imagination that embellishes what we possess, and darkens the memory of what we have lost; indeed, the reverse of the natural moral order, and the best of every state, every talent, every pleasure, separated from what accompanies them. . . . Happiness so conceived is completely impossible; happiness, such as it is obtainable, can only be acquired through the study of the surest means of avoiding great pain. This book seeks to provide that study. (Staël, *De l'influence*, 138)

These pairs function differently. Some focus on interior states, while others reflect relations with other people; the role of the imagination resembles the traditional injunction to appreciate that which is within one's means, rather than yearning for what we have not—a scenario complicated both by the reference to loss and to the idea that it is the imagination, hence a kind of fiction, that keeps us content with our lot. Staël draws a distinction between happiness as we imagine it, the impossible reunion of opposites, and happiness as it is actually possible, which is simply the avoidance of pain. To this lesser form of happiness her book proposes itself as a guide: as she tells us at the end of the introduction, "to combat unhappiness" is her only goal (Staël, *De l'influence*, 158). If we recall that the passions, defined as the loss of autonomy, constitute the chief obstacle to happiness, then it follows that the goal is to reestablish one's autonomy and thereby attain the only "possible" form of happiness.

Staël will say of love, that many people believe themselves to have been in love, but most of them are mistaken (Staël, *De l'influence*, 196); so too it

---

[49] On *De l'influence des passions* in the context of the development of Staël's political thought, see Biancamaria Fontana, *Germaine de Staël: A Political Portrait* (Princeton: Princeton University Press, 2016), esp. 132–57.

appears, as in d'Arconville, that our understanding of happiness is unclear, or, at best, understood through paradox and *via negativa*. She goes further than d'Arconville, however, in making a similar claim about our understanding of unhappiness. For Staël, no tragedies or works of the imagination can prepare us for the deep unhappiness that inevitably comes with the experience of life (Staël, *De l'influence*, 266). In an extended passage, she describes psychic pain as a self-undermining cycle of alienation: "one flees one's feelings, and this effort agitates one even more" (Staël, *De l'influence*, 267). The goal of her work will be to remedy this state, rather than providing a roadmap leading to happiness as such.

Staël's taxonomy of the passions departs from the tradition as well as from more recent schemes by Vauvenargues, Helvétius, and d'Holbach, or the extended list of passions discussed in the *Encyclopédie*. Her enumeration is less idiosyncratic than the others, as it consists of the ways in which we cede our autonomy to others, arranged in order of decreasing moral worth. Thus, the initial passion discussed, "De l'amour de la gloire," is a noble passion; subsequent passions are increasingly petty, sordid, and ultimately criminal.

Each passion displays a variation on the theme of self-dispossession. Glory is a form of renown that can only be acquired by extraordinary virtue, service to others, or genius; the ability to "exist beyond oneself" is "intoxicating" (Staël, *De l'influence*, 159). Few attain it. (Lesser souls, she will explain in subsequent chapters, are motivated by ambition and vanity.) As admirable as the desire for glory may be, it is not a pathway to happiness. Even the most disinterested public servants and benefactors of humanity—Staël has her father, Jacques Necker, in mind—must rely on others and on the hazard of circumstances to accomplish their goals. Ultimately, the will to glory is, as Émilie Du Châtelet also observed, a projection into the future, both for the realization of one's hopes and projects, and for the judgment of posterity: "This passion knows only the future, possesses only hope" (Staël, *De l'influence*, 168). Subsequent chapters examine how dispossession occurs even when the object of one's love is not another human being, but oneself. In the petty "egotistical passions" (gambling, avarice, libertinism, drunkenness), what appear to be actions taken in order to satisfy one's appetites—hence, presumably, to produce enjoyment—simply represent one's servitude to personal desire and effort to escape "the painful sensation of living" (Staël, *De l'influence*, 212).

Love is the seeming anomaly in the order of the passions' decreasing attractiveness. In her preamble to the chapter on love, Staël reminds the reader that she is not discussing ordinary affections, but rather love's extreme form that "always leads to melancholy" (Staël, *De l'influence*, 196). Thus, although it may give rise to noble impulses, love has its place amid the others because it gives rise to extreme forms of dependency in which one's only sources of pleasure reside outside the self (Staël, *De l'influence*, 201). Although love produces joy, its pain is inevitably greater.

Staël's proposed therapeutic interventions fall into two categories, the most effective being what she terms our "inner resources": a "philosophical" outlook, study, and *bienfaisance* ("charity" in the broadest possible sense—doing good for good's sake). Before taking these up, she considers the support to be gained from "intermediary sentiments," which are similar to inner resources, but also resemble the passions in that they require reliance on something or someone outside ourselves. These are friendship, family relations, and religion.

As we saw in the previous chapter, Staël praises friendship, but finds it difficult in practice. It is not a passion, because it does not inhibit personal agency as such, but its realization nevertheless depends on other people, since friendship expects reciprocity (Staël, *De l'influence*, 243). Ultimately, even the most disinterested friendship is shaped by hope, *espoir*, for a return. Staël urges inherently sensitive being to love for the sake of loving, without regard for whether or not their feelings or good actions are reciprocated, but she recognizes that the most devoted friendship cannot remain perpetually one-sided and "the only inexhaustible treasure is one's own heart" (Staël, *De l'influence*, 248). The problem is exacerbated in relations between parents and children and between spouses: the "imperious need for reciprocity" puts an end to inner peace (Staël, *De l'influence*, 250). And because "the heart seeks equality," these inherently unequal relationships give rise to stress. To the extent that affection exists in conjugal relationships, it takes the form of either love or friendship—the problems with both of which Staël has demonstrated in her previous chapters. Peace in marriage requires self-mastery ("empire sur soi-même") strength, and sacrifice (Staël, *De l'influence*, 254).[50] As for religion, although Staël recognizes that many people find consolation in religion, she notes that it too relies on forces outside our control, as we cannot persuade ourselves to have religious faith: we either have it, or we do not. Even looking at religion in its best manifestations and discounting intolerance,

---

[50] As we will see in the next chapter, d'Arconville offers a similar assessment of the prospects of happiness in marriage, both in her treatise *De l'amitié* (1760) and in her late essay "Sur le mariage," written in 1801 (PRA 1:25–53).

superstition, and fanaticism, belief remains "absolutely independent of our will" (Staël, *De l'influence*, 264). The "intermediary" resources, like the passions, thus inhibit individual agency through a reliance on forces beyond oneself. Temporal dislocation parallels the externalization of one's will, as both passions and intermediary resources draw one away from the present, beyond oneself, toward a hoped-for future. For example, although the hope (*espérance*) provided by religion is comforting to many, it offers the future "at the cost of the present" (Staël, *De l'influence*, 257).

Before undertaking the discussion of inner resources that can help tame the passions, Staël makes a distinction between a focus on "inner resources" and egoism. She defines egoism—which we have also seen condemned by Fourqueux and d'Arconville—as a kind of passion, a disposition independent of our will. One can choose to seek knowledge and wisdom, but one cannot force oneself to enjoy them ("se donner un goût") any more than one can acquire belief through an act of will. Passionate people are not egoists, because they seek happiness outside of themselves; the egoist's pursuit of self is a form of self-alienation.

Remaining firmly grounded in one's present and in command of one's will are the goals of the "inner resources," which we might liken to what Foucault called the Stoic "technologies of the self." The first of these, philosophy, refers not to a specific school of thought or even the discipline of philosophy as a whole, but rather to an attitude toward life.[51] "One must set oneself above oneself in order to master oneself; above others, so as not to expect anything from them" (Staël, *De l'influence*, 269). The philosophical stance enables us to see the world differently. Under the domination of the passions, we are only able to see things from one perspective, that of our passion; liberation from passion enables us to perceive multiple aspects of a given object or situation (Staël, *De l'influence*, 270). Staël is careful to distinguish between philosophy and a lack of feeling (*insensibilité*). The lack of sensibility is a basic character trait (in other words, requiring no effort to attain), whereas the philosophical stance is achieved only with effort, determination, and strength of character; hence the two are quite different. She emphasizes the need for inner distance: "Through a form of abstraction, which provides nevertheless real enjoyment, one attains

---

[51] We should note that in 1796, one of the chief connotations of the word *philosophie* was the ideas of the Enlightenment, giving the term loaded ideological significance in backlash of the post-Revolutionary context, when the *philosophes* were blamed in certain quarters for revolutionary violence. As Staël's editors note, Staël would offer a multifaceted definition of the word in *De la littérature* (1810), written after her encounter with Kantian thought (*De l'influence des passions*, 269 n.222).

some distance from oneself to observe one's thoughts and actions" (Staël, *De l'influence*, 272). Staël thus makes a significant distinction between the self-alienation of the passionate individual and the "philosophical" ability to examine one's thoughts and actions critically. This contemplation is entirely different from the self-involvement of the egoist or "l'homme personnel,"[52] who is in constant need of others and sensitive to slights.

Staël has to a certain extent demonstrated this ability to distance herself from her own feelings and history throughout the writing of *De l'influence des passions*. She acknowledges that although the initial chapters on the passions are based on her study of history and her observations of the world, the chapter on love comes from "my impressions alone" (Staël, *De l'influence*, 198). At the beginning of the chapter on friendship, she expresses surprise at herself for writing so calmly on matters that are close to her heart. That she is able to pursue the analysis is due to "a philosophical turn of mind" that enables her to "judge herself like a stranger" (Staël, *De l'influence*, 242).

Philosophy aside, she notes that it is difficult ("il m'en a coûté") to declare that passionate love does not bring true happiness (Staël, *De l'influence*, 282); she observes that the last of the inner resources, "goodness" or "charity" (*bonté, bienfaisance*), provides the emotional outlet of love and friendship ("les véritables jouissances du sentiment," Staël, *De l'influence*, 283), without the dissatisfaction and pain caused by the need for reciprocity. While philosophy requires strength of character and study demands intellectual application of which not all people are capable, the practice of goodness is universally available. Staël sees *bonté* as "une vertu primitive" that springs forth spontaneously; although it manifests itself differently in individuals and in different contexts, it is innate within all (Staël, *De l'influence*, 282–83). Combined with its emotional benefits, "filling the heart just as study fills the mind" (Staël, *De l'influence*, 285), *bonté* is the best and truest antidote to passion.

In its innateness and spontaneity, Staël's *bonté* resembles Rousseau's notion of pity. While acknowledging Rousseau, she distinguishes her own concept of pity from his in her conclusion. Like Rousseau, Staël sees pity as natural and involuntary, but she does not see it as reducible to biology.[53] Pity, in Staël's view, springs from our intimate knowledge and memory of ourselves,

---

[52] A late eighteenth-century dictionary defines "personnel" as a synonym of *égoïste*, noting that it is a new word and "assez à la mode" (*Dictionnaire critique de la langue française*, 1787). Fourqueux uses it as well: "la personnalité est la base de tous les vices" (Confessions, 2:210).

[53] On Staël and Rousseau's views of pity, see Nanette Le Coat, "The Virtuous Passion: The Politics of Pity in Staël's *The Influence of the Passions*," in Cuillé and Szmurlo, *Staël's Philosophy of the Passions*, 39–55.

elusive feelings that cannot be precisely articulated ("thought, or something even more elusive" Staël, *De l'influence*, 294). In an extended footnote, she further distinguishes her concept from Adam Smith's account of sympathy, the ability to place ourselves in another's situation. For Staël—as for Sophie de Grouchy, who makes a similar critique in her *Lettres sur la sympathie*—Smith's definition is constructed uniquely on the representation of the spectacle of another's pain and fails to explain how the spontaneous impulse of pity or sympathy arises in us, outside of the framework of representability.[54]

Throughout *De l'influence des passions*, Staël is at pains to distinguish between phenomena that resemble one another but need to be understood as distinct. Thus, as we have seen, the "work on oneself" ("travail sur soi"), the ability and willingness to take stock of oneself and to examine one's actions "like a stranger" is not the same as egoism, an entirely different form of self-involvement that, like the passions, vitiates the will and leaves one dependent on the opinion of others. Another important distinction is between the philosophical ability to observe oneself and the self-alienation caused by passion; the former represents self-possession, while the latter is dispossession; one produces clarity and understanding, while the other represents confusion and an inability to see oneself independently of the object of one's passion. The inner resources aim to replicate the positive aspects of passion while eliminating the need for external validation that leads to unhappiness. Thus, one may hold public office, the goal of ambition, as long as one responds to one's conscience alone, hence avoiding the pitfalls of ambition; one may embark on a literary career, as long as one finds satisfaction in being able to express oneself and to be useful, rather than expecting popular success; one may find pleasure in having made others happy, as long as one does not expect them to express gratitude (Staël, *De l'influence*, 288–89).

Finally, there is the question of time. As we have seen, the passions evacuate all meaning from the present by attaching themselves to the past or the future, either "an object that one has lost, or another that one strives vainly to acquire." The ideal, as she describes it, is analogous to a child's experience of time. As Staël sees it, it is not the case that children have no memory of the past or expectation of the future; rather, by experiencing their lives "drop by drop," they are fully engaged in the present without being distracted by the

---

[54] I discuss de Grouchy's response to Smith in "The French Theater of Sympathy," in Eric Schliesser, ed., *Sympathy: A History* (Oxford: Oxford University Press, 2015), 199–207. For the larger political ramifications of de Grouchy's response to Smith, see Eric Schliesser, "Sophie de Grouchy, Adam Smith, and the Politics of Sympathy," in O'Neill and Lascano, *Feminist History of Philosophy*, 193–219.

other two "times of existence." That engagement enables them to receive the full range of "fleeting thoughts" and "nuanced feelings" that vanish with the onset of passion and its narrow, exclusionary focus (Staël, De l'influence, 288–89).[55] It is worth noting that this ideal experience of the moment includes "sentiments passionnés"—deep feelings, distinct from passion itself. Passion, for Staël, robs us of this multilayered dimension of experience by filtering out everything that does not relate to itself.

This deeper mode of existence can help us understand the distinction between passion's intensity and a fully realized experience. Staël acknowledges that the passions inspire heroic actions and major discoveries and that they provoke an alluring sense of immensity: "there is something grand in passion" (Staël, De l'influence, 154). The passions are "humanity's leap toward a different destiny" (Staël, De l'influence, 288). Far from enhancing life, however, this "different destiny" creates "emptiness" that "tears apart" the present. Having written her book in order to regain control of her own passionate nature, Staël's admission in the end that she is not sure that she has entirely succeeded in her goal (293) might suggest that her efforts to cultivate her inner resources have left her caught in a passionate impulse and unable to realize her projected, future self.

In an earlier similar occasion, however, she had been able to call a future self into the present in a positive, affirmative way. At the end of the preface to her first major work, the 1788 Lettres sur Rousseau, the young Germaine Necker wonders if those who have sensed some future talent in her might feel that she has rushed into a subject that is still beyond her capabilities. She brushes aside the concern: "Who dares anticipate the progress of their mind? How could one agree to wait for oneself, postponing to an uncertain future the expression of an urgent feeling?"[56] In this proleptic moment, she refuses to "wait for herself" and seizes the future for the present. Analogously, despite the doubts evinced in the conclusion to De l'influence des passions that she has achieved her "philosophical self," by the act of writing, she has in fact performed that self, called it into being in the very act of doubting it. This is an affirmative "leap into a different destiny": an experience of the sublime

---

[55] Staël's "fleeting thoughts" echo the constructs of consciousness as shaped by "pensées imperceptibles" (Nicole), "petites perceptions" (Leibniz), "representations obscures" (Du Châtelet), or "idées fugitives" (Necker), which similarly evoke experience as a range of thoughts and perceptions that do not all rise to the level of conscious attention. (See Chapter 2 above 32, 67)

[56] Staël, Lettres sur les écrits et le caractère de J.-J. Rousseau, in Oeuvres completes, 1.1:38.

rooted in an enhanced apprehension of present, rather than an impoverished passionate intensity.

Staël's "future" self is a personal *Lumières à-venir*, already at work in the present. As she says in the chapter on the value of study, the pleasure of creation provides "true enjoyment in the sensation of one's self" (Staël, *De l'influence*, 277), while the examination of the broad scale of human history enables one to overcome self-absorption. Her concluding discussion of pity, a disposition that enables one to accept both others and oneself ("supporter et les autres et soi-même," Staël, *De l'influence*, 294), becomes the means to bring together the personal and the political, with a call for an end to post-Revolutionary divisions and healing in the body politic. Although *De l'influence des passions* begins with the modest goal of "avoiding pain" rather than guaranteeing happiness, the final prospect is more encouraging. The "system of perfectibility" that she would develop a few years later in *De la littérature* (1800) incorporates this forward movement into a larger narrative of historical progress.

* * *

In articulating a philosophy of happiness, seventeenth- and eighteenth-century women thinkers typically draw on Stoic and Epicurean traditions of *ataraxia* and the pleasures of studious retreat.[57] The passions, in any configuration, are seen in opposition to the happy medium, "l'heureuse médiocrité," of repose and hence antithetical to happiness. These elements are figured differently for different writers. For Marguerite de La Sablière, the passions are part of a more generalized "tumult of the world," the exteriorizing forces that distract one from confronting one's own truths and the truths of the human condition, much like Pascal's *divertissement*. But although she goes further than the others in recommending retreat from the world, La Sablière stops short of calling for an absolute retreat, instead holding out the possibility of a *refus intramondain du monde*. Even those who extol the pleasures of social life, such as Louise Dupin and Marie-Louise de Fourqueux, speak to the need for balance in social relations and the importance of cultivating intellectual pleasures; the latter especially offer a significant source of well-being for Émilie Du Châtelet, Geneviève d'Arconville, and Germaine de Staël. It is worth underscoring that Du Châtelet, who speaks the most vividly of the

---

[57] Rotraud von Kulesa, "La Philosophie du bonheur au féminin: La Philosophie morale entre stoïcisme et épicurisme," in Vanoflen, *Femmes et philosophie*, 69–77.

importance of *goûts et passions*, refers to **satisfied** pleasures and passions; among her "special skills" are techniques for determining whether a given desire is worth the risk, and she recommends quitting a situation or relationship conclusively when pain outweighs pleasure. The eighteenth-century figures reflect the evolving definition of "pleasure" and its rehabilitation as compatible with virtue, just as "passion" shifts from being understood as a force acting on the self to a feeling arising within and even revelatory of the self. For Du Châtelet and Staël, passion is ambiguous: pleasurable and lending an enhanced sense of existence, but also destabilizing and dangerous, requiring careful controls and interventions.

Ultimately, what is at stake for all these thinkers is self-possession as foundational to happiness. Self-possession is not solitude; even the greatest proponent of scholarly retreat, d'Arconville, believes that solitude leads to unhealthy thoughts and melancholy.[58] In this respect, women have a distinctly different perspective from contemporary male moralists who write on happiness, such as Levesque de Pouilly, Vauvenargues, Helvétius, or d'Holbach, for whom the question of autonomy does not arise. As we shall see in subsequent chapters, the issue arises for women in other contexts, notably that of marriage, but elsewhere as well.

In a striking and potentially far-reaching departure from the tradition, the reflection on happiness becomes a pathway into a reflection on time and temporality. Others, of course, had written on anticipation and especially regret as harmful. For Levesque de Pouilly, "regret for the past, sorrow for the present, worry for the future are the scourges that most afflict humanity" (Pouilly, 157). For Pouilly, however, these are simply causes of unhappiness, not forces that fundamentally undermine the sense of self, nor does he explore the notion of successivity in experience beyond claiming that variety contributes to *sentiments agréables* (Pouilly, 149). Momentariness and duration are merely aspects of particular events (Pouilly, 145), not constitutive of perception.

Other writers evoke happiness as a "state" of plenitude or *repos*,[59] as exemplified in Diderot's article "Délicieux" and Rousseau's *Rêveries d'un promeneur solitaire*.[60] They do not however probe the temporal complexity

---

[58] See d'Arconville, "Sur la solitude" (PRA 1: 300–309); Huguette Krief examines multiple models of retreat, as distinct from solitude, in "Retraite féminine et femmes moralistes au siècle des Lumières," *Dix-huitième siècle* 48 (2016): 89–101.

[59] Mauzi, *L'Idée du bonheur*, 125–35.

[60] Diderot imagines a state in which "time has ceased to flow, because he existed entirely within himself" (*Encyclopédie* 4:784). In the Fifth Promenade, Rousseau defines happiness as a state of perfect repose independent of past or future, but he doubts that it is truly obtainable: "In this

of happiness as we have seen in the women studied here. If duration is understood as a condition of happiness—since without duration, happiness would be reduced to the status of momentary pleasure—then one must find a way to describe duration. For Dupin, happiness is "une suite de différents plaisirs," a succession of events, but it is also "calm," which appears to be at odds with variety. She reconciles the dichotomy by distinguishing between the displacement wrought by the passions and the ability to remain grounded in a changing present. Du Châtelet and Staël similarly figure self-dispossession in terms of temporal displacement. Du Châtelet resolves the problem by advancing a conception of the present "riche du passé et de l'avenir" that is not the same as useless regret or anticipation; Staël posits a multilayered experience of the present that avoids the narrow focus imposed by passion. Like Dupin, Fourqueux sees happiness as a lasting succession of "moments agréables"; her pleasurable present time is structured by a trajectory to a defined future: a project, a purpose. As we have seen, d'Arconville similarly values projects throughout her long life. Like Du Châtelet, d'Arconville considers the idea of the future success of one's work to be a salutary illusion. Unlike the others, however, she argues that happiness is a "state" rather than a succession of events, and as such is neither imaginable nor possible.

For the women in this chapter, what is at stake is not simply a "feeling" that may come or go, but a sense of self. The central question of happiness and its relation to the passions is one of autonomy versus dependency. By framing the issue in terms of temporality, they focus the question on their sense of being in the world.

---

world we have but momentary pleasure; I doubt that anyone has known lasting happiness." Jean-Jacques Rousseau, *Rêveries du promeneur solitaire*, in *Oeuvres complètes*, ed. B. Gagnebin, 5 vols. (Paris: Gallimard, 1959), 1:1046–47.

5
On Marriage

Classical moralist thought, whether ancient or modern, has remarkably little to say about marriage. Philosophers, theologians, and legal theorists, on the other hand, have long studied its institutional and moral foundations. For Aristotle, marriage functioned as one of the building blocks of the state; while he and other philosophers would refer to spousal affection as an important component of marriage, they ultimately agreed that husbands retained authority over their wives. This view carried over through the Church fathers, who furthermore emphasized marriage as the only legitimate context for sexuality, and procreation as sexuality's only legitimate aim. Although divorce was recognized to a certain extent in Protestant countries, the Council of Trent's declaration of marriage as a sacrament meant that in Catholic countries marriage would be regarded as indissoluble, with narrowly defined exceptions for annulment or legal separation. These were expensive procedures, hence available only to the elites, and their application was typically biased in favor of men.[1] Early liberalism's ideas on equality and natural rights showed fault lines and cracks when women and the foundations of marriage came into the picture.[2] Some of the best-known feminist critiques of marriage—one thinks of those by Mary Astell and Mary Wollstonecraft—engage the question on the terrain of political and legal theory, and such responses gained traction in France as well from both men and women. As we shall see, however, moralist writing took a different approach.

Given the significance of marriage in daily life for all social classes, its role in cementing political and economic alliances, and its structural and legal implications for property law and inheritance, it is conspicuous by its absence among (male) moralists. Montaigne describes a good marriage as "representing" the conditions of friendship—as analogous to friendship, in other words, but not quite the same. He tells us that one marries not for

---

[1] For an overview, see Margaret R. Hunt, *Women in Eighteenth-Century Europe* (Edinburgh: Longman, 2010), esp. 70–78.

[2] Susan Moller Okin, *Women in Western Political Thought* (Princeton, NJ: Princeton University Press, 2010).

oneself, but rather for one's posterity, one's family. Under ideal conditions, marriage can be a source of profound happiness, but it is not to be confused with love. "These things are distantly related [*ont quelque cousinage*], but they are very different" (Montaigne, 2:274). The leading moralists of the following century are less nuanced on the subject, and indeed not particularly interested in it. As usual, in his one maxim on marriage, La Rochefoucauld sums up the thinking of an era with devastating concision: "There are good marriages, but none are delicious" (La Rochefoucauld, *Maximes*, n.113, 144). La Bruyère scatters reflections on marriage in various chapters of *Les Caractères*, where it is invariably linked to questions of wealth, social advancement, and hypocrisy. Among eighteenth-century moralists, Vauvenargues and Chamfort both take a jaundiced view of marriage, seeing it simply as a "commerce" of material interests, and hardly conducive to personal (masculine) happiness. Take Chamfort, for example: "Marriage and celibacy each have their drawbacks: I prefer the one whose drawbacks are not irreversible."[3] Much of the seventeenth- and eighteenth-century iconography of marriage further suggests ways in which the topic lent itself to comic, misogynistic, or sentimental representations. I would speculate that this treatment, or lack of treatment, of the issue stems from an understanding of marriage as primarily institutional in nature and inevitable in practice. Moralist writing lives at the intersection of the social and the psychological; for its practitioners it offered a means of gaining self-understanding outside the directives of organized religion; for readers, its insights suggested ways to maintain personal integrity while navigating the shoals of social conventions—to see below the mask. It may be that the ubiquity and inevitability of marriage rendered it largely transparent, at least to male writers.

Not surprisingly, marriage is a subject on which the female moralists differ sharply from their male counterparts. I distinguish female moralist writing from the huge volume of texts related to the "querelle des femmes" and from much salon-related cultural production. Many of these texts take a dim view of marriage without examining it in depth. Marriage may be considered "slavery" in the eyes of many elite women, but their critique remains abstract; their interest lies in analyzing the inner recesses of the human heart, the infinite variety of forms of emotional attachment and disaffection. Marriage is largely absent from Madeleine de Scudéry's world, hovering on the horizon,

---

[3] Sébastien-Roch-Nicolas de Chamfort, *Maximes et pensées* (Paris: Union générale d'éditions, 1963), 103.

urged by male suitors, but indefinitely deferred by the heroines. As I have argued in earlier chapters, passionate love or "inclination" is viewed as dangerous, less because of sexual morality than out of concern for a deeper virtue, personal integrity.

Marriage is a difficult topic. The ideology of passionate (unconsummated) love and heroic friendship left no place for it. In her 1678 novel, *La Princesse de Clèves*, Madame de La Fayette claimed that her heroine's husband was unique among men in being able to sustain passion after marriage—but only because the object of his love was never truly present. By failing to reciprocate her husband's desire, the princess ensured its continuation. La Fayette analytical eye is directed not at marriage, but at passion: what nourishes it, and what kills it. Marriage is a social and legal structure, not an emotion or feeling, yet as Montaigne observed, the two have *quelque cousinage*. For La Fayette's heroine, the moral foundations of marriage are clear in the teachings instilled by her mother: that a woman's happiness depends exclusively on loving and being loved by her husband. None of the marriages represented in the novel appear to correspond to this ideal, but as an ideal, it points to the dovetailing of social and moral understandings of marriage. As a "structure of feeling" marriage carries with it a host of assumptions, "social experiences," and unarticulated or prearticulated thoughts, thoughts "at the very edge of semantic availability," as Raymond Williams put it.[4] Needless to say, it is also a practice that channels feeling, often dramatically, and becomes the locus for heightened social anxieties that marked the rise of the novel and continue to echo in our own day.[5]

For a sense of the received wisdom on marriage, consider the pedagogical writings of Françoise d'Aubigné, marquise de Maintenon. In one of her discourses to teachers at Saint-Cyr, the academy she had founded for young girls in the 1680s, she advised instructors not to avoid the topic of marriage, but to speak of it with the utmost gravity:

> You cannot over-emphasize [to your pupils], continued Madame de Maintenon, the instruction that each owes her husband complete support, attachment to his person and all his interests, any service or attention that

---

[4] Raymond Williams, *Marxism and Literature* (Oxford: Oxford University Press), 133–34.
[5] As Tony Tanner argued in his classic study of the centrality of the topoi of marriage and adultery in the rise of the novel, "marriage is the all-subsuming, all-organizing, all-containing contract" for bourgeois society; adultery, "the possible breakdown of all the mediations on which society depends." *Adultery and the Novel: Contract and Transgression* (Baltimore: Johns Hopkins University Press, 1979), 15, 17.

she can provide, and especially a sincere, discreet zeal for his salvation, for which many virtuous women have given examples, as well as for patience.[6]

In one of Maintenon's pedagogical conversations, the girls dream of liberty and independence as rich, childless widows, but learn that dependency is universal: "men are dependent on one another, ... women even more so." We are only unhappy, they learn, when "we wish for the impossible."[7]

Over the course of the eighteenth century, thinking about marriage would evolve. Many commentators have pointed to the rise of the companionate ideal as one significant shift prompted by the valorization of affectivity and increasingly prominent views of individual choice. In France, the Revolutionary government's decision to legalize divorce in 1792—a move prompted by a combination of women's activism, anticlericalism, and the long-standing criticisms by philosophers and legal theorists—was another.[8]

In this chapter, I set the moralist critique of marriage, both implicit and explicit, in the context of contemporary philosophical and legal critiques, and in the broader context of feminist accounts of liberty. When French women moralists take up the subject of marriage, as a rule they focus less on the legal issues at stake than on the tensions, internal contradictions, and inconsistencies within both the traditional understanding of marriage and the emergent companionate ideal. Far from offering an idealized view of marriage, even in its companionate form, most women moralists emphasize its unequal power relationships and the improbability of conjugal happiness. (Suzanne Necker represents a significant exception.) The demystification of marriage norms may be unconscious, as it appears to be in the marquise de Lambert, or overt, as in Geneviève d'Arconville; yet neither contests the

---

[6] Françoise d'Aubigné, marquise de Maintenon, *Extraits de ses lettres, avis, entretiens, conversations et proverbes sur l'éducation*, ed. Octave Gréard, 4th ed. (Paris: Hachette, 1886), 113.

[7] Maintenon, "Sur la nécessité de la dépendance," in *Extraits*, 207–208. A similar lesson appears in "Sur la contrainte inevitable de tous les états," 218–22.

[8] Anne Verjus makes the point that the ideal of *conjugalité*, domestic harmony, was much more prevalent in aristocratic circles than the "myth" of aloof aristocratic marriages suggests; see her article "Conjugalité," in Huguette Krief, ed., *Dictionnaire des femmes des Lumières*, 2 vols. (Paris: Honoré Champion, 2015), 1:279–83. On the philosophes' view of divorce and the reform of marriage law, see Lieselotte Steinbrügge, *The Moral Sex: Women's Nature in the French Enlightenment*, trans. Pamela E. Selwyn (Oxford: Oxford University Press, 1995), 25–28. Among many recent studies on changes in family life under the *ancien régime* and revolution: in addition to Margaret Hunt's study cited above, see Suzanne Desan, *The Family on Trial in Revolutionary France* (Berkeley: University of California Press, 2004); Jennifer Ngaire Heuer, *The Family, Nation, and Gender in Revolutionary France, 1789–1830* (Ithaca, NY: Cornell University Press, 2005). James F. Traer's study combines legal and cultural history: *Marriage and the Family in Eighteenth-Century France* (Ithaca, NY: Cornell University Press, 1980).

institution itself or postulates grounds on which a different understanding of marriage might arise. What emerges from their writing is a call for women's individual autonomy and a meditation on the nature of freedom.

5.1. The Philosophical and Legal Critique

An early philosophical critique of marriage was laid out in Gabrielle Suchon's treatise, *Du célibat volontaire, ou la vie sans engagement* (1700), the analytic structure of which places it squarely within the realm of philosophy and theology. Suchon's work comes in the wake of earlier feminist manifestos, in particular Marie de Gournay's *Égalité des hommes et des femmes* (1622) and Poulain de la Barre's *De l'égalité des deux sexes* (1673); Suchon refers to Poulain's work. A remarkable figure, this autodidact and former nun had argued in her earlier *Traité de la morale et de la politique* (1693) that liberty, knowledge, and authority are essential God-given rights, and that their deprivation, the "constraint, ignorance, and dependency" to which women have been condemned constitute an affront to the moral order.[9] Recent philosophers have seen in Suchon a theorist of liberty who prefigures and may have inspired Rousseau[10] and whose concept of rationality has its place in the pre-Kantian "invention of autonomy."[11] Suchon's egalitarian arguments for women's moral and intellectual capacity nevertheless stop short of calling for changes in the hierarchies of Church authority or traditional marriage.[12]

Suchon's second treatise, *Du célibat volontaire*, is thus less a critique of marriage, as such, than of the inexorable rule by which women are forced to choose between two forms of dependency, marriage on the one hand and the convent on the other. Suchon argues in favor of a third way: "a situation without commitment that includes all other potential states, without their requirements."[13] In other words, a life in which a woman retains her right to determine her own fate, a life lived in the world, not the convent, and devoted to study, meditation, and conversation with friends: a life of rational

---

[9] G.S. Aristophile [Gabrielle Suchon], *Traité de la morale et de la politique* (Lyon: Chez B. Vignieu, 1693).
[10] Michèle Le Doeuff, *Le Sexe du savoir* (Paris: Flammarion, 1998), 87–88.
[11] Lisa Shapiro, "Gabrielle Suchon's 'Neutralist': The Status of Women and the Invention of Autonomy," in Broad and Detlefsen, *Women and Liberty* 50–65.
[12] Eileen O'Neill, "The Equality of Men and Women," in Clark and Wilson, *The Oxford Handbook of Philosophy in Early Modern Europe*, esp. 459–63.
[13] Gabrielle Suchon, *Du célibat volontaire, ou la vie sans engagement*, 2 vols. (Paris: Chez Jean et Michel Guignard, 1700), 1:2.

self-governance. We know that Suchon's work was well distributed; favorable reviews appeared in the *Journal des savants* and Bayle's *Nouvelles de la république des lettres*.[14] It is less clear how widely read her work was. She made no effort to conceal her gender, which may have reduced the likelihood of citation despite the positive reviews; and the dense, scholarly treatment of the subject would have made it less likely to circulate in *mondain* circles. At the same time, such a work may have significance despite the lack of evidence of "impact" through its ability to articulate an important argument, in an original manner, in a given place and time.[15] As we shall see, Suchon's vision remains a compelling one for women throughout the century to come.

A further indication of how women thinkers were considering these issues may be found in Louise Dupin's unfinished treatise from the 1740s, *Sur les femmes*, an ambitious work that aimed to cover its subject from biological, historical, and legal perspectives.[16] Arguing that biological differences cannot justify inequality between the sexes, Dupin condemns the legal constraints and unjust property laws imposed on married women. She notes that marriage law seems to have been shaped by Richelieu's vision of absolute monarchy, whereas "les principes républicains" would be better suited to the union of equal partners. Dupin points to the absurdity that although a widow of twenty-five is considered fully "adult" and able to control her own property, a married woman of fifty is treated as a minor, incapable of making decisions. She scornfully reinforces the point:

> How amusing that in a country where women are considered too old at thirty to danse or wear pink, they are considered too young at seventy to do as they wish and dispose of the slightest part of their property. (Dupin, *Des femmes*, 308–309)

---

[14] On what is known of Suchon's life, see Sonia Bertolini, "Gabrielle Suchon: Une vie sans engagement?," *Australian Journal of French Studies* 37.3 (2000): 289–308. For the details of her relations with publishers, see Wallace Kirsop, "Gabrielle Suchon et ses libraires: Une note complémentaire," *Australian Journal of French Studies* 37.3 (2000): 309–11, and "A Note on Gabrielle Suchon's Efforts to Seek Publication of Her Works," *Journal of Romance Studies* 5.2 (2005): 17–18.

[15] Shapiro, "Suchon's 'Neutralist,'" 52.

[16] Louise Dupin, *Des femmes: Observations du préjugé commun sur la différence des sexes*, ed. Frédéric Marty (Classiques Garnier, 2022); for an English translation of selected chapters, see Louise Dupin, *Louise Dupin's Work on Women: Selections*, ed. and trans. Angela Hunter and Rebecca Wilkin (Oxford: Oxford University Press, 2023).

Dupin joins a growing number of legal theorists and philosophes who draw on natural rights theory to criticize the *ancien régime*'s marriage practices as abusive and tyrannical.[17]

What I refer to as the philosophical and legal critique would fall under the category that philosopher Elsa Dorlin has termed "logical feminism," which she distinguishes from the feminism of Scudéry and the *précieuse* movement. In her reading, *précieuse* feminism ultimately paved the way for confining notions of "women's nature."[18] Dorlin focuses on Suchon and other seventeenth-century figures, but Dupin's approach has much in common with theirs. For Dorlin, logical feminism represents a usable past that was largely forgotten in the wake of the critical attention, both positive and negative, given to *la préciosité*. I will take up the question of "women's nature" in Chapter 7. In the next two sections, however, I will show how the eighteenth-century moralist account of marriage, with its roots in salon culture, also carries out much the same critique as the logical feminist critique, in a different key.

5.2. The Implicit Moralist Critique: Lambert and Puisieux

What do women moralists bring to the discussion? Their approach offers observations that are all the more powerful in that they do not necessarily present themselves as argument. As we have seen, while moralist reflections have their descriptive aspect, they bespeak an ethical or normative judgment, however subtle, in their dissection of social practices and attitudes. There is no neutral ground for the depiction of marriage. Perhaps as a sign of its noncanonicity as a subject of moralist analysis, the moralist treatment of marriage has greater generic instability than other topics, echoing didactic or polemical texts, even venturing into narrative.

Anne-Thérèse de Lambert's treatment of marriage is a case in point, blurring the boundary between moralist writing and conduct literature. Hence, we find her evocation of marriage as much or more in her didactic *Avis d'une mère à sa fille* as in her more distinctly moralist text, the *Réflexions nouvelles sur les femmes*. The subject remains implicit in both. The *Avis d'une mère à sa fille* is ostensibly addressed to a young unmarried woman; its

---

[17] Desan, *The Family on Trial*, 26–27, 39.
[18] Elsa Dorlin, *L'Évidence de l'égalité des sexes: Une philosophie oubliée du XVIIe siècle* (Paris: L'Harmattan, 2000).

complex texture of stated and unstated advice offers a dispassionate analysis of the social structures of the "world" to which she will soon gain admittance, normally through marriage. The evocation of that world includes the unavoidable fact that many married women are unfaithful to their husbands. While it is imaginable that the advice on how to flee the "attack" of love might possibly apply to an unmarried girl, clearly Lambert's discussion of how best to comport oneself in society after having committed *une faute* does not. "Women who have had the misfortune to stray from their duty, to injure decorum [*bienséance*], and to outrage virtue and modesty, owe as a sign of respect to established custom and *l'honnêteté* to appear in public with an attitude of humility; the Public demands reparation, for it remembers each fault as soon as you forget it" (Lambert, 123). While Lambert's stern injunction might also apply to widows—the only independent élite women in *ancien régime* society—the reference to "devoirs" seems a clear reference to married women.

Written well after the *Avis*, probably in the early 1720s at the time of the Regency of Philippe d'Orléans—which would explain both the sense of a decline in morality and nostalgia for the great salons of the previous century—the focus of the *Réflexions nouvelles* is on women's intellectual abilities and their superior imagination, taste, and sensibility. With the latter comes a particular propensity for passion and love, leading Lambert to reflect on a series of character types, categories of women in love: women who are interested only in pleasure, virtuous women who nevertheless find themselves inexorably drawn into grand passion, and "tender and sensitive" women, who maintain sexual virtue, but ultimately feel the most deeply of all (Lambert, 228–30). The discussion is clearly focused on the social and affective lives of adult women—hence predominantly married women, although their marriage is never mentioned as such. (Granted, her example of a badly behaved woman, "Madame de C***"—"'I wish to enjoy,' said she, 'the loss of my reputation'" [Lambert, 228]—is thought to be her mother, Madame de Courcelles, who was widowed young.) Lambert observes that, given women's temperament and men's tendency to "love in a vulgar manner" (Lambert, 232), many women will be tempted by love. For most, the unstated understanding is that she is speaking of adulterous love. Even in the case of independent widows, like Madame de Courcelles or Lambert herself, love is a temptation best avoided. Conjugal love is simply not a topic. Women who let themselves be touched by love "pass from folly to folly" (Lambert, 229), to the detriment of their reputation and, more damagingly, to their sense of personal integrity.

A similar, but far more explicit understanding of marriage informs *Conseils à une amie*, a text that blurs the line between conduct literature and moralist writing. Madeleine d'Arsant de Puisieux (1720–1798) was a writer of moralist works and novels. She gained a certain notoriety from a liaison with Diderot in the late 1740s. Her early prefaces echo her pleasure at being taken seriously as a writer by "Monsieur D***," but she later expresses her annoyance that others were attributing her work to him. *Conseils à une amie* is undoubtedly her best-known work among scholars today, but she would enjoy a long and prolific literary career and in her final years receive a pension from the Revolutionary government.

While ostensibly written as "advice," *Conseils* more closely resembles a parody of conduct literature and is more properly viewed as a moralist work concerned with the analysis of a wide range of social questions and human relationships, especially as they affect women. Puisieux's narrator, Madame de *** describes how eagerly she looked forward to marriage as a girl:

> The idea of my future liberty was so delightful to me, I believe that if my father had proposed the least agreeable man in the world, in order to have the carriage and diamonds, to put on rouge and high heels, I would have married him.[19]

Need it be said? Madame de *** finds herself in a disastrous marriage, from which she escapes by retiring to a convent: "I enjoy total liberty, since my retreat was voluntary" (Puisieux, *Conseils*, 173). Puisieux observes in the course of a discussion of power dynamics and dependency that women are better off if they do not owe their fortunes to their husbands—a situation she describes as "humiliating" (Puisieux, *Conseils*, 129–30)—and she has this to say about the proper behavior between married couples:

> A woman should have kindness, gentleness, and indulgence for her husband; but she degrades herself below a servant's place if she is too submissive. Submission is a mark of subordination, but in a married couple everything is equal. A husband has no fewer obligations to fulfill than a wife. . . . I could be wrong, but my heart tells me that [men] were not

---

[19] Madeleine de Puisieux, *Conseils à une amie, nouvelle edition* (n.p., 1749), 163–64.

destined to rule over us; and experience teaches me that the reverse might have occurred if the women of yesteryear had as much strength and resolution as the women of the present day. But the yoke is given, and we must submit. (Puisieux, *Conseils*, 131–32)

The grim acknowledgment of the final line clashes discordantly with the egalitarian feminism of the first part.

Ultimately, in Puisieux's view, while a woman should make every effort to remain virtuous, it remains the case that "one shouldn't count too much on one's strength" (Puisieux, *Conseils*, 142): many women will ultimately cede to their hearts and take a lover. There are mitigating circumstances: most young women are sent into marriage without having the chance to get to know their future spouse, and husbands are frequently unfaithful themselves. Puisieux's worldly narrator even assures her young friend that ultimately the wandering husband's "passions" will cool and that he'll again seek refuge in his family and appreciate the friendship of his wife ("sa meilleure amie," Puisieux, *Conseils*, 146). This less-than-rosy prospect of lukewarm domestic bliss aside, however, the fact remains that women may well seek their happiness elsewhere. Should such be the case, Puisieux advises, then one must choose well: "It is not the attachment that dishonors us, but rather the object" (Puisieux, *Conseils*, 151).

Conseils à une amie has a titillating reputation as a sort of misconduct book, whose lessons in worldliness offer at best an ambiguous account of virtue. "One cannot be happy without at least the appearance of virtue; any woman who ceases to be virtuous, must study how to appear so" (Puisieux, *Conseils*, 94). It's hard to imagine an approach farther from that of Lambert, whose writings were seen by her contemporaries as exemplifying virtue. Indeed, Puisieux cites and underscores her disagreement with Lambert's comment that a woman known to have committed *une faute* should appear "with an attitude of humility" in public—at best, she finds it old fashioned.

Such virtue is out of date; and if every woman who has had an affair appeared with a humble attitude, we'd see many downcast eyes. I think that they would do better to cease their folies and maintain the same attitude as before. (Puisieux, *Conseils*, 177)

Puisieux's breezy manner is at antipodes from Lambert's measured pronouncements, yet the two ultimately concur that adultery is a regular occurrence in married life. When it appeared, Puisieux's *Conseils* suffered by comparison with Lambert's *Avis à sa fille*; at the same time reviewers tended to minimize its morally equivocal advice, possibly because of their relationships with Puisieux's supposed collaborator Diderot.[20] It's worth noting, however, that reviewers of Puisieux's sequel to *Conseils*, her *Réflexions et avis sur les défauts & les ridicules à la mode* (1761) compared her to La Rochefoucauld and La Bruyère, correctly situating her work in the moralist genre that is implicit throughout *Conseils*. Earlier reviewers of *Conseils* who recognized its generic affiliation to moralist writing would have been less likely to judge it as a conduct book.

Neither Lambert nor Puisieux—both of whom appear to have had reasonably happy marriages—offers a particularly positive image of marriage per se. There are echoes of the companionate ideal in Puisieux's image of the wayward husband's return to his *meilleure amie*, but the picture is hardly a compelling one. Far stronger is her condemnation of wives' dependency on their husbands ("the yoke is given"). As such, her perspective is worlds apart from the view of Françoise de Maintenon, half a century earlier, for whom dependency was to be accepted as an ineluctable part of women's condition, regardless of social status.

Maintenon's insistence on women's *complaisance*, or willingness to yield to others, has been viewed as a form of "emotional self-control" and "a rational strategy for acting in a situation of dependence."[21] Such rational self-control can be seen as a form of what Isaiah Berlin famously called "positive liberty," the internal sense of personal integrity and autonomy that remains available even to individuals living under oppressive circumstances.[22] Jacqueline Broad, however, refers to positive liberty as a "sour grapes" approach to the absence of true or negative liberty, freedom from external circumstances, and argues that early modern women philosophers both recognized the limitations of positive liberty and looked beyond it in their quest for autonomy.[23] Maintenon's approach was to cultivate acceptance: "Gentleness [*la douceur*]

---

[20] Nadine Bérenguier, *Conduct Books for Girls in Enlightenment France* (Farnham, UK: Ashgate, 2011), 135–42.

[21] Andreas Blank, "Complaisance and the Question of Autonomy in the French Women Moralists, 1650-1710," in Sandrine Bergès and Alberto L. Siani, eds., *Women Philosophers on Autonomy: Historical and Contemporary Perspectives* (New York and London: Routledge, 2018), 44–45.

[22] Isaiah Berlin, "Two Concepts of Liberty," in *Four Essays on Liberty* (Oxford: Oxford University Press, 1969), 118–72.

[23] Jacqueline Broad, "Marriage, Slavery, and the Merger of Wills: Responses to Sprint, 1700–1701," in Broad and Detlefsen, *Women and Liberty*, 79.

is the virtue of our sex."[24] As the morganatic spouse of Louis XIV, she knew something about the complex interplay between autonomy and dependency. Later figures would find the situation less tolerable.

5.3. The Explicit Moralist Critique: Verzure and d'Arconville

As we have seen, the mid-century thinker Louise Dupin was highly critical of the structural and legal constraints on married women. Her observations are echoed in the works of her moralist contemporaries. Henriette de Marans complains of the double standard that obtains in broken marriages and engagements, from which women emerge dishonored, regardless of the cause, while men "come out of it as white as snow," adding that it is abundantly clear that men wrote these laws.[25] Elsewhere, despite a favorable comparison between the status of a married Frenchwoman and a member of a Turkish seraglio, she observes nonetheless that, if one's husband prefers a mistress to his wife, the only recourse is to close one's eyes to the situation: "for honor and duty's sake, one must behave correctly with the person to whom one is joined for life" (Marans, *Pensées errantes*, 131). Marie-Louise de Fourqueux focuses on the tension and overall unhappiness created in a household by a single difficult (*difficultueux*) individual, moody and tyrannical. The autobiographical elements in her *Confessions* tell us that her father-in-law was the model, but the chapter on family life is also a broader analysis of the extensive and exhausting mental and emotional work required to manage such situations: "The greatest effort of one's reason is required to endure habitual unreason with tranquility" (Fourqueux, 2:206). Unlike Maintenon's resigned attitude from a half-century earlier, Fourqueux typically denounces the family situation as "tyrannical" and "despotic."

In one of the most extensive moralist critiques, Marie de Verzure offers neither advice nor solutions, but casts a scathing eye on the existential situation of the married woman. Her chapter, "Sur le célibat et le mariage," offers a thoroughly disenchanted outlook. Like Geneviève d'Arconville, Verzure holds a generally pessimistic view of humanity as enslaved by passion,

---

[24] Maintenon, "Entretien avec la classe verte: Sur la douceur," in *Extraits*, 111. See also her conversation "Sur la douceur" (*Extraits*, 248–53), on how to disagree with others' opinions "avec douceur."

[25] Marans, *Pensées errantes*, 114–15. On the genesis and attribution of the *Pensées errantes*, see above, Chapter 2, note 57.

driven by *amour-propre* and venal interests. She makes it clear at the outset of her essay that her personal preference is for the single life—a version of Suchon's Neutralist pathway—but that she will do her best to remain objective in her assessment of the married state. "Being attached to my personal idea regarding marriage and the single life, I fear that I may not clearly perceive arguments against it, but I will try to set aside my prejudice" (Verzure, 1:136). Even the best marriages are nevertheless beset by anxiety—over one's children and their future, for example—and the potential for disaster is ever present. She then goes on to describe the numerous ways in which marriage has been perverted by the social and economic interests of noble and elite nonnoble families. Primogeniture, which discourages families from allowing younger sons to marry, is an egregious example of the ways in which marriage and inheritance practices among the elite go against natural inclinations and the divine injunction to perpetuate the species.[26] Although the married state favors males, it is hardly conducive to happiness for either partner. Women, however, have the worst of it.

> Girls are victims who are raised with care so that they may be sacrificed to the pride of those who gave them life—I refer to people of consequence in the world...
>
> The fate of the female sex and its destiny is to be deprived of liberty. One cannot therefore begin too early to accustom young girls to dependency; they must regard it as a legal matter against which it is useless to rebel.
>
> Fortunate are those who are allowed to choose the nature of their enslavement. (Verzure, 1:147–48)

For Verzure, even though most women would likely be happiest "simply to remain single," the convent represents the only form of the single life available to women of her class; being allowed a choice between marriage and the convent makes them no less "slaves to prejudice" (Verzure, 1:147). Unmarried women suffer from their dependency on others and lack of a place in society; the convent is "an eternal prison." Women thus desire marriage, since it is the only means of ensuring even a modicum of liberty (Verzure, 1:150). In "Sur

---

[26] On Verzure's critique of primogeniture in the context of eighteenth-century debates over population and family law, see Carol Blum, *Strength in Numbers: Population, Reproduction, and Power in Eighteenth-Century France* (Baltimore: Johns Hopkins University Press, 2002), 199; Elizabeth Fox-Genovese and Eugene Genovese, *Fruits of Merchant Capital: Slavery and Bourgeois Property in the Rise and Expression of Capitalism* (Oxford: Oxford University Press, 1983), 295.

le bonheur," she goes even further, claiming that a young woman married off to satisfy her parents' ambition "is unhappy for life; she is a slave that we honor with the name of *wife*" (Verzure, 2:66).

Verzure discusses freedom and constraint in several chapters in *Réflexions hazardées*. In "La liberté," she puts forth the Stoic principle that the only true freedom consists in mastery of one's passions. We willingly submit to them, even though we know instinctively what we should do to free ourselves. Our attachment to them stems from our inability to distinguish between our passions and our innermost selves: "Conquering one's passions, separating from them entirely, means separating from oneself" (Verzure, 1:178). Only a deep spiritual awakening will allow us to overcome the emptiness, *un vide*, that the passions leave in their wake. Turning to the "phantom" that most people take to be liberty, Verzure observes that internal freedom or positive liberty ("libres de nos idées") does not suffice for most people, who wish to be able to act on their inclinations. For Verzure, true liberty is not simply the ability to act according to our *goûts* and *penchants*, however appealing that prospect may be. Like Locke, she distinguishes between liberty and license. In her analysis, the wish for so-called freedom is a cover for a deeper drive: the wish to dominate others (Verzure, 1:181).

She argues that it is not only logically impossible for anyone to be both master of others and free of any external constraint but also morally repugnant, because "Men's duties to one another are reciprocal" (Verzure, 1:182). Liberty at the expense of others is thus pure injustice; none of us can survive in such a state. Verzure then describes the forms of legitimate and illegitimate freedoms available to us. In the chapter that follows, "Sur l'usage qu'on fait du Temps" (Verzure, 1:188–92), her focus is the interior life and the use (and misuse) of one's leisure; while not explicitly connected to the discussion of liberty, her recommendation that one devote oneself to study, not simply for the accumulation of knowledge, but for "the study of oneself," indicates the path forward. Through self-understanding and self-awareness, one maintains a perspective on one's relationships and prevents one's own individual interests from turning into overriding "passions" (Verzure, 1:187).

Other essays consider the interplay of freedom and constraint in society. "Sur les préjugés" attacks the folly of imagining that one's own customs and habits are better than those of other nations. Early education is key to overcoming such prejudices, but Verzure sees both boys' and girls' education as problematic. (Raising girls to believe in the necessity of pleasing others is especially egregious.) "Sur la subordination" and "Sur les loix" argue that subordination is a necessary evil, key to maintaining order; were we creatures of reason, laws would not be necessary, but like our secret drive for domination, our unruly vices and passions require restraint. Verzure is no republican: she sees social hierarchy as part of the moral order of things and resistance to it as symptomatic of a dangerously self-interested "spirit of independence" that hides a will to power (Verzure, 2:24). That said, it is worth noting her conviction that social relations create reciprocal duties and responsibilities. She remains consistent in her assertion that women's dependence within marriage is anything other than painful and unnatural.

Verzure thus complicates any simple notion of positive and negative liberty. As Broad observes of Mary Astell and Mary Chudleigh, she too finds that external forces, such as girls' education and the debilitating effects of "prejudice," make it difficult for women to experience even mental freedom. Furthermore, both men and women must contend with the force of unacknowledged passions and desires. Self-knowledge, *l'étude de soi-même*, becomes the key to the labyrinth.

Like Verzure, Geneviève d'Arconville sees the loss of liberty as a central truth of marriage, even companionate marriage. Reflections on the married state arise throughout her writing career, and while her thinking is generally consistent, it is also nuanced and complex, suggesting an ongoing effort to reconcile singularity and belonging, autonomy and dependence. The key texts are an early essay in her *Pensées et réflexions morales* (1760), a chapter in *De l'amitié* (1761), and several of the late essays from the years 1801–1805.

The topic of marriage arises in several of the essays in *Pensées et réflexions*. In "Sur les femmes," d'Arconville offers a series of portraits of adulterous women: Lucinde, who takes lovers out of sheer boredom; Pauline and Zénobie, who delude themselves into believing that they love both their husbands and their lovers; and Dorothée, whose fall into a series of superficial affairs is the fault of her unpleasant, jealous husband. While she condemns infidelity and promiscuity, d'Arconville sees mitigating circumstances in the cases of women who are lucid about their desires (unlike Pauline and Zénobie) or who experience a profound passion, which Dorothée's constricted life precludes (D'Arconville, 1:379–83).

The asymmetry of marriage reveals itself in a paradox:

There are more husbands who love their wives, than wives who love their husbands. I believe that I have discovered the reason in humanity's love of liberty. Women depend on their husbands, but husbands do not depend on their wives. (D'Arconville, 1:385)

Echoes of the companionate ideal can be heard elsewhere, as when a woman is said to lose more in the death of a husband for whom she feels "esteem and trust" than in the loss of the most passionate lover. Even so, d'Arconville points out, a woman who loses a good husband "at least acquires her liberty" (D'Arconville, 1: 387).

Marriage fares no better in the chapter in *De l'amitié* on friendship between husbands and wives. Marriage ought to be the source of greatest felicity to which mortals might aspire, according to d'Arconville, but all too often self-interest and passions conspire to wreck marriages (D'Arconville, 2:73). The discussion of any kind of conjugal friendship vanishes in a series of paralipses in which the speaker repeatedly refuses to name or describe what is happening: the failure of the marriage, the inevitability of adultery. "Let us cover with an impenetrable veil these topics that make modesty blush. . . . Let us forget these misfortunes that perversity has rendered all too common. . . . Let us distance ourselves from scandals so humiliating for humanity" (D'Arconville, 2:74–75). The heightened language renders the rupture of the marriage all the more dramatic—and repeatedly underscores its presence.

Marriage enters the discussion only indirectly in d'Arconville's second moral treatise, *Des Passions*, as one of the sites where lives are shipwrecked by the twin passions of desire and ambition. It is in the moralist essays left among her late manuscripts that she turns again to the topic with attentiveness, complexity, and depth. I first consider three pieces in which the question of marriage is central, then turn briefly to pertinent passages in other late essays and autobiographical writings.

One of the earliest pieces in the late manuscripts, "Sur le mariage" offers a vision of the institution of marriage even bleaker than Verzure's. Beginning with the historical observation that marriage was hardly "respectable" prior to being elevated by Christianity to a sacrament, she goes on to critique it as irretrievably damaged by social norms and familial ambitions. Young people are never consulted on the choice of a partner, she observes, and girls in particular have no basis for judgment because of their sheltered upbringing, especially if they have received a convent education. A young bride, touched by her husband's attention and thrilled by her new clothes and jewels—an image reminiscent of Puisieux's narrator's eagerness for the married state—may be inclined to fall in love, but such feelings are not made to last. A husband's self-interest consists not in seeking not his wife's love, which is unpredictable and dangerous, but rather in deserving her esteem, which lays the groundwork for mutual affection and respect. A wife's self-interest lies in obeying her husband, since his "absolute empire" over her grants him the power to "make her unhappy with impunity" (D'Arconville, *PRA* 1:50).

Describing marriage as "a yoke" imposed by religion, d'Arconville notes that it furthermore requires a constancy not found in nature (D'Arconville, *PRA* 1:46–47). In her essay "Sur la constance et l'inconstance," in the same manuscript volume as "Sur le mariage," d'Arconville elaborates on this notion, arguing that inasmuch as both depend on desires and drives that are not under our control, fidelity is not a virtue, nor infidelity a vice (*PRA* 1:54–65; see also "Sur l'inconstance en amour," D'Arconville, *PRA* 4:346–57). Given the severity of the moral code manifest throughout her writings, it comes as something of a surprise that d'Arconville, like Lambert and Puisieux, appears to acquiesce to the quasi inevitability of marital infidelity, though she imputes the blame for the majority of unfaithful wives to their unsatisfactory husbands (D'Arconville, *PRA* 1:43, 48), a point to which she returns in "Sur l'intérieur des ménages" (D'Arconville, PRA 6:38). She concludes with a scathing image:

> I conclude from these reflections that the conjugal state rarely fulfills a young girl's expectations of the felicity that she hopes to enjoy once she is married, and once she is bedecked with a collar inscribed like a dog's, "*I belong to Mr. So-and-So.*" (D'Arconville, *PRA* 1:52)

Happy—or at least bearable (*supportables*)—marriages exist, but they require much patience, flexibility, a clear mind, and iron-clad virtue ("une vertu à toute épreuve"; D'Arconville, *PRA* 1:52).

How does d'Arconville envision freedom? In "Sur la liberté" (D'Arconville, *PRA* 1:349–59), she describes freedom as the highest good, to which all creation aspires. She points to the animal kingdom, noting the difficulty of taming animals and observing that horses, freed of the harness, manifest their joy by prancing and jumping; even a broken-down old nag becomes a magnificent Bucephalus once relieved of its burden. Humans, on the other hand, claim to love liberty, but in reality they spend a lifetime pursuing different forms of voluntary servitude. D'Arconville takes as her example the typical life of males of her class: burdened by the need to become established, whether at court, in the law, in finance, or in the Church; then married "without knowing the person whom they marry" (D'Arconville, *PRA* 1:353). If children come, then one must solicit favors for their establishment, and so on. In other words, marriage is burdensome for both sexes.

> I have always been struck by this so-called love of liberty of which I have seen men so enamored. More than anyone else, I have considered it, and continue to do so, to be a mental figment [*être de raison*] a dream [*chimère*] that their imagination caresses from pure illusion, without ever realizing what they truly mean by the word *Liberty*. But having long reflected on it, I am tempted to believe that that which they decorate with the word is actually *License*, to which youths give themselves over with such abandon. Nothing could be further from it, however: the spirit of *Liberty* requires a strong character [*âme forte*] free from prejudice and courageous enough to sacrifice everything in order to maintain virtue. *License*, on the other hand, is a degradation that abases man by making him a slave to every vice. (D'Arconville, *PRA* 1:356–57)

Like others, d'Arconville denounces the tendency to confuse liberty with license. Freedom thus consists not only in the absence of external constraints, whether physical, like the horse's harness, or societal, like the duties and responsibilities of rank and marriage, but also, and more importantly, in strength of character and ability to recognize and adhere to virtuous behavior. Even given her assessment of marriage as oppressive for both sexes, she clearly does not recommend overthrowing it or any other institutions—that would be license. But although her definition of true liberty focuses on its mental aspect, the notion of positive liberty alone does not capture it in its entirety, as we have seen.

Despite d'Arconville's largely negative assessment of human relationships, her writings abound with heartfelt evocations of moments of intimacy and mutual understanding, as in her essay "Sur la tête-à-tête," (D'Arconville, *PRA* 3:256). Such deep connections are possible through friendship, but, as we have seen, friendship rarely makes it into marriage at all, and never, apparently, with any intensity. The essay "Sur l'intérieur des ménages" begins with an evocation of how difficult in general it is to be happy, then considers the chances for happiness in different social classes. Although manual labor drives away inappropriate thoughts that might lead one astray, conjugal happiness is infrequent among *le peuple*, where the men too often squander their substance on drink and are brutal to their wives and children. Prospects for happiness in wealthy families are no better: arranged marriages leave no place for individual desires, and young wives are often either humiliated by their husbands' bad example or corrupted by it. She returns to the image, present in many evocations of marriage among the wealthy, of the young woman whose head has been so turned by the prospect of new clothes and jewels that she doesn't immediately realize the burden she has taken on (D'Arconville, PRA 6: 30). Only those of "the middling sort" have a solid chance at true conjugal happiness, although the principles of even the bourgeoisie, formerly "the seat of virtue," have foundered in the wake of the Revolution. Nevertheless, d'Arconville sees in this group, free on the one hand from the stress of poverty and on the other from the ambitions and frivolous desires that accompany great wealth, the best chance for happy households where "reciprocal trust unites hearts." Love is not necessary and indeed could only disturb the state of plenitude.

In one of the last volumes, written close to the end of her life, d'Arconville echoes this thought in her essay "Du célibat," adding an autobiographical reference. Happy marriages do exist, she tells us:

> I have known several, particularly in my family. In such cases, it is certain that this redoubtable bond ... is paradise on earth. All that could potentially trouble the union instead contributes to its happiness: common interests, the eagerness of the couple to satisfy their mutual desire and to reciprocate, the births of children and the progress of their education.... All this renders their days delicious; their lives are never empty. (D'Arconville, PRA 11:145–46)

The essay as a whole, however, is an extended plea in favor of the single life. Feelings of love can obviate the loss of freedom in marriage, but they cannot last when sexual pleasure is no longer *une faveur* bestowed willingly, but rather *un devoir*, a duty. In short, she tells us, marriage is not a natural state.

> I come back to my *refrain* that liberty is the greatest of goods, and that we *prostitute* it, so to speak, by abandoning it to chance through marriage.

Personal observations of happy marriages notwithstanding, d'Arconville's first allegiance, like Verzure's, is to the ideal of the unattached life.

The personal observations at the beginning and end of "Du célibat" might appear somewhat at odds with one another. Should we make something of the fact that the "several" happy marriages that she has observed do not appear to include her own, at least not explicitly? The references to her marriage in her autobiographical writings are rare and extremely brief. Her marriage "at fourteen years, four and a half months" puts an abrupt end to the account of her childhood, "Histoire de mon enfance" (D'Arconville, PRA 3:488–89). The story of her intellectual development, "Histoire de ma littérature" (D'Arconville, PRA 5:169–226), contains a passing reference to her marriage at fourteen as the occasion of a temporary pause in her writing. That essay goes on to detail her self-education in literature, translation, and science, as well as the progress of her writing and publishing career, but says nothing of her personal and family life.

Louis-Lazare Thiroux d'Arconville, président du Parlement de Paris, was eight years her senior, hence a young man at the time of their marriage. Their three sons were born within quick succession, and it is likely that d'Arconville's turn to self-education coincided with the birth of her third son at age twenty. She refers with deep affection to her sister, her brother-in-law Denis François Angran d'Alleray, and her husband's brother François Thiroux d'Epersenne. One of her autobiographical essays, "Mes Voyages" (PRA 5:226–92), includes an amusing anecdote from the early months of their marriage about a misadventure at a friend's country house: after she walked into a swamp and was unable to extricate herself, her husband came to help her and found himself similarly trapped, so both had to be rescued by their host. The husband surfaces occasionally in other essays, but his death in May 1789 is mentioned only as the occasion for her decision to leave Paris and retire to her beloved estate in Meudon.

Such references tell us little, but should warn against a simplistic biographical reading of her discussions on marriage. Reticence, *pudeur*, would seem to be one of the primary traits of this woman who avoided *le grand monde* for a select group of friends and mentors, who always published anonymously or elected not to publish at all, and for whom public revelations of either the joys or chagrins of married life must have seemed unthinkable. We may assume that le président d'Arconville offered no obstacles to his wife's determined quest for knowledge, but whether he actively supported her efforts and took pride in them, we cannot know.[27] He is absent from her accounts of her of projects philosophical, literary, scientific, and historical; not he but

---

[27] In her *Confidences générales et particulières*, Henriette de Marans describes "Sapho," who, the editors suspect, may represent d'Arconville (Marans was close to the d'Alleray and d'Arconville

her brother-in-law d'Alleray offers advice on setting up her study at Meudon. Although she complains in some of her late essays about social obligations, she appears to have had considerable autonomy in arranging her life and determining the use of her time.

Such a life would not appear, at least, to inspire the devastating image discussed earlier of the young bride "decorated" with a dog collar, "I belong to Mr. So-and-So" ("*j'appartiens à M*^{r}*. un tel*"). On the other hand, it is clear that wealth, autonomy, and the ability to select her friends and pursue her interests did not in any way constitute "liberty." Writing at the end of her long life, she speaks of her "penchant" for the single state and describes even a good marriage as antithetical to personal liberty. Some women writers and intellectuals came to writing in the wake of unhappy marriages—one thinks of Françoise de Graffigny and Marie-Jeanne Riccoboni—or after widowhood left them free to write or hold salons, like Lambert. For Émilie Du Châtelet, born in a higher social class and in the generation of d'Arconville's parents, marriage seems to have been a simple fact of life, but hardly one that limited her in any way; like d'Arconville, she complains of the late start of her "real" education, her self-education, but this seems to be the only limitation against which she struggles. Marriage is not viewed as a constraint for the aristocrat, but for d'Arconville, marriage is an existential and moral reality. Hence even marriage with a high degree of autonomy constitutes a form of voluntary (or involuntary) servitude, and had she been offered the choice, she would not have chosen it.[28]

5.4. Suzanne Necker on Marriage and Divorce

Part of a series of sweeping changes to family law passed by the Assemblée nationale, the divorce law of September 1792 marked an extraordinary rupture from the past. The law emerged from a campaign pursued over decades "to identify indissoluble marriage with despotism and the dissolution of

---

families): a wealthy intellectual woman, beloved by her husband and family, who is nevertheless unhappy because of her husband's limited intellect: "un homme sans talents, genie mediocre, qui ne se distingue en rien." Chollet et Krief, eds., *Une femme d'encre et de papier*, 417 n.162.

[28] It is worth noting that d'Arconville's late essays "Sur le mariage" and "Sur la liberté" were written in the period 1801–1805, while divorce was still available, despite restrictions imposed by the 1803 Code Civil, but she never mentions it. Given the association of divorce with Revolutionary politics, it is likely to have been anathema to her.

marriage with liberty."[29] In contrast to the Church's position on the indissolubility of marriage, the Revolutionary government decreed that it was a civil institution; divorce became streamlined, inexpensive, and equally available to men and women on a variety of grounds, including incompatibility and mutual consent. The law proved highly popular, with a "flood" of divorces occurring in the first year of its existence and a steady stream continuing until significant restrictions were imposed by the Napoleonic Code Civil in 1803.[30] (After the restoration of the monarchy and the return of Catholicism as state religion, the law would be abolished in 1816; divorce would not be legalized again in France until 1884.) The passage of the divorce law represented both the Revolution's secularization of French society and the culmination of the century's rethinking the nature of marriage. The 1792 law "validated the growing expectation that the couple share a loving or affectionate relationship."[31] Given that women often stood most to benefit from the dissolution of bad marriages, it is hardly surprising that women activists had been among the chief proponents of the legalization of divorce. Nor is it surprising that women appear to have initiated divorce proceedings more often than men.[32]

Suzanne Necker takes a contrary view, however, in her *Réflexions sur le divorce*, published a few months after her death in 1794. At the time of the passage of the 1792 law, the Neckers had been living in Switzerland, where they had returned in 1790 following Jacques Necker's brief term as minister of finances under the revolutionary government. Their daughter, Germaine de Staël, remained in Paris until the fall of the constitutional monarchy in 1792; the rift with her mother had deepened and would not heal. Some commentators have suggested that Suzanne Necker's tract on divorce was at least in part motivated by anger with her daughter, who was said to be considering a divorce from the Baron de Staël.[33]

---

[29] Heuer, *The Family, Nation, and Gender*, 27.

[30] James Traer finds a ratio of one divorce for every three marriages in Paris at the height of the Revolution (1793–94); the large number of divorces reflects pent-up demand, the conversion of existing judicial separations to divorce, and the need for women to protect their property rights by divorcing émigré husbands, since otherwise their property would be seized (Traer, *Marriage and the Family*, 131–32).

[31] Desan, *The Family on Trial*, 94.

[32] Desan, 99–118.

[33] While many have pointed to the discussion of divorce in Staël's novel *Delphine* (1802) as a response to her mother, Catherine Dubeau notes the connections between *Réflexions sur le divorce* and Staël's defensive, possibly guilt-ridden posture in *De l'influence des passions* (1796). Dubeau, "The Mother, the Daughter, and the Passions," 26–29.

In his brief editorial preface to the *Réflexions*, Jacques Necker tells us that illness prevented his wife from expanding and polishing the manuscript; he notes that it is a highly moral text distinguished by its purity of style.[34] Both her passionate defense of indissoluble marriage and her spouse's endorsement fueled the posthumous construction of the portrait of Suzanne Necker as the emblem of the devoted wife, an image that Jacques Necker would go on to promote in his prefaces to the *Mélanges* and *Nouveaux mélanges*. Sonja Boon notes that Jacques Necker and others "strategically positioned" Suzanne Necker as a "counter-Enlightenment voice ... a generous, virtuous, and moral being who stands in direct contrast to the secular (and even decadent) worldliness that characterized French Enlightenment culture, society, and thought." The *Réflexions* were weaponized through successive reeditions during the ongoing debates over divorce throughout the nineteenth century.[35]

Although written as a passionate response to events of the day, Necker's *Réflexions sur le divorce* are also precisely what the title indicates, a reflection both on what she sees as the lamentable consequences of the divorce law and, more profoundly, on the nature of marriage itself. Following a brief introduction, the work explores what Necker takes to be the four aims of marriage: the happiness of the spouses during their youth; children; moral purity; and consolation, support, and happiness in old age. She contends that the mere existence of the divorce law undermines all four.

The first chapter offers a vision of conjugal harmony. Good marriages are based commonalities of education, character, tastes, and wishes. She argues that each member of the couple will be not only happier but also more virtuous, than had they remained single, as the spouses will help one another overcome their less desirable qualities. Interestingly, Necker does not consider children to be the primary goal of marriage; she observes that God told animals to be fruitful and multiply, but he created Eve so that Adam would not be lonely. Marriage is foundational to human happiness because it offers "effective resources against the solitude of existence" (Necker, *Réflexions*, 17) To base marriage solely on the perpetuation of the species would be to put humans on a level with animals; children are thus of secondary importance. Her reference to marriage as "conjugal society" emphasizes her point that the couple is the foundation of the state, *la Patrie* (Necker, *Réflexions*, 5) as

---

[34] Jacques Necker, "Avertissement" to Suzanne Necker, *Réflexions sur le divorce* (Lausanne: Durand Ravanel, 1794), 3–4.
[35] Boon, "Does a Dutiful Wife Write?," 65.

well as a broader point that a happy individual is in harmony with the universe (Necker, *Réflexions*,14). Marriage equals society. True marital happiness extends beyond pleasure of the senses to complete harmony of feeling.

All very well for a happy couple like Suzanne and Jacques Necker, one might say, but why would couples who have no thought of divorce suffer from the existence of a divorce law? Because, she argues, the bonds of marriage—common interests, shared purpose, a shared identity—would disappear if divorce were an ever-present possibility (Necker, *Réflexions*, 18–19). Unlike the prodivorce activists who claimed that the possibility of divorce would cause spouses to be more affectionate with one another, Necker argues that they will have less reason to make an effort, since they can always leave the marriage if they are not happy: "I assume that they will seek less to please one another" (Necker, *Réflexions*, 19). The understanding that a marriage will persist through time is a key factor, since not simply the phenomenon of duration, but a belief in durability, "the accessory idea of duration," is necessary to human happiness; a married couple's affections "increase, becoming ennobled and strengthened by means of their own duration" (Necker, *Réflexions*, 20–21).

For Necker, the divorce law "changes the structure of what is *thinkable*."[36] As such, its mere existence affects the conditions of happiness for every couple, however attached to one another they may be. As Necker will go on to explain in her second chapter on the problems created by divorce when children are involved, families are part of a larger continuum. Referring to the naturalist Bernardin de Saint-Pierre's evocation of the immensity of nature revealed by the insect life on a single strawberry plant,[37] she evokes humanity as part of the Great Chain of Being ("la grande chaîne de l'Univers"); if any link, any connection is broken, it all falls apart (Necker, *Réflexions*, 37–38). The third chapter pursues the same theme from another angle. Marriage takes us outside of ourselves ("nous oblige à vivre hors de nous"), she tells us; married couples have "a double conscience" that makes them morally responsible for one another (Necker, *Réflexions*, 62).

Necker recognizes (briefly) that some women are truly unhappy in their marriages and suffer from the abuse of bad husbands, but she is adamant that such cases are rare, and that legislation cannot be based on such exceptions.

---

[36] Janet Whatley, "Dissoluble Marriage, Paradise Lost: Suzanne Necker's *Réflexions sur le divorce*," *Dalhousie French Studies* 56 (2001): 147.

[37] Henri Bernardin de Saint-Pierre, *Études de la nature*, nouvelle edition, 5 vols. (originally published 1784; Paris: Chez Déterville, 1804), 1:104–109.

Time, experience, and one's virtue can improve most situations. As far as Necker is concerned, the majority of women who have been advocating for divorce are acting out of a deep-seated disquiet ("l'inquiétude dévorante de leur caractère") that will not be assuaged, as they hope, with another spouse (Necker, *Réflexions*, 63–64). When "conditional marriage" replaces indissoluble marriage, the specter of divorce creates fault lines and pitfalls for all by encouraging spouses to look at one another with a critical eye, to compare one another to others, and to awaken the imagination to the mirage of better options elsewhere.

Réflexions sur le divorce is interwoven with literary allusions. Somewhat surprisingly, given that he had been thought to favor divorce, Necker quotes her friend Diderot's essay "Sur les femmes" (which he had written as a rejoinder to the work of one of her closest friends, Antoine Thomas), observing that despite an overblown poetic style ("un peu recherchée") he succeeded in describing women's exquisite moral sensibility (Necker, *Réflexions*, 73). Rousseau surfaces in a reference to parents' responsibility for their children's education in *Émile* (Necker, *Réflexions*, 47), and in Julie's lament for virtue lost in *La Nouvelle Héloïse* (Necker, *Réflexions*, 65). Most of the references, however, are classical: the desperation of Medea, who killed her children when abandoned by Jason (Necker, *Réflexions*, 35); the social chaos unleashed by the crimes of Helen and Clytemnestra (Necker, *Réflexions*, 57); Psyche, who looked too closely at her husband (Necker, *Réflexions*, 67); Lucretia and the Roman vestals, exemplars of purity (Necker, *Réflexions*, 69); and in a striking image, the Bacchantes in an evocation of the bloodthirsty revolutionary mob (Necker, *Réflexions*, 59). The most extended such passage, however, is the most moving, Necker's retelling of Ovid's story of Baucis and Philemon, the worthy old couple whose greatest wish was that neither would survive the other (Necker, *Réflexions*, 95–97).

The many references provide additional textual density to Necker's argument that time and duration are intrinsic not only to the social fabric, but to humans' larger sense of belonging, of their being in time. Today, she laments, women no longer take the long view: "their new morality teaches them to fix all their thoughts on the present." They live in a perverted temporality, "separated" from both past and future (Necker, *Réflexions*, 75–76), driven by factitious desires and *inquiétude dévorante*.

Necker's vision is of connectedness, belonging, extension of the self via another human being. She emphasizes the importance of that unique connection at the beginning of the first chapter, where she evokes the multiple "centers of existence" created in us by love:

> But the feelings that transport us into another, that vary our pleasures by means of this felicitous exchange, lose part of their charm, their energy, and their influence, when we spread them out over a large number of objects. (Necker, *Réflexions*, 8)

She returns to this idea later, arguing that the benefits of indissoluble marriage are lost when we casually live "through and for others," rather than devoting ourselves to "one other" (Necker, *Réflexions*, 81). Children afford us happiness because they allow a couple to "extend themselves" ("étendre son existence autour de soi") and to see themselves and each other mirrored in their offspring—an observation that offers insight into the limitations of Necker's relationship with her daughter (Necker, *Réflexions*, 30–31). At the half-way point in the *Réflexions*, Necker interrupts her analysis for an emotional pair of apostrophes, first to her long-deceased parents, evoked as the inspiration for her hopes and dreams, and to her husband, for whom she finds language insufficient to describe the closeness of their relationship (Necker, *Réflexions*, 50–54). There is no similar evocation of her own child.

While it is certainly both a political statement and a moralist reflection on the nature of marriage, *Réflexions sur le divorce* is also a consideration of the nature of happiness. If solitude is the great misfortune of life, especially in old age, then connectedness and belonging to a larger universal order, achieved through connection to a particular individual, represent happiness. It cannot be reached, however, without effort and a willingness to accept the other's imperfections and to concede one's own wishes ("à soumettre nos goûts et à exercer notre indulgence," Necker, *Réflexions*, 99). In such a worldview, liberty is "a dangerous word" (Necker, *Réflexions*, 29).

5.5. On Liberty

Necker was well aware that she had taken a position contrary to *la philosophie*; her cultural critique, like Rousseau's, is energized by its explicitly oppositional stance. Given the historical moment, the political resonance of the word, and the circumstances under which she was writing, it is not surprising that she would dismiss *liberté* as dangerous and indeed tantamount to license. But for all her insistence on women's domestic complementarity to their husbands' activity in the world, she herself had known considerable autonomy in her charitable work and in her prominence as a salon hostess.

The moralist critique of marriage foregrounds questions of liberty and autonomy, as well as pointing out the ways in which actual marriage falls short of the "marriage myth" foisted on young girls. If liberty is a "dangerous word" for Necker, it is because, in addition to its revolutionary connotations, it represents a completely different vision of what it means to be human: for Necker, happiness involves integration into a world of relation, literally the Great Chain of Being. Hers is a powerful vision, but it is, at least in this context, a minority view. Although a full discussion of women's accounts of liberty outside the genre of moralist writing lies beyond the scope of this study, it is worth noting echoes and parallels that highlight the political significance of the theme in the moralists' critiques of marriage.

Émilie Du Châtelet, particularly in her unpublished/clandestine work, offered often daring views on the social order. Her explorations of the concept of liberty emerge primarily outside her moralist writing, such as her critique of women's subordination in the preface to her translation of Mandeville. In the *Institutions de physique*, the concept of liberty emerges as part of her goal of working out the relation between physics and metaphysics; here she defines free will as *sagacité*, the exercise of one's reason.[38] Of particular interest is a short manuscript, "Sur la liberté," an early draft for the *Institutions de physique* not included in the final version.[39] In this text, she defines liberty as "the ability to think of something or not to think of it, to move or not to move, in conformity with one's choice"; she further argues that for the compatibility of human liberty with divine omniscience.[40] One can discern an

---

[38] See Le Ru, *Émilie Du Châtelet philosophe*, 51–60. For Du Châtelet's broader social critique, see Judith P. Zinsser, "Émilie Du Châtelet's Views on the Pillars of French Society: King, Church, and Family," in Lisa Curtis-Wendlandt, Paul Gibbard, and Karen Green, eds., *Political Ideas of Enlightenment Women: Virtue and Citizenship* (Farnham, UK: Ashgate, 2013), 17–31; Ruth Hagengruber, "If I Were King! Morals and Physics in Émilie Du Châtelet's Subtle Thoughts on Liberty," in Broad and Detlefsen, *Women and Liberty*, 195–205.

[39] Du Châtelet, "Sur la liberté," in *The Complete Works of Voltaire*, vol. 14 (Oxford: The Voltaire Foundation, 1989), 484–502. On the complexity of the attribution of "Sur la liberté," see the editorial discussion by W. H. Barber, in the same volume, 14:483–84. Although some scholars believe the text to be a discarded draft of the *Traité de métaphysique*, Linda Gardiner Janik argues persuasively that it was intended for the *Institutions*; see Janik, "Searching for the Metaphysics of Science: The Structure and Composition of Madame Du Châtelet's *Institutions de physique*, 1737–1740," *SVEC* 201 (1982): 88–89. As for the *Traité de métaphysique*, Andrew Brown and Ulla Kölving conclude that it represents a collaborative effort. "Qui est l'auteur du *Traité de métaphysique*?" *Cahiers Voltaire* 2 (2002): 85–94.

[40] For a detailed analysis of "Sur la liberté," see Julia Jorati, "Du Châtelet on Freedom, Self-Motion, and Moral Necessity," *Journal of the History of Philosophy* 57.2 (2019): 255–280; see also

implicit argument about the nature of freewill in the discussion of calculation and choice in the *Discours sur le bonheur*,[41] but she explores the topic in greater detail and depth in her work in science and metaphysics.

Social and political ramifications of the philosophical issues emerge in Octavie Belot's 1756 *Réflexions d'une Provinciale*, a riposte to Rousseau's *Discours sur les origines de l'inégalité*. In her analysis of the state of nature, she questions Rousseau's claim that natural man differed from animals not because of understanding, but rather because of his status as a free agent (*agent libre*). For Belot, the capacity to be a free agent is entirely dependent on the capacity for thought, viewed through a Lockean lens: comparison, reflection, and choice. Against Rousseau's contention that it is man's free agency, not his understanding, that distinguishes him from animals, she argues:

> The capacity to will [*vouloir*] appears to me very close to the capacity to know [*connaître*]; the understanding could well be the basis for man's free agency ... [since] in order to choose, he must deliberate, and in order to deliberate, he must make comparisons; in order to make comparisons, he must examine and analyze.[42]

The argument that freedom is a function of the capacity for reflection proves to be emblematic of Belot's overall critique that Rousseau presupposes the cognitive abilities of social man in his depiction of natural man, and inversely, that he underplays both the misery of the natural state and the advantages brought by the social order. Neither the *Réflexions* nor Belot's other philosophical essay, her *Observations sur la noblesse et le tiers état* (1758) is an extended reflection on liberty per se, but, like Verzure, she argues in favor of maintaining the basic social structure with an emphasis on the fair and just application of laws and, tellingly, a reimagined aristocracy based on merit.[43]

Katherine Brading, *Émilie Du Châtelet and the Foundations of Modern Science* (New York: Routledge, 2019), 68–69.

[41] See above, Chapter 4, 132.

[42] Octavie Belot, *Réflexions d'une Provinciale sur le discours de M. Rousseau, Citoyen de Genève, touchant l'origine de l'inégalité des conditions parmi les hommes*, edited with an introduction by Édith Flammarion (Arras: Artois Presses Université, 2015), 278. See Flammarion's excellent introduction for biographical information on Belot, a discussion of the philosophical context of her response to Rousseau, and a dissection of the arguments in her *Réflexions*.

[43] Karen Green is doubtless correct to assert that Belot "suspects republicans of promoting unfettered license" (Green, "Locke, Enlightenment, and Liberty in the Works of Catherine Macaulay and her Contemporaries," in Broad and Detlefsen, *Women and Liberty*, 84). At the same time, Belot's critique of luxury, her sensitivity to poverty (which she had experienced), and her ideas for a renewed nobility point to a nuanced, complex political stance. See Paul Gibbard, "Royalist and

Far more pointed is Sophie de Grouchy's *Lettres sur la sympathie* (1798), a strongly republican text.[44] In her Lettre VI, de Grouchy lays out a theory of positive and negative rights, the former of which involves the retention of a particular good, such as property, protected by law as "a preference founded on reason" (De Grouchy, 80). A fundamental "negative right," on the other hand, is personal liberty, because no other person's claim to supersede it can be greater than one's own interest in maintaining it, "because there is no reason for this man to exercise power over me that I do not have over him" (De Grouchy, 80). Natural equality follows from the same reasoning, "because submission to the will of others and any form of inferiority to them, is in itself a greater evil than gaining superiority through power over the will of another is a good" (De Grouchy, 80).[45] De Grouchy distinguishes between natural inequality of intelligence or talent and social inequality, such as that created by the class system of the *ancien régime*. Legal reform is important to the social order that she envisions, since individual liberty is best protected by the equitable application of just laws. Verzure, too, despite her mistrust of "the spirit of independence" (Verzure, 2:24), argued that laws exist to restrain evildoers and protect individuals ("What other recourse would one have against injustice?" Verzure, 2:26), but that reform was needed when the complexity of the legal system rendered it incomprehensible to those whom it should protect ("It is absurd for men to be subject to laws that they do not know," Verzure, 2:26).

One could hardly touch on the topic of liberty without a mention of Germaine de Staël, another of the "mothers of liberalism" for whom liberty, personal and political, was a theme running throughout her life, her political engagement, her philosophical writings, and her fiction.[46] The ideal of liberty, "the irresistible progress of enlightenment and

---

Radical: Octavie Belot on Rousseau and the Social Order," in Curtis-Wendlandt, Gibbard, and Green, *Political Ideas of Enlightenment* Women, 33–48.

[44] See Sandrine Bergès and Eric Schliesser, "Introduction," to *Sophie de Grouchy's Letters on Sympathy: A Critical Engagement with Adam Smith's The Theory of Moral Sentiments* (Oxford: Oxford University Press, 2019), esp. 39–43. I cite a modern edition of the French text, Sophie de Grouchy, *Les Lettres sur la sympathie*. (As elsewhere, the translation is my own.)

[45] Eric Schliesser argues that de Grouchy's account of positive and negative rights prefigures (with the terminology reversed) Berlin's famous "Two Concepts" distinction, thus making her one of the key forerunners of modern liberalism. "Sophie de Grouchy, the Tradition(s) of Two Liberties, and the Missing Mother(s) of Liberalism," in Broad and Detlefsen, *Women and* Liberty, 109–122.

[46] "S'il fallait caractériser d'un mot l'oeuvre de Mme de Staël, c'est le mot *liberté* qui conviendrait." Simone Balayé, *Madame de Staël: Lumières et liberté* (Paris: Klincksieck, 1979), 240. Balayé's political biography of Staël remains a standard reference. See also Fontana, *Germaine de Staël* (cited above, Chapter 4, note 49).

reason,"[47] remains her compass point, from her early letter praising Rousseau's ability to inspire readers with "the liberty that places no distinctions among men other than those made by Nature" (*Lettres sur Rousseau*, 83) to her powerful statement on the role of writers and intellectuals in building and maintaining democracy in *De la littérature*: "The progress of literature, that is, the continuing improvement [*perfectionnement*] of the arts of thought and expression is necessary to the establishment and conservation of liberty" (*De la littérature*, 121). Few of the women considered here, especially those of earlier generations, could have imagined the turbulence, the sense of a new world coming into being, that the Revolution represented for Staël—and of those who lived through it, not all welcomed it with republican fervor—but at the heart of their critiques of marriage lies a deeply felt sense of the structural injustices of the *ancien régime* and a wish for something more.

One of Pauline Guizot's moralist essays, "L'Indépendance," published posthumously in her *Essais et conseils de morale* (1828), bespeaks ambivalence. It is not an overtly political essay, although we know that she took a deep interest in politics and wrote on political topics in the years after her husband entered public life as a moderate liberal leader, champion of *le juste milieu*, during the Restoration. Adjectival forms identify the narrator as male, but "L'Indépendance" does not examine gender issues per se. Here as in her essays on friendship, an adopted perspective provides her with flexibility as a moralist. The narrator is presented as a rational, responsible citizen, a firm believer in respecting the independence of others: "the way to be free is to leave those around us free . . . we shackle ourselves with the chains we impose on others" (Guizot, *Essais et conseils*, 1:250). He describes situations often associated with dependency: the decision to live in society, rather than in solitude; to defer to others' wishes, rather than following one's own preference; to fall in love; to obey the dictates of duty. He likens these to natural phenomena: "These obligations are part of the condition of any decent man [*honnête homme*], just as the laws imposed by nature are part of the human condition" (Guizot, *Essais et conseils* 1:253). In other words, none of the situations commonly thought to impinge on personal liberty represent limitations to him; from his detached perspective, "most of one's existence is filled with actions that are indifferent in and of themselves"

---

[47] Staël, *Réflexions sur la paix, adressées à M. Pitt et aux Français* (1794), ed. Lucien Jaume, in *Oeuvres complètes* III.I (Paris: Honoré Champion, 2009), 92.

(Guizot, *Essais et conseils*, 1:253). The problem? Other people's inability to make their own decisions. His siblings consult him on the simplest matters, then quarrel with him when his advice differs from what they truly wanted all along. The scenario is not without a comic element, but the message is entirely serious: most humans are incapable of assuming their own liberty ("incapable of tolerating the weight of their liberty," Guizot, *Essais et conseils*, 1:254). Their refusal creates a dilemma for the rational narrator: either to impose his will by making decisions for them, or, more subtly, to impose his will by insisting that they make their own decisions. Either way, he finds himself unable to live up to his goal of respecting the freedom of others. "Am I free? No, because I cannot avoid being in charge" (Guizot, *Essais et conseils* 1:255). Stoic detachment is to no avail: others' weakness of character undermines his goal of freedom.

My purpose in this brief review of women's reflections on liberty is to cast the overarching aims of the moralist consideration of marriage into relief. Financial independence (Puisieux), personal integrity (Lambert), and, ultimately, the ability to choose one's path, from Suchon to d'Arconville, dovetail with calls for freedom of thought and expression, political and social equality. While much of the political debate over marriage during the Enlightenment sprang from the widespread perception of the rift between practice and the growing understanding of social relations viewed through social contract theory and natural law, the moralists focused on a central element, the basic desire to choose one's pathway in life.

But just as Pauline Guizot's account of "independence" points to the concept's frailty and ambiguity in practice, so too Constance de Salm offers a nuanced reflection on the dynamics of marriage in her *Pensées*, published after the Bourbon restoration. De Salm, we might note, was the only woman studied here known to have sought and obtained a divorce while it was still relatively available in the late 1790s. (Her second spouse, Joseph de Salm, had also divorced his first wife.) Following a pair of *pensées* on the delicate balance between the interior life and one's interface with the world, she turns her attention to the equally delicate equilibrium in familial relations. Even an ill-suited (*mal assorti*) couple, she comments, may find advantages in remaining together: "in order to provide assistance to one another, it is not sufficient to have the same feelings and the same way of looking at things; one needs to have the same interests" (Salm, *Pensées*, 150). Common interests, more than shared affection, assure the continuity of the couple and provide a measure of power to the woman. Since husband and wife have equal stake in the couple's "self-interest, honor, fortune, and happiness," her constant presence and advice give her opinion a weight and a power "stronger than male pride has ever been able to imagine" (Salm, *Pensées*, 151). Finally, Salm turns to society's tendency to pity men who are viewed as being "led" by their wives. Although, she concedes, there might be gentle, easygoing men who find themselves married to difficult, demanding women, the real question is, "Why does he allow himself to be led?" since, after all, it is unlikely that a woman's will power alone could reverse a pattern established by both custom and law. Indeed, she goes on to say, if the man being "led" is completely lacking in character or decisiveness, but is happy to turn over all responsibilities to his wife's *esprit supérieur*—why then, it's she who should be pitied (Salm, *Pensées*, 152)!

Known for the strong feminist positions in her *Épître aux femmes* (1797) and other works, Salm's approach to marriage in the *Pensées* may appear uncharacteristically understated. Her point, however, is that marriage need not—*pace* Suzanne Necker—represent a total union of souls in order to function, and that power dynamics are not always what they appear to be.[48]

* * *

Not surprisingly, given all that was at stake, marriage is a considerably weightier subject for women moralists than for their male counterparts. They offer no witty jabs at convention, no clever wordplay. As we've seen, there is considerable overlap between the advice of conduct writing and the analysis of more thoroughly moralist texts. All underscore the asymmetrical power relations of marriage and young women's—and young men's—lack of choice. Suzanne Necker's rare exception undoubtedly stems from philosophical conviction, but also from the fact that she had made a love match. Over the course of the eighteenth century, the terms of the argument echo the seventeenth-century *querelle des femmes* and the critique of marriage levied by Scudéry and her contemporaries, but the evolving social and political context lends them a different meaning by setting them in a different horizon of expectations. It is one thing to compare marriage to slavery at the height of the absolute monarchy; it is another, to make the same comparison a century later, in a world where concepts of natural rights and natural law

---

[48] Salm offers a series of portraits of bad marriages in her *Épîtres à Sophie*, begun in 1801 and completed three decades later, a series of poetic epistles in which she warns a young woman of the dangers of ill-assorted ages, jealousy, and infidelity. *Oeuvres completes*, 4 vols. (Paris: Didot Frères, 1842), 1:167–222. (N.B. Salm's *Oeuvres complètes* do not include the full text of her *Pensées*, which were published in their complete form after her death.)

held increasing currency, where companionate, freely chosen marriage was the ideal, even if arranged marriages were still largely the norm.

Over the course of the long eighteenth century, the confluence of the new affectivity and new social and political ideas produced a "sea change" in the constitution of personal identity on both sides of the English Channel.[49] Here we have seen a double movement: first, women writers' turn to marriage as a legitimate object of moralist inquiry, rather than as a subject of satire; second, a shift in the attitudes of these women writers over the course of the eighteenth century. All recognize the centrality of the institution to the shape of women's lives—how could they not?—but whereas Lambert and Puisieux unblinkingly acknowledge the likelihood of infidelity by both partners, but do not see infidelity in itself as an indication of a broken marriage, or marriage as a poor choice, Verzure and especially d'Arconville discuss presumably "intact" marriages in much bleaker terms. In other words, the earlier writers appear to expect less of marriage by way of sexual or emotional fulfillment, but view it with equanimity. Verzure and d'Arconville, on the other hand, assume companionate marriage as the basic model, but find it unsatisfying and confining.

Marriage is one form of "emotional refuge" from the pressures of social hierarchies and intense self-regulation.[50] Other forms include the entire range of practices linked to the period's new emphasis on affectivity: spiritual self-examination, salon conversation, letter writing, biography and autobiography, and, of course, the reading of novels.[51] As we have seen, however, marriage offers little or no refuge for the women of this study.

There is a tension in the works discussed here between the moralist tradition's emphasis on cold observation and mastery of self and others, and our writers' desire to explore lived experience and personal vulnerability. It is the novel that will ultimately take on the cultural analysis performed by moralist writing: not the moralists' sometime will to power, but their quest to understand human motives and interactions. The entwinement of novel and moralist analysis emerges with the rise of extended prose fiction over the course of the seventeenth century; even the novel's earliest theoreticians

---

[49] Dror Wahrman, *The Making of the Modern Self: Identity and Culture in Eighteenth-Century England* (New Haven: Yale University Press, 2004), xiii, 312–21. See similar comments on the political thrust of the new affectivity in Reddy, *The Navigation of Feeling*, 154; and Seigel, *The Idea of the Self*, 83.
[50] Reddy, 148–49.
[51] Reddy, 149–54; see also Louis Dupré, *The Enlightenment and the Foundations of Modern Culture* (New Haven: Yale University Press, 2004), 45–67.

propose that fiction may indeed be the bearer of truth. A century later, in her *Essai sur les fictions* (1795), Staël will claim that fiction's inner truth exceeds both the facts of history and the disciplined analysis of philosophy.[52]

The discourse of self-regulation remains important for the women moralists, particularly Verzure and d'Arconville, for whom it stems from the Stoic tradition of the mastery of the passions—and the Augustinian distrust of *amour-propre*—rather than from models of court behavior. Stoic self-discipline, however, ultimately repeats and converges with the Ancien Régime's worldly disciplines of self-control, which may explain part of the reason why the ideal of freedom, even when internalized and separated from social institutions such as marriage, remains elusive. D'Arconville's sense of self may be bound up in the world of the *ancien régime*, but her expectations for marriage are subtly colored by a profound sense that this world was not enough.

---

[52] Staël, "Essai sur les fictions," ed. Stéphanie Genand, in *Oeuvres complètes* I.II (Paris: Honoré Champion, 2013), 39–65.

6
On Age and Experience

The topic of old age has a distinguished history in the moralist tradition. The seventeenth- and eighteenth-century moralists typically looked to Cicero's *De Senectute* in particular, as well as to Seneca's letters and to Montaigne's essays. What begins as a combination of exhortation to virtue and consolation in the face of the inevitable in the classical texts shifts subtly in the modern period, where the loss of social status among the elderly is felt more keenly. And, as Madame de Lambert put it sharply in her *Traité de la vieillesse*, referring to Cicero, but also the entire tradition, moralist writers write with men in mind: "They work on men's behalf only" (Lambert, 181). In this chapter, I will look at the ways in which women moralists considered the question of age through the lens of gender.

Let us begin by considering a foundational work, Cicero's *De Senectute*. Like his *De Amicitia*, also composed during the year preceding his assassination, the reflections on old age are addressed to Cicero's friend Atticus. As in *De Amicitia*, the dialogue purportedly takes place among men of earlier generations. Here, although the primary speaker is Cato the Elder, Cicero makes it clear that he has chosen Cato, whose name was synonymous with uncompromising moral rectitude, to be the mouthpiece for his own views, underscoring the point by observing that Cato, who was known for his rough speech, will speak "more learnedly" than in life. In the dialogue, when asked to describe the secrets of a happy old age, Cato reflects on four "complaints" that are often made about old age: the loss of the management of one's affairs, the loss of bodily strength, the loss of sensual pleasures, and, ultimately, the impending loss of one's own life. Cato argues that each of these losses is more than compensated by gains: old men are not called to do more than they are physically able, and their wisdom and experience enable them to take on new roles, "vastly more significant and more worthwhile."[1] Similarly, the advantages of a properly cultivated mind outshine those of mere physical strength at any age. Since sensual pleasures such as food or sex produce

---

[1] Cicero, "On Old Age," in *On Old Age and On Friendship*, 11.

Women Moralists in Early Modern France. Julie Candler Hayes, Oxford University Press. © Oxford University Press 2024.
DOI: 10.1093/oso/9780197688601.003.0006

chaos in our lives, "we should be very grateful to old age, which causes us no longer to want what we ought never to have wanted" (Cicero, 22). Cato recommends the higher pleasures of conversation and, in an extended lyrical passage, agriculture (Cicero, 27). As for the fear of death, Cato/Cicero explicitly takes a page from Plato, arguing that death is either nothingness or immortality spent in the company of those who have gone before, hence nothing to be feared—indeed, the prospect of immortality lends us hope. The dialogue ends on an unexpectedly poignant note. By situating the conversation in the last year of Cato's life, Cicero has it take place in the aftermath of the death of his eldest son—a loss that no parent can wish to contemplate, and that Cicero himself knew well. Like the conversation in *De Amicitia*, *De Senectute* takes place at a time of mourning, lending the entire conversation a compensatory, consolatory aura.

Cato thus denies the most serious charges against old age and minimizes concerns about infirmity or diminished mental capacity. Although these concerns are adumbrated in the exhortation to "resist old age" through a healthy lifestyle and continued mental exercise (Cato has been learning Greek in old age), Cato ascribes old age's losses to "faults of character," and maintains that one's "best defense" lies in "the knowledge and practice of the virtues."

The themes and injunctions of *De Senectute* will echo in later philosophers, in particular the emphasis on the different responsibilities and duties at different life stages, the importance of making the best use of one's brief time on earth, the advantage of being freed from the tyranny of the senses, and the need to lay the foundations for a successful old age during one's youth. Thus Seneca enjoins his friend Lucilius to come to terms with life's "natural boundaries" as well as to appreciate the present moment, rather than "living for tomorrow" or being "about to live." Another major touch point for early modern moralists, Montaigne discusses attitudes toward death in his well-known "Philosopher, c'est apprendre à mourir"; he emphasizes the different activities appropriate for the different seasons of life in "De l'aage" and "Toutes choses ont leur saison." (He however dismissed Cato's decision to learn Greek as a schoolboy's subject, unworthy of an old man.) As he makes clear in his final essay, "De l'expérience," Montaigne views practical experience as an indispensable component of knowledge: "When reason is lacking, we turn to experience"—in other words, to practice, a direct encounter with the world that can advance our understanding when reason cannot suffice (Montaigne, 2:516).

All these topics become part of the *materia prima* drawn on by the seventeenth-century moralists, but subtle differences begin to emerge. Old age becomes framed as a reminder of mortality, a reality that humans cannot tolerate for Pascal; or, as La Bruyère puts it simply, "One hopes to grow old, and one fears old age; which is to say that one loves life, and flees death" (La Bruyère, *Caractères* ch.11, n.41, 849). We also see more of a focus on contrasting patterns of behavior in the different life stages, as well as a less overtly prescriptive approach. The reader must draw his or her conclusions. As we have seen, however, moralist "descriptions" are rarely entirely neutral. Witness a pair of echoing maxims in La Sablière and La Rochefoucauld, both of whom find the "habits" of old age to be as detrimental as youthful "passion."

The habits of old age are no less obstacles for one's salvation/ well-being [*salut*] than the passions of youth. (La Sablière, *Maximes chrétiennes*, n.20, 286)

The passions of youth are hardly more opposed to one's *salut* than the lukewarm attitude of old people. (La Rochefoucauld, *Maximes*, n.34, 165)

Implicitly, both push back on the received notion that old age is good in itself.

In addition to old people's "lukewarm" response to life and their reliance on habit, age is increasingly figured as a disability, a loss of status that may be viewed as either comic or tragic. Old men who wish to marry are a stock figure of comedy, as are amorous older women. Whereas Cicero's Cato praised the peace and beauty of rural life, La Rochefoucauld sees a rural retreat as the recourse of those who no longer have any role to play and are completely disregarded at court: "Each day removes a part of themselves" (La Rochefoucauld, *Réflexions* n.14, 218). Not that all views were as somber as those of the ex-Frondeur La Rochefoucauld. In a letter to his friend the maréchal de Créqui, a text that would be much reprinted in the eighteenth-century, Saint-Évremond describes his later years in exile with equanimity, focusing on the pleasures of reading, conversation (especially with women), and study.[2] Saint-Évremond's correspondence is also the source for one of

---

[2] Charles de Saint-Évremond, "À Monsieur le maréchal de Créqui, qui m'avait demandé en quelle situation était mon esprit et ce que je pensais sur toutes choses," *Oeuvres en prose*, ed. René Ternois, 4 vols. (Paris: Classiques Garnier, 1969), 4:103–39; see also his "De la retraite," *Oeuvres en prose*, 4:287–99.

one of La Rochefoucauld's most infamous witticisms—a remark that never appeared in any of the editions of the *Maximes* that he supervised, but that he reportedly said to Ninon de Lenclos: "Old age is the hell for women" ("La vieillesse, c'est l'enfer des femmes").[3] Saint-Évremond's advice to Lenclos was to ignore "l'enfer de Monsieur de La Rochefoucauld": "Say the word 'love' boldly, and never let the term "old age" pass your lips."[4] But Saint-Évremond was kinder to women than most.

Women, as Lambert would observe, are not especially present in moralist writing on aging, other than as comic figures like La Bruyère's portrait of an old coquette who believes that age is something that befalls other women and who wears age-inappropriate finery on her death bed (La Bruyère, *Caractères*, "Des femmes" n.7, 724). For the seventeenth-century moralists, then, there is nothing especially appealing about old age for either men or women, but the idea that old age would be "hell" for women in particular acknowledges an unspoken difference: that whatever slights or inconveniences might be experienced by men, women were defined by their age—and their looks—in a more forceful way. Whether evoked by Cicero, Montaigne, or La Rochefoucauld, the life stages reflect male activities and careers; even the "loss of sensual pleasures" is reframed for women, since the code of sexual virtue places strict limits on the expression of desire for women of any age. Older women's sexual desire is viewed as perverse or ridiculous. The compensations of age, Cato's "higher and better things," such as being able to play the role of elder statesmen and mentor, are not part of the standard picture for women. In her study of women and aging during the French Enlightenment, Joan Hinde Stewart rightly points to examples of women writers whose lives belied the period's conventional wisdom about older women. Stewart observes, however, that although older women may appear as sympathetic characters in novels, they do not display romantic feelings: "It was the stuff of which novels were not yet made."[5]

Unlike novelists, however, women moralists write older women back into the picture. In considering the traditional questions—"What is experience, and what does each stage of life teach us?" and "What is lost, and what is gained, as we age?"—they seek to provide answers that speak to women's lives. They critique the power imbalance and misogyny underlying traditional

---

[3] On the provenance of the remark, see the editorial note by Jean Lafond, *Moralistes du XVIIe*, 1085.
[4] Saint-Évremond, "Lettre à Mademoiselle de Lenclos," *Oeuvres choisies*, 346.
[5] Joan Hinde Stewart, *The Enlightenment of Age: Women, Letters, and Growing Old in Eighteenth-Century France* (Oxford: Voltaire Foundation, 2010), 252.

norms governing female behavior; and while they have a deep interest in the human condition writ large, they shine a light on those elements from the moralist tradition that are not universals, but reflect a male perspective.

Many women wrote on the subject of old age, some in brief maxims and others in extended essays and dialogues. I will look first at works that consider the related subjects of life stages, the value of experience, and the forms of learning that occur over time; then turn to texts that take on the thorny issue of the social codes that shape women's opportunities in later life. I will conclude with a reading of Geneviève d'Arconville's late essay, "Sur la vieillesse et la mort." Although several of the women discussed in this chapter lived into old age, d'Arconville's piece is one of only two texts discussed here—the other is Scudéry's "De l'expérience"—whose author was in her eighties at the time of writing. Her essay, although somber in its outlook, bears witness to the exceptional qualities of mind that she carried to the end.

6.1. Experience, Knowledge, and the Seasons of Life

Written in the later decades of the seventeenth century, Dauphine de Sartre's maxims gathered under the rubrics "Expériance" and "Vieillesse" speak to a positive view of the former and a more nuanced view of the latter. Experience may or may not be linked to age: Like Montaigne, Sartre comments that practical or lived experience is essential to understanding: "the philosophy of the eyes and ears and the palpable demonstration of the truth." While experience provides a short-cut to the reasoning process, Sartre also notes that it has a temporal dimension: "Experience bears late-season fruit." Lastly, it is said to "complete" or "refine" the knowledge gained through study (Sartre, 110). In Sartre's essay on old age, wisdom is said to reflect the "experience" of age; she observes that advice from old people is more reliable ("plus seür") than that of the young. At the same time, she notes that the aesthetic appreciation of ancient ruins, temples, and palaces does not extend to the signs of age in human faces, where age is seen as "hideous and despised" (Sartre, 173). Sartre's short observations point to the different forms of temporality inherent in the word "experience," which refers both to the immediacy of perception and to the accumulation and working-through of knowledge acquired over time. Although she values the wisdom of age, she notes that its visible manifestation is shunned.

The ambivalence and multiple meanings inherent in age and experience all come to bear in Madeleine de Scudéry's conversation, "De l'expérience," which appeared in her final collection, *Entretiens de morale* (1692). This conversation takes place in the salon of the wise and virtuous Chrysante. It is she who calls the company's attention to the fact that among them are represented all the seasons of adult life: the young Célinte, "brilliant and playful," as Spring; the accomplished Anacrise, as Summer; Clariste, "still handsome and possessing an enlightened spirit," as Fall; and as Winter Chrysante herself, who despite her age "retains all the charms and refinement of her spirit" (Scudéry 1692, 1:216–17). The group also includes a younger man, Timante, and an older man, Poliandre, who like Chrysante enjoys excellent health in body and mind (Scudéry 1692, 1:218). Both Célinte and Timante are pleasant young people, and while neither is said to disdain the advice of their elders (Scudéry 1692, 1:222), both exemplify the carefree thoughtlessness of youth.

While focus of the conversation is ostensibly to analyze the meanings of "experience" and to reflect on its significance, it also points to the differences in old age for men and for women. Whereas older men retain social consideration and are sought after for their advice, aging "is more disadvantageous" for women (Scudéry 1692, 1:235), who lose status when they lose their looks. As Chrysante makes this point, Célinte respectfully disagrees, pointing out that Chrysante herself has maintained her standing and the respect of others (Scudéry 1692, 1:237). How she achieved this state leads into a series of questions: What is experience, what can it teach us, and what are its limits? Scudéry's map of the conversational territory is a densely plotted garden of forking paths in which the unifying topic becomes the role of time in a theory of knowledge.

Chrysante points to several habits that have contributed to her happy and respectable old age: choosing her friends wisely, "making provision" for old age by improving her mind and listening to the advice of her elders. She gently attempts to guide Célinte by recalling that in her own youth, she was befriended by an older woman: "I was fortunate enough to follow her advice and to want to imitate her" (Scudéry 1692, 1:223). Célinte, despite her evident respect and affection for Chrysante, does not take the hint. Instead, her reluctance to think about old age ("I think about other things," Scudéry 1692, 1:234) and her skeptical attitude toward the value of experience propel the dialogue.

Célinte makes two objections. First, she claims that "experience" is of no value to someone who exercises no leading social or professional role in life and whose actions presumably have no effect on others—"neither public nor private affairs to govern, nor causes to defend, nor patients to treat, nor a family to lead"—in other words, someone who is not a man (Scudéry 1692, 1:225). In a second objection, she goes straight to the empirical basis of the subject by calling into doubt the hitherto unquestioned relationship between knowledge and time. Even if I concede that experience is of practical use, she argues, why should we assume that it requires a great deal of time to achieve?

> For why would my mind not know everything that it needs to know as soon and as thoroughly as my eyes know what is presented to them? I see all the objects in the world as they are, without excepting the sun. Why, therefore, she continued, would a person of excellent mental capacity not know everything that the mind encounters? (Scudéry 1692, 1:225–26)

As in the debate between Télésile and Céphise in "De la connoissance d'autruy et de soy-mesme," the sun serves as the figure for the seemingly unproblematic object of knowledge that is ultimately more complicated than at first thought. Although it is clear that Célinte is mistaken, and one cannot know everything as soon as it comes into view, it is also clear that her objection is a serious one that forces the others to ask just what time contributes to our understanding of the world.

Thus, while the older characters Poliandre and Chrysante will be at pains to show Célinte that she is wrong, her query has the effect of forcing them to complicate their notion of "experience." They concede that not all experience need be "personal": one can learn from the experiences of others, whether recounted at first hand, or in books—but this concession does not answer her objection. Although they continue to maintain that time is a necessary component of the wisdom brought by experience, they concede that it is not sufficient, as evinced by numerous examples of people who have grown old and presumably experienced much, but who are not wise (Scudéry 1692, 1:228–29). Poliandre then proposes a broader definition: "Experience . . . consists in the ideas we form of all that we have seen or read, upon which our judgment has reflected in order to better understand them or to make good use of them; the social world, books, and travel all contribute to shape experience." As Célinte promptly points out, however, if one lacks judgment, all this experience is worthless and the definition falls apart (Scudéry 1692, 1:231–32).

What does experience contribute in Scudéry's theory of knowledge? In her account, *connaissance* is produced by the intersection of experience and judgment. Scudéry's model echoes Locke's near-contemporaneous model of understanding as conjoined sensation and reflection, but with a difference. Whereas the Lockean model is structural and ahistorical, Scudéry's emphasis on "experience" rather than "sensation" is inherently temporal, linking sensation inextricably to time and repetition. The French word *expérience* also points to an "experimental" aspect of knowledge. As members of the group observe, although it is possible to benefit from the experiences of others, some things simply cannot be known until we have encountered them ourselves. Thus, the aging process itself and the various seasons of life, however much they may be described, commented on, or observed, are fundamentally incomprehensible to anyone who has not lived them. The pair Chrysante and Célinte exemplify the dilemma: despite the younger woman's affection and admiration for the older woman, she has no desire to become like her, since in order to do so, she must grow old. Chrysante further complicates the issue by claiming that one does not "know" youth when one is young (Scudéry 1692, 1:234); in other words, Célinte has no concept of time, her own or anyone else's. According to Chrysante, were it not for a portrait she had seen of her late mother in old age, Célinte would never believe it possible that she herself might grow old (Scudéry 1692, 1:234).

It is a curiously overdetermined moment in the dialogue: Chrysante's implicitly maternal role with respect to Célinte made manifest in the reference to the latter's biological mother, who we learn is dead. Why could not the same point have been made à propos of a living mother? Célinte's avoidance of thinking about aging suddenly appears to be less that of a coquette who fears the loss of her beauty, than that of a daughter who is unwilling or unable to think about her mother's death. Chrysante's immediate response is to paint the passage of time in a positive light and to proclaim her own happiness, which is due in part to her having listened to her older, wiser friends in her youth and "made provision" ("faire provision") of relationships that would support her throughout her life (Scudéry 1692, 1:238), and in part—we learn later—to her having survived an unhappy marriage (Scudéry 1692, 1:252).

No amount of wise advice from others can give us knowledge of certain things, the characters reflect. Death cannot be known. Simply knowing that people die every day, "as the leaves fall one after another from the trees," gives us no insight and "does not enable us to know death itself" (Scudéry 1692, 1:248). Célinte having expressed her horror at the idea of facing death on a battlefield, another woman, the mature Clariste (representing Fall in the seasonal allegory), immediately comments that "there is another very important thing to which we are exposed without any prior experience, and I am persuaded that one would expose oneself to it less, if one knew it well: I mean marriage" (Scudéry 1692, 1:252). And thus, in a sudden shift, sex (marriage) becomes the other event that cannot be known before it is encountered directly. (I cannot help thinking of the remark by one of the characters in Don Delillo's novel *White Noise*: "There was only one topic of conversation. Sex and death.") Although one of the men, Antenor, has described his own sentimental education at the hands of "a few fair ones that I used to see" ("quelques belles que je voyois") whose snares he avoided only through the intervention of an older, wiser friend (Scudéry 1692, 1:241–42), all agree that for a woman, at least, no number of warnings or examples of bad marriages can have the slightest effect: "one always imagines that one will be happier than others" (Scudéry 1692, 1:253). The fact that Antenor was able to learn from multiple romantic experiences, while women must stake everything on marriage, is not discussed.

Timante, the younger man, points out that if we insisted on knowing everything ("tout éprouver") ahead of time, we would never attempt anything or take chances: "one would upset the normal order of things, one would scarcely make any friends, and one would hardly tell one's secrets to anybody" (Scudery 1692, 1:255)" (1:255). The others concur, and launch a series of anecdotes that bear on various kinds of "secrets" both kept and revealed. Anecdotes about secrets underscore the role of the "secret" within "experience": the degree to which fundamental things cannot be known otherwise than through experience or "experimentation." The scene closes with Chrysante and the other older women extolling the pleasures of age. Timante declares himself ready to follow the advice of his elders, but Célinte respectfully declines to join him: "I sincerely confess that I am not unhappy to have this serenity [*repos*] still distant from me, and I hope that it will remain so for a long time" (Scudéry 1692, 1:263-4).

Célinte thus appears unready to accept mentorship, one of the principal elements of the "provisions" that Chrysante made for herself during her own youth. Célinte's reluctance demonstrates her older friend's observation that youth cannot know youth, but it creates a dilemma and opens an aporetic structure in the conversation. If youth is not aware of itself as youth, how then can it prepare for a future that it is not ready to acknowledge? The older characters describe finding happiness through their friendships and by having abandoned illusions, "being disabused of all the false pleasures and frivolous hopes of youth" (Scudéry 1692, 1:263): in other words, through a series of discoveries, presumably painful ones. Implicitly, the loss of illusion or "frivolous hope" joins death and marriage as a phenomenon that cannot be known until it occurs.

Ultimately, then, Scudéry argues that although the accumulation of practical and intellectual knowledge is useful, indeed necessary, there are certain basic things that must be encountered directly. Experiential learning, as we might call it, reveals more than any amount of education or mentorship can prepare us for. It is clear, however, that Célinte was incorrect to suppose that one could "know everything" with the instantaneity of vision. Understanding requires time. Although youth cannot know youth, the passage from one life stage to another brings the awareness of temporality. That awareness is the gift of time; the wisdom of age is to understand and accept that transition. Célinte will receive Chrysante's mentorship, if she receives it at all, only in retrospect.

Marie de Verzure's pair of essays on youth and age similarly pursue the question of how to "make provision" for later life. In "La Jeunesse," Verzure underscores the importance of early training and education. She focuses on moral education, which needs to begin early, prior to "l'instant où la nature se développe" (Verzure, 2:76). Her phrase reminds us that, in certain contexts, the word *nature* refers to the genitals and sexuality. Ostensibly the discussion concerns boys as well as girls; the feminine pronouns that follow refer to the antecedent *jeunesse*. Nevertheless, it soon becomes clear that Verzure's primary interest is in girls, as the educative process she envisions is intended to help them "flee from danger," a coded phrase for the avoidance of seduction, generally not viewed as a danger for boys. She criticizes early training that focuses exclusively on "graces and talents"—in other words, the lessons in music, dance, and singing that were typical for girls of her rank. Rather, she admonishes, "From the beginning, one must shape the mind and the reason to watch over the heart, in order to shield it from the seduction of the senses" (Verzure, 2:78). If one waits until the senses are awakened, it will be too late.

Although Verzure sees benefits in the study of history, with its exemplars of vices and virtues, the key to virtuous self-possession is rigorous training in self-examination—not surprising, given the overall aims and methods of her *Réflexions hazardées*. The child who regularly looks within, identifies her faults, and learns from them "to her sorrow" (*à ses dépens*), will take it upon herself to improve. *Amour-propre* propels her, because we all wish to be happy with ourselves and to gain the approval of others (Verzure, 2:80).

Youth has distinct advantages in Verzure's view. Newness and innocence are the principal advantages because they facilitate learning. Even youth's attractiveness, "l'avantage de plaire," is helpful, as long as it is directed toward eliciting positive reinforcement for "solid and durable" attributes. "Pleasing" is, of course, double-edged, since the *désir de plaire* is often assumed to be a quality of women in general and underlies morally dubious coquetry. In a series of agricultural and architectural metaphors, Verzure describes a pedagogy for cultivating that which is inherent in the child and building solid foundations for later life. "La Jeunesse" concludes by foreshadowing those later years, with the warning that if one waits too long to properly provision oneself with qualities that go beyond superficial *agréments*, then one risks finding oneself without a social network. People are happy to share ideas with other intelligent, thoughtful people, but not with others: "one always gives to those who already have; but those to whom everything must be given are tiresome" (Verzure, 2:87). Thus, in order to continue to please others in later life, one must have something of one's own to contribute.

The essay "La Vieillesse" extends these ideas. If youth's advantages are malleability and the ability to please, the advantage of age is to have successfully absorbed the lessons inculcated in youth and "learned self-knowledge through one's own faults" (Verzure, 2:89). Old age must come to terms with the realization that it is not in itself pleasing ("la vieillesse déplaît"), but self-sufficiency, a clear conscience, the satisfaction of doing good, and the absence of distraction by the passions are among the "provisions for old age." Those who lack these provisions are unhappy; they remain mired in regret at a time when they could make the best use of their understanding and judgment (Verzure, 2:90).

Verzure provides both positive and negative images of old age. In the short essay "L'Ingénuité et l'innocence," one of several pieces that parse the distinction between two closely related terms, she observes that *ingénuité* has nothing to do with age: "There are people who at sixty are artless and childlike [*ingénus*]; in whom candor and openness take the place of innocence; whose ideas, mind, and heart are so far from cruelty or even the slightest malice, that they mature with the simplicity of first innocence" (Verzure, 2:151–52). The candid, open-hearted old person is in sharp contrast with the bitter, demanding figure evoked in "Des Vieillards" (Verzure, 2:192–95), who wishes to be loved by young people, but whose insistence on rights and prerogatives alienates them.

Verzure, then, defines the compensations of old age in terms of self-sufficiency and lessons learned—"provisions" received. At the same time, she tends to frame her arguments in terms of exchange, such as the idea that one must "give" something to be accepted in a group in "La Jeunesse." While the attention to exchange may seem at odds with the mistrust of manipulative forms of exchange expressed in her writings on friendship, it echoes the complex interplay of self and other that we saw in her account of self-understanding. In "Des Vieillards," the economic aspect is even clearer: "the attentions and deference that one demands are a debt; pleasant, freely given attentions are a gift" (Verzure, 2:194). If one requires respect for one's age, like payment on a debt, it cannot bring the happiness that only a gift can provide. Although Verzure does not frame her reflections on old age in terms of gender, it is striking to note the extent to which she envisions a successful old age in terms of self-sufficiency and the ability to thrive without making assumptions about the respect or affection of others—gifts that cannot be forced.

Others emphasize the grim side of old age. In her *Réflexions et avis sur les défauts et les ridicules à la mode* (1761), the sequel to her *Conseils à une amie*, Madeleine de Puisieux signals that women's lives from cradle to grave are beset by pain and unequal treatment: physical and mental constraints, a lack of education, an arranged marriage, which lead only to the "the moment so feared by pretty women, the loss of their charms." The only solution for many is a turn to the trappings of religion, "fake devotion in which ... they find neither true satisfaction nor compensation for what they have lost."[6] Constance de Salm views old age as loss and privation. In her *Pensées*, written over the course of many years but first published when she was in her sixties, she expresses disdain for the "resignation of age" that many take for the fruit of wisdom, but is only "the first stage of the declining mind and strength of character" (Salm, *Pensées*, 25). Similarly, she sees *le repos* as "the opposite of life," leading directly to "stagnation, old age, and death" (Salm, *Pensées*, 76). There appears to be no compensating gain for the loss of "the happy illusion in youth that lets us believe in the affection and boundless devotion of our friends" (Salm, *Pensées*, 133–34). In Salm's account, experience may even be a negative force: "To have seen much, voyaged much, observed much, is to have robbed oneself, without realizing it, of the means to be truly

---

[6] Madeleine de Puisieux, *Réflexions et avis sur les défauts et les ridicules à la mode* (Paris: Chez la Veuve Brunet, 1761), 5–8.

happy" (Salm, *Pensées*, 201). Salm finds one advantage to old age, especially for women: "being able to speak freely about any number of things that one could never say when one was young without a frustrating constraint that disturbed one's heart and mind" (Salm, *Pensées*, 301). As we will see, the promise of a loosening of constraints on female behavior will also give hope to others.

In *De Senectute*, the losses of old age are more than made up by gains: whereas the losses are material and physical, the gains are the "higher" goods of knowledge, experience, and the respect of one's peers. Those who did not hold the appropriate values in their younger years will not be happy in old age, as we see in Cato's example of the strongman Milo of Croton, who was devastated by his declining physical strength, having cultivated no other virtue. Through "the knowledge and practice of the virtues," men may expect that their advanced years will be marked by new roles of mentorship, teaching, and the giving of wise counsel, and the pleasures of conversation, study, and a leisured retreat.

Although early modern moralists evince doubts as to the inherent good of attaining old age, the moralist evocation of life stages strives to provide a similar road map for achieving what happiness might be possible. The virtues enjoined by women moralists are simple: heed the advice of elders, observe those around you, practice scrupulous self-examination, do not be driven by the passions. Implicit in most, and explicit in both Verzure and Puisieux, is the need for a solid education to avoid an overreliance on the transitory charms of youth. While it is certainly true that women's virtue was defined by sexual morality to such an extent that it need not even be mentioned, the degree to which the examples and implicit advice of these texts focus on self-reliance is significant, as we saw in the chapter on happiness.

The object of knowledge has shifted over the course of these readings. For all, "experience" is constitutive of "knowledge," but the understanding of "experience" has shifted, as different zones of the word's broad semantic field come into focus. While for all our writers, "experience" is always more than (mere) "sensation," the emphasis shifts from experience of the natural, phenomenal world, to experience of one's own sense of being, to experience of the social world. These thinkers also seek to define the "experiential" dimension of knowledge, the degree to which we must encounter something for ourselves, with or without the participation of others; or the degree to which it remains "experimental," discovered through trial and error, without a clear idea (or only a weak hypothesis) to guide us to a conclusion. In Puisieux's

Réflexions, the gradual introduction of a narrative element, a series of letters addressed to a young woman friend interspersed among the "reflections," suggests a more strongly determined trajectory to the search for knowledge, which is also more clearly defined as something transmitted from one (older, wiser) person to another. It is significant that the scope of knowledge in Puisieux is more clearly linked to gender than ever before and that the notion of "experience," when applied to women, has taken on a distinctly sexual connotation. All this can be linked to the evolution of *mondanité*, worldliness, and the territorializing effects of the novel. But as we have seen in Scudéry, there were other forms of understanding available.

I can do no more than gesture here toward works where an autobiographical component provides a roadmap for attaining wisdom at different life stages. Prior to the advent of modern autobiography, Montaigne had woven his personal experience into his analysis of the human condition: "I myself am the matter of my book" (Montaigne, 1:1). Montaigne does not however narrate his life as a sequence of events; the great confessional narratives, beginning with Augustine, offer a defined trajectory, a pathway to salvation, rather than to the construction of an identity situated in time. In the final decades of the eighteenth century, Rousseau's *Confessions*, in which the Genevan presented himself as simultaneously unique and exemplary, were taken by many readers as a new model for authenticity and self-disclosure, a challenge that would be taken up notably by Madame Roland in her *Mémoires*. Moralist writing, while distinct from autobiography, similarly takes an interest in psychological evolution at different life stages. The very public authorial persona in Madeleine de Puisieux's prefaces charts her career from a novice writer and friend of "Monsieur D***" (Diderot) to a worldly, combative author who responds to her critics and is tired of having her work attributed to a man.[7] The manuscripts of both Henriette de Marans and Geneviève d'Arconville, written for friends and family, rather than for publication, include extended reflections on their childhood and early intimations of a literary career. Such works display the stages of a life and a career that emphasize turning points, intellectual milestones, paths taken and not taken, that could become available to others.[8]

---

[7] "If the Editor of the *Encyclopédie* is more than capable of leading that great work, it would still likely be impossible for him to compose anything as insignificant as my trifles, which have no merit other than a light-hearted tone, a sense of honor, and a style that is mine alone and no one else's." (Puisieux, *Des caractères*, 2 vols. (Londres: n.p., 1751), 2:viii

[8] For example, Henriette de Marans, "Histoire de mon esprit depuis 12 ans jusqu'à 16 ans," *Mémorial à mon usage particulier*, in Chollet and Krief, *Une Femme d'encre et de papier*, 203–207.

6.2. Codes of Conduct

Reflections on time, temporality, and life stages touch indirectly on gender differences in the experience of old age, as Scudéry's understated comment that old age is "more disadvantageous" to women than to men. When women moralists turn to the codes of conduct regulating women's behavior, an overtly critical stance emerges. In this section, I will first look at Anne-Thérèse de Lambert's two pieces on women and old age. The first is an "experimental" search for the foundations of successful aging; the second, a polemical indictment of society's attitudes toward older women.

Lambert's *Traité de la vieillesse* was undoubtedly one of the best-known works on old age from the eighteenth century. Although not published until well after her death, it is thought to have been written not in her later life, but rather sometime around the year 1700, when she was in her early 50s.[9] That she addressed her reflections on age to her daughter further suggests that this work may have been written about the same time as the *Avis d'une mère à sa fille*, written near 1700, but published (against the author's wishes) in 1728. While a fifty-something Lambert hardly strikes us (me, in any case) as "old"—particularly inasmuch as she would live well into her eighties—it may well have been the case for her, as for Scudéry's "summer" and "fall" characters, Anacrise and Clariste, that the initial sensations of age and change are most vivid to one who has already experienced the passage of one life stage and thus temporality. Anacrise is the only character in "De l'expérience" to express either regret for the past or apprehension for the future: "I have often regretted that when I was twelve or thirteen I so fervently wished to be seventeen or eighteen; for although I am only at what Chrysante calls the Summer of my life, I seem to feel the approach of Autumn, just as Clariste sees the coming of Winter" (Scudéry 1692, 1:219).

Lambert's vision of age is considerably more somber than that of Scudery's "winter" character, Chrysante. Her introductory statement sets the tone: "as I near that age where everything slips away from us, I hope to find through

---

Although her papers were "private," numerous prefaces and passages in her papers make it clear that she intended them for the eyes of future generations. D'Arconville left numerous autobiographical pieces among her late essays (*PRA*), also intended for the eyes of family and friends.

[9] Lambert, *Traité de la vieillesse*, in *Oeuvres*, 181–204. Although her editor Granderoute places the writing of the *Traité de vieillesse* near the end of Lambert's life, I agree with Roger Marchal, who argues for an earlier time of composition, nearer the time of Lambert's other "Ciceronian" essay, the *Traité d'amitié*, from the early 1700s (Marchal, *Madame de Lambert et son milieu*, 192–93).

reasoning the value of all that I will lose" (Lambert, 181). Loss is the principal motif from the outset, coloring her view of women's entire lifespan: "women are left on their own at every age: their education is neglected in their youth, and over the course of their life they are deprived of the guidance and support needed for old age" (Lambert, 181). Although Lambert promises herself and her daughter to seek to discover what compensations there might be to make up for the loss of youth, few options present themselves. Citing Montaigne ("From the ardent passions... we move on to chilly ones"; Lambert, 182), she reflects on the pains and indignities of the aging body, and the ever-narrower range of pleasures that are permitted, since "what is permissible at one age is indecent in another" (Lambert, 183).

Lambert seems to feel little compassion for the harsh fate of the aging *femme galante*, but women of feeling fare no better. Even though older women's capacity for feeling is as lively as ever ("the heart does not fade like the senses"; Lambert, 184), passion and love no longer have their place among the "duties of old age."

> All that slips away at a certain age, when, if you hope to make use of your heart, you no longer have any feeling but pain. There comes a time when one must lead a life in accordance with the decorum [*bienséances*] and the dignity of one's age: one must renounce any sort of lively pleasure... one must break off any relation with one's feelings: one feels those ties when it becomes necessary to end them. (Lambert, 185)

The other "duties" consist in the realization that social rules are stricter than ever: "When you lose your youth, you lose the right to make mistakes; you are no longer allowed to be wrong" (Lambert, 186). Since none of society's amusements, whether gambling, flirtation, elegant clothes, or witty conversation, are suitable, the only real option appears to be staying home: "one's pride suffers less there than elsewhere" (Lambert, 186). At which point, Lambert's daughter or any other reader might be justified in taking Célinte's position and deciding that she is quite happy to keep her distance from this subject.

It is worth recalling, however, that Lambert has stated explicitly that she is not writing from experience ("I am nearing that age where everything slips away") and that she has announced two purposes in writing: on the one hand, a grim desire to "find... the value of all that I will lose" and on the other, to discover what might replace that which she has lost—or more precisely, that which she expects to lose. Unlike Scudéry's characters, whose research is collective, participatory, and inductive, based on the empirical data of evidence and anecdotes, Lambert's method harkens back to an earlier mode: speculative, deductive. And yet her writing too is "experimental" in a very broad sense: exploratory, geared at finding something new.

Lambert's scientific model reminds us of Descartes, "seul dans un poêle," mentally shearing one idea away from another until he had reached a foundation. For Lambert, too, the bleak account of the privations of old age leads to thinking about the ways in which solitude is productive and how, once shorn of its worldly accretions, the self may be known and cultivated. She draws on both Christian and Stoic traditions in stressing the need to cultivate one's soul and detach oneself from the senses.

> One must allow nature to take its course imperceptibly; nature is our surest guide.
> We live to lose and to detach ourselves. (Lambert, 189)

In many ways, even this more positive account of old age appears to represent no more than a positive spin or attitude adjustment of the mournful depictions of the first part of the essay. The loss of pleasure is repositioned as freedom from the bonds of sensuality (Lambert, 189) and unhappiness is attributed to "the imagination" (Lambert, 188). Since Lambert offers no argument or technique for achieving this altered consciousness other than enjoining the reader to yield to necessity, the result may be less than totally convincing. The second half of the essay, however, provides a path forward.

Lambert's reflections lay a special emphasis on time and temporality. On the one hand, *De la vieillesse* is about the inexorable damage wrought by time: "There is nothing so useless as rebelling against the effects of time; time is stronger than we are" (Lambert, 189). On the other hand, she echoes Seneca in a call to make use of time ("faire usage du temps"; Lambert, 190) in the search for ourselves. As in Scudéry, awareness of time is ultimately and paradoxically the gift of age. In other stages of life, "We possess the capacity for enjoyment, but not for understanding." We are limited principally because we are distracted, constantly drawn this way and that, and "we run after truths that are not appropriate for us" (Lambert, 190). It is only as our time grows short that we succeed in grasping it. Like Scudéry's "experienced" women, Lambert recognizes that we are typically unable to perceive a particular temporal situation until we are no longer in it, until we reach the final stage. "We come to each life stage without knowing how to conduct ourselves in it or to enjoy it; when it is over, we see what we could have done" (Lambert, 181). Beset by desires and incapable of living otherwise than in terms of others' ideas of us (Lambert, 193), youth has no sense of self and no firm purchase on the here and now: "Society is no more than a herd of fugitives from themselves" (Lambert, 195), whereas "In later life, we return to ourselves" (Lambert, 193)—indeed we arrive there for the first time. Like Scudéry, Lambert emphasizes the importance of the will, *la volonté*, in transforming the sensation of transience ("tout nous échappe") into one of deliberate detachment (Lambert, 196).

Lambert does not see detachment as a turn away from living. Against Montaigne, she argues that meditation on death is only another way of avoiding the present. Despite the importance she places on Christian spirituality and confidence in the afterlife, she also differs with Pascal's claim that "the future is our sole object" (Lambert, 192). Instead, in another Senecan echo: "One must hasten to live one's life: it is unwise to say, 'I will live'; and it is living too late to say, 'I will live tomorrow'" (Lambert, 192).[10] It is only in this vivid evocation of a fully conscious life that the past can have any meaning. Rather than simply attempting to give a euphemistic glow to the privations of age, Lambert asserts a positive quality, the ability to live in the present. Her discourse is so authoritative that it is easy to forget that it is not based on "experience," but instead on a projection, a speculation as to what the future might hold. We might liken her approach to a thought experiment in which she imagines the resources that would be available to her in the darkest future imaginable, an old age beset by pain and depression. "Experience" is the term that captures that meaning; presented as "one of the advantages of later life," it is a form of meaning, of knowledge, that for Lambert as for Scudéry is uniquely bound up with self-possession and a sense of time.

Because the *Traité de la vieillesse* is shot through with echoes, allusions, and quotations from the moralist tradition, some commentators have viewed it as a derivative work, less interesting than her powerful *Réflexions nouvelles sur les femmes* (which will be discussed in the next chapter). Such a judgment, however, misses the explicit goal of the essay, which is to synthesize

---

[10] Seneca: "Observe individuals, and study people in general, and you will find every one of us living for tomorrow. 'Is there any harm in that?' you say. Yes, endless harm. For they are not living; they are only about to live. Everything is deferred. Even if we were paying attention, life would slip by us; as it is, we put off living, and our lives race past us as if they belonged to someone else—ending on the last day, yet lost to us every day." Lucius Annaeus Seneca, Letter 45, *Letters on Ethics to Lucilius*, 133.

nearly two millennia of advice offered to men on the subject of old age and to translate it in terms appropriate for women living at the dawn of the eighteenth century. The *Traité* also demonstrates in clear terms the appeal of moralist writing as a conversation with the past—as if Cicero, Seneca, Montaigne, Pascal, and Saint-Évremond had become regular members of Lambert's salon. She interweaves the voices, formulates her responses, and gives shape to the whole.

Although its classical echoes lend the *Traité de vieillesse* a certain timeless quality, it speaks to its own time, as Lambert's pointed remarks on the inequalities of men's and women's education and social roles indicate. This is especially true in Lambert's other essay on the subject of older women, the *Discours sur le sentiment d'une dame qui croyait que l'amour convenait aux femmes lors même qu'elles n'étaient plus jeunes* ("Discourse on the opinion of a lady who believed that love was appropriate to older women").[11] The *Discours* is a more complex text than at first appears. The title announces the topic as if it were a resolution in a formal debate, with arguments for and against by the two principals, the narrator and her friend Ismène, who believes that women should be allowed to engage in love relationships in later life. The text is however entirely a "discourse" in the first person, with the narrator presenting Ismène's views and commenting on them. The narrator's role is not what one might expect: she introduces the text by announcing that she agrees with Ismène, but that she will present the views of "public opinion" rather than her own.

Joan Hinde Stewart oversimplifies both the *Traité de vieillesse* and the *Discours* when she claims that Lambert "concludes unambiguously" as to "the unsuitability of love" for older women.[12] Stewart elides the fact that the narrator of the *Discours*—let's refer to her as Lambert—is unambiguously in agreement with Ismène: "I shall not attack Ismène's opinions; she has established them too firmly and with great refinement for me to argue against them" (Lambert, 317). Finding herself incapable of marshalling arguments against her friend's view, she elects to present the commonly received idea

---

[11] Lambert, *Discours sur le sentiment d'une dame qui croyait que l'amour convenait aux femmes lors même qu'elles n'étaient plus jeunes*, Oeuvres, 317–28. Published a decade after her death, the *Discours* is another text that has proven difficult to date. Based largely on the idea that the character Ismène is inspired by Ninon de Lenclos, whose salon was in its glory when Lambert acquired the Hôtel de Nevers, home of her future salon, in the late 1690s, Roger Marchal places the *Discours* among Lambert's earlier works (Marchal, *Madame de Lambert et son milieu*, 109–11; 196). Granderoute, on the other hand, suggesting that Ismène may be modeled on the duchesse du Maine, who joined the salon in 1726, places it among the later works, written sometime after the *Réflexions nouvelles*.

[12] J. Stewart, *The Enlightenment of Age*, 16.

that older women should abandon all thoughts of love. She refers to this view as "a prejudice"; she advances it not because she agrees with it, but because public opinion is too powerful to be denied: "Custom [*l'usage*] is stronger than I am" (Lambert, 317). This is prime moralist territory: an ostensibly neutral description of the manners of the day.

As we have seen elsewhere, however, moralist "description" comes with a normative slant. I would term it "critical" rather than "prescriptive." Let us consider the word that Lambert uses to refer to the received view, *l'usage*, which carries a complex set of meanings. From Latin *usus*, the word is defined in seventeenth-century dictionaries as "custom, received practice," as one might expect. In the second half of the century, however, one of its primary connotations had come to be linguistic usage, thanks to the profound influence of Claude Favre de Vaugelas's 1647 treatise, *Remarques sur la langue française*. Vaugelas's focus on *l'usage*—"the King, or the Tyrant, the arbiter, or the master of languages"[13]—represented an understanding of the historicity of language and the idea that it was determined by speakers and writers, not rules and systems of grammar. The broader implications of this insight ripple throughout the century and feed the antisystematic trend.[14] The 1743 Dictionnaire de Trévoux sets *l'usage* in opposition to *raison* in social contexts, giving precedence to *usage*; Nicolas Beauzée's article on the subject for the *Encyclopédie* argues that it demonstrates "that much in language is arbitrary, that the signification of words and phrases is accidental, [and] that reason alone is insufficient to devine it."[15] *L'usage* thus bespeaks the powerful influence of "opinion," but it also carries the notions of historicity and arbitrariness. By aligning *usage* with *opinion reçue* and, especially, with *préjugé*, Lambert implies that it is subject to change, contrary to reason, and subtly sides against it.

Is there really a debate between Lambert and Ismène? Lambert announces the "rule": "According to the rule, one must cease loving once one has ceased to please [*plaire*]" (Lambert, 317), which she promptly undercuts by observing that men are the arbiters of what "pleases."

> They imposed on us a law to be beautiful, and they gave us nothing else to do. They destined us to be a pleasant spectacle for their eyes; once we no

---

[13] Claude Favre de Vaugelas, "Préface," *Remarques sur la langue françoise* (Paris: Chez la Veuve Jean Camusat, 1647), ã verso.
[14] See above, Chapter 1, 10–13.
[15] Nicolas Beauzée, "Usage (Grammaire)," in Diderot and d'Alembert, *Encyclopédie*, 17:516.

longer offer that pleasure, we have neither their gaze nor their attention. (Lambert, 318)

There can be no doubt as to Lambert's irony here. She offers the "public's" weak attempts to refute Ismène's talking points, indicating that she personally agrees with her friend. In a powerful passage, she presents Ismène's view that older women possess superior qualities of mind and heart: "As for deep feelings, they are scarcely to be found among the young; they are far more delicate and profound at the age we are discussing" (Lambert, 319). Later in life, having experienced much, a woman of solid character returns to herself ("renvoyée à elle-même," 320) and, if she chooses to love, her feelings are deep and constant.

In the end, Lambert finds only two arguments against Ismène's views, independent of the dictates of *l'usage*: first, that few if any men are able to appreciate "women's true merit" (Lambert, 321); and second, that Ismène is uniquely admirable, cultivated, and reasonable—and as such has largely withdrawn herself from society—hence inimitable, not a model for others. Neither argument speaks to the basic truth of Ismène's view, of course. In effect, both arguments return us to the imperfect social world of the opening paragraphs, in which men judge women entirely on their ability to please them and girls and women internalize this standard.

Given her analysis of the state of the world—the moralist's task—it is not surprising that Lambert concludes that the best approach for one's own peace of mind and happiness is to accept the status quo. As she explained at the outset, "I take the world as it is, not as it should be (Lambert, 317). Even so, the *Discours* ends with a scathing indictment of a world in which men dictate the rules of feminine virtue:

> Custom has served them so well that everything is for them and against us. However shameful their conduct, we can never complain; our testimony has no effect against them. And as a consequence of their unjust laws, we cannot make any treaty with them that respects equality. (Lambert, 324)

Although it was likely written in the early years of the eighteenth century, Lambert's *Traité de la vieillesse* and *Discours sur le sentiment d'une dame* would not be published until the 1740s; her work paved the way for midcentury reflections on youth and age among later women moralists.

Suzanne Necker's *Mélanges* include many comments on youth and age from different perspectives. Some echo her interest in the operations of the mind:

> At the beginning and the end of life, material things are merely accessory. In youth, we are distracted from external objects by our internal feelings; in old age, the soul breaks free of all that surrounds it, since it has learned from experience that physical objects derive value only from people and their ideas. (Necker 1798, 1:111)

Elsewhere, she comments on how the passage of time affects our perception of the phenomenal world, making it impossible to say that we "know" another individual "by heart":

> But how can one predict the movements of the mind? Even physical objects produce new results over time; how could it be possible for thought to remain the same. (Necker 1798, 1:92)

Other remarks, however, focus on the diminished social status of older women. One of the grimmer reflections has been cited as an example of Necker's austere code of conduct.

> Women of a certain age have nothing better to do than to [let themselves] be forgotten; but that is only possible to the extent that they never forgot themselves in their youth. (Necker 1798, 1:195)

Whether Necker was endorsing this view or simply reporting on it, it's undoubtedly the case that her maxim is inspired by the purely linguistic pleasure of playing the two meanings of *s'oublier*, "forgetting oneself" (both "to recede from view" and "to behave immorally"), against one another. A more substantive discussion of the changing norms for old age places the focus on the need for self-reliance at a time of diminished worldly status: "the world is no longer interested in them; they should therefore have only indifference for the world." Although the first part of the reflection concerns old people in general (subsumed under the masculine noun, "le vieillard"), the second half turns specifically to women: "Young women seek to please by their looks; old women must strive not to displease, but any pretention is forbidden them." Youth expects everything of others; in old age, "one must tolerate everything except evil, and demand nothing" (Necker 1798, 3:24–25). Furthermore: "When one is no longer young, one has nothing but religion, morals, friendship, and one's mind; one should therefore live in retreat and often in solitude, because these benefits can only be cultivated far from other people and are often lost in their company" (Necker 1798, 2:17).

Necker joins a long tradition of recommending a retreat from the world in old age. As we have seen, whereas Cicero/Cato viewed the rural retreat as the opportunity to enjoy the higher pleasures of conversation and study, La Rochefoucauld saw it as a step down in order to avoid the public embarrassment of one's loss of status. Even Saint-Évremond, who describes retreat in positive terms, ultimately prefers a "retreat" within the world: "au milieu du monde je me retire du monde même" (Saint-Évremond: "In the midst of the world, I retreat from the world, 4:298). Lambert describes retreat as a blissful "calme sans interruption" (Lambert, 196)—but she never apparently felt the need to avail herself of it, having guided her salon until the end. Similarly, one questions whether or not Necker would have followed this path and discontinued her salon, had the Revolution not forced her and her husband into exile.

For Necker, as for others, among the virtues of old age are detachment from sensual pleasures and from the expectation that the world owes us anything. "An old woman must be strong and have need of no one" (Necker 1801, 1:238). Despite some of her austere pronouncements, her vision of later life has a strongly positive dimension as the time when we are at last allowed to be ourselves: "One is *oneself* at the end of life; one no longer seeks to please, and one loses both the desire and the right to do so" (Necker 1798, 1:109). It is a time to exercise and refresh the mind (Necker 1798, 2:331; 3:33). In an extended reflection, she observes that we have four "educations" at different life stages: that which we receive from our parents; that which we discover ourselves, which often corrects the first; a moral education derived from our experience in society; that of old age, the culmination and "the best of all" (Necker 1801, 2:62–64). Although we retain new information less readily in old age, we have the capacity to return to what we know and come to a new, more complete understanding that is also an "apprenticeship" as we prepare for the next life. "It is then that one must gather together all the moral and sensible ideas one acquired in one's maturity and join to them the reflections to which the circumstances of old age and the proximity of the end have necessarily given rise" (Necker 1801, 2:64).

Society's behavioral norms for older women had not changed greatly in the decade when Pauline de Meulan, later Guizot, was writing essays for Suard's *Le Publiciste* (1801–1810) and after. The topic of old age surfaces in several of the pieces published under the general rubric "Des Femmes" in the posthumous collection of her work edited by her husband. The first essay in the series, "De la manière dont les hommes jugent les femmes, et les satires qu'on a faites contre elles" ("On the way men judge women, and the satires they make against them") is written in the persona of "an old woman" of sixty that we saw her adopt in several of her essays on friendship (Guizot, *Essais et conseils*, 2:1–27). There is something poignant in Guizot's imagining herself at an age that she never reached. She was only in her midfifties at the time of her death and was likely in her thirties when she wrote many, if not all, of the essays in the *Essais et conseils de morale*.

The purported age of the narrator provides her with a strong platform for lecturing her addressee, a young man. Warning him that she plans to address him "like a grandmother," she admonishes him firmly, but affectionately, regarding his recent behavior, in particular a scene at which she was present, when he uttered a number of inane clichés about "all women." The narrator found his remarks all the more offensive inasmuch as he seemed oblivious to her presence. Evidently, she notes, having passed the age of fifty she no longer counts as part of "that corporation people refer to as 'women'" (Guizot, *Essais et conseils*, 2:2). Furthermore, she finds her young friend ridiculous in his pretentions that he knows anything about "women in general"—he is far too young. Had he more experience of the world (or a better education), he would know that it has all been said before. With which she embarks on a scathing history of men's accounts of women, ancient, medieval, and modern. The invisibility of the old woman is but the first example of one of the overarching arguments of the essay: that although men make distinctions among other men based on a whole gamut of relationships (familial, social, political, national), they make no such distinctions among women: "For a man, a woman is just a woman." Or, more precisely, a woman is a member of a species "that men judge, not for what she is in herself, but only in relation to them" (Guizot, *Essais et conseils*, 2:8). By reducing women to their sex, and depriving older women of any sexual identity, they have effectively erased older women from their notice. As Guizot will observe in one of the later reflections in "Des femmes," not only are older women not supposed to feel passion, they should not respond to it in others: "At the age where one must renounce any claim to pleasing, any love that one inspires is almost ridiculous" (Guizot, *Essais et conseils*, 2:35).

The last piece in "Des femmes" offers a brighter, although hardly less ironic, perspective. The narrator of "Les agréments de la vieillesse" ("The pleasures of old age," *Essais et conseils*, 2:63–68) is a "a woman who does not yet enjoy them"—a younger woman. This narrator looks forward to old age, because she will at last be free of the expectations and social roles imposed on young women. She will not be required to be pretty, to laugh at bad jokes, or to appear interested simply out of politeness; all she will need to do in order to be accepted in a group is to appear to lend her approval. Others' rudeness and slights will not matter, for she has nothing to prove and no status to achieve. Guizot's satire cuts two ways, revealing both the stress of the behavior imposed on young women and the lack of consideration granted older women. "At sixty, one should shrug off others' approval, so that they do not shrug at you. I can hardly wait to be sixty"[16] (Guizot, *Essais et conseils*, 2:66). In effect, Guizot's projected old age echoes earlier moralists who recommended detachment and retreat, but not without a sharp criticism of the reasons why society's treatment of women might lead one to opt out. The most telling passage describes the older woman's freedom of speech:

> Her gaiety can be less circumspect, her manners freer, her generosity more personal, her feelings more expressive. . . . She is able to describe her former advantages, her former mistakes, the impulses that she tamed, the penchants that she overcame; she can recall them without being ashamed, because she remembers them without regret, blending the charm of her weakness with the merit of her virtue. (*Essais et conseils*, 2:68)

If only, she adds, one could have all that and be young and pretty as well! For all the irony, the picture she paints of old age is an attractive one, but it speaks to the strict limitations on what (younger) women are able to say and on the feelings that they can express. Constance de Salm, it will be recalled, also wrote of older women's ability to speak freely on subjects that would have been embarrassing to them in their youth. In this hoped-for version of old age, Guizot's *vieille femme* does not enter into a retreat, but is able to indulge her younger acquaintances when it pleases her to do so, to ignore them when

---

[16] Guizot's witticism plays on two meanings of the verb *se moquer*: not to care about something, and to make fun of someone.

it does not, and to speak as freely as she likes, without the troubling *réserve* of which Salm complained.

Like Lambert, Guizot's moralist project is "descriptive" insofar as it consists in showing "the world as it is," but it is hardly neutral. The code of conduct outlined is the world's, not the writer's: one may conform to it out of external necessity, or simply because nonconformity will result in unhappiness, but the outlines of a better world, "the world as it should be," are clearly delineated.

How, then, do women moralists confront the "hell" of old age? As we have seen, they offer a number of approaches. Chief among them is the notion that one should "make provision" during one's youth. The concept of "provision" assumes that old age is a season of loss and privation, like winter. It also assumes that youth has a role to play and something to contribute to one's later life. The relationship between youth and age thus has a dual temporal dynamic: the contributions of youth to age, and the contributions of age to youth in the form of mentorship. Teaching and mentorship are among the "vastly more significant" roles featured among the compensations of old age for Cicero, and the mentorship of older women for younger women plays an important part for Scudéry and Puisieux.

The mentorship model cannot be taken for granted, as we see when Scudéry's Célinte turns down Chrysante's offer of mentoring. It is not universal. Most women moralists see solitude or social isolation as the defining aspect of old age. This is where "making provision" comes into play, either as cultivating one's intellect (thereby making oneself acceptable in society, for Verzure, or keeping one's mind active, for Necker) or by developing one's self-sufficiency. Both of these may constitute a "compensation" for old age, but they are very different from the social integration and the respect of the greater community envisioned by Cicero. The theme of loss is never far. Lambert regrets that social codes forbid women the full exploration and expression of tender feelings, especially inasmuch as older women have achieved an emotional depth and integrity beyond that of younger women. The satisfaction of having reached that state is in itself is however one compensation. "One is *oneself* at the end of one's life," as Necker says (Necker 1798, 1:109). Abandoning the need to *plaire* is not simply making the best of a painful situation, but is instead felt as a liberation and freedom from "the tyranny of public opinion" (Lambert, 193). In this way, retreat may be viewed as positive, "uninterrupted calm" (Lambert, 196).

6.3. Not Her Last Word: D'Arconville on Old Age

D'Arconville's essay "Sur la vieillesse et la mort" appears in the second volume of the *Pensées, réflexions et anecdotes*, the late manuscripts composed from 1801 to 1805, when she was in her eighties. Her family had suffered during the Revolution: her eldest son and brother-in-law Denis Angran d'Alleray had been guillotined; she and her sister had spent months in prison and were released only after the fall of Robespierre. She had lost many friends over the years. In poor health and relatively reduced circumstances, she had fallen into depression, describing herself as "sad and melancholy," when one of her great-nieces encouraged her to begin writing again, suggesting that she put her "uncommon memory" to use: "I could set in writing all that I remembered, adding the reflections that my all too lively imagination might offer."[17] Before the Revolution, d'Arconville had published extensively in a broad range of fields—moralist writing, chemistry, literary and scientific translations, fiction, and history—but she had renounced writing for publication in the early 1780s. Although she mentions additional projects, little of her work from the 1780s or the revolutionary decade has survived. Her young relative's suggestion unleashed a remarkably creative phase, during which she produced over 200 essays on moralist topics, literary criticism, anecdotes, history, science, and, gradually, autobiography.

"Sur la vieillesse et la mort" (PRA 2: 162–76) proceeds in two stages. First, d'Arconville looks at humans' paradoxical attitudes to time and mortality and draws conclusions regarding human nature. Why, she asks, given our claim to be attached to life, do we constantly wish for time to hurry its pace—wishing to grow older, in effect? We are impatient to know the outcome of events, either to achieve a hoped-for goal, or to end an unpleasant or painful episode. We appear to forget that in order to arrive at this anticipated moment, we have hastened through our allotted days, effectively shortening our existence. At the same time, the wish for a long life is a further manifestation of our inconsistency (*inconséquence*), given that life is typically filled with physical and emotional pain: "for most people, wishing for a long life means wishing for the continuation of their misfortunes, even as they do their utmost to prolong their days" (PRA 2:163).

D'Arconville imagines the balance sheet of an individual's life, with "illnesses, accidents, and sorrows" on one side and "happy moments,

---

[17] D'Arconville, "Histoire de ma littérature," PRA 5:223–24.

pleasures, even calm states when one had nothing to complain of." A simple calculation shows that misfortune easily outweighs happiness. Young people do not think of such things, because the end of life seems remote, but as we age, the fear of death deepens within us. We wish to continue our existence, despite increasing infirmities (PRA 2:164–65). Worse, we may lose our mental capacities. She describes the sorry state of creative geniuses, "the greatest, most fertile minds, who gave us works as instructive as they were delightful," reduced by dementia, unable to remember or understand their own work. Coming as the final, culminating point in her list, this is clearly the worst fate that she can imagine.

Given that we cannot know if such a fate awaits us, d'Arconville concludes that "the love of life" must simply be innate. Like all other animals, we simply want to live; we flee danger. "The fear of death is thus natural and inherent to every living being" (PRA 2:170). Furthermore, it must have been implanted in us by God, because there is no rational explanation for it. In spite of all that we know and the pain we have experienced, we seek to preserve life. D'Arconville's attitude toward time echoes Seneca's injunction not to lose sight of the present moment by living for tomorrow. Her view that one should accept the boundaries of one's life without seeking to extend it echoes the Stoics as well, but her view of old age and of humanity's approach to it is considerably bleaker.

After this unflinching account of the end of life, d'Arconville states that she has no interest in getting into a theological discussion. However, she adds, if eternity exists, then we will be either happy or unhappy, rewarded or punished, contingent on our actions in life. Were people to take this account of the afterlife seriously, she goes on to observe, then they would live like saints. But even though most claim to believe the Christian account of the afterlife, they do not behave accordingly, providing a further example of human *inconséquence*: "Ah! How small and contemptible is man when he is left to his own devices and gives himself over to all the passions that drag him over the bottomless precipice, that make his present life miserable, and that leave him a future so fearsome that the very idea makes one shudder" (PRA 2:172–73). The Pascalian echo reminds us of the formative influence of Jansenism in d'Arconville's childhood; as she recounts in "Histoire de mon enfance," she found the Saint-Médard convulsionaries that she witnessed absurd (as she did other forms of popular cult), but a strict Augustinianism would characterize her lifelong moral outlook.[18]

---

[18] "Histoire de mon enfance," PRA 3: 311–489. For a modern edition of "Histoire de mon enfance," see Bernier and Swiderski, *Madame d'Arconville*, 33–73; an English translation is included

The end of life becomes a moment for d'Arconville to reflect less on the afterlife than on the human condition: petty, beset by passion, and in denial of ultimate reality. And yet, she goes on to reflect, there are worse prospects, such as "le Spinosisme" (PRA 2:173). Since it is unlikely that d'Arconville had encountered Spinoza's works directly, she appears to have absorbed the common eighteenth-century attacks on him as an atheist. D'Arconville argues that the hope for eternal bliss can make life's challenges easier to bear, whereas the "spinozist," believing in nothing, has no recourse other than suicide when life becomes unbearable, and no possible future other than nothingness (*néant*). Her account of humanity's plight has reached its nadir.

At this point, d'Arconville takes a surprising step, given the seriousness of the topic. She quotes the airy response of seventeenth-century Madame de Cornuel[19] to a friend who evinced skepticism as to the Christian account of the afterlife: "I am far from sharing your opinion; to the contrary, I think that even if it were no more than a rumor [*un bruit de ville*], it merits that we pay attention and go deeper into it" (PRA 2:175). Particularly given the Pascalian overtones of the description of humanity as "petit et méprisable," the decision to quote Cornuel rather than Pascal—whom d'Arconville greatly admired—is perhaps in keeping with her claim not to be doing theology. The echo of Pascal's wager is clear in her gloss on Cornuel's *bon mot*: "one runs no risk in believing the dogmas of the Christian religion and in leading a life in conformity with its principles; since to stray from them not only exposes us to eternal suffering, but also deprives us of the resources and consolations that faith and piety alone can procure, and that are necessary to be able to tolerate the bitterness of life" (PRA 2:175–76).

D'Arconville ends her essay with an intriguing misquotation:

Monsieur de Montesquieu begins his chapter on religion* [*D'Arconville's footnote: "See *The Spirit of the Laws*"] thus: "The atheist," he says, "and the believer both speak constantly of religion. One speaks of what he loves, the other of what he fears." Indeed, I am inclined to believe that the atheist is often in contradiction with himself, that he is an unbeliever in his own disbelief and that his supposed [*prétendu*] calm is a pretence. (PRA 2:176)

in d'Arconville, *Selected Philosophical, Scientific, and Autobiographical Writings*, trans. J. Hayes (Toronto: Iter, 2018), 155–84.

[19] Anne-Marie Bigot de Cornuel (1605–1694), salonnière known for her witticisms.

Despite her normally excellent memory for quotations, d'Arconville has reversed the terms of Montesquieu's aphoristic one-sentence chapter: "The pious man and the atheist speak constantly of religion; one speaks of what he loves, the other of what he fears."[20] I had initially thought to regard the misquotation as a simple error, but given the care with which the manuscript is prepared, with footnotes and inserted corrections, and particularly given her gloss on the quotation, I am inclined to see it as a more meaningful "slip." Not that she is deliberately parodying Montesquieu, but that she unconsciously rewrote the text in keeping with her own opinion. The atheist "loves" religion as a debate topic with which he can badger others, while the believer "fears" because he has no certitude of a heavenly reward. For d'Arconville, the atheist is in contradiction with himself, since by speaking constantly ("toujours") about religion, he demonstrates his own obsession with the subject. In other words, he manifests what Paul Tillich would famously call "the state of being ultimately concerned"[21]—and so is not an atheist at all. Or, in d'Arconville's expression, "incrédule sur son incrédulité." She may claim that she is leaving theology to the theologians, but she has also countered the specter of atheism adumbrated earlier.

For d'Arconville, we might say that old age is a state of being ultimately concerned. If her meditation on the end of life contains a recommendation on how to live, it is to live realistically, with hope for the afterlife, but without certitude. Although neither the volumes nor the individual essays of the PRA are dated, occasional references to her age and other events allow us to situate them in time. The earliest pieces are from 1801. The piece immediately following "Sur la vieillesse" is a deeply felt lament on the death of d'Arconville's sister, which occurred in 1802. We cannot know how much time elapsed between the composition of "Sur la vieillesse" and her sister's death, but it is reasonable to suppose that her sister's final illness cast a shadow on her reflections. "Sur la mort de Madame d'Alleray" is painful to read and in certain ways illustrates key points of "Sur la vieillesse et la mort." D'Arconville evokes a "dreadful emptiness" of overwhelming physical and mental pain; expresses the hope that death will soon "put an end to my pains"; and offers a prayer that God will show mercy in allowing her to join her sister, "whose

---

[20] Montesquieu, *De l'esprit des lois*, ed. Robert Dérathé, Book 25, Chapter 1 (Paris: Garnier Frères, 1973).
[21] Paul Tillich, *The Dynamics of Faith* (New York: Harper, 1957), 1.

virtues, I hope, will have deserved eternal happiness" in the afterlife (PRA 2:179–80). It is the human condition as she has described it.

But these are not d'Arconville's last words. "Sur la vieillesse et la mort" is in the second volume of the PRA, relatively early in what would become twelve volumes of "thoughts, reflections, and anecdotes."[22] Although initially reluctant, or too exhausted, to envision new compositions after her sister's death, she rallies and produces another dozen essays in the second volume, including a return to her habitually wry, self-deprecating description of her writing process. Thus begins an essay on the subject of Commerce:

> My old brain cannot seem to come up with anything to feed my pen, despite my unfortunate need, even if 82 years of existence should excuse me from the effort, from going to the trouble of splattering ink on paper. But my pen's nature is to have a doglike appetite, so I am forced to throw it at least some bones to gnaw so that it will not die of starvation. (PRA 2:340–41)

However bleak her philosophy of existence, d'Arconville's sense of humor, delight in quirky language, and endless desire to "feed her pen" carry her forward. Words to live by.

---

[22] Or thirteen volumes; see above, chapter 4 note 48.

7
On Women's Nature and Capabilities

In the previous chapters, we have seen how women moralists framed long-standing topics in philosophy and ethics in terms of their own experience of the world. In this chapter, we come to the subject that is at the heart of all the others, the question of "women's nature" and its implications for debates over women's cognitive abilities and their roles both public and private.

I explore women moralists' engagement with this vast topic through several lenses, taking a roughly diachronic approach. Early modern approaches to the question of women's nature emerge in the context of the *querelle des femmes*, a centuries-old polemic on the supposed inferiority or superiority of women. During our period, the *querelle* gives rise to arguments for women's equality.[1] My focus here is less on the issue of equality per se than on the entwinement of theories of sociability with evolving concepts of biological determinism during the period. After considering the larger cultural context, I take a detailed look at a fascinating and understudied work on female "characters" by Jeanne-Michelle de Pringy and the use of the literary genre of *caractères* to explore philosophical issues. Although she finds much to criticize in women's attitudes and comportment, Pringy shifts the focus away from biology to the social world, foreshadowing the arguments of eighteenth-century moralists to whom I turn next. In the final section, I turn to the post-Revolutionary period and the acrimonious debates over the woman writer, *la femme auteur*, that erupted in the first decade of the nineteenth century. Although that debate is most often remembered as a chapter in the history of authorship and the status of women writers, I argue that its implications are much broader, representing the culmination of two centuries of arguments over women's abilities, virtues, and proper role in society.

---

[1] On the relation of the *querelle* to arguments for women's equality, see O'Neill, "The Equality of Men and Women," 445–74.

7.1. Politeness and Embodiment

Because women were traditionally believed to possess innate qualities of gentleness (*douceur*) and meek dispositions, they play a crucial role in the period's conduct literature, in which politeness (*politesse*) and *honnêteté* are considered key to social advancement. As we will see, women moralists are embedded in these traditions, but depart from them in distinctive ways.

Elsa Dorlin has argued that the seventeenth century saw the emergence of two forms of feminism, that of the *précieuse* movement exemplified by Madeleine de Scudéry and a *féminisme logique* advanced by Marie de Gournay, François Poulain de la Barre, Anna Maria van Schurman, and Gabrielle Suchon; she identifies the two forms with modern-day difference feminism and equality feminism.[2] While Dorlin's exegesis of Suchon's and the others' arguments is helpful, she understates the complexity of the salon-oriented *précieuse* position that serves as a foundation for moralist analysis. As we will see, even when the moralists take the notion of "feminine nature" as a starting point, it is never an easy given. Women moralists continuously question the relation of nature to culture; their accounts become increasingly critical over the course of the eighteenth century.

I can do no more than gesture toward the immense volume of writing related to the *littérature de l'honnêteté*, which extends through many genres, but receives a major impetus from Nicolas Faret's *L'Honneste homme, ou l'art de plaire à la cour* (1630), inspired by Baldassare Castiglione's immensely influential *Il Libro del cortegiano* (1528). Faret, a regular member of the salon of the intellectually inclined Mme des Loges and one of the first members of the Académie française, borrowed freely from Castiglione's advice in order to address his own generation; his work would in turn inspire numerous other manuals of savoir-vivre that would proliferate throughout the century and beyond.[3] These are how-to books aimed at a public more heterogeneous than Castiglione's, offering not simply a guide to good manners, but strategies for success in the complex world of the court. Faret's reader learns that although conversation with women is "the nicest / gentlest [*la plus douce*] and most agreeable" of all forms of conversation, it is also "the most difficult and

---

[2] Dorlin, *L'Évidence de l'égalité des sexes*, 14.
[3] Craveri discusses the relation of Faret's book to Castiglione (*L'Âge de la conversation*, 342–45). On the relationship between *politesse* and classical humanism in the elaboration of *honnêteté*, see Emmanuel Bury, *Littérature et politesse: L'Invention de l'honnête homme* (Paris: Presses Universitaires de France, 1996), and Maurice Magendie's encyclopedic study, *La Politesse mondaine et les theories de l'honnêteté au France au XVIIe siècle de 1600 à 1660* (1925; reprint Geneva: Slatkine, 1970).

delicate." Women are more sensitive to nuances than men, as their minds are both quicker ("l'esprit plus prompt") and less "encumbered" than men's. Women are also more likely to notice and call attention to verbal lapses.[4] The connection between women and the foundations of civility was set.

Women's special role in maintaining standards of polite conversation would continue to be linked to the constitution of their minds. One of the two interlocutors in the *Entretiens d'Ariste et d'Eugène* (1671) by Dominique de Bouhours, a friend of Scudéry's, would argue that women, although especially adept in their mastery of language, were physiologically unsuited to wit (*bel esprit*). The character Eugène bases his account of women's nature on humoral medical theory, claiming that their "cold and humid" constitutions make them "weak, timid, indiscreet, flighty, impatient, and talkative" and that "nothing is more limited" than their minds. Ariste, the wiser of the pair, agrees "in general," but observes that there have been many exceptions, citing examples from throughout history.[5] At the end of the century, Jean-Baptiste Morvan de Bellegarde's *Réflexions sur la politesse des moeurs* (1698) would give women a central place in establishing polite society as naturally "gentler, more accommodating, more gracious than men." Although he acknowledges that they are perhaps unfairly excluded from major roles in public life ("des grands emplois & des grandes affaires") he notes that it is also the case that they have a penchant for trivial matters, *la bagatelle*.[6] The worldly value of effortlessness, *nonchalance*—a latter-day version of Castiglione's *sprezzatura*—facilitated an association between politeness and leisured aristocratic women, but led to the argument that women were congenitally incapable of intellectual "work," as we see in Bouhours.[7]

Complaisance, the willingness to accommodate oneself to others' wishes, is a key element of *politesse* for both sexes, but a particular virtue for women. Like the related verb *complaire*, *complaisance* indicates both pleasing and being pleased: it is a social virtue.[8] An eighteenth-century etiquette guide, Paradis de Moncrif's *Essai sur la nécessité et sur les moyens de plaire*,

---

[4] Nicolas Faret, *L'Honneste homme ou l'art de plaire à la cour* (Paris: Chez Toussaincts du Bray, 1630), 220–21.

[5] Dominique de Bouhours, *Les Entretiens d'Ariste et d'Eugène*, ed. Bernard Beugnot and Gilles Declercq (Paris: Honoré Champion, 2003), 265–67.

[6] Jean-Baptiste Morvan de Bellegarde, *Réflexions sur la politesse des moeurs* (Paris: Chez Jean Guignard, 1698), 5, 397.

[7] See Anthony J. La Vopa, *The Labor of the Mind: Intellect and Gender in Enlightenment Cultures* (Philadelphia: University of Pennsylvania Press, 2017), 19–43.

[8] On women's social virtues, see La Vopa on the "relational intelligence" often ascribed to women (La Vopa, 8, 41, 103).

described the act of pleasing as a central element of sociability, "appropriate for every rank and every age," as long as it was based on reason and honorable motivations.[9] The characters in Madeleine de Scudéry's "De la complaisance" note that it is a vice when taken to excess, but that it is expected of women: "Il faut qu'une femme le soit," states one character flatly (Scudéry 1680, 1:319). As we saw à propos of Maintenon, *complaisance* can be seen as "a rational strategy for acting in a situation of dependence."[10] "Pleasing" is clearly less pleasurable when it becomes an obligation, however, and freedom from the obligation to please is viewed as an advantage of old age. It should also be noted that the semantic field of *plaire* is broad, extending to different shades of attraction from acts of civility and platonic *galanterie* to flirtation and seduction.

The learned abbesse de Fontevraud, Gabrielle de Rochechouart de Mortemart (1633–1693), distinguished between *civilité*, which is a matter of language and "certaines cérémonies arbitraires" and can be learned, from *politesse*, which requires an innate "disposition" refined through social interactions.[11] A descendent of one of the oldest noble families in France and older sister of Madame de Montespan, the abbesse is thought to have written her "Question sur la politesse" in 1674; the work circulated among her friends, among them Mme de Sablé.[12] For her, the etymology of *politesse*— to smooth, polish, and "remove whatever is rough or unpleasant"—is key to pleasing interactions and inextricably linked to virtue.

The abbesse does not see *politesse* as a special attribute of either sex. Neither does Scudéry, in her conversation "De la politesse," but she refers to the marquise de Rambouillet as "the woman who understood *politesse* better than anyone," crediting her with having established it by inspiring others at Court and throughout the kingdom (Scudéry 1684 1:121). Scudéry expands on the social context of *politesse*, which she describes as emerging from the political and cultural environment created by absolute monarchy. Although

---

[9] François-Augustin Paradis de Moncrif, *Essai sur la nécessité et sur les moyens de plaire* (Paris: Prault, 1738), 52.

[10] Blank, "Complaisance and the Question of Autonomy," 44. (See above, Chapter 5, 225–30.) Although I agree with Blank that coquetry similarly offers women a means to preserve autonomy, I believe that he too hastily associates it with *complaisance*, especially in Scudéry. "Pleasing" has a far broader purview than flirtation.

[11] Marie Madeleine Gabrielle de Rochechouart de Mortemart, "Question sur la politesse," in Saint-Hyacinthe, *Recueil de divers écrits*, 84b–93. The same volume included the first publication (posthumous) of Lambert's *Traité de l'amitié* and the first publication of Lévesque de Pouilly's *Théorie des sentiments agréables*.

[12] Pierre Clément, *Gabrielle de Rochechouart de Mortemart, étude historique* (Paris: Didier, 1869), 40.

she would concur with Rochechouart de Mortemart that its natural home is the Court, her interlocutors propose that it can spread beyond through the intermediary of books. The friends suit the action to the word by deciding to write down their conversation for the benefit of others (Scudéry 1684, 1:119–87). For Scudéry, then, *politesse* is not seen as a particularly feminine trait, and may be imparted to those who lack direct contact with the court, but it is nevertheless associated with a woman, the emblematic founding mother of seventeenth-century salon culture.

At the end of the seventeenth century, the stage was set for a particular configuration of women's essential "character" that combined features of the worldly social code with traditional humoral theories of women's bodies, even as the older physiological theory had begun to give way to an understanding of bodies operating via "fibers" and sensibility.[13] *Politesse* would be an increasingly contested notion,[14] but the notion that women's temperament was key to sociability and grounded in biology remained strong. Whether the differences between men's and women's bodies should imply differences in ability to reason or differences in status was, however, deeply contested. As the Cartesian philosopher François Poulain de la Barre famously wrote in *De l'égalité des deux sexes* (1673), "The mind has no sex."[15] That women possess capacity equal to men for learning and rational thought does not, however, imply that they possess the same character or nature: Poulain too accepted the theories of women's hypersensitivity, arguing that women's constitution renders them "imaginatives et spirituelles" and gives them an advantage for learning (Poulain de la Barre, 122). Claude Buffier, a regular in Madame de Lambert's salon, included the idea of women's intellectual weakness as a "vulgar prejudice" to be rejected; like Poulain, he argued that women's "delicacy and discernment" enhanced their aptitude for study.[16]

But although difference need not entail inequality, biological difference became increasingly accented over the course of the eighteenth century. This process culminated in the dominance of what Thomas Laqueur calls

---

[13] On the complex and evolving interrelation between Enlightenment medical science and "sensibility" in a wide range of contexts, see Anne C. Vila, *Enlightenment and Pathology: Sensibility in the Literature and Medicine of Eighteenth-Century France* (Baltimore: Johns Hopkins University Press, 1998).

[14] Peter France, *Politeness and Its Discontents: Problems in French Classical Culture* (Cambridge: Cambridge University Press, 1992), esp. 53–73.

[15] François Poulain de la Barre, *De l'égalité des deux sexes*, ed. Marie-Frédéric Pellegrin (Paris: Vrin, 2011), 99.

[16] Claude Buffier, *Examen des prejugez vulgaires, pour disposer l'esprit à juger sainement de tout* (Paris: Chez Jean Mariette, 1704), 62.

the "two-sex model" of sexual incommensurability, exemplified in the surgeon Pierre Roussel's *Système physique et moral de la femme* (1775).[17] For Roussel, sexual difference is not limited to primary or even secondary sexual characteristics: "woman is not woman simply in one part, but in every aspect under which she can be considered."[18] Roussel's pronouncements would be cited throughout the nineteenth century as proof that women's intellectual weakness was innate, rather than the product of defective education (Vila, 253–54). Such theories would weigh heavily in nineteenth-century legislation curtailing the rights and activities of women (Laqueur, 194–207). While there are obvious ways in which the earlier understanding of women's bodies and character figure as precursors to these developments, they are not the same. It was possible to argue that the mind has no sex, while arguing that women's different bodies provided certain mental advantages. As we shall see, for Anne-Thérèse de Lambert, women's vivacity and *délicatesse* become the basis of an argument for cognitive superiority. Later women would question the degree to which such characteristics were innate or learned in response to social conventions. As Louise Dupin succinctly put it: "That which distinguishes men from women does not appear to have any effect on differences of merit, intelligence, understanding, or any quality whatsoever" (Dupin, *Des femmes*, 59).

7.2. Portraits and Mirrors: Pringy's *Les Differens caracteres des femmes du siècle*

Let us consider a 1694 work, *Les Differens caracteres des femmes du siècle*, by Jeanne-Michelle Hamonin de Maranville, madame de Pringy. Steeped in the theological and philosophical debates of late seventeenth-century France, Pringy's criticisms of women's behavior should be understood in terms of her psychological theory. Her work shows how a particular moralist subgenre, the *caractère*, may be deployed to critique social practices (its usual role), to explore the damaging psychological effects of those practices, and to offer a mechanism for change.

---

[17] Thomas Laqueur, *Making Sex: Body and Gender from the Greeks to Freud* (Cambridge, MA: Harvard University Press, 1990), 149–92. See also Steinbrügge on the "sexualization of female existence" in Roussel (Steinbrügge, *The Moral Sex*, 41–43).

[18] Pierre Roussel, *Système physique et moral de la femme, ou Tableau philosophique de la constitution, de l'état organique, du temperament, des moeurs, & des fonctions propres au sexe* (Paris: Chez Vincent, 1775), 2.

Little is known of Pringy's life, including the dates of her birth and death. A daughter of the minor nobility, married, widowed, and remarried, she enjoyed a solid reputation as a woman of letters. Published in 1694, with a second edition in 1699, *Les Differens caracteres* was favorably reviewed in *Le Mercure* and *Le Journal des savans*, as were her other works. She was close to the influential Jesuit Louis Bordaloue and published a *Vie du Père Bourdaloue* in 1705, the year following his death. Her piety infuses the *Differens caractères*, as does her sharp social analysis. Appearing in the wake of the tremendous success of La Bruyère's *Les Caractères ou les moeurs de ce siècle* (1688), Pringy's book has often been viewed by modern scholars as a less humorous, more didactic echo of her predecessor. Her goals and methods are, however, quite different from La Bruyère's, and bespeak a carefully delineated educational psychology.

The notion of *caractère* as a "character type" did not originate with La Bruyère, who claimed classical inspiration, and had long been familiar to the theater-going public in works inspired by the stock characters of Italian commedia dell'arte and, importantly, in Molière's comedies. Molière presented contemporary social "types," to which La Bruyère alluded most notably in his hypocrite Onuphre, an explicit reimagining of Tartuffe. The moralist "character" genre aims for sociological accuracy, but also for didactic utility, "to instruct while entertaining," as Molière put it. In the celebrated opening lines of La Bruyère's preface, he claimed to be "returning" to the public the material that it had "lent" him, inviting the public to "examine at its leisure this portrait that I have drawn from nature, and if it recognizes some of the defects that I touch upon, correct them" (La Bruyère, 693).

Recognition and self-correction, a common trope of the Horatian injunction to combine the pleasing with the useful, receive only a passing nod from La Bruyère, but they are foundational for Pringy:

> My goal being to contribute to the improvement [*la perfection*] of those whose true Characters I describe, I thought to compensate them for the discomfort of recognizing themselves in these portraits, by giving them the means to correct their defects.[19]

---

[19] Jeanne-Michelle de Pringy, *Les Differens caracteres des femmes du siècle*, ed. Constant Venesoen (Paris: Honoré Champion, 2002), 69. Venesoen's introduction is marred by his evident lack of sympathy for the text, in which he finds "une emphase morale et spirituelle qui rique d'agacer" (10), but his bio-bibliographic scholarship, which presents what is known of Pringy's life and examines her theological affinities with Bossuet, Senault, and others, is extremely useful.

Pringy's "perfection" should be understood in the etymological sense of a process of improvement, becoming complete or wholly realized. She makes two important assumptions: first, that women will be able and willing to recognize themselves in her harsh portraits; second, that they will be induced to follow the models for self-improvement that she proposes, achieving "a transformation of morals [*moeurs*]" (70). It is worth noting that she has a specific group of women in mind, and that she uses a term that indicates her worldview: *femmes du siècle*. Unlike La Bruyère's reference to the *moeurs de ce siècle* (emphasis added) or "our time," the phrase *femmes du siècle*, like *gens du siècle*, refers not to a period of time or an epoch, but to the "world" of those who are not in religion, as in English "secular": in other words, *femmes du monde*.[20]

Pringy's project relies on two basic assumptions: that women will be capable of seeing themselves in her depictions of flawed character types, and that they will be capable of aligning themselves with virtuous models. Both actions face obstacles: the external obstacle of society's encouragement of poor behavior, and the internal obstacle of *amour-propre*. As I will show, Pringy develops a psychological theory and a pedagogy to show how change is possible; underlying all is her positive assessment of women's potential to attain a virtuous ideal. I examine her work in detail, first because it is sophisticated and substantial, yet understudied; second, because Pringy's critique of female behavior foreshadows later writers, including Lambert and d'Arconville, whose criticisms have also been misconstrued as either misguided or misogynist.

The work is divided into two main parts. The first contains the six "characters," along with their corresponding corrective virtues or "perfections":

I.	Les Coquettes	II.	La Modestie
III.	Les Bigotes	IV.	La Piété
V.	Les Spirituelles	VI.	La Science
VII.	Les Économes	VIII.	La Règle
IX.	Les Joüeuses	X.	L'Occupation
XI.	Les Plaideuses	XII.	La Paix

---

[20] She further underscores the social status of those she studies in the section on Coquettes: "Je parle des mieux élevées, je laisse là celles du commun people, et toute celles qui ne connoissent la galanterie que sous le nom de débauche, je parle aux personnes distinguées" (Pringy, 70).

The second half consists of a discourse on the nature of *amour-propre*, the "dominant passion in women," according to Pringy, and its role in each of the *caractères* of the first part. What first appears to be a neat set of binaries proves to be more complex. The relations among the "characters" and "perfections" are not always symmetrical. For example, the excesses of "Les Économes" (Misers) are set off against the need for a well-balanced economy at the macro level in "La Règle," then linked to a larger social and psychological problem of *déréglement*. "L'Occupation" (Industriousness), intended as a counterweight to the compulsive gambling described in "Les Joüeuses," spends more time in describing the vice of idleness, *oisiveté*, one of the fundamental causes of gambling addiction. The *caractères* vary in the degree of social acceptability, and some are actively encouraged by society. A firm hand in one's household expenditures is generally considered a virtue, for example, but taken to miserly excess it harms both oneself and others. Each *caractère* represents the dark side of behaviors that women are encouraged to practice.

In Pringy's psychology, each of us has a *tempérament*, sometimes called a *disposition*, that is a given and that can be either good or bad, as when we are told that the inclination to gamble stems from *un mauvais naturel* (Pringy, 97). Dispositions lead to "penchants" or "inclinations" that are then "fortified" by habit and become "custom" (*coûtume*). The basic temperament decides one's dominant passion, which in women is almost invariably *amour-propre*. Why would this be the case? For Pringy, self-love is "the most natural, the most useful, and the most common" passion, regardless of sex, but in women it is encouraged and cultivated from early childhood and throughout their lives (Pringy, 135). Starting in girlhood, women are discouraged from physical activity, developing a taste for indolence (*molesse*), "voluptuous inclinations," and an understanding that their looks are their most important attribute. These qualities produce the dysfunctional behaviors analyzed as *caractères*.

Temperament is not destiny. Pringy's goal is to reveal the depths of misery created by these character flaws in order to inspire women with the desire for change, then to demonstrate the corrective virtue that will lead to their improvement or "perfection": becoming truly themselves. Given the strength and tenacity of *amour-propre*, it is remarkable that Pringy believes women capable of recognizing themselves in the unflattering mirror—hence, perhaps, the reason for her scathing descriptions, intended to shock the reader into recognition. She emphasizes the need for active, conscious effort. Some may be born with "fortunate inclinations" that lead one naturally in the right path, but few people "find virtue without a guide" (Pringy, 74). Modesty, for example, is rarely a given disposition, but instead emerges as the result of conscious efforts to overcome the inertial forces that make us listen to the blandishments of *amour-propre*. The need for effort explains why "idleness" is such a grave defect. Like *amour-propre* itself, it stems from a natural inclination to rest, but it is inculcated in women to such an exaggerated extent that it prevents them from developing a sense of duty to others and from engaging in healthy mental exercise.

The first chapter, on Coquettes, sets up the structure:

Flirtation [*la galanterie*] is popular in society and as a pleasure in general, and this trifling attitude is born with the sex. Her temperament contributes to this character and her education confirms it, making her focused on the nothings that fill it . . . without bothering to make of her a woman of substance, they seek to make her amiable; she is instructed in pleasing, not in living. (Pringy, 70)

In the basic scenario, "temperament" contributes to a character flaw that is reinforced by education and socialization. Pringy offers the first of several indications of what she sees as women's basic mental equipment or "nature": here, the "esprit de bagatelle" or tendency to be taken by small matters and details. She returns on several occasions to the notion that women's minds operate differently from men's. Whereas men, once they have found what they consider to be the truth of a given matter, remain set on the idea (whether it be right or wrong), women typically come to conclusions more quickly, but are also more likely to change their minds (Pringy, 87). Their "vivacity" is not a virtue in Pringy's thinking, since it often leads them to make up their minds without thinking through ("déterminer sans reflechir," Pringy, 88), which leads to faulty reasoning.

Pringy emphasizes that women have "no less mental capacity than men," but that it is too often put to bad use and exacerbates character flaws (Pringy, 72). The sexes' different social roles also lead to different manifestations of bad character. The chapter on religious hypocrisy, "Les Bigotes," notes that men assume this persona for financial gain (remember Tartuffe!), while women are led to it out of pride (*orgueil*) and *amour-propre* (Pringy, 76). Similarly, although both men and women are capable of wrecking their household economy, men typically err in the direction of excessive expenditure for pleasure and to make a show of ostentation; women's form of *déréglement* goes in the opposite direction, that of avarice (Pringy, 96–97).

The first three "characters"—Coquettes, *Bigotes* (religious hypocrites), and *Spirituelles* ("femmes d'esprit" as opposed to women of true learning), point to inner flaws that show themselves in relationships with others. The narcissism of the Coquette is a form of alienation, played out through meaningless flirtation: "she seeks herself in external objects." Her lack of authentic engagement is mirrored in her partner: "under the image they present of loving one another, they only love themselves" (Pringy, 136). The Coquette's extreme behavior and exaggerated expressions are symptoms of a profound unhappiness (Pringy, 72–73). Coquetry's opposite, Modesty, acquired through conscious practice, restores relationships and ensures courteous relationships with one's peers, superiors, and inferiors. Relationships are also key to the second pair, "Les Bigotes" and "La Piété." Women turn to hypocrisy because the appearance of religious devotion enables them to maintain worldly connections and "reconcile God and the world." The *bigote* enjoys the reputation of being a "dame de charité" without needing to make the effort required of a true "dame charitable" (Pringy, 77). More darkly, however, hypocrisy also enables her to dominate others. Pringy emphasizes the sadistic element in such "charity": "making the miserable suffer" (Pringy, 80). True Piety is defined in terms of action: searching, following, constantly renewing one's faith ("point de repos"), and above all squelching one's *amour-propre* (Pringy, 81–85).

In the next pair, Pringy's juxtaposition of facile, superficial knowledge and true *science* offers insights both into the formation of ideas and the ways in which our intellectual lives affect others. The *spirituelle* is in many ways less overtly problematic than either the coquette or the *bigote*, as her wit evinces neither the dubious moral qualities of *galanterie* nor the outright cruelty of religious hypocrisy. Nevertheless, "A woman who takes pride in her wit [*se pique d'esprit*] is unbearable" (Pringy, 85). She is unbearable because when she speaks, she does so with easy eloquence and so persuades her listeners, even though she is likely to lead them into error. The essay is thus an account of the genesis of error. Picking up the theme of women's natural vivacity, Pringy makes an observation that some commentators have taken to be misogynistic: "A woman touches on her studies without ever going into depth" (Pringy, 85). The context and overall structure of *Les Differens caracteres* make it clear, however, that the passage refers not to all women, but to those who possess this particular character flaw.[21] They may be numerous, but this is an analysis of a particular "character," not Woman as such. What makes the *femme d'esprit* dangerous? Pride and *amour-propre* play their role in her constitution: she limits her reading to authors with whom she knows that she will already agree, and those who cultivate an elegant prose style: "all the erudition in the world cannot please her if it lacks *politesse*" (Pringy, 85). She is highly critical, because she views criticism as a sign of intelligence. The source of her errors and faulty reasoning, however, is deeper than a question of "taste":

> Here is how witty women [*femmes spirituelles*] proceed. A big mental idea forms in the imagination. Neither knowledge, nor a rule, nor a concept—it is an idea, which is an extended space that encompasses all great things. In this vast space, they imagine that they see assembled all the beauties of the mind. They create a confused mixture of everything they know, and this pile of imperfect knowledge fills their heart as badly as it fills their mind. Opinion vitiates the will, while the disorder of the heart solidifies the mind's errors and will not allow them to change. (Pringy, 86)

In Pringy's epistemology of fuzzy thinking, a "big idea" is a beautiful fantasy, composed of bits and pieces of knowledge and stitched together with desire. Preconceived opinion overrides the will; misguided emotion sets it in stone. In such a mental framework, each new idea becomes a further obstacle to finding the truth: "Every image that she notices, every idea that she forms, every opinion that she hears, become so many obstacles to the truth that she proposes and of which she is ignorant" (Pringy, 87). The pernicious effects of habit and custom here manifest themselves as faulty thinking, rather than poor personal choices. "The habit of opinion is stronger than all the passions together" (Pringy, 88). Women who are thus misguided are more likely than men to misguide others, because of their communicative skills and ability to use "colorful" language to persuade their listeners.

---

[21] I am in total disagreement with the reading of this passage by Pringy's modern editor, Constant Venesoen, for whom the chapter "renoue avec la vieille tradition phallocratique" of women's intellectual inferiority (Avant-propos, in Pringy, 43). Venesoen then professes astonishment at the "contradiction" in the first sentence of "La Science," "L'esprit et de tout sexe" (Pringy, 88). Eliane Viennot similarly accuses Pringy of misogyny in *La France, les femmes et le pouvoir: Les résistences de la société (XVIIe–XVIIIe siècles)* (Paris: Perrin 2008), 370. Both readings fail to consider the context of the passage and Pringy's overall argument.

Now, it may be that Pringy, whose sympathies appear to lie with the cultural conservatives of her day, was aiming her satire at a well-worn image of salon women and *précieuses*: there are echoes of Molière's *Précieuses ridicules* in the *spirituelle*'s concern with language and style, and even more echoes of *Les Femmes savantes*; she echoes Nicolas Boileau's infamous *Satire X* on women in her choice of *caractères*. But there can be no doubt that Pringy had a high idea of women's intellectual potential, as she makes clear at the beginning of "La Science": "Mind belongs to every sex [*L'Esprit est de tout sexe*]. The soul is a spiritual being equally capable of operating in women as in men" (Pringy, 88).

As Linda Timmermans put it, Pringy owes more to Poulain de la Barre than to La Bruyère.[22] Even if women are "rightly excluded" from certain "laborious" professions, she finds no reason to exclude them from the realm of erudition (Pringy, 89). Indeed, she goes on to argue, women need serious study more than men in order to balance their natural vivacity, "to lift up their understanding in an orderly manner and to fix their ideas with certitude" (Pringy, 90). Even with the best possible temperament ("le plus beau naturel du monde"), study is needed in order to come to an understanding of oneself and the world. In an extended passage, Pringy extols the pleasures and the pure happiness of learning, of being able to confront "a thousand confused ideas" on a topic and determine which is the best reasoned, to establish principles that enable one to avoid error. Poised on the cusp of the Enlightenment, Pringy draws strength from traditional faith and culture, but in the spirit of the age to come, she sees truth as the goal of a laborious journey, not as the starting point.[23]

With one's judgment properly informed, one has the freedom (*liberté*) to choose among the whole range ideas bequeathed to us by Antiquity. Here as elsewhere, *amour-propre* is the enemy: "In order to know much, one should love oneself little" (Pringy, 91). She hastens to say that this does not mean that we must inevitably set others' opinions above our own, but intellectual modesty means that we should proceed with caution if our opinion diverges from the ancients and the best of the moderns. Learning is an ongoing process, never complete: the greatest thinkers "are constantly learning and are rarely

---

[22] Timmermans, *L'accès des femmes à la culture*, 209. In addition to the arguments that Pringy presents for women's intellectual strength in *Les Differens caracteres*, she continued to present counterarguments to misogynist "prejudice" in a later work, *Critique contre la prevention* (Paris: J. Musier, 1702), which was reviewed in the *Mercure*.

[23] On the period's shift in the epistemology of truth, see David W. Bates, *Enlightenment Aberrations: Error and Revolution in France* (Ithaca, NY: Cornell University Press, 2002).

content with themselves." The pursuit of knowledge ultimately leads us to understand ourselves better and to come closer to God.

If Pringy's first three "characters" demonstrate the ways in which *amour-propre* and sloth produce behaviors that corrode the self and distort relationships with other people, the next three involve dispositions that, while similarly destructive of interpersonal relationships, manifest themselves through one's relationship to material objects, especially money. Because saving money is generally viewed as a laudable goal, "les Economes," misers, suffer from "an acceptable vice" and thus find it all the more difficult to extricate themselves from an endless grinding effort to create ever more "surplus" (*superflus*), even though they deprive themselves and their families of necessities and fail in their charitable obligations. Relationships with friends and family members turn exclusively on monetary considerations (Pringy, 92–94). Gambling creates similar havoc in "Les Joüeuses" (Pringy, 97–100). Here, any "surplus" is swallowed up at the gaming table, but the financial ruin brought about by a gambling addiction is little different from the misery wrought by avarice. Last, similarly compulsive behavior characterizes "Les Plaideuses," whose endless litigations are not intended to lead to justice, but are an exercise in vanity and an end in themselves (Pringy, 103–106).

The three have much in common and reveal Pringy's psychological insight. All are compulsive behaviors, addictions, driven by inner anxiety and desire. "Disturbed by her desire, she is more restless than others," we are told of the miser (Pringy, 92). Gambling is "a passionate preoccupation" (Pringy, 98) that, like avarice, has its roots in its social acceptability. *Plaideuses* suffer from "troubled thoughts and disquiet" (Pringy, 103). Unlike the first three characters, who are at least superficially content with their lives, these three are deeply unhappy, but unable to break the destructive cycles in which they find themselves. A further common feature to all three is that their disquiet is focused on fantasy and imaginary gain. The gambler gives free rein to "eagerness for riches" and loses all sense of self in the "nocturnal empire" (Pringy, 98). For the *plaideuse*, "she counts on what she is hoping for, her desire assures her of possession, and on that basis she takes action" (Pringy, 103). The miser is "insatiable," finding pleasure in "a future hoard" that she can never adequately realize (Pringy, 138). Last, these disorders lead to "the loss of time, estrangement from God, forgetting oneself" (Pringy, 105). Time can be regained, as it were, when we recognize its importance in our own salvation. "Time is the way to eternity" for Pringy, hence wasted time and the forgetfulness of time cause one to wait until it is too late to change. "There is no longer enough time to come to know yourself once you are no longer able to put knowledge into practice, and it is no longer possible to put knowledge into practice when there is no more time to know yourself" (Pringy 102).

Although the final chapter of Part One, "La Paix," corresponds to "Les Plaideuses" in the logic of the book's structure, it also sums up the solution to all the ills that Pringy has diagnosed. True peace is a divine gift, "a state in which external objects no longer have power over us, and which is enlightened, separated, detached from things of this world and able to rise above the fears and desires that they elicit" (Pringy, 106). Freed from fear and desire, we are able to see beyond the disquiet and hypersensitivity brought on by *amour-propre* (Pringy, 107).

Part Two is entirely dedicated to a study of *amour-propre*'s causes and effects, recapping its manifestations in each of the six "characters" of Part One. In Pringy's account, which reflects the widespread diffusion of "cultural Jansenism" despite her Jesuit connections, self-love stems from a perversion of our innate desire to be happy, or inability to understand that happiness can only be found in the love of God, rather than the love of self (Pringy, 134). Love is "the noblest of the passions," but through the Fall has degenerated into "the bonds of the misplaced love of self" (Pringy, 141). Redemption is the defeat of *amour-propre*.

For Pringy, women's innate qualities—"weak, fragile, changeable, inconstant" (Pringy, 143)—make them susceptible to the trap of *amour-propre*, but their plight is exacerbated by their restricted education and society's encouragement of multiple forms of self-involvement. *Amour-propre* "so completely erases all womens' good qualities" that even those who are eminently capable of erudition and governance allow pride and vanity to prevent them from achieving their potential. In the final section, however, she offers a vision of what is possible to those who free themselves from the limiting perspective of *amour-propre*. The qualities that made them susceptible to self-love become virtues once they are freed of it.

> An intelligent woman would certainly go farther than any man; her vivacity, her penetration, her delicacy, her fiery courage, the subtlety of ideas whose movement is quicker than those of men, would render her capable of conceiving and executing the greatest projects.... Women have so many advantages over men that they should be eager to conquer a passion that makes them inferior to the stronger sex. (Pringy, 149–50)

For Pringy, the moralist *caractère* enables her not only to critique a particular social reality, but also to integrate her critique into a pedagogy and an implicit psychology: she expects that her women readers will see themselves in her portraits, be shocked into recognizing their profound and often unconscious unhappiness, and find the inspiration to fulfill their potential as moral beings and members of society.

The lasting popularity of La Bruyère ensured that "characters" would continue to appear in moralist works in the eighteenth century. In Madeleine de Puisieux's *Les Caractères* (1750), the title appears to be no more than a signifier for "moralist writing," since the text is a series of reflections, not character portraits. As we saw above in the chapter on marriage, Geneviève d'Arconville includes several named "characters" in the chapter on women in her early *Pensées et réflexions morales*; other chapters include male portraits, usually exemplifying intellectual pretentiousness. D'Arconville's *caractères* are interspersed amid the short maxims and reflections that compose her work; they reflect a tendency toward narrative that will appear in her later *Des Passions*.

Marie de Verzure offers an arresting use of the technique in the last two chapters of her *Réflexions hazardées*. The *Réflexions* end with a double portrait, "La Femme raisonnable" and "La Femme du Monde." At first glance, the two seem rather obviously paired to highlight the modesty and retiring nature of the "reasonable" woman and the superficiality of the society woman, not unlike Pringy's "Les Spirituelles" and "La Science." Verzure's reasonable woman displays both modesty and "une liberté honnête." She prefers the company of her books to that of other people, but she is neither a recluse nor a prude; all of her readings are "good books" because even when she reads frivolous books (presumably novels), they enable her to deepen her understanding and perfect her mastery of language (Verzure, 2:274). She practices Verzure's method of examining herself in order to understand others: "By learning to know herself, she acquires understanding of the human heart" (Verzure, 2:275). She achieves the goal proposed by Lambert and others: "she makes provision of resources so that, if it becomes necessary someday, she may make up for a lack of friends by becoming self-sufficient" (Verzure, 2:276). The woman of the world, on the other hand, is all about appearances: her looks, her company, and her furnishings are carefully planned in order to project a certain image—and to avoid any appearance of being planned: "She carefully hides the care that she takes with everything" (Verzure, 2:281). The final contrast with the "reasonable woman" is damning: "One wishes to be thought perfect; the other seeks to become so" (Verzure, 2:282).

What is interesting about this portrait is that the society lady's carefully wrought public image is that of an intellectual. We are told that she is completely up to date on the latest books and plays, that she offers patronage to young writers, and that next to her favorite chair can be found a selection from her personal library "composed of new publications and a few books of metaphysics, which show that this is a woman who thinks, but who hides what she knows, because nothing is more ridiculous than a woman who displays her knowledge" (Verzure, 2:280). The last sentence is striking: we do not know, in the end, if the *femme du monde* actually reads and thinks or not; a mask lies behind the mask. While many features of this portrait are clearly antithetical to the reasonable woman's studious existence and select circle of friends, the two have elements in common. It is curious, after all, that the book ends with this worldly vision, rather than with the "correct" paragon of reason. Is the worldly woman the self-deprecating parody of the reasonable woman, her inner other? Or is she the ultimate mask, a disguise perhaps even more effective than that of "an ignorant woman who knows the world only through hearsay"? Just as the *Réflexions* represent the fruit of introspection that must nevertheless be offered to the public for confirmation, the women readers of the final two essays find themselves at the intersection of self and society, mind and heart.

7.3. Nature, Culture, and the *désir de plaire*

In this section, I examine eighteenth-century women moralists' understanding of the relationship between what were perceived to be women's innate abilities or nature and the social world. As we have seen, although Pringy ascribes much of the blame for women's bad behavior to the toxic effects of social conditioning, she nevertheless sees certain cognitive characteristics— vivacity, penetration, *délicatesse*, and quick thinking—as distinctively feminine. Although she clearly would not have agreed with his conclusions, Pringy may have been echoing elements of Malebranche's much discussed account of women's minds in Book II of *De la Recherche de la verité* (1674), where he argued that the delicacy of women's brain "fibers" prevented them from making the effort required for serious intellectual labor. Poulain's argument for the advantageous quickness of women's brains becomes in Malebranche's hands a means to discredit women's ability to reason.[24] Women, according to Malebranche, have more aptitude than men for fashion, style, and taste, but they are incapable of sustained reflection. "Everything relevant to taste is in their hands, but in general they are incapable of penetrating truths of any difficulty."[25]

The marquise de Lambert responded directly to Malebranche's account in her *Réflexions nouvelles sur les femmes*. Probably written around 1720, the text was published without her permission in 1726 and drew both praise and blame for its intense "metaphysics of love" in the final section.[26] Lambert's rebuttal of Malebranche is dual: she inverts his values by underscoring the importance of taste and language in polite culture, and she uses his physiological model to demonstrate the opposite of his argument. In Lambert, "sensibility became the lynchpin of a gendered psychology."[27]

Lambert begins by quoting Malebranche: "A very respectable author attributes to women all the graces of the imagination: 'Everything relevant to taste is in their hands,' he says, 'and they are the judges of the best language'" (Lambert, 219). Superiority in imagination, taste, and language, she notes, is no small advantage. After setting forth the role of imagination and taste in the formation of judgment, she takes on the matter of women's brain fibers. She begins by summarizing the argument that women's innate distractibility renders them incapable of following a line of reasoning that leads to the truth. Women, she argues, do not require the reasoning process employed by men: "in women, ideas arrive by themselves and organize themselves more from feeling than from reflection: nature reasons for women and spares them the trouble" (Lambert, 221). Sentiment is thus no enemy of reason. To the contrary, it speeds the mind toward the truth and assists in the creation of

---

[24] See Nicole Pellegrin on the ways in which Poulain and Malebranche represent two divergent paths from the Cartesian legacy. Although biological difference did not necessitate inequality for Poulain and others like him, it increasingly was used to support arguments for inequality. Pellegrin, *Pensées du corps et différences des sexes à l'époque moderne* (Paris: ENS Éditions, 2020). See also La Vopa, *The Labor of the Mind*, 47–51.

[25] Nicolas Malebranche, Book Two, "De l'imagination," Chapter 1, *De la recherche de la vérité*, in *Oeuvres complètes*, ed. Pierre Clair and Geneviève Rodis-Lewis (Paris: Vrin, 1962), 1: 266-67. On Malebranche's position vis a vis salon culture, see La Vopa (*The Labor of the Mind*, 63–96) and on Lambert's response to Malebranche (110–14).

[26] On the publication history and Lambert's unsuccessful attempt to purchase the entire publisher's stock, see Marchal, *Madame de Lambert et son milieu*, 174–77; Granderoute's editorial introduction, 205–11.

[27] Katherine Hamerton, "A Feminist Voice in the Enlightenment Salon: Madame de Lambert on Taste, Sensibility, and the Feminine Mind," *Modern Intellectual History* 7.2 (2010): 226. In addition to a careful reading of the *Réflexions*, Hamerton offers a thorough account of Lambert's intellectual milieu and the salon debates that led up to the writing of the work.

new ideas. Such "effortless feminine cognitive excellence" (Hamerton, 237) is not simply an alternative to male ratiocination, but superior. If the ability to reason is universal among humans, while "vivacity" is simply an accidental mental feature, then it is not the case that Lambert "emotionalizes" the female mind, as Steinbrügge argues.[28] The afterlife of this line of thought will, however, be different.

Thought to have written the *Réflexions* in the context of lively debates on women's intelligence in her salon, Lambert sets her critique of Malebranche in a broader critique of the double bind facing women, who are condemned for engaging in intellectual activity on the one hand, and for expressing the feelings that are supposedly their province, on the other: "while shaping them for love, we forbid them its use" (Lambert, 222). Lambert seeks to defend women's cultural authority and establish their role as critics, while upholding the values of salon sociability against academic efforts to establish rules for aesthetic excellence.[29]

In order to lay claim to respect for women's intellect as well as acknowledgment of the place of sensibility in judgment, Lambert distinguishes between two types of personal qualities, the *estimables* and the *agréables* (Lambert, 223–24). Qualities worthy of respect are "real" and "intrinsic" characteristics whose claim on us is a matter of justice. Agreeable qualities are "external" in that they depend on the mental or physiological disposition of the individual viewer or interlocutor; they produce pleasure. Their location in the viewer explains why different people respond differently to a given object. (Individual viewers' dispositions and more or less finely tuned perceptions determine the perspicacity of their judgment.) Love, then, can never be "deserved," as a matter of justice. At the same time, Lambert asks, is it possible that love has nothing to do with justice or esteem, and only pleasure? Surely not. "We have as much need to love as to esteem" (Lambert, 224). Just as she had argued in the opening passages of the *Réflexions* that women's writing and scholarship have enriched French culture, here she claims that a full appreciation of women as thinking and feeling individuals in whom *estime* and *amour* are united is in the best interests of all. The concluding section of the *Réflexions*, the "metaphysics of love," represents a platonic ascent of

---

[28] Steinbrügge, *The Moral Sex*, 18–20.
[29] As Faith Beasley puts it, "Lambert is defending the right of women and worldly culture in general to pass judgment on works and to determine literary standards according to different criteria." Beasley, "Anne-Thérèse de Lambert and the Politics of Taste," *Papers on French Seventeenth-Century Literature* 19.37 (1992): 342.

love motivated not simply by pleasure, but by virtue (Lambert, 227). Lambert regrets the decline in morals of the present age, looking back to "l'ancienne galanterie" of the great seventeenth-century salons, upon which her own was modeled, for examples of mixed-sex friendship both dignified and pleasurable.

Lambert's account of women's nature involves both critical and positive elements. She attacks the "tyranny" of men who mock women's intellectual accomplishments and endeavor to reduce them to "a pleasant spectacle," all the while falsely claiming to appreciate women who are "reasonable and intelligent" (Lambert, 222–23). That women should accommodate themselves to male dictates is hardly surprising, she observes, but society is the poorer for it. Like Poulain, she makes the case for valorizing women's vivacity and enhanced sensitivity. As we shall see, these generally accepted features of sexual difference in early eighteenth-century science will ultimately be absorbed in later theories of women's biologically based limitations; the argument that they might constitute a cognitive advantage would be lost from view.

Writing a generation later, Geneviève d'Arconville had even less patience with the social world and the role that women were expected to play in it. Whereas Lambert had approvingly cited a description of Madame de La Sablière as a woman of feeling ("She never thought, . . . she simply feels," Lambert, 222), d'Arconville would dismiss any such idea with a concision worthy of La Rochefoucauld: "There are things that one believes one thinks, but that one merely feels" (*Pensées et réflexions morales*, 1:357). She expressed her frustration with society women in the preface to her translation of Alexander Monro's *The Anatomy of the Humane Bones*, published as the *Traité d'ostéologie* in 1759.

> Women trendsetters especially, who pronounce judgment even on things about which they know absolutely nothing, not content with the power bestowed by their grace and beauty, wish to extend their authority even to Medicine. A doctor concerned only with his art is incapable of pleasing them; he neglects little social graces and idle prattle strewn with supposed witticisms, the usual recourse of mediocrity. In order to please such ladies, one must charm them. A truly learned man strikes them as an idiot; whereas they see someone with the requisite social skills as a modern-day Hippocrates. (D'Arconville, 3:195–96)

I give the passage in its entirety because it has been cited as evidence of d'Arconville's "sexism." In context, it is clear that d'Arconville's ire is directed against the superficiality and arrogant ignorance of society people, men as well as women; it is an egregious misreading of the text to claim that she "railed against women who wished to study medicine and anatomy."[30] The women she complains of here have no interest in knowledge, only in witty conversation: they are the latter-day embodiment of Pringy's *spirituelles*.

The chapter "Sur les femmes" in her *Pensées et réflexions morales* of 1760 is a blistering critique of women's behavior, but also an indictment of the society that requires it. D'Arconville's first published work that was not a translation, *Pensées et réflexions morales* lays out the basic view of humanity that she explores in her later moralist treatises: driven by passions and *amour-propre*, unwilling to benefit from the teachings of religion, unlikely to experience true friendship. She is dubious of the claim by "our modern philosophers" that freedom from organized religion could make us happy. "Sur les passions," the chapter that immediately precedes "Sur les femmes," ends with a comparison of men's and women's susceptibility to the passions. Men's education encourages the empire of their senses more than women's, she observes, and thus licentious books pose a greater danger for men, especially in their youth. Women and girls are more likely to be moved by "decent novels where love is always subordinate to virtue," whereas these have little effect on boys. Her point is that, despite these differences, both sexes are drawn to depictions of love, whether by sentiment or sensuality. In men, the physical acts on the mental, whereas women experience the reverse (D'Arconville, 1:366–67).

In "Sur les femmes," vanity and coquetry, both manifestations of *amour-propre*, appear to be women's chief characteristics:

Men are proud, but most women are merely vain. (D'Arconville, 1:368)

Coquetry is not limited to the artifice and flirtatious behavior of pretty women: plain women develop an even greater talent for it, not having the benefit of a face that, as d'Arconville puts it, accomplishes three-quarters

---

[30] Londa Schiebinger, *The Mind Has No Sex? Women in the Origins of Modern Science* (Cambridge, MA: Harvard University Press, 1989), 249. Schiebinger's accusation of sexism also comes in response to the illustration of a female skeleton, whose head appears unnaturally small and hips unnaturally wide, that d'Arconville commissioned for the *Traité d'ostéologie*. As Nina Rattner Gelbart points out, however, the illustration was likely produced under the supervision of the surgeon Jean-Joseph Sue, who selected the skeletons and provided the measurements (Gelbart, *Minerva's French Sisters*, 225–26).

of the task; for those who lack beauty, laying claim to "l'esprit et les talents" offers an alternative approach, one which men make use of as well. Women are the experts, however, because "the desire to please is innate in them" (D'Arconville, 1:374). To what extent are the features of this unflattering portrait innate and distinctly female? The comparison at the end of the previous chapter, with its emphasis on reading and education, suggests that such behavior is learned. According to the final lines of "Sur les femmes," the supposedly innate *désir de plaire* is, her earlier jibe notwithstanding, cultivated and encouraged by men:

> I am hardly surprised that women are coquettes, since it is the surest means to please men. . . . Men admire virtue, but coquetry subjugates them. (D'Arconville, 1:383)

Similarly, a discussion of "pretty women" is less about women and more about the way that people respond to them; seen through the distorting lens of the public gaze, it is impossible to assess their character and abilities with equity until later in life (D'Arconville, 1:372–73).

In a famous passage often cited as the rationale for her decision to publish anonymously, d'Arconville levels her strongest criticism at the society that disrespects women and curtails their options.

> Women have hardly any public role to play, save by indecency, intrigue, or ridicule.
>
> In the private sphere, women assume no role with impunity. Are they flirtatious? They are despised. Do they engage in intrigue? They are dreaded. Do they display learning or wit? If their work is bad, they are mocked. If the work is good, others take the credit, leaving them only the ridicule of having claimed to be authors. (D'Arconville, 1:370–71)

D'Arconville's tone is harsh, but her criticism of society's treatment of women is not far removed from Lambert's. ("What male tyranny! They do not wish for us to use either our minds or our feelings"; Lambert 217).

Given the consolidation of a medical consensus on sexual incommensurability, the insistence of Roussel and his followers that women's difference extended to every aspect of their being, and the rise of arguments promoting naturally established separate spheres for men and women, it is noteworthy that d'Arconville and other women moralists emphasized a view of women's behavior and characteristics as learned, not innate. Henriette de Marans imagines founding an empire with women in charge. Let men not imagine for a moment that they possess greater abilities than women, she argues with an imagined interlocutor: men simply have greater opportunity to learn, both from their education and the professions open to them.[31] Unlike her friend Antoine Thomas, whose *Essai sur le caractère, les moeurs et l'esprit des femmes* (1772) caused an uproar in Paris salons,[32] Suzanne Necker holds that women's "quickness" and "vivacity" were learned behaviors: "Women have been taught to live, to feel, to judge, and to speak for the present moment; thence comes the quickness in our thoughts and responses that people call instinct" (Necker 1801, 1:79). In a longer passage, she reflects on the role of education in women's aptitudes:

> If I were arguing for the cause of women, I would begin by proving that men cannot attribute the superiority of their talents to biological differences, and that it can only be attributed to education.
>
> I would go on to describe the aims of women's education; I would demonstrate that the nature of these aims modifies our minds and our inclinations [*penchants*] but does not require less intelligence or capacity. (Necker 1801, 1:76)

She goes on to suggest that even if it were the case that women were less capable of steady concentration than men, their patience is equally valuable, and their strength is the same sort that produces genius. Constance de Salm would agree, noting the flagrant contradiction between women's upbringing and education, which are entirely geared for meekness and dependency and the very real responsibilities that they will assume in adult life, whether managing a household, educating children, or as an independent widow. Elsewhere, she scoffs that the "duty" imposed by men to dress to please them is an "insult" and "one of the strongest pieces of evidence of men's absurd and ridiculous pride" (Salm, *Pensées*, 104–108; 153–54).

The late eighteenth-century novelist Françoise-Albine Benoist offers what initially appears to be a contrary, or contrarian, perspective in her *Lettres sur*

---

[31] Henriette de Marans, *Confidence générales et particulières*, in Chollet and Krief, *Une femme d'encre et de papier*, 411.

[32] As noted above (Chapter 5, 181), Necker sided with Diderot's critique of Thomas; Louise d'Épinay wrote a stronger rejoinder in a letter to Ferdinando Galiani. The three texts are collected in Elisabeth Badinter, ed., *Qu'est-ce qu'une femme?* (Paris: P.O.L., 1989).

le désir de plaire (1786), a moralist text disguised as an epistolary novel. There is no plot; the "letters" are a series of scenes in which the narrator gleefully relates her interactions with a broad range of social "characters," both men and women. Her ability to flatter some, listen to others, and nod approval as needed enables her to succeed socially while remaining free of emotional attachments: "I owe my liberty to the desire to please; it has shielded my heart from the weaknesses of love."[33] Benoist's narrator has qualities in common with Clarice, the coquette at the center of Scudéry's "Histoire de la coqueterie" (Scudéry 1688, 2:755–844), whom the "reasonable" characters attempt to cure of her coquetry. Clarice too enjoys freedom from emotional entanglements. (It helps that she is independently wealthy and in no need of a husband). Even so, she does not imagine remaining in her present situation for more than a few years, perhaps less; although the conversation ends inconclusively, Clarice has given indications that she may change. Scudéry and Benoist, writing a century apart, have very different aims; Scudéry seeks to analyze coquetry's underlying motivations, while Benoist uses her heroine's *désir de plaire* as a device to satirize various social types, such as the Provincial, the Aging Coquette, and an entire dinner table of characters from the literary world. Docility is her special talent: "by sacrificing my vanity to the glory of those around me I am certain to please them, and that is enough for me" (Benoist, 83). For Benoist, docility is a means to a satirical end. By placing herself in the moralist's position, observing and judging others, she pleases herself above all and furthers her will to power.

Satire aside, women moralists have nothing kind to say about docility or gentleness, which by the dawn of the nineteenth century was being framed as a behavior imposed on women by men. Few attain the intensity of Fanny Raoul's 1801 feminist manifesto, *Opinion d'une femme sur les femmes* (1801), in which she denounces *douceur* as a code word in male vocabulary: "I have noticed that this word, coming from men, is a synonym for weakness; so that, according to them, a gentle woman is one who does exactly what they want, and who lowers herself so much that she truly believes herself inferior to them, has neither feelings nor principles of her own, and believes that she should meekly accept whatever ideas are handed to her."[34] Pauline Guizot observes that "pleasing" is the only form of ambition that women have been allowed to express, hence their supposed "feminine rivalries." Men's rivalries

---

[33] Françoise-Albine Benoist, *Lettres sur le désir de plaire* (n.p. [Amsterdam?], 1786), 18.
[34] Fanny Raoul, *Opinion d'une femme sur les femmes*, in Geneviève Fraisse, ed., *Opinions de femmes de la veille au lendemain de la revolution française* (Paris: Côté-femmes, 1989), 143.

are equally intense, but their ambitions are framed heroically (Guizot, *Essais et conseils*, 2:1314).

Over the course of her many moralist essays, journalistic pieces, and literary criticism, Guizot calls attention to the ways in which women's behavior and intellectual development have been framed by the male perspective. As a critic, she levels a scathing analysis of the paternalist condescension in Joseph-Alexandre de Ségur's magnum opus, *Les Femmes, leur condition et leur influence dans l'ordre social* (1803) and the casual misogyny of Gaston de Lévis's *Maximes et réflexions* (1807)—commentary that is all the more biting through her satirical assumption of the "girly" persona that they ascribe to all women.[35] For Guizot, women's characteristics are embedded in social structures: "I am aware that men are in the habit of attributing to us various customs to which we have been obliged to comply, and imposing rules on us that they claim we invented" (Guizot, in Suard, ed. 4:224–25). Or, in her essay "De la manière dont les hommes jugent les femmes,"[36] she observes that the feminine vices mocked by male writers from Juvenal to Boileau represent "the spirit of the age" which manifests itself equally in men, who determine the norms. "If our virtues do not take the same shape [as men's], it is because our situations are not the same; if our defects appear different, it is because they lead us to stray from different duties" (Guizot, *Essais et conseils*, 2:26).

A shift takes thus place in women moralists' analysis of women's character. In the late seventeenth century "the mind has no sex" was understood as a confirmation of women's ability to reason; while their temperament and character were held to be biologically determined, these features did not negatively affect intellectual function. Women moralists of the eighteenth century would extend the concept of "women's nature" to the full range of attitudes, behaviors, and thought processes, but claim that these are induced by social convention and education, even as the "scientific" consensus swung to the views of Roussel and his followers and the cultural consensus coalesced around Rousseau's view of women's domestic role. Women moralists are often impatient with the roles assigned to them, setting the stage for the feminist manifestos of the Revolution and afterward. In the final section of this chapter, I will turn to the ways in which the tensions over

---

[35] Guizot's review of Ségur, "Lettres d'une femme à M. A. de Ségur sur son ouvrage intitulé *Les Femmes*," originally appeared in *Le Publiciste* and was included with a number of her essays in J.-B.-A. Suard, ed., *Mélanges de littérature*, 5 vols. (1804; reprint Geneva: Slatkine, 1971), 4:219–38; her piece on Lévis, presumably also written for Suard, would not be republished until many years after her death: "Réflexions d'une femme sur le recueil de Maximes de M.D.L.," in *Le Temps passé* 1:470–74.

[36] See above, Chapter 6, 214–15.

female characteristics come to bear in the bitter debates on the status of the woman intellectual, *la femme auteur*, in the early nineteenth century.

7.4. *Comment peut-on être femme auteur?*

The early years of the nineteenth century saw a striking increase in the use of the phrase *femme auteur*.[37] Although the abbé Mallet's article "Auteur" for the *Encyclopédie* explicitly applied the (masculine gender) word to women as well as men, citing Antoinette Deshoulières and Anne Dacier as examples, the word *auteur* retained a certain "professional" connotation that even male writers would sometimes avoid in favor of the more elevated term, *gens de lettres*.[38] An anonymous 1757 comedy, *Le Public vengé, ou La Femme auteur*, portrays the titular character as a vain, pretentious woman who will do anything to get her work in print; she is ultimately humiliated when her manuscript is circulated without her permission, making her the laughingstock of Paris.[39] Although women writers and intellectuals had long been a prominent feature of the cultural landscape, as witnessed by the rise in popular anthologies and compendia of women writers,[40] the emergence of the "professionalized" term and attendant controversies marked a new site of contestation for women's place in the public sphere. Even as women lost social and political ground during and after the French Revolution, their numbers in print expanded dramatically during the revolutionary decade and thereafter.[41]

The status of the woman writer—intellectual, philosopher, novelist, historian, critic—occupies a zone of the cultural landscape that exceeds the limits of this study of women moralists; the debates it occasions extend beyond moralist writing as defined here. The evolving image of the woman writer matters for philosophy as for literary and cultural studies, however,

---

[37] The ARTFL database shows occurrences of "femme auteur" starting in the mid-eighteenth century, but the highest frequencies are from 1784 to 1890. "Femme de lettres" follows a similar curve.

[38] On the ways in which evolving literary culture retained seventeenth-century class attitudes, see Gregory S. Brown, *A Field of Honor: Writers, Court Culture, and Public Theater in French Literary Life from Racine to the Revolution* (New York: Columbia University Press, 2005).

[39] *Le Public vengé, ou la femme auteur* (Lyon: Chez la Veuve d'Antoine Olier, 1757). Despite the unsanctioned release of her manuscript, the central character learns that her book will actually appear in print, providing her with a measure of grim satisfaction, but she must leave Paris in order to avoid those whom she has angered by her criticisms.

[40] See above, Chapter 1, 21–22.

[41] Carla Hesse, *The Other Enlightenment: How French Women Became Modern* (Princeton: Princeton University Press, 2003), 37.

because it speaks directly to the question of women's nature and mental capacity. Geneviève Fraisse has analyzed the peculiar intensity of the period 1800–1820, observing that during this time, an insistence on women's practical reason, "a combination of innate and acquired traits" acquired through experience, rather than study, and exercised exclusively in the domestic sphere collides with the reality of women's role as cultural producers and the ambitions of "exceptional" women of widely varying political views.[42] These cultural tensions ignite two centuries of debates over women's abilities and place in the world. Although much of the *femme auteur* controversy took place in and around novels, it is also shaped in the moralist and philosophical writings of Germaine de Staël, Félicité de Genlis, and Pauline Guizot. Coming at the end of the great age of moralist writing that was a legacy of the *ancien régime*, it provides a fitting conclusion to this study.

Needless to say, French women had been writing since the emergence of the French language and publishing since the dawn of print. They had also long complained of the stigma attached to their activity. Although much admired by her contemporaries, the poet Antoinette Deshoulières advised a young friend, "Mademoiselle ****" to avoid a literary career:

Seek not a frivolous glory
That causes such pain and so little pleasure.[43]

A century later, Madeleine de Puisieux would offer much the same advice—citing the poem by Deshoulières—to the ostensible recipient of her *Réflexions et avis*, a young woman whose sentimental education provides a novelistic plot woven into the moralist analysis. Puisieux also responds sharply to her own critics, observing that women are often the most vicious of all: "they consider it a crime to know how to write, and even more to publish" (Puisieux, *Réflexions et avis*, 250). Geneviève d'Arconville, as we saw earlier, notes that women who display knowledge or wit risk having their work attributed to others. And one might add Elisabeth Guibert's comment,

Men rarely pardon women for taking up the pen; it appears to be a toy they want for themselves. (Guibert, 104)

---

[42] Geneviève Fraisse, *Reason's Muse: Sexual Difference and the Birth of Democracy*, trans. Janet Marie Todd (Chicago: University of Chicago Press, 1994). 148.
[43] Antoinette Deshoulières, "Epistre chagrine à Mademoiselle ****," *Poësies de Madame Deshoulieres* (Paris: Chez la Veuve de Sébastien Mabre-Cramoisy, 1687), 51.

In 1797, the poet Ponce-Denis Lebrun, known to his contemporaries as "the French Pindarus," offered this advice to women poets:

Do you wish to resemble the Muses?
Inspire, but do not write.[44]

Lebrun's verse is remembered, not for the response printed with it from his friend the dramatist La Chabeaussière, who archly warned him to beware of "the ire of our *femmes-auteurs*" but rather because it inspired Constance Pipelet (later de Salm) to riposte with her *Épître aux femmes*, calling on women to take up the pen.

Come and show posterity
That we, too, will gain immortality. (Salm, *Oeuvres*, 1:6)

For Pipelet/Salm, men and women are fundamentally the same: "When nature made two different sexes / She changed the form, not the elements" (Salm, *Oeuvres*, 1:6). She concedes men's role in governance and defense, but concludes that "the arts are for all, just as is happiness" (Salm, *Oeuvres*, 1:20).[45]

Authorship, then, takes on a particular energy and the catch-phrase *femme auteur* becomes a renewed locus of controversy in this context where even visible, culturally powerful women have not yet taken the step of demanding political rights. As Christine Planté put it in her study of women's authorship during the nineteenth century, the *femme auteur* becomes a new character type, "invested with the ideologies and fantasms of the nineteenth century, which invented the figure."[46] Like Montesquieu's Persians, the woman writer is both visible and somehow unthinkable: "Comment peut-on être Persan?"

Let us first consider how the fantasmatic *femme auteur* engaged two of the most visible and culturally powerful women of the post-revolutionary period, Germaine de Staël and Félicité de Genlis. In them we see efforts to

---

[44] Ponce-Denis Écouchard Lebrun, "Ode aux belles qui veulent devenir poètes," in *L'Esprit des journaux françois et étrangers*, 26e année, vol. 2 (March–April): 245–46. The "response" from August-Étienne-Xavier Poisson de La Chabeaussière appears below Lebrun's poem on page 246.

[45] Geneviève Fraisse points out the fundamentally subversive dimension of women's right to "the arts": "What is really at stake here in imitation is the individual's right to express herself and, what is more, the right to invent" (Fraisse, *Reason's Muse*, 43).

[46] Christine Planté, *La Petite soeur de Balzac: Essai sur la femme auteur*, nouvelle edition (Lyon: Presses universitaires de Lyon, 2015), 15. See also Vicki Mistacco, "Femme auteur," in Krief and André, *Dictionnaire*, 465–73.

tease out the entwined problems of women's nature, authorship, and audience. Their writing reminds us that the "moralist impulse" had increasingly abandoned the moralist forms—essay, maxim, character type—that have provided the corpus for this study for other genres, especially the novel. I conclude with the reflections on women's authorship, both moralist essays and criticism, by the woman whom the nineteenth-century critic Sainte-Beuve termed the greatest moralist of the age: Pauline Guizot.

In 1800, opposing visions of *la femme auteur* were cast in sharp relief. In *De la littérature considerée dans ses rapports avec les institutions sociales*, Germaine de Staël—who does not use the expression—offers a broad cosmopolitan vision of intellectual and political progress, looking into the post-Revolutionary future to assess what will be needed to further the cause of progress. *De la littérature* takes a capacious view of "literature" that encompasses philosophy, history, drama, poetry, and fiction. As she had indicated a few years earlier in her "Essai sur les fictions," here she expands on the potential for works of the imagination to carry forth "moral and philosophical truths" (Staël, *De la littérature*, 332). Fiction should be mindful of a higher purpose: "It is not enough to move the soul; one must enlighten it" (Staël, *De la littérature*, 325). Staël, who had published several short fictions and plays in the 1790s, but was primarily known for philosophical and political works, would deliver on her vision two years later with her novel *Delphine*.

She dismisses the Gothic novels that were in vogue as "useless," but speaks warmly of "novels that depict manners [*moeurs*] and characters," particularly those by women. She cites Isabelle de Charrière's *Caliste*, Sophie Cottin's *Claire d'Albe*, Adelaide de Souza's *Adèle de Sénanges*, and calls attention to the works of Félicité de Genlis for "her ability to paint situations and observe sentiments" (Staël, *De la littérature*, 330–31n.). She observes that women excel as novelists because of their ability to understand the human heart; inasmuch as novels typically focus on love and sentiment, "women alone understand all the delicate nuances" (Staël, *De la littérature*, 331n.). As she points out in the chapter "Des femmes qui cultivent les lettres," however, women's ability to carry forth an ambitious literary and philosophical program is constrained by their "uncertain" role, "neither in the natural order, nor the social order" (Staël, *De la littérature*, 310). Staël lays out the ways in which French society has failed women by denying them education and consideration, "reducing women to the most absurd mediocrity" (Staël, *De la littérature*, 312). She looks back to the *ancien régime* and to salons like her mother's, where women "distinguished by their minds and their character" shaped opinion with wisdom and courage (Staël, *De la littérature*, 313). She lays the sad decline of post-Revolutionary society to a lack of intelligent, educated women; instead, women who have nothing but "insipid gaiety" reduce the most brilliant gatherings to "young men who have nothing to do and young women who have nothing to say" (Staël, *De la littérature*, 314). Women whose abilities enable them to rise above the herd are roundly criticized: "As soon as a woman is considered to be distinguished, the general public is prejudiced against her" (Staël, *De la littérature*, 315).[47]

Staël's diagnosis of the fate of the exceptional woman evidently draws on her own experience, but also on her views on women's character and potential. "It is to the benefit of the enlightenment and happiness of society that women be able to develop their mind and their reason with care" (Staël, *De la littérature*, 315). It is true that Staël seems unable to draw connections between the exceptional woman and women in general: how does one close the gap between individual freedom and general enlightenment (Fraisse, 114–15)? For Staël, women's dilemma lies in the contradictory claims of self-actualization and happiness; the former requires the will to develop one's mind and to pursue one's ambition, but subsequent harsh treatment of society makes enduring love, hence happiness, impossible. As we saw in *De l'influence des passions*, Staël describes love as "women's only passion" (Staël, *De l'influence*, 207), which is consistent with her view that women are the best novelists because of their understanding of the emotions—a view that has a long ancestry. Like Lambert, Staël finds it ironic that women are more easily forgiven a lapse in morals than the exercise of their intellect. In her novels, Staël will intensify the dilemma, exploring the tragic incompatibility of female talent and happiness.

In the same year that Staël published *De la littérature*, the popular writer Sophie Cottin—whose earlier *Claire d'Albe* Stäel had mentioned as one of the better recent novels—advanced the claim in her new novel, *Malvina*, that women should avoid writing for publication, and confine themselves to writing novels. As the character "mistriss Clare" says to the protagonist, "I believe that novels are women's territory . . . they are better suited to it than anyone, because it is they who are able to seize all the nuances of a sentiment that is their entire life, whereas it is simply an episode in the life of a man."[48]

---

[47] Similarly, in *De l'influence des passions*: "De quels sentiments de jalousie et de haine les grands succès d'une femme ne sont-ils pas l'objet!" Staël, *De l'influence*, 190.

[48] Sophie Cottin, *Malvina*, 2 vols. (Paris: Maradan, 1800), 2:86–87.

Clare's argument that women should not publish their writing—she is vague on the reasons that are leading her to seek publication for her own work—are actually not so different from Staël's account of the difficulties and unfair criticisms confronting women writers, nor do they differ on the question of women's emotional intelligence. Cottin's reservations about publication, although startling in a best-selling novelist, would perhaps have attracted less attention had she not gone on to deny women's ability to write anything other than novels. Asked by Malvina why she doesn't write about "more useful topics" (Cottin, 2:86), Clare explains that women are not capable of writing on weighty matters: "Having neither depth in their observations nor order in their ideas, women are incapable of genius." In Clare's view, faulty education does not explain the situation. Men have shown themselves able to overcome the disadvantages of low birth and poor education, but "no woman, as far as I know, has taken this route." Clare's comments are reinforced by a footnote in which the author herself adds,

> Let someone show me a woman who has written a philosophical work, a play, or any large-scale work that requires long and patient reflection, and that would even be at the level of our second-best writers? If there is one, I will hold my tongue and concede that this woman is able to resemble men, but I will be sorry for her, because she will be the loser. (Cottin, 2:88n.)

Given Staël's considerable celebrity as a public figure and author of political and philosophical works, Cottin's comments are stunning and provocative, to say the least—all the more so inasmuch as she clearly borrowed from Staël the remark about love being an "episode" for men.[49]

Both Pauline de Meulan (later Guizot, the name that I will continue to use here) and Félicité de Genlis responded to Cottin within the year. Guizot evidently thought well enough of her essay, one of her first for *Le Publiciste*, that she included it in a collection of her pieces, *Essais de littérature et de morale*, published anonymously, but with her portrait, in 1802. In "Réflexions sur les femmes, par une femme," she expresses dismay over Cottin's footnote, observing that it is difficult to imagine that she did not have *De la littérature* in mind.[50] She then dismisses Cottin in order to discuss Staël. The essay is a commentary on the role of reviewers, who are more apt to criticize a work

---

[49] Staël: "Love is the entire history of a woman's life, an episode in men's lives." *De l'influence*, 207.
[50] Anon. [Pauline de Meulan Guizot], *Essais de littérature et de morale* (Paris: n.p., 1802), 85–95.

than to signal what is praiseworthy. Gesturing toward larger philosophical issues, such as Staël's notion of perfectibility, that cannot be addressed in the space of a short essay, she quotes several passages of historical analysis that she finds especially well drawn, then focuses on Staël's chapter, "Des femmes qui cultivent des lettres," and the passage where Staël describes the pain inflicted by vicious criticism. The essay is a call for even-handedness and civility in criticism; it is also a full-bodied endorsement of Staël and what she represented for intellectually ambitious women of the day, as well as an expression of hope that celebrity and happiness would not always be mutually exclusive: "Superior to nearly all women and to most men by the strength of her mind, the breadth of her knowledge, and the brilliance of her talent, if she uses these rare gifts to instruct and to please us, she will surely reap not only glory, but also happiness" (Meulan Guizot, *Essais de littérature*, 95).

Although Pauline de Meulan's essays were widely read and she participated in numerous critical debates, her anonymity prior to marriage enabled her to avoid becoming a public figure like Staël, whom she admired, or like Félicité de Genlis, with whom she differed on key issues. She and Genlis agreed, however, on Cottin's footnote. Genlis, a highly successful educational theorist and author of best-selling works for young people, responded in a work whose title aligns it with moralist writing, *Le Petit La Bruyère* (1801). As she indicates in the preface, the first part of the book, consisting of positive and negative character portraits, is intended for children, but the second part, consisting of "maximes et réflexions," is for their elders. It is here that she comments on the recently published "injurious attack on *femmes auteurs*," quoting the offending passage in *Malvina* at length.[51] Like Guizot, Genlis praises Staël's comments on women writers: "Of all the writers that I know, Madame la baronne de Staël is the author who, in my opinion, has spoken to this issue with the greatest dignity, rationality, nuance, and intelligence" (Genlis, *La Bruyère*, 225). It quickly becomes evident, however, that she takes Cottin's criticism of women who write on education as directed at herself; in addition to refuting Cottin, she suggests that a number of features of *Malvina* have been borrowed from her own work (Genlis, *La Bruyère*, 228).

Genlis had not finished with Staël, however. Even in *Le Petit La Bruyère*, a chapter on suicide critiques Staël's defense of suicide in *De l'influence des passions* (Genlis, *La Bruyère*, 316–41). In a footnote to the 1824 edition of

---

[51] Félicité de Genlis, *Le Petit La Bruyère, ou Caractères et moeurs des enfans de ce siècle* (Paris: Maradan, 1801), 225–26

her work, Genlis takes credit for Staël's later retraction—although there is no evidence that Staël gave much thought to Genlis's critique. And there are unflattering portraits of a pseudo-intellectual woman thought to represent Staël in Genlis's novella, *La Femme auteur* (1802) and *La Femme philosophe* (1804), a response to *Delphine*.[52] Both Staël's emblematic stature as a woman intellectual and Genlis's willingness to engage in polemical battles reveal much about the ability of women to hold public roles. For present purposes, however, Genlis's critical preface to her work *De l'influence des femmes sur la littérature française* (1811) speaks directly to the question of women's nature, their ability to exercise their intellect and to express themselves as writers.

Genlis's preface, "Réflexions préliminaires sur les femmes," is constructed in three movements: she examines first the claim that women are incapable of producing works of genius; second, the "natural character" of women's writing; and last, the rules that should govern both women writers and their critics. The first issue she dismisses fairly quickly. While conceding that men's overall literary production surpasses that of women, she argues that women possess the requisite attributes of genius: "imagination, sensibility, elevated spirit [*âme*]."[53] Women surpass men in certain genres, such as epistolary writing and the novel; they possess the native ability to produce works of genius in other genres, such as tragedy, but have lacked educational opportunity. Furthermore, she observes, men have determined the hierarchy of genres; men control the institutions that determine criteria for excellence, such as the Académie française.

When she turns to the question of whether women have a "natural" style of writing, she notes first the contradictory claims in male judgments of women's writing; second, she disputes the claim that women have an innate sensitivity (*sensibilité, délicatesse*) that no man can possess. On the other hand, both "education and decorum" impose self-constraint on women, leading them to hide their feelings and develop indirect means of communicating, "a touching and mysterious language" (Genlis, *Influence*, xii). For Genlis, the social and moral imperative of modesty is also an aesthetic imperative, creating intense effects through restraint. She argues against the claim that a "natural" expression of desire, freed from social conventions, is truly

---

[52] The one-sided relationship—Genlis was much more focused on Staël than the reverse—has attracted recent scholarly interest. See Lotterie, *Le Genre des Lumières*, 263–80; Amélie Legrand, "Les Ambiguïtés de l'exemplarité dans *La Femme auteur* de Félicité de Genlis et *Corinne ou l'Italie* de Germaine de Staël," *Cahiers staëliens* 63 (2013): 215–38.

[53] Félicité de Genlis, *De l'influence des femmes sur la littérature française* (Paris: Chez Maradan, 1811), iii.

"natural." To the contrary, since the creator intended humans to live in society, then the civilized state (*pace* Rousseau) is that which corresponds to human nature. Socialized modesty is therefore "natural." Women's only significant physiological difference from men is to be weaker, from which Genlis concludes that they should not govern, and to bear children, which leads her to determine that they have right to be protected (Genlis, *Influence*, xix).[54] She also concludes, however, that given that the advancement of civilization is part of the order of things, women should be allowed the education that enables them to develop their natural abilities and talent as artists and writers: "Why should they be forbidden to write and become authors?" (Genlis, *Influence*, xxi).

Genlis concedes that she herself had offered arguments against women's literary ambition—a reference to her 1802 novella, *La Femme auteur*, in which the protagonist sacrifices love and financial security in pursuit of her literary career. Genlis writes that she had "pushed impartiality to the point of exaggeration" at the time, but now, at the "end of my career" (although she would continue writing for nearly two more decades), she may speak more freely. It is not simply the case that women possess the requisite qualities needed to become great writers; they, their families, and society at large are better served if they cultivate the arts, rather than indulging in frivolous pastimes.[55] "Thus all true creative dispositions and clear aptitude for an art deserve cultivation" (Genlis, *Influence*, xxiii).

Having established that women are able to make important literary contributions and that they deserve the education that will enable them to do so, Genlis turns to the conditions under which women may become published authors and the rules governing their conduct vis-à-vis critics and the reading public. While Genlis imposes strict limits on what she considers acceptable behavior for women, she discusses at greater length the rules of civility that should govern all critics, male or female. She gives a withering rebuttal to an unnamed critic who claimed that women writers deserved no special consideration, "since in becoming authors, they have abjured their sex and renounced all their rights" (Genlis, *Influence*, xxxi). She distinguishes,

---

[54] It is worth noting that Louise Dupin had argued that physical strength has nothing to do with ability to govern in the modern era (Dupin, *Des femmes*, 113).

[55] As Christine Planté observes, Genlis, like virtually all other commentators, male or female, on "la femme auteur," imagines *la femme* as a leisured upper-class woman (Planté, *La Petite soeur de Balzac*, 60–61). To set Genlis's views on women, style, and literary genre in the context of the long nineteenth century, see Planté, chapter 7, "Écrire comme un homme, écrire comme une femme," 181–221.

however, between a woman who writes "useful and moral works" (like Genlis herself), who deserves "all the respect due her sex," and women who write inappropriate or blameworthy works, who might not. The preface ends with a nostalgic look back at the era of Louis XIV, when women writers flourished and men of letters did not attack them. The ground thus continues to shift as Genlis and her contemporaries parse the interrelation of nature and culture. Staël and Genlis were at opposite ends of the political spectrum, but they agreed that the climate for women writers was a hostile one.

As we have seen, Pauline Guizot carried on the moralist tradition through essays and criticism written in a wide range of voices; her interests were broad, but she would return on numerous occasions to women's issues and to the situation of women intellectuals. Her political views were closer to Staël than to Genlis. If Genlis tended to blame the ills of the present day on the pernicious ideas of the Enlightenment, Guizot remained "attached to the cause of the philosophy of the last century," as Charles de Rémusat wrote in his biographical essay for the *Essais et conseils de morale*.[56] Like her novels of the 1790s, her essays and journalistic pieces of the early 1800s appeared anonymously. Her anonymity was apparently not total, however. After Suard included a number of her pieces in his *Mélanges littéraires* (1803–1804), Staël wrote to him to ask if the essays signed "P." were indeed by "Mademoiselle de Meulan" and contacted her to express her appreciation.[57]

Guizot was as formidable a critic as essayist. We have already had occasion to look at her sharp critiques of antifeminist works by Ségur and Lévis and her praise for Staël. She does not spare Genlis, whose tendency to infuse any topic with bitter comments about the moral failings of the *philosophes* irritated her considerably. Her review of *Le Petit La Bruyère*, written in the persona of a widower seeking to educate his three young daughters, calls attention to the contrast between Genlis's insistence on modest deportment and the vehemence of her denunciation of freethinkers (*esprits forts*). In her review of Genlis's novel, *Les Mères rivales*, she finds well-drawn characters, an engaging plot, and an elegant style (albeit "a bit uniform"), but she also points out Genlis's gratuitous barbs leveled at Condillac and d'Alembert.[58] Her most pointed criticism of Genlis, however, comes in what is ostensibly

---

[56] Charles de Rémusat, "Notice sur la vie et les ouvrages de Mme Guizot," in Guizot, *Essais et conseils de morale*, 1:xxxvi–xxxvii.
[57] Sainte-Beuve, *Portraits de femmes*, 287.
[58] Both of Guizot's reviews were included in her anonymous essay collection of 1802, when both of Genlis's works were still quite recent. "Lettre sur *Les Mères rivales* de madame de Genlis" and "L'Éducation des filles," in *Essais de littérature et de morale*, 23–32; 110–16.

a review of Louis-Simon Auger's 1806 edition of the letters of Madame de Maintenon. Although she does ultimately comment (favorably) on Auger's book, she opens with an ironic response to the claim made by Genlis that the Enlightenment *philosophes* had dimmed Maintenon's reputation: "In the old days, when something bad happened, they blamed witches; nowadays, it's the *philosophes*."[59] Historically, Guizot points out, Maintenon's reputation suffered much more from the attacks by contemporaries like Saint-Simon than from *philosophes* writing half a century after her death.

Guizot's recurring criticisms of Genlis are of interest, not simply because they remind us of Guizot's identification with *le parti philosophique*, but because they are a significant instance of an action that she had reflected on and took seriously: criticizing another woman writer. In the series of essays and maxims collected under the title "Des Femmes," she offers this thought:

> Among women, we should criticize one another in the same way that one criticizes family members in public, being careful not to attack the other in a way that would dishonor the family name. (Guizot, *Essais et conseils*, 2:30)

Similar reflections on women's seeming inability to fight fair appear in one of Guizot's pieces reprinted in Suard's *Mélanges*, "Sur les femmes auteurs," in which a male persona claims to be deeply disturbed by women's public disputes ("they print every nasty thing that they know about each other"), especially two writers identified as "Madame de G. and Madame de S."—Genlis and Staël. Women don't know how to fight properly, he sighs, and he regrets the bygone days when they pretended that they never intended to publish, but the manuscript was stolen. A similar observation appears in her review of *Le Petit La Bruyère*, when a male friend of the male narrator makes the same comment. "They go too far, exhaust their resources, and rip the enchanting veil that enhanced their natural grace" (*Essais de littérature et de morale*, 116). In both these pieces, Guizot's irony is aimed at the attitudes of the male speakers themselves, as the cliché "the enchanting veil" makes clear. She may indeed be irked that women cannot seemingly criticize one another without "dishonoring the family name"—but as we have seen, she is more

---

[59] Guizot, "De Mme de Maintenon et de la nouvelle édition de ses lettres," *Le Temps passé*, 1:462–63. Genlis had just published her *Madame de Maintenon* (Paris: Maradan, 1806), on which she would draw a few years later for *De l'influence des femmes*. She and Auger engaged in an acrimonious exchange of articles and pamphlets following his criticism of the 1811 book; an exchange undoubtedly fueled by her earlier quarrel with the editors, of whom he was one, of the *Biographie universelle*.

irked by men's tendency to reduce all women to "that corporation referred to as *women*" (Guizot, *Essais et conseils*, 2:2). Criticisms among male writers do not produce comments about all men. For men, the "family honor" of the sex is irrelevant, but it is an inescapable part of the cultural system that women must confront.[60]

The difficulties facing women critics are the topic of Guizot's "Lettre d'une femme journaliste à un ami" (Guizot, *Le Temps passé*, 2:543–48).[61] Writing in the persona of a female theater critic (one of her numerous roles for *Le Publiciste*), she expresses surprise that others seem more interested in attacking her as a woman rather than for her aesthetic judgments, which are invariably interpreted as purely "personal." Working women, she notes, do not expect to have respect accorded to their embroidery, a symbol of leisured femininity; it should be based on their professional activity, "respect that is due solely to the work itself."

She continues to reflect on the ethical dimension of criticism in her essays on Anne-Thérèse de Lambert and Émilie Du Châtelet.[62] As the title indicates, "Lettre d'une femme sur les femmes qui ont de la réputation, et en particulier sur Mme du Châtelet" focuses on the status of the woman intellectual. Guizot's immediate impetus was the 1806 publication of Du Châtelet's letters to Argental.[63] Guizot's essay is not a review of the new edition, but a commentary on its critical reception by men with a certain view of femininity.

> A woman with a reputation, for those who have heard of her, is a strange sort of animal of indefinite sex; one knows that it is not a man, but one does not quite consider it to be a woman either. If she were observed to be sewing, it would be a source of astonishment; if she were said to have children, that would be a freak of nature. (Guizot, *Le Temps passé*, 2:500)

---

[60] Genlis had indeed prefaced her criticism of Staël's attitude toward suicide by claiming that it "pained" her to criticize another *femme auteur* (Genlis, *La Bruyère*, See Lafond, *Moralistes* 316–17).

[61] The editor notes the original date of publication, December 18, 1807.

[62] Guizot, "Des femmes qui ont écrit, et de Mme de Lambert en particulier," in Suard, *Mélanges*, 4:252–71; "Lettre d'une femme sur les femmes qui ont de la reputation, et en particulier sur Mme du Châtelet," *Le Temps passé* 2:500–504. The essay in *Le Temps passé* includes the publication date, April 7, 1806, indicating that it would have appeared at least two years later than the essay on Lambert, republished by Suard in 1804. (Neither Suard's *Mélanges* nor the *Conseils de morale* provide original publication dates.)

[63] Du Châtelet, *Lettres inédites de madame la marquise Du Chastelet à M. le comte d'Argental*, ed. Claude Hochet (Paris: Chez Xhrouet, 1806). As editors of the recent edition of Du Châtelet's correspondence observe, Hochet appears to find the letters' greatest value in what they reveal about Voltaire; the edition is significant, however, as it contains letters whose autographs have since disappeared. See Ulla Kölving and Andrew Brown, "Histoire éditoriale de la correspondence," in Kölving and Brown, *La Correspondance d'Émilie Du Châtelet*, 1: 49–50.

Guizot takes aim at one critic who had dismissed Du Châtelet's celebrity as "borrowed," and wonders what she would need to earn a reputation—are her scientific works and Newton commentary not enough? In a commentary on Du Châtelet's *Sur le bonheur*, which Hochet included in his edition of the correspondence (along with the second chapter of the *Institutions de physique*, "De l'existence de dieu"), Guizot is taken with Du Châtelet's call to divest oneself of prejudice, although she finds that it contradicts the recommendation to be "susceptible to illusion." That and other seeming inconsistencies lead Guizot to comment that Du Châtelet "let her mind be dazzled by maxims that contradicted her heart," adopting certain notions intellectually without integrating them into her lived experience. It is that experience, as revealed in the letters, that Guizot finds the most engaging and with which she identifies strongly. Du Châtelet is reassuring proof that a brilliant intellectual woman is not a strange creature of indeterminate gender. Critics, however, are irritating: Guizot mocks the reviewer who pointed to a passage where Du Châtelet expresses pleasure in her victory over Mairan in their debate on *vis viva*: "The journalist is thrilled to seize upon a single passage where, he claims, *Madame Du Châtelet reveals her secret pride* [*amour propre*]. What a clever man! He knew that Madame Du Châtelet was an author, so he had to discover that she had an author's pride." Guizot also finds the editor Hochet's extended comparison between Du Châtelet's letters and those of Madame de Sévigné out of place. For Guizot, both editor and reviewers have missed the point and shown that they have been unable to come to terms with an exceptional woman as a human being.

The ability of an exceptional woman to thrive in the world is the central topic of Guizot's "Des femmes qui ont écrit, et de Mme de Lambert en particulier," one of the essays republished by Suard. Guizot finds much to admire in Lambert, whose work she knows well. She turns to Lambert less to praise the causes of her literary fame, however, than to understand how she succeeded in being "pardoned" for it. In the midst of the controversies over women writers, the question is timely and urgent. She notes that Lambert writes about women in general, never about herself. "She understood how to be simultaneously a woman and a writer; these days, one is a woman-writer [*femme-auteur*], which is not the same thing" (Suard, *Mélanges*, 4:254). The key for Guizot lies in a certain reticence, which Guizot associates with Lambert's notion of *pudeur*, both in personal relationships and in her reluctance to publish: "Reserve is women's armor" (Suard, *Mélanges*, 4:255). Women should publish, of course—but not in haste, and only after having striven to ensure that their work is truly excellent. ("There is no middle ground for them between success and ridicule," Suard, *Mélanges*, 4:252). One hears echoes of the complaints that women's writing has flooded the market, that every woman considers herself an *auteur*. The danger, as Guizot sees it, is that the existing tendency to lump all women together in the female "corporation" will associate all women writers with mediocrity. The *ancien régime*'s conventions offered a useful restraint: "It was a prejudice more useful than is generally thought, the ridicule attached to women whose literary occupations were too public" (Suard, *Mélanges*, 4:256). She cites the great Hellenist Anne Dacier as an example of a woman who, having "left the path" that society destined for her and having no models to guide her, was unable to manage public opinion when she engaged in a heated public debate, "compromising" her womanly reserve. One may find that Guizot herself goes too far in advising reticence, especially when she recommends that women avoid humor in their writing: as we have seen, she was a keen satirist with an expert sense of irony! Anonymity appears to have been her personal form of *réserve*, allowing her to engage in debate, parody critics, and reflect on the state of the world under one of her pseudonyms or the characters whose voices she assumed: "la douairiaire du Marais," a father writing to his son, a "woman of a certain age," or, simply, "P."

Like Genlis, Guizot breathes a sigh of regret for Lambert's era (Suard, *Mélanges*, 4:264): for Genlis, it was a time when men treated women writers with the respect that she finds lacking in the present; for Guizot, a time when a woman could describe "love without weakness" and be understood. Lambert's writing holds another important truth for Guizot as a moralist, in her ability to draw on her own experience, yet efface herself, in order to write about the female condition. Paradoxically, Guizot argues, the restrictions on women's lives make them better able to understand others and to generalize. For a statesman, the life of a man of letters is "pure speculation," but women's limited experience provides insight into one another's lives. At first glance, her statement that "one woman resembles all others" (Suard, *Mélanges*, 4:265) appears to be precisely the "corporation" idea that she has resisted. Her point, however, is that the restrictions on women's activities result in greater similitude among their lives and duties: "their virtues and their defects flow from the same sources; their weaknesses, whether they give in to them or conquer them, all have the same origin." This being the case, "No woman can speak of other women without thinking a bit about herself; none can think about herself without thinking a great deal about others" (Suard, *Mélanges*, 4:266).

Very much in the manner with which Lambert turned Malebranche's dismissive account of women's minds into an advantage, Guizot explains why women's constricted lives lead them to focus on concrete realities and make them better observers of the human condition.

She comes back to this idea in several of the short pieces included under "Des femmes" in the *Essais et conseils de morale*. For example, she takes the potentially misogynist notion that women are self-centered: "Women have never thought or imagined anything that had no relation to themselves." A woman may indeed be less interested in the broader world because it is largely closed to her, but when her gaze turns inward, "nothing will be hidden from her; let her not fear to plumb the depths of the heart, for they will not resist her efforts" (Guizot, *Essais et conseils*, 27). Because she is herself a universe worthy of her study, "It is rare that a woman gains anything by leaving the house!" Guizot pursues the same logic in reflecting that women's writing, more than men's, exemplifies the character of an age: "To understand the manners of an era, one should consult works written by women" (Guizot, *Essais et conseils*, 28). Again, the conventions of women's socialization being infinitely more circumscribed than men's, women's writing is less likely to reflect idiosyncratic thought and to show greater insight into broad trends and social relations.

In a word, women make better moralists.

Conclusion

In 1769, Denis Diderot dashed off a brief review of *Le Temple du bonheur*, an anthology of ancient and modern writing on happiness, for the *Correspondance littéraire*.[1] Instead of discussing the work, he relates a conversation with the abbé Galiani, to whom he attributes the quip, "all those treatises on happiness are simply the story of the happiness of those who wrote them."[2] Although Galiani dismisses the genre, Diderot later reflects that although the notion of happiness varies from individual to individual, it ultimately depends on an ideal political environment ("neither king, nor judge, nor priest, nor laws, nor yours nor mine . . .") and the ability to adjust one's desires ("disdaining pleasures that aren't meant for us")—the latter being, of course, a classical moralist trope.

Galiani dismisses moralist writing on happiness because it appears too "personal"; like De Jaucourt, he evidently favors a "scientific" approach to *la morale*. As it happens, *Le Temple du bonheur* was originally intended to include a piece that would seem to prove his contention, Du Châtelet's *Discours sur le bonheur*, which had been withheld by the original editor, J.-B.-A. Suard.[3] The autobiographical dimension of the *Discours sur le bonheur* has often distracted commentators from its substantial philosophic arguments.

It is precisely that ability to frame larger observations and judgments from the starting point of the individual that characterizes moralist writing. Introspection has value for the individual—and as we have seen, several moralist projects began as purely personal exercises—but the decision to

---

[1] *Le Temple du bonheur, ou Recueil des plus excellens traités sur le bonheur, extraits des meilleurs auteurs anciens et modernes*, 3 vols. (Bouillon et Paris: Aux dépens de la société typographique, 1769). The BNF catalogue incorrectly lists the editor as J-F Dreux du Radier, evidently by confusion with a 1740 anthology with the same title.

[2] Diderot, "Le Temple du bonheur," DPV 18: 343. The *Correspondance littéraire* chose not to publish the review.

[3] Georges Mangeot, "Les 'Réflexions sur le bonheur' de la marquise Du Châtelet," in *Mélanges offerts . . . à Gustave Lanson* (Paris: Hachette, 1922), 280–81. Suard appears to have handed the project to Jean-Louis Castilhon, *encyclopédiste* and author of one of the longer pieces.

make one's "thoughts and reflections" public is heavy with significance. First, organizing one's thoughts on a particular topic, writing them, and sharing them, publishing them, or simply imagining them shared (as when Henriette de Marans designs a title page and frontispiece for her daily writings) is to allow oneself a certain status, to attribute worth to one's experience, and to enlarge one's horizon of expectations for one's place in the world. In response to Montaigne's question "Que sais-je?," the answer is not abstract theorizing: what I know is what I have experienced. My experience is a worthwhile object of knowledge.

Just as the moralist observes herself, she observes the world. She reflects on the qualities that contribute to a good life, such as friendship and social relations. She questions the legal and philosophical structures that shape her world. None of this reflection is simply "descriptive," as we have seen. Descriptions, whether in essays, portraits, or maxims, are constructed from a carefully developed point of view; it is the reader's responsibility to detect the normative framework animating the perspective. If there is a unifying thread in these women's analyses of the self, of friendship, of happiness, of marriage, of age, of the female condition, it is the recurring claim of personal integrity, autonomy, and liberty. Moralist writing, through its form and content, supports women in that search.

Bibliography

Agamben, Giorgio. "Friendship." *Contretemps* 5 (2004): 2–7.
Arconville, Marie-Geneviève-Charlotte Thiroux d'. SEE Thiroux d'Arconville.
Ariew, Roger. "What Descartes Read: His Intellectual Background." In *The Oxford Handbook of Descartes and Cartesianism*, ed. Steven Nadler, Tad M. Schmaltz, and Delphine Antoine-Mahut, 25–39. Oxford: Oxford University Press, 2019.
Arnauld, Antoine, and Pierre Nicole. *La Logique ou l'art de penser*, introduction by Louis Marin. Paris: Flammarion, 1970.
Aronson, Nicole. *Mademoiselle de Scudéry, ou le voyage au pays de Tendre*. Paris: Fayard, 1986.
ARTFL Project (American and French Research on the Treasury of the French Language). Database. https://artfl-project.uchicago.edu
Bachaumont, Louis-Petit de. *Mémoires secrets pour servir à l'histoire de la République des Lettres en France depuis 1762 jusqu'à nos jours*. 36 vols. Londres: J. Adamson, 1777–1789.
Badinter, Elisabeth, ed. *Qu'est-ce qu'une femme?* Paris: P.O.L., 1989. [Texts by Antoine Thomas, Denis Diderot, and Louise d'Épinay.]
Balayé, Simone. *Madame de Staël: Lumières et liberté*. Paris: Klincksieck, 1979.
Bates, David W. *Enlightenment Aberrations: Error and Revolution in France*. Ithaca, NY: Cornell University Press, 2002.
Bates, Robin. "Madame Guizot and Monsieur Guizot: Domestic Pedagogy and the Post-Revolutionary Order in France, 1807–1830." *Modern Intellectual History* 8.1 (2011): 31–59.
Beasley, Faith. "Anne-Thérèse de Lambert and the Politics of Taste." *Papers on French Seventeenth-Century Literature* 19.37 (1992): 337–44.
Beasley, Faith. *Salons, History, and the Creation of 17th-Century France: Mastering Memory*. Aldershot: Ashgate, 2006.
Beauzée, Nicolas. "Usage (Grammaire)." In Diderot and d'Alembert, 17:516.
Belot, Octavie. *Réflexions d'une Provinciale sur le discours de M. Rousseau, Citoyen de Genève, touchant l'origine de l'inégalité des conditions parmi les hommes*, ed. Édith Flammarion. Arras: Artois Presses Université, 2015.
Benoist, Françoise-Albine. *Lettres sur le désir de plaire*. n.p.: n.p., 1786.
Bénouville, Bonne-Charlotte de [and Henriette de Marans]. *Pensées errantes; avec quelques lettres d'un Indien*, ed. Huguette Krief. Paris: Classiques Garnier, 2014.
Benrekassa, Georges. *Le Langage des Lumières: Concepts et savoir de la langue*. Paris: PUF, 1995.
Bérenguier, Nadine. *Conduct Books for Girls in Enlightenment France*. Farnham, UK: Ashgate, 2011.
Bergès, Sandrine, and Eric Schliesser. "Introduction." In *Sophie de Grouchy's Letters on Sympathy: A Critical Engagement with Adam Smith's The Theory of Moral Sentiments*, trans. S. Bergès, 1–53. Oxford: Oxford University Press, 2019.

Berkel, Tazuko Angela van. *The Economics of Friendship: Conceptions of Reciprocity in Classical Greece*. Leiden and Boston: Brill, 2020.

Berlin, Isaiah. "Two Concepts of Liberty." In *Four Essays on Liberty*, 118–72. Oxford: Oxford University Press, 1969.

Bernardin de Saint-Pierre, Henri. *Études de la nature, nouvelle edition*. 5 vols. Paris: Chez Déterville, 1804 (1784).

Bernier, Marc André. "Mme d'Arconville et la question des limites de l'esprit humain." In *Femmes et philosophie des Lumières*, ed. L. Vanoflen, 43–54. Paris: Classiques Garnier, 2020.

Bernier, Marc André, and Marie-Laure Girou Swiderski, eds. *Madame d'Arconville, moraliste et chimiste au siècle des Lumières*. Oxford University Studies in the Enlightenment. Oxford: Voltaire Foundation, 2016.

Bertolini, Sonia. "Gabrielle Suchon: Une vie sans engagement?" *Australian Journal of French Studies* 37.3 (2000): 289–308.

Blanchot, Maurice. *L'Amitié*. Paris: Gallimard, 1971.

Blank, Andreas. "Complaisance and the Question of Autonomy in the French Women Moralists, 1650–1710." In *Women Philosophers on Autonomy: Historical and Contemporary Perspectives*, ed. Sandrine Bergès and Alberto Siani, 43–60. New York and London: Routledge, 2018.

Blum, Carol. *Strength in Numbers: Population, Reproduction, and Power in Eighteenth-Century France*. Baltimore: Johns Hopkins University Press, 2002.

Boon, Sonja. "Does a Dutiful Wife Write; or, Should Suzanne Get Divorced? Reflections on Suzanne Curchod Necker, Divorce, and the Construction of the Biographical Subject." *Lumen* 27 (2008): 59–73.

Boon, Sonja. *The Life of Madame Necker: Sin, Redemption, and the Parisian Salon*. London: Pickering and Chatto, 2011.

Boros, Gabor. "The Passions." In *The Oxford Handbook of Philosophy in Early Modern Europe*, ed. Desmond M. Clark and Catherine Wilson, 182–200. Oxford: Oxford University Press, 2011.

Bouhours, Dominique de. *Les Entretiens d'Ariste et d'Eugène*, ed. Bernard Beugnot and Gilles Declercq. Paris: Champion, 2003.

Bourgeois-Courtois, Muriel. "Réflexion morale et culture mondaine (matériaux pour une synthèse)." *Dix-septième siècle*, no. 202 (Jan–March 1999): 9–19.

Brading, Katherine. *Émilie Du Châtelet and the Foundations of Modern Science*. New York: Routledge, 2019.

Brewer, Daniel. "Virtue and the Ethics of the Virtual." In *Enlightenment Virtue, 1680–1794*, ed. James Fowler and Marine Ganofsky, 235–51. Oxford University Studies in the Enlightenment. Oxford: Voltaire Foundation, 2020.

Briquet, Fortunée. *Dictionnaire historique, des Françaises connues par leurs écrits* (1804), ed. Nicole Pellegrin. Strasbourg: Presses de l'université de Strasbourg, 2016. Available online: http://books.openedition.org/pus/4124.

Broad, Jacqueline. "Marriage, Slavery, and the Merger of Wills: Responses to Sprint, 1700–1701." In Broad and Detlefsen, 66–81.

Broad, Jacqueline, and Karen Detlefsen, eds. *Women and Liberty, 1600–1800*. Oxford: Oxford University Press, 2017.

Brown, Andrew, and Ulla Kölving. "Qui est l'auteur du *Traité de métaphysique*?" *Cahiers Voltaire* 2 (2002): 85–94.

Brown, Gregory S. *A Field of Honor: Writers, Court Culture, and Public Theater in French Literary Life from Racine to the Revolution.* New York: Columbia University Press, 2005.

Brunn, Alain. *Le Laboratoire moraliste: La Rochefoucauld et l'invention moderne de l'auteur.* Paris: Presses universitaires de France, 2009.

Buffier, Claude. *Examen des prejugez vulgaires, pour disposer l'esprit à juger sainement de tout.* Paris: Chez Jean Mariette, 1704.

Burch, Laura. "New Pleasure in Life Unfolding: Madeleine de Scudéry's Friendship Fan." *Seventeenth-Century French Studies* 36.1 (2014): 4–17.

Bury, Emmanuel. *Littérature et politesse: L'Invention de l'honnête homme.* Paris: Presses Universitaires de France, 1996.

Cassirer, Ernst. *The Philosophy of the Enlightenment*, trans. Fritz C.A. Koelln and James P. Pettegrove. Princeton, NJ: Princeton University Press, 1951.

Chamfort, Sébastien-Roch-Nicolas de. *Maximes et pensées.* Paris: Union générale d'éditions, 1963.

Chédozeau, Bernard. *Le Baroque.* Paris: Nathan, 1989.

Chollet, Mathilde, and Huguette Krief. *Une femme d'encre et de papier à l'époque des Lumières: Henriette de Marans (1719–1784).* Rennes: Presses universitaires de Rennes, 2017.

Cicero, Marcus Tullius. *On Old Age* and *On Friendship*, trans. Frank O. Copley. Ann Arbor: University of Michigan Press, 1971.

Clément, Pierre. *Gabrielle de Rochechouart de Mortemart, étude historique.* Paris: Didier, 1869.

Coleman, Patrick. *Anger, Gratitude, and the Enlightenment Writer.* Oxford: Oxford University Press, 2011.

Condillac, Etienne Bonnot de. *Essai sur l'origine des connaissances humaines*, ed. Charles Porset, introduction by Jacques Derrida. Paris: Galilée, 1972.

Conley, John J. "Madeleine de Scudéry." In *The Stanford Encyclopedia of Philosophy* (Fall 2019 Edition), ed. Edward N. Zalta. Available online at https://plato.stanford.edu/archives/fall2019/entries/madeleine-scudery/.

Conley, John J. *The Other Pascals: The Philosophy of Jacqueline Pascal, Gilberte Pascal Périer, and Marguerite Périer.* Notre Dame: Notre Dame University Press, 2019.

Conley, John J. *The Suspicion of Virtue: Women Philosophers in Neoclassical France.* Ithaca, NY: Cornell University Press. 2002.

Correspondance littéraire, philosophique et critique par Grimm, Diderot, Raynal, Meister, etc. (1877)., ed. Maurice Tourneux. 16 vols. Reprint Nendeln: Kraus Reprints, 1968.

Cottin, Sophie. *Malvina.* 2 vols. Paris: Maradan, 1800.

Coulet, Henri. "Qu'est-ce qu'un petit moraliste?" In *La Morale des moralistes*, ed. Jean Dagen, 221–34. Paris: Honoré Champion, 1999.

Cousin, Victor. *Madame de Sablé: Nouvelles études sur les femmes illustres du dix-septième siècle.* 3rd ed. Paris: Didier, 1865.

Craveri, Benedetta. *L'Âge de la conversation*, French trans. by Éliane Deschamps-Pria. Paris: Gallimard, 2002.

Croq, Laurence. "Mme de Fourqueux (1728–1798), femme du monde et écrivain." In *Histoire et civilization du livre: À travers l'histoire du livre et des Lumières*, ed. Frédéric Barbier, 157–77. Geneva: Droz, 2011.

Cuillé, Tili Boon, and Karyna Szmurlo, eds. *Staël's Philosophy of the Passions.* Lewisburg, PA: Bucknell University Press, 2013.

Cureau de la Chambre, Marin. *Le Système de l'âme.* Paris: J. d'Allin, 1664.

Darmon, Jean-Charles. "Moralistes en mouvement: L'Amitié entre morale et politique." In *Le Moraliste, la politique et l'histoire de La Rochefoucauld à Derrida*, ed. J.-C. Darmon, 31–68. Paris: Desjonquères, 2007.

DeJean, Joan. *Fictions of Sapho 1546–1937*. Chicago: University of Chicago Press, 1989.

Deprun, Jean. *La Philosophie de l'inquiétude au XVIIIe siècle*. Paris: Vrin, 1979.

Deprun, Jean. "La Réception des *Maximes* dans la France des Lumières." In *Images de La Rochefoucauld: Actes du tricentenaire, 1680–1980*, ed. Jean Lafond and Jean Mesnard, 39–46. Paris: Presses Universitaires de France, 1984.

Derrida, Jacques. "Cher Jean-Luc, cher Simon." Afterword to Simon Hantaï and Jean-Luc Nancy, *La Connaissance des textes: Lecture d'un manuscrit illisible (Correspondances)*, 143–56. Paris: Galilée, 2001.

Derrida, Jacques. *Donner le temps: 1. La Fausse monnaie*. Paris: Galilée, 1991.

Derrida, Jacques. *Politiques de l'amitié*. Paris: Galilée, 1994.

Derrida, Jacques. *Voyous*. Paris: Galilée, 2003.

Desan, Suzanne. *The Family on Trial in Revolutionary France*. Berkeley: University of California Press, 2004.

Deshoulières, Antoinette. "Epistre chagrine à Mademoiselle ****." In *Poësies de Madame Deshoulieres*, 44–51. Paris: Chez la Veuve de Sébastien Mabre-Cramoisy, 1687.

Destutt de Tracy, Antoine-Louis-Claude. *Élemens d'idéologie, Première partie: Idéologie proprement dite*. 2nd ed. Paris: Chez Courcier, 1804.

Diderot, Denis. *Oeuvres completes*, ed. Herbert Dieckmann, Jacques Proust, Jean Varloot, et al. (DPV). 25 vols. Paris: Hermann, 1975–2004.

Diderot, Denis, and Jean Le Rond d'Alembert, eds. *Encyclopédie ou dictionnaire raisonné des sciences, des arts et des métiers*. 17 vols. Paris: chez Briasson [et al.], 1751–1772. Available online via the ARTFL Project: https://encyclopedie.uchicago.edu.

Dixon, Thomas. *From Passions to Emotions: The Creation of a Secular Psychological Category*. Cambridge: Cambridge University Press, 2003.

Domenech, Jacques. *L'Éthique des Lumières: Les Fondements de la morale dans la philosophie française du XVIIIe siècle*. Paris: Vrin, 1989.

Dorlin, Elsa. *L'Évidence de l'égalité des sexes: Une philosophie oubliée du XVIIe siècle*. Paris: L'Harmattan, 2000.

Du Châtelet, Gabrielle-Émilie Le Tonnelier de Breteuil, marquise. *Discours sur le bonheur*, ed. Robert Mauzi. Paris: Les Belles lettres, 1961.

Du Châtelet, Gabrielle-Émilie Le Tonnelier de Breteuil, marquise. *La Correspondance d'Émilie Du Châtelet*, ed. Ulla Kölving and Andrew Brown. 2 vols. Ferney-Voltaire: Centre international d'étude du XVIIIe siècle, 2018.

Du Châtelet, Gabrielle-Émilie Le Tonnelier de Breteuil, marquise. *Lettres inédites de madame la marquise Du Chastelet à M. le comte d'Argental*, ed. Claude Hochet. Paris: Chez Xhrouet, 1806.

Du Châtelet, Gabrielle-Émilie Le Tonnelier de Breteuil, marquise. *Selected philosophical and Scientific Writings*, trans. Judith Zinsser and Isabelle Bour. Chicago: University of Chicago Press, 2009.

Du Châtelet, Gabrielle-Émilie Le Tonnelier de Breteuil, marquise. "Sur la liberté," in *The Complete Works of Voltaire*, ed. W.H. Barber et al., vol. 14: 484–502. Oxford: The Voltaire Foundation, 1989.

Dubeau, Catherine. "L'Épreuve du salon ou Le monde comme performance dans les *Mélanges* et les *Nouveaux mélanges* de Suzanne Necker." *Cahiers staëliens* 57 (2006): 201–25.

Dubeau, Catherine. "Les *Mélanges* (1798) et *Nouveaux mélanges* (1801) à rebours: Un florilège à quatre mains . . . et deux voix?" In *Ventriloquie: Quand on fait parler les femmes (XVe–XVIIIe siècles)*, ed. Diane Desrosiers and Roxanne Roy, 209–29. Paris: Hermann, 2020.
Dubeau, Catherine. "The Mother, the Daughter, and the Passions," trans. Sylvie Romanowski. In Cuillé and Szmurlo, 57–73.
Dubeau, Catherine. "Mrs. Spectator: Journal, comptes moraux et tyrannie de l'introspection dans les *Mélanges* et les *Nouveaux mélanges* de Suzanne Necker." In *Influences et modèles étrangers en France sous l'Ancien Régime*, ed. Virginie Dufresne and Geneviève Langlois, 145–62. Québec, QC: Presses de l'université Laval, 2009.
Duclos, Charles Pinot. *Mémoires pour servir à l'histoire des moeurs du XVIIIe siècle*, ed. Henri Coulet. Paris: Desjonquères, 1986.
Dufour-Maître, Myriam. *Les Précieuses: Naissance des femmes de lettres en France au XVIIe siècle*. New ed. Paris: Honoré Champion, 2008.
Dupin, Louise. *Des femmes: Observations du préjugé commun sur la différence des sexes*, ed. Frédéric Marty. Paris: Classiques Garnier, 2022.
Dupin, Louise. *Le Portefeuille de Madame Dupin, Dame de Chenonceaux*, ed. Gaston de Villeneuve-Guibert. Paris: Calmann Lévy, 1884.
Dupin, Louise. *Louise Dupin's Work on Women: Selections*, ed. and trans. Angela Hunter and Rebecca Wilkin. Oxford: Oxford University Press, 2023.
Dupré, Louis. *The Enlightenment and the Foundations of Modern Culture*. New Haven: Yale University Press, 2004.
Épinay, Louise d'. *Mes moments heureux*. Genève: De mon imprimerie [Gauffecourt], 1759.
Encyclopédie, ou dictionnaire raisonné *des sciences, des arts et des métiers*. See under Diderot, Denis, ed.
Faret, Nicolas. *L'Honneste homme ou l'art de plaire à la cour*. Paris: Chez Toussaincts du Bray, 1630.
Fontana, Biancamaria. *Germaine de Staël: A Political Portrait*. Princeton, NJ: Princeton University Press, 2016.
Fourqueux, Marie-Louise Auget de Monthyon de. *Confessions de Madame ****. 2 vols. Paris: Chez Maradan, 1817.
Fowler, James, and Marine Ganofsky. "Introduction: Virtue and the Secular Turn, 1680–1794." In *Enlightenment Virtue, 1680–1794*, ed. J. Fowler and M. Ganofsky, 1–36. Oxford University Studies in Enlightenment. Oxford: Oxford University Press, 2020.
Fox-Genovese, Elizabeth, and Eugene Genovese. *Fruits of Merchant Capital: Slavery and Bourgeois Property in the Rise and Expression of Capitalism*. Oxford: Oxford University Press, 1983.
Fraisse, Geneviève. *Reason's Muse: Sexual Difference and the Birth of Democracy*, trans. Janet Marie Todd. Chicago: University of Chicago Press, 1994.
France, Peter. *Politeness and Its Discontents: Problems in French Classical Culture*. Cambridge: Cambridge University Press, 1992.
Fumaroli, Marc. *L'Age de l'éloquence* (1980). Reprint Paris: Albin Michel, 1994.
Gamaches, Etienne de. *Système du coeur*. Paris: D. Dupuis, 1704.
Gardner, Catherine Villanueva. *Rediscovering Women Philosophers: philosophical Genre and the Boundaries of Philosophy*. Boulder, CO: Westview Press, 2003.
Gargam, Adeline. *Les Femmes savantes, lettrées et cultivées dans la littérature française des Lumières, ou la conquête d'une légitimité (1690–1804)*. 2 vols. Paris: Honoré Champion, 2013.

Gelbart, Nina. *Minerva's French Sisters: Women of Science in the French Enlightenment.* New Haven: Yale University Press, 2021.

Genlis, Stéphanie-Félicité du Crest, comtesse de. *De l'influence des femmes sur la littérature française.* Paris: Chez Maradan, 1811.

Genlis, Stéphanie-Félicité du Crest, comtesse de. *Le Petit La Bruyère, ou Caractères et moeurs des enfans de ce siècle.* New ed. Paris: Maradan, 1801.

Gibbard, Paul. "Royalist and Radical: Octavie Belot on Rousseau and the Social Order." In *Political Ideas of Enlightenment Women: Virtue and Citizenship*, ed. Lisa Curtis-Wendlandt, Paul Gibbard, and Karen Green, 33–48. Farnham, UK: Ashgate, 2013.

Glucker, John. "Cicero as Translator and Cicero in Translation." *Philologica* 10 (2015): 37–53.

Goldmann, Lucien. *Le Dieu caché.* Paris: Gallimard, 1959.

Goldsmith, Elizabeth C. *Exclusive Conversations: The Art of Interaction in Seventeenth-Century France.* Philadelphia: University of Pennsylvania Press, 1988.

Goldstein, Claire. *Vaux and Versailles: The Appropriations, Erasures, and Accidents That Made Modern France.* Philadelphia: University of Pennsylvania Press, 2008.

Goodman, Dena. *Becoming a Woman in the Age of Letters.* Ithaca, NY: Cornell University Press, 2009.

Goodman, Dena. "Le Spectateur intérieur: Les Journaux de Suzanne Necker." In *L'Invention de l'intimité au siècle des Lumières*, ed. Benoît Melançon, 91–100. Nanterre: Université Paris X, 1995.

Goodman, Dena. "Suzanne Necker's *Mélanges*: Gender, Writing, and Publicity." In *Going Public: Women and Publishing in Early Modern France*, ed. Elizabeth Goldsmith and Dena Goodman, 210–23. Ithaca, NY: Cornell University Press, 1995.

Green, Karen. *A History of Women's Political Thought in Europe, 1700–1800.* Cambridge: Cambridge University Press, 2014.

Green, Karen. "Locke, Enlightenment, and Liberty in the Works of Catherine Macaulay and Her Contemporaries." In Broad and Detlefsen, 82–94.

Grouchy, Sophie de. *Les Lettres sur la sympathie (1798) de Sophie de Grouchy: Philosophie morale et réforme sociale*, ed. Marc André Bernier and Deidre Dawson. Oxford: Voltaire Foundation, 2010.

Grouchy, Sophie de. *Sophie de Grouchy's Letters on Sympathy: A Critical Engagement with Adam Smith's The Theory of Moral Sentiments*, trans. S. Bergès. Oxford: Oxford University Press, 2019.

Guibert, Elisabeth. *Pensées détachées.* Bruxelles: Couturier fils, 1771.

Guion, Béatrice. *Pierre Nicole, moraliste.* Paris: Honoré Champion, 2002.

Guizot, Pauline de Meulan. *Essais et conseils de morale: Oeuvres diverses et inédites de Madame Guizot*, ed. François Guizot. 2 vols. Paris: Pichon et Didier, 1828.

Guizot, Pauline de Meulan. [Anon.]. *Essais de littérature et de morale.* Paris: n.p., 1802.

Guizot, Pauline de Meulan, and François Guizot. *Le Temps passé, mélanges de critique littéraire et de morale par M. et Mme. Guizot*, ed. Henriette de Witt. 2 vols. Paris: Perrin, 1887.

Hadot, Philippe. *Philosophy as a Way of Life: Spiritual Exercises from Socrates to Foucault*, ed. Arnold I. Davidson, trans. Michael Chase. Malden, MA, and Oxford: Blackwell Publishing, 1995.

Hagengruber, Ruth. "If I Were King! Morals and Physics in Émilie Du Châtelet's Subtle Thoughts on Liberty." In Broad and Detlefsen, 195–205.

Hamerton, Katherine. "A Feminist Voice in the Enlightenment Salon: Madame de Lambert on Taste, Sensibility, and the Feminine Mind." *Modern Intellectual History* 7.2 (2010): 209–38.

Hannin, Valérie. "Une Ambition de femme au siècle des Lumières: Le Cas de Madame Necker." *Cahiers staëliens* 36 (1985): 5–29.

Harth, Erica. *Cartesian Women: Versions and Subversions of Rational Discourse in the Old Regime*. Ithaca, NY: Cornell University Press, 1992.

Harth, Erica. *Ideology and Culture in Seventeenth-Century France*. Ithaca, NY: Cornell University Press, 1983.

Hayes, Julie Candler. "The Body of the Letter: Epistolary Acts of Jean-Luc Nancy, Simon Hantaï, and Jacques Derrida." *Postmodern Culture* 13.3 (2003).

Hayes, Julie Candler. "The French Theater of Sympathy." In *Sympathy: A History*, ed. Eric Schliesser, 199–207. Oxford: Oxford University Press, 2015.

Hayes, Julie Candler. *Reading the French Enlightenment: System and Subversion*. Cambridge: Cambridge University Press, 1999.

Hayes, Julie Candler. "Unconditional Translation: Derrida's 'Enlightenment to Come.'" *Eighteenth-Century Studies* 40 (2007): 443–55.

Hébrail, Jacques, and Joseph de La Porte, eds. *Supplément à la France littéraire*. Paris: Chez la Veuve Duchesne, 1778.

Helvétius, Claude-Adrien. *De l'esprit* (1758), ed. François Châtelet. Paris: Marabout université, 1973.

Henderson, Christine Dunn. "Passions, Politics, and Literature: The Quest for Happiness." In Cuillé and Szmurlo, 57–73.

Hesse, Carla. *The Other Enlightenment: How French Women Became Modern*. Princeton, NJ: Princeton University Press, 2003.

Heuer, Jennifer Ngaire. *The Family, Nation, and Gender in Revolutionary France, 1789–1830*. Ithaca, NY: Cornell University Press, 2005.

Hinds, Leonard. "Female Friendship as the Foundation of Love in Madeleine de Scudéry's 'Histoire de Sapho.'" *Journal of Homosexuality* 41.3–4 (2001): 23–35.

Holbach, Paul-Henri Thiry, baron d'. *La Morale universelle, ou les devoirs de l'homme fondés sur sa nature*. 3 vols. Amsterdam: M.-M. Rey, 1776.

Hui, Andrew. *A Theory of the Aphorism: From Confucius to Twitter*. Princeton, NJ: Princeton University Press, 2019.

Hunt, Margaret R. *Women in Eighteenth-Century Europe*. Edinburgh: Longman, 2010.

James, Susan. *Passion and Action: The Emotions in Seventeenth-Century Philosophy*. Oxford: Oxford University Press, 1997.

James, Susan. "Reason, the Passions, and the Good Life." In *The Cambridge History of Seventeenth-Century Philosophy*, 2 vols., ed. Daniel Garber and Michael Ayers, 2:1358–96. Cambridge: Cambridge University Press, 1998.

Janik, Linda Gardiner. "Searching for the Metaphysics of Science. The Structure and Composition of Madame Du Châtelet's *Institutions de physique*, 1737–1740." *Studies on Voltaire and the Eighteenth Century* 201 (1982): 88–89.

Jorati, Julia. "Du Châtelet on Freedom, Self-Motion, and Moral Necessity." *Journal of the History of Philosophy* 57.2 (2019): 255–280.

Kavanagh, Thomas M. *Enlightenment and the Shadows of Chance: The Novel and the Culture of Gambling in Eighteenth-Century France*. Baltimore: Johns Hopkins University Press, 1993.

Keralio, Louise-Félicité de. *Collection des meilleurs ouvrages françois composés par des femmes*. 12 vols. Paris: Chez Maradan, 1786–1789.
Kirsop, Wallace. "Gabrielle Suchon et ses libraires: Une note complémentaire." *Australian Journal of French Studies* 37.3 (2000): 309–11.
Kirsop, Wallace. "A Note on Gabrielle Suchon's Efforts to Seek Publication of Her Works." *Journal of Romance Studies* 5.2 (2005): 17–18.
Kölving, Ulla, and Andrew Brown. "Histoire éditoriale de la correspondance." In *La Correspondance d'Émilie Du Châtelet*, 2 vols., ed. Kölving and Brown, 1: 49–50. Ferney-Voltaire: Centre international d'étude du XVIIIe siècle, 2018.
Kostroun, Daniella. *Feminism, Absolutism, and Jansenism*. Cambridge: Cambridge University Press, 2011.
Krief, Huguette. "Retraite féminine et femmes moralistes au siècle des Lumières." *Dix-huitième siècle* 48 (2016): 89–101.
Krief, Huguette, and Valerie André, eds. *Dictionnaire des femmes des Lumières*. 2 vols. Paris: Honoré Champion, 2015.
Kulesa, Rotraud von. "La Philosophie du bonheur au féminin: La Philosophie morale entre stoïcisme et épicurisme.": In *Femmes et philosophie des Lumières*, ed. L. Vanoflen, 69–77. Paris: Classiques Garnier, 2020.
Kwass, Michael. "Consumption and the World of Ideas: Consumer Revolution and the Moral Economy of the Marquis de Mirabeau." *Eighteenth-Century Studies* 37.2 (2004): 187–213.
La Bruyère, Jean de. *Les Caractères ou les moeurs de ce siècle*. See Lafond, *Moralistes*, 693–960.
La Fayette, Marie-Madeleine Pioche de la Vergne, Comtesse de. *La Princesse de Clèves*. Paris: Garnier-Flammarion, 1966.
Lafond, Jean. "La Marquise de Sablé et son salon." In *Images de la Rochefoucauld: Actes du tricentenaire, 1680–1980*, ed. Jean Lafond and Jean Mesnard, 201–16. Paris: Presses universitaires de France, 1984.
Lafond, Jean, ed. *Moralistes du XVIIe siècle*. Paris: Robert Laffont, 1992.
Lambert, Anne-Thérèse de Marguenat de Courcelles, marquise de. *Oeuvres*, ed. Robert Granderoute. Paris: Honoré Champion, 1990.
La Porte, Joseph de, and J-F de la Croix. *Histoire littéraire des femmes françoises*. 5 vols. Paris: Lacombe, 1769.
Laqueur, Thomas. *Making Sex: Body and Gender from the Greeks to Freud*. Cambridge, MA: Harvard University Press, 1990.
La Rochefoucauld, François VI, duc de. *Réflexions diverses*. See Lafond, *Moralistes*, 197–231.
La Rochefoucauld, François VI, duc de. *Réflexions ou sentences et maximes morales*. See Lafond, *Moralistes*, 134–93.
La Sablière, Marguerite de. *Maximes chrétiennes*. In *Réflexions ou sentences et maximes morales de monsieur de la Rochefoucault. Maximes de madame la marquise de Sablé. Pensées diverses de M.L.D. et les Maximes chrétiennes de M. ****. Amsterdam: Chez Pierre Mortier, 1705.
La Sablière, Marguerite de. *Pensées chrétiennes*. In *Madame de La Sablière, ses pensées chrétiennes et ses lettres à l'abbé de Rancé*, ed. Samuel Menjot d'Elbenne, 265–66. Paris: Plon-Nourrit, 1923.
Lascano, Marcy P. "Émilie Du Châtelet on Illusions." *Journal of the American philosophical Association* 7.1 (2021): 1–19.
La Vopa, Anthony J. *The Labor of the Mind: Intellect and Gender in Enlightenment Cultures*. Philadelphia: University of Pennsylvania Press, 2017.

Lebrun, Ponce-Denis Écouchard. "Ode aux belles qui veulent devenir poètes." In *L'Esprit des journaux françois et étrangers*, 26e année, vol. 2 (March–April 1797): 245–46.

Le Coat, Nanette. "The Virtuous Passion: The Politics of Pity in Staël's *The Influence of the Passions*." In Cuillé and Szmurlo, 39–55.

Le Doeuff, Michèle. *Le Sexe du savoir*. Paris: Flammarion, 1998.

Legrand, Amélie. "Les Ambiguïtés de l'exemplarité dans *La Femme auteur* de Félicité de Genlis et *Corinne ou l'Italie* de Germaine de Staël." *Cahiers staëliens* 63 (2013): 215–38.

Le Ru, Veronique. *Émilie Du Châtelet philosophe*. Paris: Classiques Garnier, 2019.

Le Ru, Veronique. "*Le Discours sur le bonheur* ou le déploiement d'une morale hédoniste et matérialiste à travers deux questions." *La Lettre clandestine* 30 (2002): 87–97.

Levesque de Pouilly, Louis-Jean. "Deuxième état du texte." In *Théorie des sentiments agréables*, ed. Françoise Gevrey, 131–61. Reims: Université de Reims Champagne-Ardenne, 2021.

Levi, Anthony. *French Moralists: The Theory of the Passions, 1585–1649*. Oxford: Clarendon Press, 1964.

Lilti, Antoine. *Le Monde des salons: Sociabilité et mondanité à Paris au XVIIIe siècle*. Paris: Fayard, 2005.

Lotterie, Florence. *Le Genre des Lumières: Femme et philosophe au XVIIIe siècle*. Paris: Classiques Garnier, 2013.

Lougee, Carolyn. *Le Paradis des femmes: Women, Salons, and Social Stratification in Seventeenth-Century France*. Princeton, NJ: Princeton University Press, 1976.

Luhmann, Niklas. *Love as Passion: The Codification of Intimacy*, trans. Jeremy Gaines and Doris L. Jones. Cambridge, MA: Harvard University Press, 1986.

Magendie, Maurice. *La Politesse mondaine et les theories de l'honnêteté au France au XVIIe siècle de 1600 à 1660* (1925). Reprint Geneva: Slatkine, 1970.

Maintenon, Françoise d'Aubigné, marquise de. *Mme de Maintenon: Extraits de ses lettres, avis, entretiens, conversations et proverbes sur l'éducation*, ed. Octave Gréard. 4th ed. Paris: Hachette, 1886.

Malebranche, Nicolas. Book Two, *De la recherche de la verité*. In *Oeuvres complètes*, vol. 1, ed. Pierre Clair and Geneviève Rodis-Lewis. Paris: Vrin, 1962.

Mangeot, Georges. "Les 'Réflexions sur le bonheur' de la marquise Du Châtelet." In *Mélanges offerts par ses amis et ses élèves à M. Gustave Lanson*, 281–82. Paris: Hachette, 1922.

Marans, Henriette de. *Confidences générales et particulières*. In *Une femme d'encre et de papier*, ed. Mathilde Chollet and Huguette Krief, 327–446. Rennes: Presses universitaires de Rennes, 2017.

Marans, Henriette de. *Mémorial à mon usage particulier*. In *Une femme d'encre et de papier à l'époque des Lumières*, ed. Mathilde Chollet and Huguette Krief, 110–253. Rennes: Presses de l'université de Rennes, 2017.

Marans, Henriette de. *Pensées errantes, avec quelques lettres d'un Indien*. See under Bénouville, Bonne-Charlotte de.

Marchal, Roger. *Madame de Lambert et son milieu*. Oxford: Voltaire Foundation, 1991.

Marty, Frédéric. *Louise Dupin: Défendre l'égalité des sexes en 1750*. Paris: Classiques Garnier, 2021.

Mathieu-Castellani, Gisèle. *La Rhétorique des passions*. Paris: Presses universitaires de France, 2000.

Mauzi, Robert. *L'Idée du bonheur dans la littérature et la pensée françaises au XVIIIe siècle* (1960). Reprint Paris: Albin Michel, 1994.

McMahon, Darrin M. *Happiness: A History*. New York: Grove, 2006.
Méchoulan, Éric. "Le Métier d'ami." *Dix-septième siècle* 205.4 (1999): 633–56.
Méchoulan, Éric. "La Prudence de l'homme de cour: De Gracián à Amelot de la Houssaye." In *Le Moraliste, la politique et l'histoire de La Rochefoucauld à Derrida*, ed. Jean-Charles Darmon, 95–105. Paris: Desjonquères, 2007.
Menjot d'Elbenne, Samuel. *Madame de La Sablière, ses pensées chrétiennes et ses lettres à l'abbé de Rancé*. Paris: Plon-Nourrit, 1923.
Mercer, Christia. "Prefacing the Theodicy." In *New Essays on Leibniz's Theodicy*, ed. Larry M. Jorgensen and Samuel Newlands, 13–42. Oxford: Oxford University Press, 2014.
Mercer, Christia. "The Contextualist Revolution in Early Modern Philosophy." *Journal of the History of Philosophy* 57.3 (2019): 529–48.
Mistacco, Vicki. "Femme auteur." In Krief and André, 1:465–73.
Moncrif, François-Augustin Paradis de. *Essai sur la nécessité et sur les moyens de plaire*. Paris: Prault, 1738.
Montaigne, Michel de. *Essais*, ed. Maurice Rat. 2 vols. Paris: Classiques Garnier, 1962.
Montesquieu, *De l'esprit des lois*, ed. Robert Dérathé. 2 vols. Paris: Garnier Frères, 1973.
Moriarty, Michael. *Disguised Vices: Theories of Virtue in Early Modern French Thought*. Oxford: Oxford University Press, 2011.
Moriarty, Michael. *Early Modern French Thought: The Age of Suspicion*. Oxford: Oxford University Press, 2003.
Moriarty, Michael. *Fallen Nature, Fallen Selves: Early Modern French Thought II*. Oxford: Oxford University Press, 2006.
Morlet-Chantalat, Chantal. "Parler du savoir, savoir pour parler: Madeleine de Scudéry et la vulgarization galante." In *Femmes savantes, savoirs des femmes: Du crépuscule de la Renaissance à l'aube des Lumières*, ed. Colette Nativel, 177–95. Genève: Droz, 1999.
Morvan de Bellegarde, Jean-Baptiste. *Réflexions sur la politesse des moeurs*. Paris: Chez Jean Guignard, 1698.
Necker, Suzanne. *Des inhumations précipitées*. Paris: De l'imprimerie royale, 1790.
Necker, Suzanne. *Mélanges extraits des écrits de Mme Necker*, ed. Jacques Necker. 3 vols. Paris: Charles Pougens, 1798.
Necker, Suzanne. *Nouveaux mélanges extraits des écrits de Mme Necker*, ed. Jacques Necker. 2 vols. Paris: Charles Pougens, 1801.
Necker, Suzanne. *Réflexions sur le divorce*. Lausanne: Durand Ravanel, 1794.
Nicole, Pierre. *Essais de morale: choix d'essais*, ed. Laurent Thirouin. Paris: Encre marine, 2016.
Okin, Susan Moller. *Women in Western Political Thought*. Princeton, NJ: Princeton University Press, 2010.
O'Neill, Eileen. "Disappearing Ink." In *Philosophy in a Feminist Voice: Critiques and Reconstructions*, ed. Janet A. Kourany, 17–62. Princeton, NJ: Princeton University Press, 1998.
O'Neill, Eileen. "The Equality of Men and Women." In *The Oxford Handbook of Philosophy in Early Modern Europe*, ed. Desmond M. Clarke and Catherine Wilson, 445–74. Oxford: Oxford University Press, 2011.
O'Neill, Eileen. "Women Cartesians, 'Feminine Philosophy,' and Historical Exclusion." In *Feminist Interpretations of René Descartes*, ed. Susan Bordo, 232–57. University Park: Pennsylvania State University Press, 1999.
O'Neill, Eileen, and Marcy P. Lascano, eds. *Feminist History of Philosophy: The Recovery and Evaluation of Women's philosophical Thought*. Cham, Switzerland: Springer Nature, 2019.

Pal, Carol. *The Republic of Women: Rethinking the Republic of Letters in the Seventeenth Century*. Cambridge: Cambridge University Press, 2012.

Papasogli, Benedetta. *Le 'Fond du coeur': Figures de l'espace intérieur au XVIIe siècle*, trans. from Italian by Claire Silbermann and Marie-Pierre Benveniste. Paris: Honoré Champion, 2000.

Parmentier, Béatrice. *Le Siècle des moralistes de Montaigne à La Bruyère*. Paris: Seuil, 2000.

Pascal, Blaise. *Pensées*. See Lafond, *Moralistes*, 321–604.

Patin, Madeleine Hommetz. *Réflexions morales & chrestiennes, tirées la pluspart des epistres de Saint Paul*. Padua: Imprimerie de Jean Baptiste Pasquati, 1682.

Pellegrin, Marie-Frédérique. *Pensées du corps et differences des sexes à l'époque moderne: Descartes, Cureau de la Chambre, Poulain de la Barre et Malebranche*. Paris: ENS Éditions, 2020.

Pellegrin, Marie-Frédérique, ed. *Repenser la philosophie du XVIIe siècle: Canon et corpus* (Special issue). *Dix-septième siècle* 296 (2002/3).

Piqué, Barbara. "Les Cadres allégoriques dans les *Conversations* de Madeleine de Scudéry." In *Madeleine de Scudéry: Une femme de lettres au XVIIe siècle*, ed. Delphine Denis and Anne-Elisabeth Spica, 59–67. Artois: Artois presses université, 2002.

Planté, Christine. *La Petite soeur de Balzac: Essai sur la femme auteur*. New ed. Lyon: Presses universitaires de Lyon, 2015.

Plisson, Marie Prudence. *Maximes morales d'un philosophe chrétien*. Paris: Chez Lamy, 1783.

Poulain de la Barre, François. *De l'égalité des deux sexes*, ed. Marie-Frédéric Pellegrin. Paris: Vrin, 2011.

Pringy, Jeanne-Michelle de. *Les Differens caracteres des femmes du siècle*, ed. Constant Venesoen. Paris: Honoré Champion, 2002.

Le Public vengé, ou la femme auteur. Lyon: Chez la Veuve d'Antoine Olier, 1757.

Puisieux, Madeleine d'Arsant de. *Les Caractères*. 2 vols. Londres: n.p., 1750.

Puisieux, Madeleine d'Arsant de. *Conseils à une amie*. New ed. n.p., 1749.

Puisieux, Madeleine d'Arsant de. *Réflexions et avis sur les défauts et les ridicules à la mode*. Paris: Chez la Veuve Brunet, 1761.

Pujol, Stéphane. *Morale et science des moeurs dans l'Encyclopédie*. Paris: Honoré Champion, 2021.

Racine, Nicole, and Michel Trébitsch, eds. *Intellectuelles: Du genre en histoire des intellectuels*. Bruxelles: Editions Complexe, 2004.

Raoul, Fanny. *Opinion d'une femme sur les femmes* (1801). In *Opinions de femmes de la veille au lendemain de la revolution française*, ed. Geneviève Fraisse, 142–74. Paris: Côté-femmes, 1989.

Raphael, David Daiches, ed. *British Moralists, 1650 to 1800*. 2 vols. Oxford: Clarendon Press, 1969.

Rapin, Rene, "Réflexions sur la morale." In *Oeuvres du P. Rapin*, 2 vols. Paris: les frères Barbou, 1725.

Reddy, William. *The Navigation of Feeling: A Framework for the History of the Emotions*. Cambridge: Cambridge University Press, 2001.

Reuter, Martina. "François Poulain de la Barre on the Subjugation of Women." In Broad and Detlefsen, 33–49.

Ribard, Dinah. *Raconter vivre penser: Histoires de philosophes 1650–1766*. Paris: Vrin, 2003.

Robertson, Ritchie. *The Enlightenment: The Pursuit of Happiness, 1680–1790*. New York: Harper Collins, 2021.

Rochechouart de Mortemart, Marie Madeleine Gabrielle de. "Question sur la politesse." In *Recueil de divers écrits, sur l'Amour et l'amitié, La Politesse, la Volupté, Les Sentimens agréables, L'Esprit et le coeur*, ed. Thémiseul de Saint-Hyacinthe, 86–93. Paris: Chez la Veuve Pissot, 1736.

Rodis-Lewis, Geneviève. *Le Problème de l'inconscient et le cartésianisme*. Paris: Presses universitaires de France, 1985.

Rodrigues, Ana. "Du Châtelet und La Mettrie: Letzte Replik in Potsdam." In *Émilie du Châtelet und Die Deutsche Aufklärung*, ed. Ruth Hagengruber and Hartmut Hecht, 389–413. Wiesbaden: Springer Vieweg, 2019.

Rorty, Amélie. "From Passions to Emotions and Sentiments." *Philosophy* 57.220 (1982): 159–72.

Roukhomovsky, Bernard "Portrait du moraliste en optician." In *L'Optique des moralistes de Montaigne à Chamfort*, ed. B. Roukhomovsky, ix–xix. Paris: Honoré Champion, 2005.

Rousseau, Jean-Jacques. *Rêveries du promeneur solitaire*. In *Oeuvres complètes*, 5 vols., ed. B. Gagnebin, 1:1046–47. Paris: Gallimard, 1959.

Roussel, Pierre. *Système physique et moral de la femme, ou Tableau philosophique de la constitution, de l'état organique, du temperament, des moeurs, & des fonctions propres au sexe*. Paris: Chez Vincent, 1775.

Rutler, Tracy. "Happiness and Disability: Émilie Du Châtelet's Adaptive Worldbuilding." *Esprit créateur* 61.4 (2021): 140–52.

Sablé, Madeleine de Souvré, marquise de. "De l'amitié." In *Maximes de Madame de Sablé* (1678), ed. Damase Jouaust, 57–61. Paris: Librairie des bibliophiles, 1870.

Sablé, Madeleine de Souvré, marquise de. *Maximes*. See Lafond, *Moralistes*, 246–55.

Sacy, Louis de. *Traité de l'amitié*. The Hague: Chez Louïs et Henry van Dole, 1703.

Saint-Évremond, Charles de Marguetel de Saint-Denis de. *Oeuvres choisies*, ed. Jacques Prévot. Paris: Hermann, 2016.

Saint-Évremond, Charles de Marguetel de Saint-Denis de. *Oeuvres en prose*, ed. René Ternois. 4 vols. Paris: Classiques Garnier, 1969.

Saint-Hyacinthe, Thémiseul de, ed. *Recueil de divers écrits, sur l'amour et l'amitié*. Paris: Veuve Pissot, 1736.

Sainte-Beuve, Charles-Augustin. *Portraits de femmes*, ed. Gérald Antoine. Paris: Gallimard, coll. Folio classique, 1998.

Salm, Constance de. *Oeuvres complètes*. 4 vols. Paris: Didot Frères, 1842.

Salm, Constance de. *Pensées*. New ed. Paris: A. René, 1846. (Although the first two sections of Salm's *Pensées* had appeared in earlier editions, the final section was published only in this posthumous edition.)

Sartre, Dauphine de. *De sa propre main: Recueils de choses morales de Dauphine de Sartre, marquise de Robiac (1634–1685)*, ed. Nancy M. O'Connor. Birmingham, AL: Summa Publications, 2003.

Schiebinger, Londa. *The Mind Has No Sex? Women in the Origins of Modern Science*. Cambridge, MA: Harvard University Press, 1989.

Schliesser, Eric. "Sophie de Grouchy, Adam Smith, and the Politics of Sympathy." In O'Neill and Lascano, 193–219.

Schliesser, Eric. "Sophie de Grouchy, the Tradition(s) of Two Liberties, and the Missing Mother(s) of Liberalism." In Broad and Detlefsen, 109–122.

Schneider, Robert A. *Dignified Retreat: Writers and Intellectuals in the Age of Richelieu*. Oxford: Oxford University Press, 2019.

Scudéry, Madeleine de. *Conversations nouvelles sur divers sujets*. Paris: Chez Claude Barbin, 1684.
Scudéry, Madeleine de. *Conversations sur divers sujets*. 2 vols. Paris: Chez Claude Barbin, 1680.
Scudéry, Madeleine de. *Entretiens de morale*. 2 vols. Paris: Chez Jean Anisson, 1692.
Scudéry, Madeleine de. *La Morale du monde, ou Conversations*. 2 vols. Paris: Chez Thomas Guillain, 1686.
Scudéry, Madeleine de. *Nouvelles conversations morales, dédiées au Roy*. 2 vols. Paris: Chez la Veuve de Sébastien Mabre-Cramoisy, 1688.
Seifert, Lewis C. "The Marquise de Sablé and Her Friends: Men and Women between the Convent and the World." In *Men and Women Making Friends in Early Modern France*, ed. Lewis C. Seifert and Rebecca M. Wilkin, 219–45. London: Routledge, 2015.
Seigel, Jerrold. *The Idea of the Self: Thought and Experience in Western Europe since the Seventeenth Century*. Cambridge: Cambridge University Press, 2005.
Seneca, Lucius Annaeus. *Letters on Ethics to Lucilius*, ed. and trans. by Margaret Graver and A.A. Long. Chicago: University of Chicago Press, 2015.
Seneca, Lucius Annaeus. *Anger, Mercy, Revenge*. Trans. Robert A. Kaster and Martha Nussbaum. Chicago: University of Chicago Press, 2010.
Seth, Catriona, ed. *La Fabrique de l'intime: Mémoires et journaux de femmes du XVIIIe siècle*. Paris: Robert Laffont, 2013.
Shapiro, Lisa. "*L'Amour, l'Ambition* and *l'Amitié*: Marie Thiroux d'Arconville on Passion, Agency, and Virtue." In O'Neill and Lascano, 175–91.
Shapiro, Lisa. "Canon, genre et historiographie." In Pellegrin, 417–33.
Shapiro, Lisa. "Gabrielle Suchon's 'Neutralist': The Status of Women and the Invention of Autonomy." In Broad and Detlefsen, 50–65.
Shapiro, Lisa. "Princess Elizabeth and Descartes: The Union of Soul and Body and the Practice of Philosophy." *British Journal for the History of Philosophy* 7.3 (1999): 503–20.
Shapiro, Lisa. "Revisiting the Early Modern philosophical Canon." *Journal of the American philosophical Association* 2.3 (Fall 2016): 365–83.
Shapiro, Lisa. "Some Thoughts on the Place of Women in Early Modern Philosophy." In *Feminist Reflections on the History of Philosophy*, ed. Lili Alanen and Charlotte Witt, 219–50. Dordrecht: Kluwer Academic Publishers, 2004.
Shoemaker, Peter. "From My Lips to Yours: Friendship, Confidentiality, and Gender in Early Modern France." In *Men and Women Making Friends in Early Modern France*, ed. Lewis C. Seifert and Rebecca M. Wilkin, 247–65. London: Routledge, 2015.
Soumoy-Thibert, Geneviève. "Les Idées de Madame Necker." *Dix-huitième siècle*, no. 21 (1989): 357–68.
Staël, Germaine de. "Essai sur les fictions," ed. Stéphanie Genand. In *Oeuvres completes* I.II, 39–65. Paris: Honoré Champion, 2013.
Staël, Germaine de. *De la littérature considérée dans ses rapports avec les institutions sociales*, ed. Jean Goldzink. In *Oeuvres completes* I.II, 103–388. Paris: Honoré Champion, 2013.
Staël, Germaine de. *De l'influence des passions sur le bonheur des individus et des nations*, ed. Florence Lotterie and Laurence Vanoflen. In *Oeuvres completes* I.I, 131–302. Paris: Honoré Champion, 2008.
Staël, Germaine de. *Lettres sur les écrits et le caractère de J.-J. Rousseau*, ed. Anne Brousteau and Florence Lotterie. In *Oeuvres completes* 1.1, 35–110. Paris: Honoré Champion, 2008.

Staël, Germaine de. *Réflexions sur la paix, adressées à M. Pitt et aux Français*, ed. Lucien Jaume. In *Oeuvres complètes* III.I, 83–119. Paris: Honoré Champion, 2009.

Stanton, Domna. "The Ideal of 'repos' in Seventeenth-Century Literature." *Esprit Créateur* 15.1/2 (Spring–Summer, 1975): 79–104.

Starobinski, Jean. "La Rochefoucauld ou les morales substitutives." *La Nouvelle revue française* 163–164 (July–August 1966): 16–34, 211–29.

Steinbrügge, Lieselotte. *The Moral Sex: Women's Nature in the French Enlightenment*, trans. Pamela F. Selwyn. Oxford: Oxford University Press, 1995.

Stewart, Joan Hinde. *The Enlightenment of Age: Women, Letters, and Growing Old in Eighteenth-Century France*. Oxford: Voltaire Foundation, 2010.

Stewart, Philip. *L'Invention du sentiment*. Oxford: Voltaire Foundation, 2010.

Suard, Jean-Baptiste-Antoine, ed. *Mélanges de littérature*. 5 vols. 1804; reprint Geneva: Slatkine, 1971.

Suchon, Gabrielle. *Du célibat volontaire, ou la vie sans engagement*, 2 vols. Paris: Chez Jean et Michel Guignard, 1700.

Suchon, Gabrielle [pseud. G.S. Aristophile]. *Traité de la morale et de la politique*. Lyon: Chez B. Vignieu, 1693.

Talon-Hugon, Carole. *Les Passions rêvées par la raison: Essai sur la théorie des passions de Descartes et de quelques-uns de ses contemporains*. Paris: Vrin, 2002.

Tanner, Tony. *Adultery and the Novel: Contract and Transgression*. Baltimore: Johns Hopkins University Press, 1979.

Taylor, Charles. "The Politics of Recognition." In *Multiculturalism: Examining the Politics of Recognition*, ed. Amy Gutman, 25–73. Princeton, NJ: Princeton University Press, 1994.

Taylor, Charles. *The Sources of the Self: The Making of Modern Identity*. Cambridge, MA: Harvard University Press, 1989.

Thirouin, Laurent. "Paradoxe et contradiction dans le discours des moralistes du XVIIe siècle." In *De la morale à l'économie politique*, ed. David Morgan. Paris: Presses universitaires de France, 1996. 1–14.

Thiroux d'Arconville, Marie-Geneviève-Charlotte. *Mélanges de littérature, de morale et de physique*. 6 vols. Amsterdam: Au dépens de la Compagnie, 1775.

Thiroux d'Arconville, Marie-Geneviève-Charlotte. *Pensées, réflexions et anecdotes* (PRA). Manuscript. Morisset Library, University of Ottawa. (Several essays from the PRA are available in Bernier and Swiderski, *Madame d'Arconville*.)

Thiroux d'Arconville, Marie-Geneviève-Charlotte. *Selected philosophical, Scientific, and Autobiographical Writings*, ed. and trans. Julie Candler Hayes. Toronto: Iter Press, 2018.

Thompson, Ann. "Émilie Du Châtelet and La Mettrie." In *Époque Émilienne*, ed. Ruth Hagengruber, 377–89. Cham: Springer, 2011.

Tillich, Paul. *The Dynamics of Faith*. New York: Harper, 1957.

Timmermans, Linda. *L'accès des femmes à la culture sous l'ancien regime* (1993). New ed. Paris: Champion, 2005.

Todd, Janet. *Women's Friendship in Literature*. New York: Columbia University Press, 1980.

Toinet, Raymond. "Les Ecrivains moralistes du XVIIe siècle." Published in a series of issues of the *Revue d'histoire littéraire de la France*. RHLF 23. 3–4 (1916): 570–610; RHLF 24.2 (1917): 296–306; RHLF 24.4 (1917): 656–75; RHLF 25.2 (1918): 310–20; RHLF 25.4 (1918): 655–71.

Traer, James F. *Marriage and the Family in Eighteenth-Century France*. Ithaca, NY: Cornell University Press, 1980.

Tyson, Sarah. *Where Are the Women? Why Expanding the Archive Makes Philosophy Better*. New York: Columbia University Press, 2018.
Van Delft, Louis. "Caractère et style." In *Caractères et passions au XVIIe siècle*, ed. Jean-Pierre Collinet, 13–32. Dijon: Éditions universitaires de Dijon, 1998.
Van Delft, Louis. *Le Moraliste classique; Essai de définition et de typologie*. Paris: Droz, 1982.
Van Delft, Louis. "La Rochefoucauld et l'anatomie du coeur." *Littératures classiques* 35 (Jan 1999): 37–62.
Van Kley, Dale. *The Religious Origins of the French Revolution*. New Haven: Yale University Press, 1996.
Vanoflen, Laurence. "Le *genre* et la philosophie des Lumières." In *Femmes et philosophie des Lumières: De l'imaginaire à la vie des idées*, ed. Laurence Vanoflen, 7–27. Paris: Classiques Garnier, 2020.
Vaugelas, Claude Favre de. *Remarques sur la langue Françoise*. Paris: Chez la Veuve Jean Camusat, 1647.
Vauvenargues, Luc de Clapiers, marquis de. *Introduction à la connaissance de l'esprit humain* (1747), ed. Jean Dagen. Paris: Flammarion, 1981.
Vauvenargues, Luc de Clapiers, marquis de. *Oeuvres complètes de Vauvenargues*, ed. Jean-Baptiste-Antoine Suard. 2 vols. Paris: Dentu, 1806.
Verjus, Anne. "Conjugalité." In Krief and André, 1:279–83.
Verzure, Marie Pannier d'Orgeville de. *Réflexions hazardées d'une femme ignorante, qui ne connoît les défauts des autres que par les siens, et le monde que par relation et par ouï-dire*. 2 vols. Amsterdam and Paris: Chez Vincent, 1766.
Viala, Alain. *La Naissance de l'écrivain: Sociologie de la littérature à l'âge Classique*. Paris: Editions de minuit, 1985.
Vieillard-Baron, Jean-Louis. "L'Âme et l'amour selon Malebranche." *Les Études philosophiques* 4 (1996): 453–72.
Viennot, Eliane. *La France, les femmes et le pouvoir: Les résistences de la société (XVIIe–XVIIIe siècles)*. Paris: Perrin, 2008.
Vila, Anne C. *Enlightenment and Pathology: Sensibility in the Literature and Medicine of Eighteenth-Century France*. Baltimore: Johns Hopkins University Press, 1998.
Vincent-Buffault, Anne. *L'Exercice de l'amitié: Pour un histoire des pratiques amicales aux XVIIIe et XIXe siècles*. Paris: Seuil, 1995.
Wahrman, Dror. *The Making of the Modern Self: Identity and Culture in Eighteenth-Century England*. New Haven: Yale University Press, 2004.
Whatley, Janet. "Dissoluble Marriage, Paradise Lost: Suzanne Necker's *Réflexions sur le divorce*." *Dalhousie French Studies* 56 (2001): 144–53.
Whitehead, Barbara. "The Singularity of Mme Du Châtelet: An Analysis of the *Discours sur le bonheur*." In *Émilie Du Châtelet: Rewriting Enlightenment Philosophy and Science*, ed. Judith Zinsser and Julie C. Hayes. Oxford: Voltaire Foundation, 2006.
Wilkin, Rebecca. "Impact, influence, importance: Comment mesurer la contribution des femmes à l'histoire de la philosophie?" In Pellegrin, 435–50.
Williams, Raymond. *Marxism and Literature*. Oxford: Oxford University Press, 1977.
Zinsser, Judith P. "Émilie Du Châtelet's Views on the Pillars of French Society: King, Church, and Family." In *Political Ideas of Enlightenment Women: Virtue and Citizenship*, ed. Lisa Curtis-Wendlandt, Paul Gibbard, and Karen Green, 17–31. Farnham: Ashgate, 2013.
Zinsser, Judith P. *La Dame d'esprit: A Biography of the Marquise Du Châtelet*. New York: Viking, 2006.

Index

For the benefit of digital users, indexed terms that span two pages (e.g., 52–53) may, on occasion, appear on only one of those pages.

affectivity, 8–9, 26–27, 71–72, 189
  and friendship 71–73, 84–85, 104, 105
Alembert, Jean le Rond d', 11, 256–57
Amour-propre (self-love), 32, 65–66, 116–17, 190
  in d'Arconville, 33, 97–98
  in La Rochefoucauld, 32–33
  in Pringy, 229, 230–31, 236
  in Scudéry, 38, 39, 41
  in Verzure, 47, 48, 52, 200
Arconville, Marie Geneviève Charlotte d' [Thiroux d'Arconville], 13, 38–39, 137, 237
  Des passions, 140–43, 172
  on friendship, 97–101, 108–9, 110, 111, 172
  on happiness and unhappiness, 139–40, 143–46
  and Jansenism, 14–15, 33, 218
  on liberty, 171, 173–74, 175, 177
  on marriage, 171–73
  on old age, 217–21
  Pensées, réflexions et anecdotes (PRA), 19–20, 145–46, 172–76, 217
  on women, 100–1, 106, 241–44
Aristotle, 72, 73, 94–95, 105, 157
Aristotle: Diogenes Laertius quote, 80–81, 99–100, 104, 108
Arnauld, Antoine: 5–6, 13, 16
Augustinian revival. *See* Jansenism
authorship, women's, 18–22, 247–61
autonomy, 72, 108, 156, 167–68, 183
  in d'Arconville, 139–40, 171, 177
  in Staël, 146–47, 148
  See also integrity; liberty

Belot, Octavie, 184
Benoist, Françoise-Albine, 244–45

Caractère (moralist genre), 9–10, 98, 227–28, 237
Carte de Tendre (Scudéry), 77f–78
Chamfort, Sébastien-Roch-Nicolas de, 157–58
Cicero, Marcus Tullius, 72, 107, 191–92, 203
Condillac, Etienne Bonnot de, 11–12, 13, 29, 52–53, 256–57
Cottin, Sophie, 251–52
Cureau de la Chambre, Marin, 14–15, 115–16

Dacier, Anne, 21–22, 24, 25, 247, 259–60
Descartes, René: 8–9, 27, 34–35, 115–16
Deshoulières, Antoinette, 248
Destutt de Tracy, Antoine, 53–54
Diderot, Denis, 11–12, 52–53, 97n.36, 112, 155–56, 262
  and Necker, 58, 60–61, 181
  and Puisieux, 165, 166–67, 204
divorce, legalization of, 55–56, 157, 160, 177–82, 187–88
  See also Necker; "*Réflexions sur le divorce*"
Du Châtelet, Émilie, 17–18, 86–87, 148, 177
  Discours sur le bonheur, 128–36, 262
  reputation as intellectual, 24, 25, 137, 258–59
  "Sur la liberté," 183–84
Dupin, Louise, 24, 42–45, 226–27
  Des femmes, 23, 42, 162–63
  on friendship, 87, 91, 101, 105
  "Idées sur le bonheur." 124–28

education, women's and girls', 133, 159–60, 170–71, 234, 254–55

Encyclopédie
  "Auteur," 247
  "Bonheur," 117–18
  "Délicieux," 155–56
  "Discours préliminaire," 11
  "Morale," "Moraliste," 12
  "Passions." 117, 124–25
  Système figuré (Tree of knowledge), 42–43, 142
  "USAGE," 210
Epinay, Louise de, 9n.21, 244n.32
Esprit, Jacques, 6

femme auteur. *See* woman writer (*femme auteur*)
Fourqueux, Marie-Louise, 19–20, 24–25, 69, 137, 168
  on friendship, 88–89, 91, 101, 105
  on happiness, 136–39, 154–56

Genlis, Félicité de, 21–22, 249–51, 256–258, 260–61
  on women writers, 252–56
Gournay, Marie de, 161, 223
Goût, 49, 95–96, 98, 102, 129–30, 131–32, 150
  See also inclination
Grouchy, Sophie de, marquise de Condorcet, 85, 151–52, 185
Guibert, Elisabeth, 84–85, 92, 106, 248
Guizot, Pauline (née de Meulan), 24–25, 65–66, 186–87
  on Cottin and Staël, 252–53
  on Du Châtelet, 131, 258–59
  on friendship, 90, 101–3
  on Lambert, 259–61
  on old age, 214–16
  on women, 245–46
  on women writers, 256–58

Helvétius, Claude-Adrien, 13, 72–73, 117
Holbach, Paul-Henri Thiry, baron d', 4–5, 117–18, 137–39
honnêteté, 15–16, 223–24

inclination (*Inclination*), 76–77, 84, 103, 118–19, 158–59
  in Scudéry, 77–83, 109
  See also Goût

integrity, personal, 103, 157–59, 164–65, 167–68, 187
  See also autonomy; liberty

Jansenism, 5–6, 32–34, 41, 116, 122, 123–24, 236
  and d'Arconville, 33, 218

La Bruyère, Jean de, 9–10, 50, 73, 107, 157–58, 193, 194, 228–29, 234
Lafayette, Marie-Madeleine Pioche de la Vergne, marquise de, 103, 123–24, 159
Lambert, Anne-Thérèse de, 14–15, 22–23, 24, 163–64, 166
  Discours sur le sentiment d'une dame, 209–11
  Réflexions nouvelles sur les femmes, 96, 164–65, 239–41
  Traité de l'amitié, 93–97, 106–7
  Traité de la vieillesse, 205–8
La Mettrie, Julien Offray, 124–25, 132
La Rochefoucauld, François VI, duc de, 4–5, 14–15, 50, 116, 157–58
  on *amour-propre*: 32–33
  on friendship, 75, 90–91
  and moralist genre, 7–8, 17
  on old age, 193–94, 213
  and Sablé, 6, 16–17, 74–75
La Sablière, Marguerite de, 7, 9, 119–24, 154–55, 193
Lenclos, Anne ("Ninon") de, 14–15, 193–94
Levesque de Pouilly, Louis-Jean, 124–25, 127, 130–31, 143–44, 155
liberty, 91, 161, 182–90, 263
  in d'Arconville, 139, 142–43, 171–72, 173–74, 175, 177
  "positive," 167–68, 171
  in Puisieux, 165
  in Verzure, 169–71
  See also autonomy

Maintenon, Françoise d'Aubigné, marquise de, 23, 159–60, 167–68
Malebranche, Nicolas, 59, 238–40
Marans, Henriette de, 24–25, 69–70, 101, 168, 204, 243–44, 262–63

INDEX 283

Montaigne, Michel de, 14–16, 204
  "De l'amitié," 72, 73, 75–76, 80, 85–86, 92, 94–95, 99–100, 107, 108
  on marriage, 157–58, 159
  on old age and death, 132, 192, 205–6, 208

Necker, Suzanne, 19–20
  on liberty, 182–83
  Réflexions sur le divorce, 178–82
  "Sur l'âme," 58–62
  on women's nature, 243–44
  on youth and age, 212–13
Nicole, Pierre, 5–6, 7, 12, 13, 16, 32

Pascal, Blaise, 7, 9, 43, 116, 135, 193, 219
Patin, Madeleine, 7, 16–17
pleasing (*plaire, complaisance*), 89, 138–39, 216, 224–25, 231, 242–43, 244–46
  in Dupin, 91, 126
  in Verzure, 170–71, 201
  See also sociability
Poulain de la Barre, François, 28–29, 161, 226, 234, 241
Pringy, Jeanne-Michelle de, 227–37
Puisieux, Madeleine de, 173, 187, 189, 202–4, 216, 248
  Conseils à une amie, 7, 165–67

Raoul, Fanny, 245–46
Rochechouart de Mortemart, Gabrielle de, 24–25, 225–26
Rousseau, 11–12, 42, 86, 155–56, 161, 181
  Belot's critique of, 184
  and Staël, 151–52, 153–54, 185–86

Sablé, Madeleine de Souvré, marquise de, 6, 14–15, 16–17, 18–20, 33, 106–7, 110, 225
  on friendship, 74–76, 81, 108
Saint-Evremond, Charles de Marguetel de Saint-Denis de, 4–5, 193–94, 213
Salm, Constance de, 202–3, 244, 249
  on friendship, 103, 105–6
  on marriage, 187–88
salons, salon culture, 1, 5–6, 14–16, 17–18, 20–21, 92, 104, 119, 137–38, 226, 234
  Dupin's salon, 42, 124, 226, 240
  Lambert's salon, 93, 213, 226, 240

Necker's salon, 24–25, 55, 56, 61, 63–64, 182–83, 250–51
Sablé's salon, 6, 16–17, 74, 223–24
Scudéry's salon, 34–35, 41, 116
  See also pleasing (*plaire*); sociability
Sartre, Dauphine de, 19–20, 69–70, 76–77, 195
Scudéry, Madeleine de: 14–15, 22–23, 24, 116, 224–26, 244–45
  "De la connoissance d'autruy et de soy-mesme," 36–41
  "De l'expérience," 196–200
  on friendship, 77–83
self-possession, 62–63, 118–19, 152, 155, 200, 208
  See also autonomy; liberty
Seneca, Lucius Annaeus, 72, 85–86, 90–91, 93–94, 106–7, 112, 140–41, 192, 207–8
sensibility (*sensibilité*), 88, 100, 106, 126, 136–37, 150–51, 254–55
  in Lambert, 164–65, 226–27, 239–41
sociability, 71–72, 104, 126, 127–28, 136, 225, 226–27
  in Scudéry, 34–37, 40–41
  See also pleasing (*plaire*); salons
Staël, Germaine de, 22–23, 24, 256
  De l'influence des passions, 112–13, 146–53
  De la littérature, 4–5, 250–51
  Essai sur les fictions, 112–13, 190, 250
  on friendship, 84–85, 101, 149–50
  Lettres sur Rousseau, 153–54, 185–86
  on liberty, 185–86
Stoic tradition, 27, 57–58, 63, 150–51, 154–55, 190
  in d'Arconville, 14–15, 139–40, 141, 142, 218
  and friendship, 72–73, 75–77, 84
  in Lambert, 94–95, 207
  and the passions, 114–15, 117–18, 123–24, 170, 190
Suard, Jean-Baptiste-Antoine, 24–25, 56, 64–65, 128–29, 256, 259–60
Suchon, Gabrielle, 23, 161–62

unconscious ideas, 32, 62–63, 67–68, 153n.55

Vauvenargues, Luc de Clapiers, marquis de, 13, 67–68, 72–73, 116–17
Verzure, Marie de, 45–55, 237–38
   on friendship, 87–88
   on girls' education, 200
   on marriage, 168–70
   on youth and age, 200–2

will (*volonté*)
   and friendship, 73, 75–76
   in Lambert, 207–8
   in Scudéry, 40–41
   in Staël, 150–51, 251
   in Verzure, 49, 52
   See also liberty